Kenneeth Cal
106 Joyner

Teaching the learning disabled

A COMBINED TASK-PROCESS APPROACH

Teaching the learning disabled

A COMBINED TASK-PROCESS APPROACH

BILL R. GEARHEART

Professor of Special Education,
University of Northern Colorado,
Greeley, Colorado

with 35 illustrations

The C. V. Mosby Company
Saint Louis   1976

Library of Congress Cataloging in Publication Data

Gearheart, Bill R
    Teaching the learning disabled.

    Includes bibliographies and index.
    1. Learning disabilities. I. Title. [DNLM:
1. Education, Special. 2. Learning disorders. LC4661
G292t]
LC4704.G42   371.9   75-42478
ISBN 0-8016-1762-6

CB/CB/B 9 8 7 6 5 4 3 2 1

PREFACE

Learning disabilities as a recognized sub-area of the larger field of special education is scarcely more than 10 years old. At this time it appears to hold much promise, but some of its efforts (many of which grew out of highly specialized work with the brain injured, severe dyslexics, and others) have received sharp criticism. In some cases this has been due to well-intentioned but inappropriate application of methods designed for one highly specific type of disability to children with quite different educational needs. Some criticism has been directed at attempts to capitalize commercially on this new interest in learning problems with relatively little concern for the actual effectiveness of the various types of "dramatic new approaches" and miraculous "cures" that are advertised much as a new laundry detergent might be. A third concern has related to efforts to remedy learning process disabilities without sufficient attention to application of process in academic learning tasks such as reading and arithmetic.

The problems inherent in the application of inappropriate methods are in the process of being corrected as more and more educators understand that learning disabilities include a variety of problems and require a similarly wide variety of methods for remediation. The problem of commercial capitalization on the problems of humanity may never be solved, but better programs in the public schools, increased awareness, and frank discussion may reduce its negative effects. The problem of overemphasis of process to the exclusion of task can be greatly reduced through careful analysis and application of knowledge already available. One major purpose of this book is to propose a combined task-process approach and to provide guidelines for planning programs based on such an approach. In addition, a number of specific approaches that have been effective with learning-disabled children will be reviewed along with the variables that may make each method likely to be useful. A discussion of how children learn and an outline of assessment models that appear to be particularly valuable in providing the necessary data base for learning disabilities program planning are also included.

It would be difficult to overemphasize the fact that although teachers are in dire need of practical classroom methods and approaches to assist the child with learning disabilities, "the approach," that is, a single educational approach that is likely to be effective with nearly all learning-disabled children, is like the elusive pot of gold at the end of the rainbow. Failure to fully understand this has been a major factor in the problems mentioned.

In an earlier volume, *Learning Disabilities: Educational Strategies,* I provided an overview of the major educational systems in learning disabilities and the work of recognized leaders in the field. In that book the main thrust is objective presentation of these theories and systems, with an emphasis on the positive aspects of each. This book is dedicated to the presentation of methods and

v

approaches that I have observed to be effective, and much of the presentation is keyed to disabilities that cause significant problems in reading, arithmetic, and other academic skill areas. It is my hope that with an understanding of the concepts presented here, at least average teaching skill, and a generous amount of applied logic and common sense, teachers will be able to more effectively plan programs for children with learning disabilities.

Bill R. Gearheart

Acknowledgments

I gratefully acknowledge the contributions and assistance of a variety of individuals in completing this volume. A number of educators in various parts of the nation provided valuable assistance through the provision of information about existing programs. These included Jean Averette, Norma Boekel, Dee Clyne, Roger Clyne, Barbara Coloroso, Jean Jackson, Lila Mills, Blanie Moye, William Mullineaux, Michael Preslar, Betty Quinn, Ruth Sebrell, Alan Sheinker, and Jan White.

Nancy Golden Hanck and George E. Marsh II greatly enhanced the value of this text by contributing Chapters 5 and 7, respectively. Various co-workers at the University of Northern Colorado assisted in a variety of ways, both direct and indirect. Finally, and most importantly, I wish to recognize the contributions of Ruth Perkins in manuscript typing and management.

CONTENTS

Learning disabilities: what, how, and why

HISTORICAL REVIEW

The study of what is today called learning disabilities had its origin in the 1800's in a variety of diverse areas of interest, but acceptance of the term "learning disabilities" came as recently as the mid-1960's. Dember (1964) provides an account of investigations relating to visual perception as early as 1801. These efforts could now be considered research in learning disabilities. Another early nineteenth-century effort was that of Gall, a Viennese physician who postulated an association between parts of the brain and various disorders of mental ability (Head, 1926). Although his efforts were mainly theoretical, they were based on his work with brain-injured adults and grew into later, more scientific efforts by others. Specifically, Gall attempted to describe what would now be called aphasia, a part of the present area of learning disabilities.

By the turn of the century at least three accounts of word blindness (which might now be called severe dyslexia) had been published. One such report was made by James Hinshelwood, a Scottish ophthalmologist, another by James Kerr, a British physician, and the third by W. P. Morgan, a British ophthalmologist (Gearheart, 1973).

By 1930 considerable additional investigation had been conducted in (1) predictable losses of specific abilities caused by damage or lesions in specific areas of the brain and (2) severe reading disabilities, mirror writing, and unusual visual perception problems in children who had no apparent or known brain damage and possessed at least average intellectual ability. This work formed the basis for many of our present programs for children with learning disabilities and is part of the reason for confusion as to whether the field of learning disabilities is the primary concern of the neurologist, the ophthalmologist, the psychologist, the reading specialist, or the special educator.

Wiederholt (1974) has provided one of the more complete reviews of the history of learning disabilities in a chapter in *The Second Review of Special Education* (an effort sufficiently timely and comprehensive to be reprinted as a separate bonus publication of the Division for Children with Learning Disabilities of the Council for Exceptional Children). Wiederholt calls the years from 1800 to 1930 the foundation phase of the learning disabilities movement. The time from 1930 to 1960 is viewed as a transition phase, with 1960 to the present called the integration phase.

Between 1930 and 1960 the work of earlier investigators (including pretwentieth-century efforts cited previously) plus theoretical efforts by individuals such as Samuel Orton (1925) grew into highly developed remedial systems. (See pp. 93-95 for discussion of a system that grew out of Orton's theoretical rationale.) Orton was a professor of psychiatry who discovered that a number of individuals with normal or above-normal intelligence were nonreaders. Many of these individuals exhibited severe problems in memory for word pattern and letter orientation, which he labeled strephosymbolia (twisted symbols). He reported his work to an American Neurological Association meeting in 1925, and the later work of remedial reading specialists such as Anna Gillingham and Bessie Stillman and the extensive use of the term "dyslexia" are based on his work and theories (Gearheart, 1973).

Another early contributor to this yet-to-be-defined field was Grace Fernald. Fernald's work in a remedial clinic at the University of California at Los Angeles in 1921 involved all areas of the school curriculum but became best known for remedial efforts in reading. Her techniques were widely disseminated in her text *Remedial Techniques in Basic School Subjects* (1943), which is still in use in the 1970's. Her approach to reading involving systematic and simultaneous use of the visual, auditory, kinesthetic, and tactile sensory channels is reviewed briefly on pp. 90-93. (For a more complete review of Fernald's efforts, including selected case studies, see Gearheart [1973, Chapter 7].) Fernald's own account of the pupils with whom she worked clearly indicates that a large majority of these children would be called learning disabled today.

Alfred Strauss also contributed significantly to efforts that culminated in the establishment of programs for learning-disabled children. Strauss and Werner (1942) initiated a broad range of investigation into the behavior of brain-injured children, but the work of Strauss and Lehtinen (1947) generated more notable attention in that it presented comprehensive instructions for the management and education of hyperactive brain-injured children. Strauss' contributions to this area of concern were so noteworthy that the symptoms usually attributed to such children came to be commonly called the Strauss syndrome. Strauss was involved in investigative efforts with other authorities in this evolving area of interest, including Newell Kephart, who later achieved considerable eminence as a perceptual-motor theorist (Strauss and Kephart, 1955).

Kephart is one of several individuals who have been called perceptual-motor theorists because of their common belief that higher level mental processes develop out of and after the motor system and the perceptual system. In general these authorities believe that unless these motor and perceptual systems develop adequately and in the normal sequence, the higher level abilities are likely to be faulty in some way. Their theories are generally consistent with those of many developmental psychologists and child-development authorities, but their emphasis on the importance of each event taking place in a particular order and their insistence that any other developmental path may cause serious problems are not so universally accepted.

Many existing learning disabilities programs utilize components of the programs that have been advocated by Kephart and other perceptual-motor theorists, but total acceptance and utilization of such approaches for nearly all children who exhibit learning disabilities, a tendency noted in the 1960's, are much less common today. (For a more extensive review of perceptual-motor theories as articulated by Kephart, Barsch, Cratty, and Getman, see Gearheart [1973, Chapter 3].)

Another major segment in the spectrum of efforts that led to development of the area of learning disabilities is that involving language development, particularly as related to the deaf and aphasic. Helmer Myklebust is probably the best known authority who came into prominence in learning disabilities from this background.

Myklebust worked in this area for several years prior to publication of his text *Auditory Disorders in Children* (1954), but his real recognition as a learning disabilities authority came with the publication of the text *Learning Disabilities: Educational Principles and Practices* (1967), which he co-authored with Johnson. Educational approaches advocated by Johnson and Myklebust are outlined on pp. 95-98.

We see that as we approached the 1960's there were a number of efforts directed toward assisting children with serious educational problems caused by factors or syndromes such as brain injury, written language disorders, spoken language disorders, perceptual process disorders, and gross motor problems. Although some of these areas might be viewed as separate and distinct, it became increasingly obvious that there were many cases in which several of these conditions existed concurrently.

For example, many brain-injured children had severe problems in the area of written language, particularly in reading. Other children who were not obviously brain injured had similar problems. Many children who had reading problems had severe visual perception problems. Some children who had spoken language disorders had problems with auditory perception processes, and others had other combinations of disorders or disabilities. There was also continuing evidence that many people lost certain of these abilities (language, memory of numbers, etc.) after suffering strokes or after brain trauma resulting from accidents or surgery; at least in some cases the relatedness of many of these disorders appeared obvious.

RECOGNITION OF LEARNING DISABILITIES AS A SEPARATE ENTITY

During the 1950's a special educator of international renown started investigative efforts that played a major role in the recognition of learning disabilities as a subarea of special education. Dr. Samuel Kirk, known for his work with the mentally retarded and for a variety of efforts on behalf of all handicapped children, became involved in the development of a new type of diagnostic tool. Actually, this had been his interest for some time, but growing indications that some children who scored as mildly mentally retarded on an individual test of intelligence could, in fact, learn far beyond what such scores would indicate led Kirk to begin intensive efforts to find a better way to measure the individual abilities that contribute to overall learning ability.

As a result of this research the experimental edition of the Illinois Test of Psycholinguistic Abilities (ITPA) was published in 1961. This test evoked wide interest and the revised edition (Kirk et al., 1968) received acceptance that was unprecedented in the field of special education. (It was perhaps *too* widely acclaimed, leading to greater expectations of the test than had been planned and to some misuse and overuse.) At any rate, the nature of the investigation that led to the ITPA brought Kirk farther and farther into the field that was soon to be named learning disabilities.

Kirk's prominence as a special educator plus his interest in the ITPA undoubtedly played a role in his involvement in a conference convened by the Fund for Perceptually Handicapped Children, Inc., on April 6, 1963. In a speech at this conference Kirk made the point that much of the terminology that had been used to label handicapped children was essentially useless for purposes of management or educational programming. Kirk noted that terms such as brain injured and aphasic did not indicate whether a child was bright or dull, hyperactive or underactive. He further noted that these are primarily classification terms, labels that may be satisfying to professionals, and perhaps to parents, but of little value in planning remediation or program modifications. In his efforts to indicate that these were nearly useless terms for instructional purposes, Kirk noted that he had recently been using the term "learning disabilities" to describe children who had disorders in language, speech,

or reading or associated communication problems but two *did not have* sensory handicaps such as blindness or deafness. He also indicated that he did not include within this group those children who exhibited generalized mental retardation (Wiederholt, 1974).

Kirk's words fell on fertile ground. Although the group may not have fully understood his message regarding the limited value of labels, they apparently liked the new label "learning disabilities"; the next day they organized the Association for Children with Learning Disabilities (ACLD). Kirk became chairman of the first Professional Advisory Board, and its membership included a number of the leaders mentioned previously. The field of learning disabilities may thus be considered to have been officially born on April 7, 1963.

Following the formation of the ACLD a number of events seemed to assure the place of this terminology among special educators. The fact that so many individuals of influence were included on the first ACLD Professional Advisory Board undoubtedly had a considerable effect on the rapid spread of the use of the term "learning disabilities," but a related influence was the fact that many parents could accept the possibility that their child was learning disabled much better than the possibility that he was mentally retarded. In addition to avoiding the stigma that was often attached to mental retardation, there were other attractive advantages to this new terminology. Willenberg describes these advantages quite succinctly.

Anyone in frequent contact with parents of these children knows of their heartaches and frustrations. The era of the learning disabled child represents new hope bringing many changes in attitudes and service.

Instead of the child being viewed as the product of parental mismanagement and educational impotence, the new outlook is positive and emphatic on several points:

1. The child's condition is caused by factors generally beyond the scope of normal child-rearing practices. This assumption serves the useful purpose of reducing parental feelings of guilt and shame.

2. The learning disabled child behaves and functions as he does because of forces beyond his ability to comprehend or control. This assumption removes the stigma of willful and deliberate intent as the basis for inappropriate behavior and poor achievement.

3. The learning disabled child with proper attention has the potential for normal development and successful school achievement. This assumption removes the child from the ranks of the mentally retarded in perceived learning potential and social adaptability.

4. The learning disabled child's condition is amenable to treatment and specialized instruction. This assumption proclaims that the condition is remediable and that there are persons with the knowledge and skill to accomplish such results.

5. The remediation of learning disabilities is justifiable from a humanitarian and economic standpoint. This assumption provides the basis for demanding public support to underwrite the additional expense of treatment and special instruction.

The proclamation of hope for the learning disabled does not carry with it the know-how or resources to solve all problems of all children in need of specialized attention. Various disciplines are at work—psychology, psychiatry, neurology, pediatrics, internal medicine, and education. Since "learning" is the key word qualifying the disability, it would appear evident that education will constitute the major source for remediation.*

Although there were undoubtedly some, perhaps many, who embraced this new concept erroneously, this affective component of influence can scarcely be denied.

By 1966 a comprehensive task force report on minimal brain dysfunction in children was published as an NINDS Monograph (Clements, 1966). This project, jointly funded by the National Society for Crippled Children and Adults and the National Institute of Neurological Diseases and Blindness, made an attempt to clarify terminology and identification of learning-disabled children and youth. Although this was a highly useful doc-

ument, its medical orientation gave the field a more highly medical "flavor" and appearance than it was to assume later.

During 1968 three more events took place that reflect the rapid acceptance of learning disabilities as appropriate terminology within the special education area.

1. The Division for Children with Learning Disabilities (DCLD) was established within the Council for Exceptional Children (the major professional organization of special educators; it includes divisions relating to the blind, the mentally retarded, etc.).

2. The *Journal of Learning Disabilities* was first published in January, 1968.

3. The National Advisory Committee on Handicapped Children, a committee established by federal law to assist and advise the Bureau of Education for the Handicapped, made its first annual report on January 31, 1968. Ten major recommendations were included in this report; one was that the area of learning disabilities should be given special consideration by the bureau. This committee also provided an interesting and useful statement regarding a definition of learning disabilities (p. 6).

In the years that followed the Bureau of Education for the Handicapped followed these recommendations and, with strong congressional support (in the form of a learning disabilities act added to existing legislation for the handicapped), funded model learning disabilities programs in a majority of the 50 states. By the mid-1970's it could be concluded that the field of learning disabilities had "arrived." Controversies remained, but the increase in learning disabilities programs in the public schools made the large-scale national recognition of learning disabilities undebatable.

A REMAINING PROBLEM: AN ACCEPTABLE DEFINITION

Perhaps no other subarea of special education is involved in as much continued debate and confusion as there is in determining which children should be considered learn-

*From Willenberg, E. Foreword. In B. R. Gearheart, *Learning disabilities: educational strategies.* St. Louis: The C. V. Mosby Co., 1973.

ing disabled.* When Kirk referred to learning disabilities in his speech in 1963 he provided the basis for most definitions in use today, but in a speech delivered at the 1975 ACLD meeting he indicated that although he could define learning disabilities 10 years ago, he was not certain that he could in 1975. He obviously referred to the confusion that has developed as this area of interest has grown—sometimes like Topsy—since the mid-1960's.

The first "official" definition was provided in 1968 by the National Advisory Committee on Handicapped Children.

Confusion now exists with relationship to the category of special learning disabilities. Unfortunately it has resulted in the development of overlapping and competing programs under such headings as "minimal brain dysfunction," "dyslexia," "perceptual handicaps," etc.

A Federal study, sponsored jointly by the National Institute of Neurological Diseases and Blindness, the National Society for Crippled Children, and the U.S. Office of Education, is now in progress to attempt to define more clearly the nature and extent of these problems, and to provide a basis for the planning of more effective programs of research and service. Prior to the completion of this study, it is necessary for the Office of Education to formulate a definition. To serve as a guideline for its present program the committee suggests the following definition.

Children with special learning disabilities exhibit a disorder in one or more of the basic psychological processes involved in understanding or in using spoken or written languages. These may be manifested in disorders of listening, thinking, talking, reading, writing, spelling, or arithmetic. They include conditions which have *been referred to as perceptual handicaps, brain injury, minimal brain dysfunction, dyslexia, developmental phasia, etc. They do not include learning problems which are due primarily to visual, hearing, or motor handicaps, to mental retardation, emotional disturbance, or to environmental disadvantage.*

From an educational standpoint, special learning disabilities must be identified through psychological and educational diagnosis.*

This definition at first appeared to be satisfactory, but numerous problems developed with use.

Many different approaches have been used in attempts to arrive at an acceptable definition of learning disabilities, but at the present time there appears to be no totally acceptable statement. Patricia Myers, President of the DCLD, noted that "as long as we find various investigators reporting incidence figures ranging from 3% to 40% of school children as learning disabled, there is a case to be made for the non-existence of the condition." She further admits that "no one has a panacea to offer for the problems of definition and identification" (Myers, 1974). Her statement effectively summarizes the present situation, but since the concern of this book is learning disabilities, we must further consider the matter of definition. (In some recent texts on learning disabilities the authors have avoided this issue by simply *not* defining learning disabilities. This may be the easy route but seems to be a total "cop-out.")

Vaughan and Hodges (1973) completed a study in which they searched for an acceptable definition of learning disabilities by surveying field practitioners. They submitted 38 published definitions (not identified by source) to a jury of experts. The jury selected the 10 most acceptable definitions; these were in turn sent to a total of 100 individuals: special education teachers, speech clinicians, special education directors, nurses, social workers, and psychologists.

---

*One possible exception is the area of specialization that relates to children who are called emotionally disturbed, behavior problems, disruptive, socially maladjusted, etc. This area may, in fact, be even more difficult to define than learning disabilities, but the public schools are not presently attempting to serve any significantly large number of such children. There are few authorities who try to make a case for describing 20% to 30% of the school-age population as emotionally disturbed, as some have attempted to do with learning disabilities, a practice with which I strongly disagree.

---

*From *Special education for handicapped children: first annual report of the National Advisory Committee on Handicapped Children.* Washington, D.C.: Office of Education, U.S. Department of Health, Education, and Welfare, 1968.

Only the directors of special education (who were the most likely to be aware of national definitions) selected as their first choice the Department of Health, Education, and Welfare definition, which is from the language of Public Law 91-230. At that time, according to Vaughan and Hodges, 49 states and the ACLD officially recognized the definition, yet it was the fourth choice of the group of respondents to this survey. This result is another example of the variation and lack of agreement that still exist. However, this definition, a modification of the Advisory Committee definition, has received sufficient acceptance to warrant quotation here.

The term "children with specific learning disabilities" means those children who have a disorder in one or more of the basic psychological processes involved in understanding or in using language, spoken or written, which disorder may manifest itself in imperfect ability to listen, think, speak, read, write, spell, or do mathematical calculations. Such disorders include such conditions as perceptual handicaps, brain injury, minimal brain dysfunction, dyslexia, and developmental aphasia. Such term does not include children who have learning problems which are primarily the result of visual, hearing or motor handicaps, of mental retardation, of emotional disturbance, or of environmental disadvantage.*

At this point the reader may logically ask, "So what is the problem?" or "Why isn't this definition acceptable?" The question is pertinent and at least part of the answer follows.

1. The definition does not indicate *degree* of disability and thus may be used to include a very high percentage of the children in any given school. (As indicated by Myers, some have suggested that as many as 40% of all schoolchildren have learning disabilities.)

2. The definition excludes children whose primary problems are visual, hearing, or motor handicaps; mental retardation; emotional disturbance; or environmental disadvantage. Thus, by definition, a child who is blind and in addition has problems that

*From Section 602, Public Law 91-230, April 13, 1970.

would lead to the designation of learning disabled if he were not blind—problems that apparently do not relate to blindness—cannot be called learning disabled and thus cannot receive direct help from learning disabilities personnel in many states.

3. The definition makes no attempt to differentiate between temporary, symptomatic problems and more specific, long-term problems.

Other points could be made regarding problems and inadequacies of learning disabilities definitions, but this should aptly illustrate the reasons for concern. My analysis of learning disabilities definitions, including those promulgated through federal projects, committees, and laws, those used by the various states as the basis for reimbursement of special programs for the learning disabled, and those stated by authors, both well recognized and little known, has led to the following conclusions and generalizations.

1. Most definitions indicate that there must be a considerable, or significant, discrepancy between the actual level of functioning of the child (in reading, mathematics, language development, etc.) and the level of functioning that might be expected when we carefully consider the child's intellectual potential, sensory capability, and educational experiences—his opportunity to have learned.

2. Most definitions specifically exclude the mentally retarded, the visually impaired, and the hearing impaired. Many exclude the emotionally disturbed if the emotional disturbance is primary, that is, if it preceded the learning problem rather than resulted from it.

3. Many definitions exclude the culturally disadvantaged; in some cases this includes the culturally different (different from the white middle class).

4. Many definitions imply that there is a central nervous system dysfunction but do not require "proof" of such dysfunction. In like manner, many imply that one or more of the learning abilities is not functioning properly.

Problems exist in interpretation and in establishment of the existence of all of the conditions mentioned. The following comments, keyed to the previous four points, are intended to expand or clarify some of the problems posed by definitions. (They may also compound the problem for some readers, but someone once said, "The more we know, the more we know that we don't know." This is likely to be the case with learning disabilities.)

1. Significant discrepancy is, in my opinion, an important principle, but it is difficult to define with precision. For example, is a 2-year discrepancy significant? If it is significant at the fourth-grade level, then how large a discrepancy is significant at the tenth-grade level? At the first-grade level?

The concept of discrepancy rests squarely on the idea that we can determine how much a child should be able to learn. This in turn depends on his intellectual ability. Recent events and investigations have led to a widely accepted concensus that, at least for many minority and culturally different children, even the most highly respected tests of individual intelligence are inappropriate. How then are we to determine intellectual potential? If we cannot determine intellectual potential, how can we determine a degree of discrepancy?

2. The matter of exclusions is based on the presumption that many recognized handicapping conditions are provided for or can be provided for through existing programs. This has some validity for administrative and fiscal planning, but if it prevents learning disabilities specialists from assisting a deaf child who also has visual learning problems, it has negative results. This problem requires further consideration.

3. The purpose of excluding the culturally different and culturally disadvantaged was to prevent the wholesale placement of black, Mexican-American, Puerto Rican–American, and the very poor of all races in special, segregated, or semisegregated programs. It was intended to prevent confusing of educational issues and attempts by schools (for example) to use learning disabilities programs to substitute for badly needed bilingual programs. It was not intended to keep culturally different or culturally disadvantaged

children with learning disabilities out of learning disabilities programs. Unfortunately some special educators who were under pressure for having had too many such children in programs in the past have used this exclusion to avoid serving such children and thus avoid possible conflict.

4. The question of central nervous system involvement has a variety of ramifications. When a child has serious learning problems and such obvious central nervous system problems that most any physician would so certify, it seems a reasonable criterion. In many other cases in which a child with no obvious problems to which a physician could certify (in many cases, different physicians make different diagnoses in borderline cases) does have serious learning problems, this becomes a troublesome consideration. Because this is a determination outside the realm of education, it may do more to deter good programming (in some settings) than to help it.

These comments could be greatly expanded; a definite problem exists and a solution is not yet apparent. In the face of this dilemma, some would advocate "giving up the ship," literally capitulating until a better, more specific definition can be developed. This might be the easy way out, but parents of children with learning problems would not accept this; their concern is not definitions but services for children who are in need of special assistance. Since recent court decisions have tended to direct school districts to provide special services for certain handicapped children who had been previously denied such services (Gearheart and Litton, 1975), it is altogether likely that children will soon be receiving service under some other equally unsatisfactory label. It would thus appear that we will continue to serve the learning disabled, even if we cannot presently find a fully acceptable definition.

A brief discussion of the characteristics of learning-disabled children is appropriate here, although some might wonder how characteristics can be discussed if a condition cannot be acceptably defined. We will therefore note that the characteristics apply to the children we are presently serving in programs for the learning disabled. These children are hyperactive, hypoactive, unmotivated, inattentive, overattentive, uncoordinated, and perseverative; they reverse letters or symbols when copying; and they have memory disorders, language deficits, poor auditory discrimination, inconsistent recognition of visual symbols, left-right confusion, figure-ground confusion, and others. Many of these are contradictory; we will not find all of them in each learning-disabled child. *The one characteristic on which all authorities seem to agree is a significant educational discrepancy between expected academic performance and actual academic performance with no relationship to a sensory impairment.* The other characteristics mentioned appear more likely to occur among the learning disabled than among nondisabled children but do not in and of themselves indicate a learning disability.

SUMMARY

Although it may be possible to trace some efforts that we now relate to learning disabilities to even older research, it is generally accepted that present-day learning disabilities programming had its origin in efforts in the early 1800's to treat visual perception problems. Since that time a variety of investigation and theorization about children who cannot learn effectively despite apparently intact learning abilities has led to the present umbrella term "learning disabilities." Under this umbrella we find a wide variety of children whose common problem is significant educational retardation despite the fact that they appear to have had the opportunity to learn and have the abilities required for successful academic achievement.

The term "learning disabilities" dates from the early to mid-1960's and is in common use—and considerable misuse—today. Definitions of learning disabilities have been formulated and have received some official recognition, but all have inherent problems that lead to disagreement as to which children should be included in such a category.

Many estimates of the incidence of learning disabilities have been proposed; they range from 2% to as high as 30% to 40%. This fact alone has caused many problems for those who try to plan and provide for such children. Unusually high estimates appear to benefit few except those who attempt to commercialize on parental concern or those who are trying to emphasize the need for service. These latter individuals (who have good intentions) are slowly learning that such high estimates, in addition to being unrealistic, tend to discourage special help if for no other reason than the fact that special programs for nearly half of all school-age children cannot be "sold" to those who finance education.

Therefore a concerted effort is underway on a national level to develop a definition of learning disabilities that will be sufficiently specific and descriptive to delineate just which children should be considered learning disabled without excluding certain children who badly need special services. This definition must also provide an acceptable basis for the supplementary reimbursement (from state sources to local school districts) that played such a significant role in establishing present programs, without permitting school officials (who may be more interested in funds than in programs) to misuse it. Finally, it must provide a focal point for additional research to provide the basis for improving existing educational practices, both in prevention and remediation.

The remainder of this book, particularly Chapter 11, may shed further light on this problem; in the meantime, the chapters that follow are dedicated to assisting those who will serve learning-disabled children and youth (whoever they may be).

REFERENCES AND SUGGESTED READINGS

Bateman, B. Learning disabilities—yesterday, today, and tomorrow. *Exceptional Children,* 1964, *31,* 167-177.

Clements, S. *Minimal brain dysfunction in children: terminology and identification, phase one of a three-phase project* (NINDS Monograph No. 3, U.S. Public Health Service Publication No. 1415). Washington, D.C.: U.S. Government Printing Office, 1966.

Cruickshank, W., Bentzen, F., Ratzeburg, F., and Tannhausser, M. *A teaching method for brain-injured and hyperactive children.* Syracuse: Syracuse University Press, 1961.

Dember, W. *Visual perception: the nineteenth century.* New York: John Wiley & Sons, Inc., 1964.

Fernald, G. *Remedial techniques in basic school subjects.* New York: McGraw-Hill Book Co., 1943.

Frierson, E., and Barbe, W. (Eds.). *Educating children with learning disabilities.* New York: Appleton-Century-Crofts, 1967.

Frostig, M., and Maslow, P. *Learning problems in the classroom: prevention and remediation.* New York: Grune & Stratton, Inc., 1973.

Gearheart, B. *Learning disabilities: educational strategies.* St. Louis: The C. V. Mosby Co., 1973.

Gearheart, B., and Litton, F. *The trainable retarded: a foundations approach.* St. Louis: The C. V. Mosby Co., 1975.

Getman, G., Kane, E., Halgren, M., and McKee, G. *Developing learning readiness.* New York: McGraw-Hill Book Co., 1968.

Gillingham, A., and Stillman, B. *Remedial work for reading, spelling, and penmanship.* New York: Sackett & Wilhelms, 1936.

Goins, J. *Visual-perceptual abilities and early school progress.* Chicago: University of Chicago Press, 1958.

Haring, N. G., and Miller, C. A. (Eds.). *Minimal brain dysfunction in children: educational, medical, and health related services, phase two of a three-phase project* (Neurological and Sensory Disease Control Program Monograph, U.S. Public Health Service Publication No. 2015). Washington, D.C.: U.S. Government Printing Office, 1966.

Head, H. *Aphasia and kindred disorders of speech.* London: Cambridge University Press, 1926.

Hinshelwood, J. *Congenital word blindness.* London: Lewis, 1917.

Johnson, D., and Myklebust, H. *Learning disabilities: educational principles and practices.* New York: Grune & Stratton, Inc., 1967.

Kephart, N. *The slow learner in the classroom.* Columbus, Ohio: Charles E. Merrill Publishing Co., 1971.

Kirk, S., and Kirk, W. *Psycholinguistic learning disabilities: diagnosis and remediation.* Urbana: University of Illinois Press, 1971.

Kirk, S., and McCarthy, J. *Examiner's manual: Illinois Test of Psycholinguistic Abilities.* Urbana: University of Illinois Press, 1961.

Kirk, S., McCarthy, J., and Kirk, W. *Examiner's manual: Illinois Test of Psycholinguistic Abilities* (Rev. ed.). Urbana: University of Illinois Press, 1968.

Myers, P. President's message. *DCLD Newsletter,* 1974, *4*(3), 5-6.

Myers, P., and Hammill, D. *Methods for learning disorders.* New York: John Wiley & Sons, Inc., 1974.

Myklebust, H. *Auditory disorders in children.* New York: Grune & Stratton, Inc., 1954.

Myklebust, H. *The psychology of deafness.* New York: Grune & Stratton, Inc., 1960.

Orton, S. Word blindness in school children. *Archives of Neurology and Psychiatry,* 1925, *14*, 581-615.

Orton, S. *Reading, writing and speech problems in children.* New York: W. W. Norton & Co., Inc., 1937.

Orton Society: Specific language disabilities (Vol. 3). Pomfret, Conn.: The Society, 1963.

Orton Society: Dyslexia in special education (Vol. 1). Pomfret, Conn.: The Society, 1964.

Special education for handicapped children: first annual report of the National Advisory Committee on Handicapped Children. Washington, D.C.: Office of Education, U.S. Department of Health, Education, and Welfare, 1968.

Strauss, A., and Kephart, N. *Psychopathology and education of the brain-injured child* (Vol. 2). New York: Grune & Stratton, Inc. 1955.

Strauss, A., and Lehtinen, L. *Psychopathology and education of the brain-injured child.* New York: Grune & Stratton, Inc., 1947.

Strauss, A., and Werner, H. Disorders of conceptual thinking in the brain-injured child. *Journal of Nervous and Mental Diseases,* 1942, *96*, 153-172.

Vaughan, R., and Hodges, L. A statistical survey into a definition of learning disabilities: a search for acceptance. *Journal of Learning Disabilities,* 1973, *6*, 658-664.

Wiederholt, J. Historical perspectives on the education of the learning disabled. In L. Mann, and D. Sabatino (Eds.), *The second review of special education.* Philadelphia: JSE Press, 1974.

Willenberg, E. Foreword. In B. R. Gearheart, *Learning disabilities: educational strategies.* St. Louis: The C. V. Mosby Co., 1973.

2 Guiding principles in planning and programming

One of the more difficult explanations that the learning disabilities practitioner must give to the general educator, and at times to other special educators, is that there is no single method that is the foundation for must successful efforts with learning-disabled children. In educating the hearing handicapped, for example, we may assume that nearly all effective educational adaptations and specialized programming will relate to the basic problem of inability to receive and develop language in a normal manner. Certainly the problem may be complicated by other disabilities, by the lack of early (preschool) educational assistance, or by the attitudes of parents or peers. Whether the hearing loss was congenital or occurred after the development of basic language, the individual's level of intelligence and a host of other factors have a significant effect on what is required in the way of special educational services. But the fact that the basic problem is a *hearing* problem dictates certain needs and provides the foundation for educational planning. In a similar manner the visually disabled have a set of predictable needs, and educators of the blind can plan effectively for adapted and specialized educational programs based on a *visual* problem.

In learning disabilities planning all that can be counted on is that the learning-disabled individual is not achieving (usually in reading or mathematics) as well as his basic ability profile (sensory and intellectual abilities) indicates he should achieve. Some authorities indicate that to properly diagnose learning disabilities we must also have *evidence* of neurological or cerebral dysfunction or of "central processing dysfunctions." Of course, these may be inferred from behavior and from the results of educational, psychometric, and medical tests, but they are very difficult to *prove;* actual brain damage can only be proved with absolute certainty if the brain has been exposed to visual inspection (as in surgery, after an accident, or in postmortem examination). Deliberate surgery to establish the existence of brain damage and postmortem examination are acceptable with laboratory animals but seem likely to remain unacceptable to all concerned as a method of proving the existence of cerebral dysfunction in humans.

It has become fairly common to assume cerebral dysfunction or even brain damage when an individual *acts* like those for whom the fact of brain damage can be established, but for practical purposes the educator who works with learning-disabled children is working with children who exhibit unusual or significant educational deficits that cannot be explained by hearing or visual acuity problems, below-average intelligence, lack of educational opportunity, or similar, generally accepted causal factors.

What, then, can be said about these children? The following principles apply to *most* learning-disabled children. In combination they provide a starting point for program planning.

TEN PRINCIPLES FOR PROGRAM PLANNING
Principle No. 1

There is no single "right" method to use with learning-disabled children.

Children are referred for assistance in learning disabilities programs because they are *not* learning by the approach used in the classroom with the general population of boys and girls. Before further discussion we should review the manner in which it is decided which approach (or approaches) will be used in education. The area of reading will be used as an example.

Although we tend to pass through cycles of emphasis on phonic or sight recognition approaches in reading, and although individual teachers may vary their applications of written local district philosophy, the major determinant in most cases is the variety of basal readers published and the variety (or lack of variety) provided by this source of basic materials.

I do not question the effectiveness of basal readers for the 75% to 85% of children who are successful in using them. If we look into the research evidence indicating that we should use "method A" or "method B," we typically find that method A was most effective for 78% of the children who were taught in this manner, while method B was most effective for 83%. (There also may have been methods C, D, and E, which we will presume were less effective.) Obviously we should use the most effective method, method B. The only remaining problem is that even the best method was relatively ineffective for 17% of the children.

What about teacher-initiated variations in approach? In too many cases these are little more than the use of another basal reader; in others it is simply a matter of placing a child in a lower reading group with the hope that more of the same at a lower level will work. In rare cases the teacher may actually use a fundamentally different teaching approach based on careful observations of the child and how he learns most effectively. When this is done it is often quite effective, but the factor that saves public education from an even higher rate of failure is the fact that the human organism is highly resilient and learns in spite of our inadequate efforts. We must remain thankful for this fact but we can take little credit for it.

This is not intended to be an indictment of regular classroom teachers. Teachers are kept busy attempting to achieve success with the majority of the class who respond to the more general approach. They must also be concerned with maintaining order, filling out forms, writing objectives, holding fire drills, supervising the playground, and other apparently necessary evils. The fact that they do not recognize that use of another basic text series is not actually a different educational approach is not surprising, since school district guides and some supervisory personnel may assure them that it is. The practice of using the standard method (which has already proved ineffective), but applying it more precisely, was used too often in the past by teachers and by some remedial reading specialists.

It is unlikely that a teacher who knew that a child was deaf would attempt to use hearing as the major learning avenue in teaching word attack skills. However, many teachers continue to use a method that relies heavily on hearing sounds accurately, even to teach students who do not have the required ability to discriminate between the sounds being used. A student may hear sound as well as other children but be unable to discriminate between certain phonemes that are different yet somewhat similar. A similar situation may exist in the case of a child who has good visual acuity but cannot accurately discriminate between certain letters and thus does not do well with an approach based primarily on sight recognition.

If two children with the problems just described were referred to the same learning disabilities resource room, it would be unlikely that they would have the same educational program, either for remediation or to build reading skills through utilization of existing abilities. Both may be 11-year-old fifth-grade boys of average intelligence who read at the beginning second-grade level, but this does not dictate the same program or the same methodological approach.

At least to a limited extent, both might have learned to read effectively if the school had recognized their learning strengths and weaknesses and approached them appropriately at the first- or second-grade level. However, they were taught by a general "most acceptable for the average" approach and are now in trouble academically. Their obvious lack of success probably also would cause trouble in terms of unacceptable acting-out behavior.

It would be the height of absurdity to move from one "right" approach (that was not right for them) to another "right" approach that might be equally inappropriate.

The idea of one right method in learning disabilities violates common sense and is the outgrowth of lack of understanding. Present assessment techniques cannot always tell us exactly how to approach each child with learning disabilities, but we can avoid the error of belief in a single approach and can know that we may need to try a number of approaches and methods in certain difficult cases.

Principle No. 2

All other factors being equal, the newest* possible method should be used.

In gathering data relative to educational history and background, every attempt should be made to determine which approaches and materials have been used with each child. This information is not significant in all cases, but it is in many. Analysis of this information can have several applications. If certain approaches have been used with little or no success, they may be inappropriate. This is not always true; the approaches may have been poorly implemented or the child may not have had certain requisite abilities at an earlier date and may possess them now; however, this does provide a starting point for further investigation.

An equally important point that is too often overlooked is that people tend to develop a failure syndrome after trying to accomplish a task only to be met by repeated failure. In the case of learning to read, we will probably think it necessary to continue trying to help the child learn to read or to read more effectively, but *we should make a deliberate attempt to use a method that "looks" and "feels" different to the child.* The more severe the learning problem and the longer it has been recognized and felt by the child, the greater the need for this procedure. This principle dictates that when many approach paths appear possible and all other factors are approximately equal, the most different approach (from earlier methods used) is likely to be the most effective. It also dictates that we gather information as to which methods have been previously used both in the regular classroom and in any earlier remedial attempts.†

---

*"New" means new to the child.
†The importance of checking on previous remedial attempts may be seen in cases in which poorly implemented remedial efforts have tended to cancel out the effectiveness of a particular approach even though all other clues and evaluative results indicate the probable effectiveness of such an approach. Sometimes the effect of such unsuccessful efforts can be overcome, but knowledge of their existence is essential.

Principle No. 3

Some type of positive reconditioning should be implemented.

Pioneers in the learning disabilities field, such as Fernald and Gillingham, recognized the value of this principle, a value that remains today. (For a discussion of the procedures followed by Fernald and Gillingham, see pp. 90-95.) Principle No. 2 is a part of this positive reconditioning effort, but additional attempts should be directed toward convincing the child that inability to develop adequate reading (or arithmetic or language) skills is not his fault. Rather it is because schools and teachers did not recognize that he needed to learn by different methods than other children. The obvious point of this effort is to convince the child that he is "O.K."—to boost his self-concept to the point that he will approach the learning task with increased confidence—and thus maximize his chances of success.

Much has been written about the "self-fulfilling prophecy" effect on teachers when they are told that a given child is mentally handicapped and therefore will not learn as well or as much as a normal child. The result is even more devastating when the individual becomes convinced through painful experience that he cannot learn. There is a scarcity of research on the effects of planned positive reconditioning, but the experience of a number of learning disabilities teachers, the historical testimony of both Fernald and Gillingham, and simple logic would strongly support this principle.

One word of caution should be given the learning disabilities teacher who might attempt to use the specific techniques of Fernald. In her clinic, Fernald was working with children who were physically separate from the public school classroom and who usually remained in the clinic for most of a school year. Therefore she could imply or even directly state that teachers who had earlier taught the child had not used methods that were "right" for him. She would not likely have said this in a manner that would have placed specific blame on a given teacher, but she could have been fairly direct if she deemed it necessary to promote positive reconditioning of a child. Because her clinic was separate from the school in which the child had been enrolled, this would not be likely to result in blacklash from the regular classroom. In contrast, most learning disabilities teachers are employed by the public schools. Children are in their programs for only part of the day, and close cooperation with the classroom teacher is essential. Therefore care must be taken in telling the child that school methods or teachers are at fault.

Principle No. 4

High motivation is a prerequisite to success; deliberate consideration of the affective domain is essential.

Because this is such an obvious principle, it may not be emphasized properly; attempts to maximize motivation are difficult to measure or monitor and may seem unglamorous except as related to some unusual type of behavior modification system. Principles No. 2 and 3 are a part of the overall attempt to maximize motivation, but deliberate efforts beyond these two should be planned. In the case of older children who may have developed the basic learning abilities necessary for academic success several years late, a program to promote high motivation may be the only workable procedure. The fact that various behavior modification techniques are in common use, many with apparent success, attests to the validity of this principle.

This principle also dictates some sort of planned investigation of the affective domain —a look at how the child feels about himself, both in general (in the world outside the academic boundaries) and as he attempts to achieve within the school setting. Some learning-disabled children have emotional problems that are so obvious that we can scarcely overlook them. With these children we usually plan and initiate attempts to counteract, remedy, or in some manner attend to these problems.

Many of the other principles enumerated here have the effect of attending to the problems of low self-esteem; if academic achievement improves, there is an "automatic" positive effect. But beyond these positive factors, it is imperative that we deliberately look at the affective components to maximize the potential of other remedial efforts and to prevent negative emotional components, even if they are minimal in nature and extent. This investigation of the affective domain, even when there is no outer indication of problems, must be a part of our program of evaluation and planning for the learning disabled.

Principle No. 5

The existence of nonspecific or difficult-to-define disabilities must be recognized, particularly in older children.

A serious educational problem in reading or arithmetic can be defined, but if a child has experienced, for example, significant visual perception problems at an early age and did not have the visual skills necessary for success in reading at ages 6, 7, and 8 but developed them later, it may be almost impossible to pinpoint what the specific disability *was*. What may exist is significant educational retardation and, in many cases, a very negative attitude toward school. The need may be to develop second- or third-grade reading skills in a 15-year-old student who has learned many ways to circumvent his reading problem. Some authorities who want to describe learning abilities only in terms of specific disabilities that may be carefully defined might say that this is not a learning disability. My point of view is that this is a learning disability and that it requires careful consideration and planning.

One caution is necessary. In recognizing the possibility of such nonspecific disabilities we must be careful not to use this possibility as an "out," a convenient reason not to investigate each individual case fully to determine specific guidelines for remediation and skill development programming.

Principle No. 6

Complete, accurate information about learning strengths and weaknesses is essential.

Educational planning for the child with learning disabilities must be based on recent, complete, accurate information that can be used to provide the basis for determining which areas require maximum remedial efforts and which solid abilities are present that may be used as approach avenues in attacking the disabilities. Accurate assessment of strengths also indicates intact abilities that may be utilized in the continuing attempt to teach content and concepts during the major part of the day, when remedial efforts are not the point of focus.

A single assessment tool must not be used to determine strengths or weaknesses. Even if several assessment tools and techniques are used, every effort should be made to use at least two different measures to verify the existence of each specific area of dysfunction or low-level functioning. It also dictates that *when we discover one problem area, we should not automatically assume that it is the major cause of the academic retardation.* For example, there have been situations in which those conducting a learning disabilities program were so involved with the idea of visual perception problems and so intent on providing programming in this one area of remediation that for all intents and purposes it was the only type of disability they looked for. In many cases, even if such a problem could be documented, it was a less significant problem than others that were fairly evident on the basis of observational assessment.

Complete accurate information requires a comprehensive investigation of all possible causal factors, the compilation of accurate historical information, and an objective attitude on the part of those interpreting such data. It means not accepting the first evidence of problem areas as the final answer and also means a structured system whereby continual assessment and scheduled reevaluation are accomplished. (See pp. 20-22 for additional information and guidance in this important area.)

Principle No. 7

Symptoms often associated with learning disabilities do not necessarily indicate the presence of learning disabilities or predict future learning disabilities.

One of the common learning problem labels that has existed for many years is dyslexia. There are a variety of definitions for dyslexia, but usually the term indicates a severe reading disability accompanied by visual perception problems and problems in writing such as reversals and mirror writing. Reversals, mirror writing, and a variety of visual perception problems also appear quite regularly in children who are medically diagnosed as brain injured and are served in learning disabilities programs because of their severe learning problems. Reversals and mirror writing have therefore come to be associated with learning disabilities and there is a tendency to become concerned about the likelihood of future learning problems when a child consistently exhibits this type of writing. This concern may be well founded but is often overdone and may be totally inaccurate. This may be best illustrated by the following abbreviated case study. It should be noted that I am deliberately leaving out a number of details so that the reader may better appreciate the conclusion to this study, which I personally conducted.

Case study. John S. was 4 years 11 months old and was just about to start attending kindergarten. His parents had some questions about appropriate educational programming for John and were concerned that he might not enjoy school. It was decided that a minimal initial study of John would be made and that further study and investigation would be initiated as indicated.

An individual test of intelligence and a variety of additional tests to predict future educational success were given to John. Two results follow.

1. John tended to exhibit reversals when writing his name.
2. John had poorly developed motor skills.

If we were to guess about John's educational future based only on this information, we might be inclined to wonder about the reversals and whether he would have problems in reading. If we were to base educational planning on such skimpy information, we might suggest that the kindergarten teacher look into a variety of types of readiness material and training to help assure John's readiness for entrance into first-grade reading after a year of kindergarten.

Additional information revealed in this study was as follows.

3. John was reading with good understanding at midfifth-grade level.
4. John's IQ was approximately 155.
5. Although John could not do well in spelling if he were asked to write out spelling words (due to poor motor ability), he could spell aloud at the mid-third-grade level.
6. Arithmetic ability—again determined verbally—was at the upper second-grade level, but he had some fourth-grade arithmetic skills.

It should be noted that John was referred because of concern about future educational programming. The real concern, however, was that school personnel might not know how to handle this remarkable boy. He was somewhat shy, was slightly retarded in motor skill development, and did provide some beautiful examples of reversals. He also provided an excellent, if somewhat exaggreated, example of why we should not confuse the presence of certain symptoms often associated with learning disabilities with the existence of learning disabilities.

Principle No. 8

Educational time and effort must be carefully maximized for the child with learning disabilities.

The learning-disabled child is already educationally retarded in comparison to what his intelligence indicates he should be learning; therefore time is of the essence. A number of major variables must be considered in educational planning for each child; the fact of placement in a learning disabilities program is an insufficient solution. The following variables must be considered.

1. The learning disability (or disabilities) to be overcome must be determined. We must be as specific as possible in this effort, which leads to determination of abilities to be developed.
2. In addition to the learning ability to be developed (for example, auditory discrimination appropriate to age and general developmental level), we must consider academic skill areas to be emphasized and the effect of the disability on these areas. This may be broadly defined as reading, for example, or more narrowly defined as ability to hear specific phonemes accurately so as to effectively use phonetic approaches to reading.
3. We must identify the content, concepts, or both that are of prime importance at this point in educational planning for the child.

How to most effectively balance these three major variables for each child depends on such things as how and where the child is served by the educational system. If he is in a resource room for 90 minutes each day, the major task must be approached in the order given above with most of the third task to be accomplished by the regular classroom teacher. The longer the daily time period in the specialized setting, the more the specialist will likely become involved in the teaching of content.

To maximize educational time and effort these three tasks should be combined as much as possible; that is, after initial determination of disabilities and of academic areas that should receive major attention, remedial efforts should be directed first toward developing specific learning abilities and second toward developing them within the framework of the academic area that needs the most attention; then, when possible, content or conceptual development goals should be considered. The arbitrary manner in which some school systems have indicated that learning disabilities personnel should "remedy disabilities" but not "teach or remedy reading" is unacceptable, unprofessional, and wasteful of precious educational time (for the child) and expensive professional efforts (on the part of educators). The discussion of learning disabilities versus remedial reading sheds more light on this artificial and professionally unacceptable dichotomy.

Principle No. 9

Learning disabilities planning should be based on a learning theory (or theories) to be most effective.

If we are to accept the idea of a learning *disability,* then we are indicating that there are certain definable learning abilities that children must have to learn normally. Although we may be able to pinpoint the fact that a given child has significant problems in auditory discrimination and may be able to assist him to improve his auditory discrimination, we also need to help him build reading and language skills that have been retarded by the discrimination problem. We therefore need to know how children develop adequate reading and language skills so that we may postulate the manner in which the earlier problem caused retarded development in these areas.

It is my point of view that there are a number of different types of learning and that it is logical and advantageous in learning disabilities planning to assume the existence of different learning processes for these different types of learning. (For a discussion of learning theories and their application in learning disabilities, see Chapter 3.)

Principle No. 10

It is critically important to be concerned and involved with both process- and task-oriented assistance and remediation.

Principle No. 10 reflects the basic frame of reference of this text. It is of the utmost importance that it be followed to make possible the effective use of time and effort. Because of a unique and unfortunate conflict that may exist in the assigned functions of two specialized teachers who work with children with unusual reading problems (the learning disabilities teacher and the remedial reading teacher), learning disabilities teachers are sometimes prohibited from task-oriented assistance to the child or may in some cases believe that it should not be their task. Problems do exist between learning disabilities teachers and remedial reading teachers in some parts of the United States. It might be easier to avoid discussion of this problem (and certainly would be more popular in some quarters) but it has sufficient significance to the implementation of the highly important principle of involvement in both process- and task-oriented assistance and remediation that it cannot be overlooked. The following discussion will briefly indicate how this problem developed and what we must do about it for the good of boys and girls.

Learning disabilities versus remedial reading. The term "versus" is deliberately used to suggest a competitive attitude between these two areas. This competition is unnecessary and for the most part negative, as it has been applied in a profession that is dedicated to maximum assistance to the learner. It must be noted that this competition (as is the case with most competition) has had some beneficial spin-off effects, but it is time for cooperation on behalf of children to replace this atmosphere of controversy.

To better understand this phenomenon, it may be well to briefly review its historical development and the pressures, both professional and economic, that it has generated. It may then be possible to go about the business of cooperatively assisting children who are having difficulty in reading.

In the mid-1960's the fledgling professional group of learning disabilities specialists began to emerge from a number of very small, more specifically defined specialty areas. Although learning disabilities program efforts were recognized by other special educators in a manner that would indicate at least some homogeneity, they were highly varied and heterogeneous in defined function, scope, and effectiveness. They were supported by a strong, active, and effectively vocal parent group, the ACLD, and legislation at both state and national levels gave them considerable strength and encouragement.

During this same period of time the nation was involved in attempts to better recognize and attend to the needs of various minority groups, and many children who were educationally handicapped (such as the hard of hearing, the visually impaired, and the mentally retarded) were assisted by special education. It therefore seemed logical to attach the new group to special education, particularly since to do so would provide significant state reimbursement to local districts and would also permit the Bureau of Education for the Handicapped of the U.S. Office of Education to actively apply its efforts, including both research emphasis and direct funds to local districts. Since a few states had previously recognized certain children who were now considered learning disabled as belonging in special education (for example, the hyperkinetic or Strauss syndrome child), and because the ACLD directed its efforts toward special education, there was rapid national acceptance of learning disabilities as a part of special education.

So, why the problem? As is the case with many new programs, initial efforts were not always totally effective; consumers (parents) wanted immediate implementation, and in the process of starting new programs, old programs were sometimes dropped or deemphasized. Remedial reading and special education programs for the mentally handicapped were at times reduced in size or phased out entirely. This was ill-advised in most cases, and sometimes the new learning disabilities program was less effective than the program that was dropped. The results were felt at the local school district level by remedial reading teachers, who were told to get back to school to become qualified as learning disabilities specialists, and at the university level, where students were tempted to change programs "midstream."

This description may be overly dramatic, but it is what happened and what is still happening to some extent. For a local school superintendent who must balance the budget, the fact that two learning disabilities teachers can be employed for the cost of one remedial reading teacher (due to special state reimbursement) and that the local ACLD can be satisfied at the same time make the decision not too difficult.

In a majority of schools the learning disabilities specialist can work with many of the same children as the remedial reading teacher and in addition can assist children whose basic problems are in mathematics or an area other than reading. In most schools both remedial reading and learning disabilities programs continue to exist, and in some their work is carefully planned and coordinated. But in too many they are competitive at the local school level and children receive less than maximum help. It is to this point that the rest of this discussion is directed.

It would be possible to indicate that a specific cooperative plan would be ideal, but the variety of settings, local regulations, organizational plans, budgeting procedures, and state laws and regulations make any single "ideal" plan unrealistic. It is highly unlikely that remedial reading will be included in special education (most remedial reading specialists would not want that, and legislators would not be likely to accept it) or that learning disabilities will be taken out of special education in the near future. It is equally unlikely that remedial reading programs will receive the type and extent of special reimbursement now enjoyed by special education. The most likely possibility would seem to be that two relatively small subgroups in education, each dedicated to assisting children with educational problems and disabilities, could learn to define role and function so as to maximize service to children.

This should be organized on the state level, taking into account state regulations, and implemented on a local level in accordance with local conditions. State education officials have an urgent responsibility to reorganize state regulations and guidelines to encourage this type of cooperative effort. Local education officials, remedial reading staffs, and learning disabilities staffs have a responsibility to do all possible to make this happen quickly. Local decisions may lead to the establishment of guidelines as to degree of severity or acceptable case loads, criteria for multihandicapping conditions, and other guidelines that are consistent with existing state regulations and the commonsense dictates of good educational practice. Evaluation and staffing procedures should reflect local educational thinking, and *all* members of the professional staff in each local educational unit should work together to serve the needs of children.

Hartman and Hartman (1973) pinpointed the problem when they indicated that there is little if any difference between children seen by the learning disabilities specialist and those seen by the remedial reading specialist in many settings. They made the point that we (educators) have created a false dichotomy in this matter and that we must look into the matter of whether the "task-oriented" approach of the reading specialist or the "process training" of the learning disabilities specialist is most effective with the type of children typically served in these programs. After much discussion, they concluded that at this time (1973) the reading specialist is on safer ground than the learning disabilities specialist.

It should be noted that their reasoning is based on the assumption that the learning disabilities specialist is concerned only with "what's wrong with the child" and does not look into the the child's reading problems. If this is the case in learning disabilities programs, then their point about the relative effectiveness of learning disabilities programs and remedial reading programs is well made. Learning disabilities as an organized entity is a new field, but its roots go back many years. As a result the mid-1960's and early 1970's saw too much dependence on perceptual training and the remediation of faulty processes. There *are* children in whom these faulty processes are the major problem, and for these children such programming makes sense. But even here, attention must be given to the application of abilities to actual learning tasks.

The frame of reference of this book is that the learning disabilities teacher must be concerned with both process- and task-oriented

assistance and remediation. To do anything less is to shortchange the child, who is the ultimate reason for our professional existence.

PROGRAM SEQUENCE

The 10 principles may be used to guide overall program planning for the learning disabled, but some structure and sequence must be established, space must be obtained, personnel must be employed, children must be evaluated, and a host of other factors must be considered in establishing an actual program. Program models are provided in Chapter 10, but to provide further perspective for the principles discussed, a simplified flow chart indicating a possible sequence for learning disabilities programming is provided here. The flow chart is most applicable to the resource room setting but could be used with only slight modifications if service were provided through itinerant or consultative service plans. This chart, along with the program models and explanations of various types of programs provided in Chapter 10, will indicate how the public school system can provide the framework within which the methods described in much of the rest of this text can be implemented.

EXPLANATORY NOTES FOR FLOW CHART

A. Entry to program: Entry to program assumes that some sort of assessment has already taken place and that a pupil is eligible for a learning disabilities program according to local district guidelines. In most states this means that, at a minimum, it has been established that the student is above the level of mental retardation and that he has nearly normal visual and auditory acuity. It also usually means that his academic achievement is significantly below that predicted by his years in school and his apparent ability to learn. Usually this determination of eligibility is made by an evaluation and placement committee. *Program entry requires parent permission, as does the assessment that precedes it.*

B. Assessment: The variety of assessment procedures that might be completed at this time is considerable, depending on how much assessment has already taken place and the resulting indications of need for further assessment. Although in most instances it may be assumed that visual

Sequence of coordinated task- and process-oriented learning disabilities program

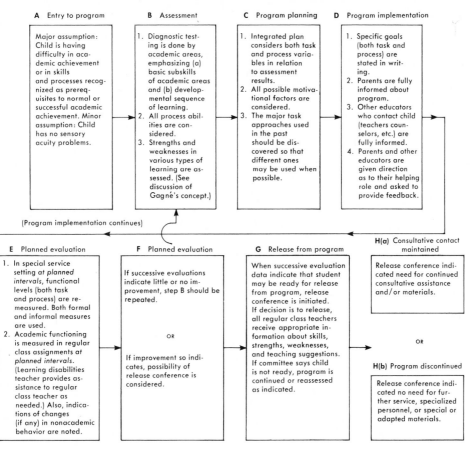

and auditory acuity have been effectively determined, such possibilities as binocular incoordination might be considered at this level, particularly as may be indicated by other assessment or careful observation.

C. Program planning: At this point there should be sufficient information to permit initial, tentative program planning. In addition to the initial program plan, at least one potentially viable alternative program should be outlined at this time in case initial programming is not successful.

D. Program implementation: Parents should receive a full explanation of the program and should have every opportunity to ask questions. Parents and other teachers who contact the child should be provided specific guidelines about the type of feedback that will be most helpful.

E. Planned evaluation: Planned, periodic, formal evaluation is essential in *all* cases, although the nature of each individual case may require varia-

tions in the time intervals between successive evaluations. Less formal, ongoing evaluation should be made continuously.

F. Planned evaluation: Three or four planned evaluations should be completed before the need for complete reassessment and new program planning is considered. If there is little or no progress after these evaluations are completed, the case should be referred back to step B (assessment).

G. Release from program: Planned consideration for release from the program is just as important as planned consideration for entry. Parents must be made a part of this action just as they were in program planning and implementation.

H. Consultative contact maintained or program discontinued: The release conference may result in a decision that the child is ready to "go it alone" with no supportive help or materials, or some degree of support and assistance may be deemed necessary. For some children this may mean the provision of adapted materials; for others it may mean that the committee was almost certain that release is indicated but elected to recommend that the learning disabilities specialist check with the regular class teacher once each week "just in case." In some instances the specialist may be directed to make regular contact for at least 6 weeks and then consider the program totally discontinued if the regular class teacher indicates that progress is satisfactory. In others the learning disabilities specialist may be directed to report back to the release committee so that a decision may be made by that group. In other words, for many children this may be a planned "phasing out" of the program rather than abrupt program discontinuance.

SUMMARY

Ten principles may be used to guide most learning disabilities programming: (1) there is no single "right" method to use with learning-disabled children; (2) all other factors being equal, the newest possible method should be used; (3) some type of positive reconditioning should be implemented; (4) high motivation is a prerequisite to success; (5) the existence of nonspecific or difficult-to-define disabilities must be recognized, particularly in older children; (6) complete, accurate information about learning strengths and weaknesses is essential; (7) symptoms often associated with learning disabilities do not necessarily indicate the presence of learning disabilities or predict future learning disabilities; (8) educational time and effort must be carefully maximized for the child with learning disabilities; (9) learning disabilities planning should be based on a learning theory (or theories) to be most effective; and (10) it is critically important to be concerned and involved with both process- and task-oriented assistance and remediation.

A presentation of models for establishment of learning disabilities programs and a discussion of service delivery alternatives will be presented in a later chapter, but a general sequence for planning learning disabilities programs was provided in this chapter as part of the guiding principles that may be used to plan programs for learning-disabled children.

REFERENCES AND SUGGESTED READINGS

Hammill, D., and Bartel, N. (Eds.). *Educational perspectives in learning disabilities.* New York: John Wiley & Sons, Inc., 1971.

Hartman, N., and Hartman, R. Perceptual handicap or reading disability? *The Reading Teacher,* 1973, *26,* 684-695.

Johnson, D., and Myklebust, H. *Learning disabilities: educational principles and practices.* New York: Grune & Stratton, Inc., 1967.

Lerner, J. *Children With Learning Disabilities.* Boston: Houghton Mifflin Co., 1971.

Mann, P., and Suiter, P. *Handbook in diagnostic teaching: a learning disability approach.* Boston: Allyn & Bacon, Inc., 1974.

Myers, P., and Hammill, D. *Methods for learning disorders.* New York: John Wiley & Sons, Inc., 1969.

Valett, R. *Programming learning disabilities.* Belmont, Calif.: Fearon Publishers, 1969.

3 How children learn

This chapter is *not* entitled "learning theories in application" for two reasons: (1) developing a total learning theory is beyond the scope of this text and (2) "learning theories" are almost as frightening to many teachers as "statistics." Our concern is how children learn, and to consider this question we must briefly enter the realm of the learning theorist while keeping at least one foot in the classroom. If readers will have faith that this short trip is necessary to better understand practical programming for learning-disabled children, perhaps it will be more easily tolerated. Every effort will be made to use nontechnical terminology, and the more complex considerations of neurological functioning will be avoided altogether.

The reason that a learning disabilities teacher must have some concept of how children learn is that the major premise underlying most learning disabilities programming is that the learning process is not working as we would normally expect it to work. Most of the procedures used to teach children in large group instruction are based on the manner in which children of a certain age normally learn. The learning-disabled child is one who is not learning effectively through these procedures; thus we may expect that many such children somehow have different learning needs than other children in the class. We cannot necessarily assume that they actually learn differently, but we do know that present teaching techniques are not effective.

It must be recognized that some children do not learn effectively because they are not motivated; they are not interested or do not see the benefits of learning. These children might learn in the "normal" way if they could be made to want to learn. A discussion of motivational systems, including some aspects of behavior modification techniques, will be provided in Chapter 10 and should be of value in planning for such children. Even in this situation, however, the motivational system can be made more effective if teachers understand *how* children learn; motivational emphasis may be implemented at critical points in the learning sequence only if we understand that sequence.

In summary, the importance of how children learn and how this particularly applies to learning disabilities is based on the following assumptions.

1. A majority of children learn in the school setting; learning-disabled children are not learning effectively in school.

2. Existing educational methods and approaches are working with at least marginal effectiveness with many children but are not working effectively with learning-disabled children.

3. Existing methods are somewhat consistent with how most children learn but *may not* be consistent with how learning-disabled children learn.

Note that we cannot assume that existing methods are inconsistent with how learning-disabled children could learn if all other factors were positive. The problem may relate to motivation, to intellectual readiness, or to readiness in specific abilities such as visual discrimination and the ability to discriminate between different but similar phonemes. Regardless of the reason, when the traditional classroom methods and approaches break down, we must look further into the learning process and thus must have some theory of learning.

LEARNING THEORIES: WHICH ONE IS BEST?

Surveys of major learning theories usually include the work of theorists in major schools of thought: Gestalt theorists, reinforcement theorists, and a number of others grouped in various ways by a variety of reviewers. Each theory makes sense to some, and many teachers apparently think that they find some truth in more than one theory, as indicated by their teaching practices. The question of which is best, most accurate, or best substantiated by research depends on whom you ask;

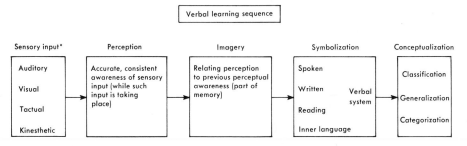

*The senses of taste and smell are not of major importance in learning disabilities.

each has its supporters and its detractors. We will consider here just two theories, a simplified version of the way Johnson and Myklebust (1967) view learning as expressed in their discussion of hierarchies of experience and Gagné's (1970) eight types of learning.

VERBAL LEARNING SEQUENCE

Johnson and Myklebust (1967) provide a relatively simple explanation of how children learn in a manner designed to be pertinent to the consideration of learning disabilities. The chart on p. 24 was derived from their narrative description of verbal learning, the most important facet of learning from the educator's point of view.

The chart is an oversimplification of a highly complex process, but it does accurately indicate what might be called the minimum sequence of events that must take place for children to learn normally. It also represents the basic assumptions that underlie most curricula. (That is, most planned sequential educational programs assume that children learn in this manner and that they have all the requisite capabilities to so learn.) Most important is the fact that as we move from left to right across the chart, each process assumes adequate functioning and development of all processes to the left.

If, for example, we are using materials and teaching approaches that require accurate auditory perception and we are providing special training or practice to develop this perception, we are assuming that auditory acuity is normal. In learning disabilities programming we are (by definition) assuming adequate sensory acuity in the auditory and visual channels, which should have been determined by comprehensive tests of hearing and vision.

A word of caution must be interjected here: this assumption of adequate sensory acuity may not be accurate. Some facets of the visual channel may be operating normally while others are not. For example, a child may have 20/20 vision as measured one eye at a time, but the two eyes may carry visual signals in such a manner that they

appear to the child as two separate, overlapping images. If such binocular incoordination is present, then it has an effect on visual perception and on all processes to the right on the chart. Such problems as binocular incoordination can usually be corrected, but they may go undetected for years.

Similar problems can, and in some children do, exist farther to the right on the chart. When a problem is discovered at any one level, it is always important to check to see if the problem originates with less than adequate functioning at a lower (farther to the left) level. For example, a test of auditory sequential memory (imagery level) might indicate that a child is functioning significantly below the level expected for a child of his age. If we attempt to develop auditory sequential memory without first checking out the possibility of auditory perception problems, we may be wasting valuable time.

Just as is true at the sensory levels, there are many components of each level represented. In following through on the example of auditory sequential memory problems we may find that all auditory perception processes appear to be functioning normally. We might then note that this child is presently located in an open classroom where there is a good deal of background noise, although the test for auditory discrimination was conducted in the silence of a small testing room. If we check auditory discrimination in a noisy environment, we may find a significant problem. This example may be paralleled at each level in relation to each of the modalities.

A final caution must be observed in the use of this type of model. *It provides a way to look at just one facet of the whole set of variables necessary for learning.* These abilities are necessary for the learning process to proceed normally, but so are motivation, language background and experience, and a host of other factors. Remediation and attention to factors and processes represented on the chart are important, but once the problem is remedied, children usually require additional help in task assistance and in relation to the affective factors that effect learning. Learning disabilities programs can be only minimally effective if they remain totally focused on process variables.

Johnson and Myklebust provide a number of highly valuable insights regarding the learning process. Most of the remainder of this discussion of their theory is taken from a description of their approach in *Learning Disabilities: Educational Strategies* (Gearheart, 1973).

Johnson and Myklebust note that disabilities may relate to any level of the various processes of learning. They place these processes into five levels, which they call hierarchies of experience. Commencing with the lowest and most simple, these levels follow.

Sensation. Sensation is the simplest and most basic level. Those who have lost or never had the use of one of the sensory channels are highly deprived in the learning process. For purposes of consideration of the learning-disabled youngster, we may assume adequacy at this level, for by definition these children have adequate sensory acuity.

Perception. Perception, the second level, is defined somewhat differently by different authors, but if it means the ability to accurately recognize sensory input, or information, then it is a relatively simple psychological process. However, it is important that the learning disabilities teacher know if the child has perceptual problems because a deficit at this level interferes with all the higher, more complex processes in the hierarchy. A misdiagnosis at this level could lead to many faulty conclusions and wasted remedial procedures.

Imagery. Imagery is the next higher process and has sometimes been confused with perception or, perhaps for the most part, overlooked. The imagery concept is necessary to explain the differences between perception and memory. Perception concerns the ability to differentiate between various similar but different ongoing sensations. Imagery pertains to information already received. When a child is exercising imagery, he is recalling aspects of a past experience or is relating to memory of past perceptions. If he describes what he saw on the way to school, he is exer-

cising visual imagery of the earlier experience. If he explains the loud explosion he heard, he is utilizing auditory imagery, or memory. Johnson and Myklebust cite the example of a child who could not recall the common features of his own bedroom or whether there were trees along the street on which he walked to school each day.

Symbolization. Symbolization is the fourth hierarchical aspect of experience among the learning processes. This next-to-the-highest level is sufficiently complex and all-inclusive to defy complete understanding. For example, it definitely includes both verbal and nonverbal categories of learning, and it may be called the ability to represent, or to trigger, the recall of experience. Symbolization is the level in the hierarchy at which all forms of life lower than humans drop out. That is, all forms of animals engage in perception; some are apparently capable of imagery, but none except humans is capable of or exercises symbolization. For purposes of discussion, symbolization may be thought of as the ability to acquire language, although, as will be pointed out later, both verbal and nonverbal symbolization are important in consideration of the learning-disabled child.

Inner language. Johnson and Myklebust recognize three major aspects of symbolization. The first, inner language, is the aspect that permits a word to have meaning. Without inner language and the experience of what a word means, the word does not transmit meaning and therefore is not, in truth, language. In a television series about outer space that was popular in past years, one regular member of the space crew is a member of a race (from another planet) that lives on the basis of pure logic and does not feel emotion. He is a highly intelligent individual, but words such as "love" are not in his language. He knows and can pronounce the word, but it has no meaning for him because he cannot experience it. In a similar manner, words such as "thank you" are meaningless, for people (from his point of view) do things because they are logical. He can say these words and understand when others say them but cannot develop effective inner language in the true sense.

Inner language is the language in which an individual thinks; bilingual individuals usually *think* in the language that is their native tongue. If faced by a particularly pressing problem, even though fluent in the second language and in the habit of using it daily, many such individuals revert to their native tongue to think through the problem. Because of long association and considerable research with the deaf, Johnson and Myklebust turn to this area to illustrate inner language. They state that a number of graduate students whose parents are deaf, who learned sign language from their parents as small children, still think in sign language when engaged in difficult mental tasks. This is the case even though the students hear adequately and outwardly use sign language only in conversing with their parents.

Because inner language is the first language to be acquired and must be learned before an individual can receive or express oral language, it may be very fixed and rigid. It is the foundation on which the rest of language acquisition and development is based.

Receptive language. A second aspect of symbolization is receptive language, which includes at least two major subparts—visual and auditory. Normally the auditory receptive language is developed first, but, for example, in the normal reading process, both are required. Impairment of auditory receptive language ability will have a reciprocal effect on the development of inner language, and both will then be retarded. A similar reciprocal relationship exists between the auditory receptive and visual receptive. If input (reception) precedes output (expression), any defect in receptive language will inhibit the development of expressive language, that is, written or vocal expression.

At this level of the language development hierarchy, small deficiencies at a lower level are multiplied by any resultant higher level deficiencies and become a major problem. For example, a deficiency in perception will result in additional deficiencies at the imagery level, and serious difficulties are likely at the symbolization level. If a child misperceives what he hears, he proceeds at the imagery and symbolic level on the basis of this misperception, and his behavior seems inappropriate or bizarre. Or, if there is enough feedback of the reactions of others to his inappropriate behavior, he may tend to cut off any auditory perception except that of which he is absolutely certain and may appear to be hard-of-hearing or selectively deaf. The teacher or clinician may misunderstand the nature of the problem because, as in the previous example, a deficit may appear to be at one level of functioning (say, the imagery level) when in fact it is at a lower (perceptual) level. This principle must be understood, for otherwise it can result in inappropriate remedial attempts and failure for both the child and the clinician or teacher.

A key point to remember when considering apparent receptive language disabilities is that the development of adequate receptive language presumes adequate memory functioning. If memory span or memory sequence ability is impaired, symbolic functions cannot be developed in a normal manner. The most common evidence of memory sequence problems is the child's inability to follow instructions that involve three or four acts to be accomplished in a particular sequence. Since sequential behavior becomes increasingly important as the child grows older and is involved in more complex activities, this disability must be remedied.

Expressive language. The third major facet of symbolization is expressive language. This may take place when the child has developed inner language, when he has become competent in receiving language, and if other lower levels of the hierarchy are intact and functional. This expressive language, like the receptive, will be primarily either auditory or visual, with the auditory developing first in nearly all cases.

Often defective expressive language is simply a direct indicator of defective receptive language. Expressive aphasia, one of the most common manifestations of a defect in expressive language, was the first of the language disorders to be separately identified and recognized as a specific condition. In many cases it is difficult to separate settings in which the output function alone is impaired from those in which output is defective, but the apparent cause, or at least a major related factor, is defective receptive language. Both expressive auditory (expressive aphasia) and expressive written (dysgraphia) language impairments are called apraxias. In apraxias, by definition, the motor system itself is not impaired. It is only that the organism cannot use the motor system effectively to express language. Johnson and Myklebust believe it is important to distinguish between the apraxias and the conditions such as dysarthria and ataxia that affect expressive language. Dysarthria is a paralytic condition and may be caused by either the central or peripheral nervous system. Ataxia is caused only by central nervous system disorders and involves no paralysis. These two are often seen concurrently with learning disabilities such as aphasia but must be viewed as separate entities.

Conceptualization. Conceptualization is the fifth and final level at which we must consider the possibility of learning disabilities. Although we may often see disabilities affecting perception, imagery, or symbolization, the conceptual ability, which humans do not share with other animals, is perhaps the most intriguing process. This behavior includes both the ability to abstract and the ability to categorize. Although abstraction can take place without conceptualizing, a person cannot conceptualize without engaging in abstraction. Conceptual reasoning is somewhat difficult to explain and may be best shown through illustration. Development of the concept of the category of objects we call dishes will be considered as an example.

To the very small child, plate refers to the plate on which he eats. It may be highly distinctive in his life, have pictures of nursery rhyme characters, be divided into sections, etc., but it is plate to him. Later he learns that other objects on which he or others eat are called plates. In the meantime he has learned about cups and learned to distinguish between cups and glasses or perhaps mugs. Then, although the word has been in his

environment for some time, he becomes aware of the word "dishes." Perhaps he first hears of it when Aunt Mary hands him a plate of food and calls it a dish. At any rate, he soon learns that all the plates, cups, bowls, etc. on the table are dishes. Through a group of experiences and through the language that has been used in these experiences, he has learned of the class of objects called dishes and that a plate may be called a plate or a dish. He has learned that all plates are not shaped alike, although they have similar uses (except for the decorative plates on the plate rail overhead), and he has learned that all plates are dishes. A plate is observable, but the category dishes is not, except as a group of experiences with a variety of items that others have called dishes. He has formed the *concept* of dishes.

Some children have trouble relating objects and ideas through experiences. These children may be said to have conceptualization difficulty.

Nonverbal disabilities. Nonverbal disabilities have been mentioned in various places in the preceding discussion. Johnson and Myklebust believe that there "is a neurology of learning which relates to verbal functions and a neurology of learning which relates to nonverbal functions" (Johnson and Myklebust, 1967). They believe that one hemisphere of the brain serves mainly the verbal learning functions, whereas the other serves the nonverbal functions. They do not believe that one side, either the one represented by handedness or the one opposite established handedness, can be predicted to be the verbal hemisphere. They note that apparently functions can be transferred from one side to the other and that apparently this is sometimes done naturally when a person loses practical competence on one side due to accident.

An example of nonverbal functioning is recognition of a flag (as in patriotism) or a religious symbol (as a cross in the Christian faith) at the symbolic level of functioning. Another example is the kind of recognition that most individuals give to such facial expressions as a smile or a frown. Although these may sometimes be misleading, social custom has resulted in general rules that provide a guide to the behavior that most children learn. Those who are not perceptive to these nonverbal cues have trouble with interpersonal relationships and have social learning disabilities.

The Johnson and Myklebust view of verbal learning has been presented for a number of reasons. It is consistent with many of the evaluative tools that are presently in use with learning-disabled children and with much of the current literature relating to learning disabilities. It does not emphasize the motor realm as do some theories but does use a middle-of-the-road approach in explaining language development and verbal learning. It is consistent with the majority of well-accepted research findings relating to neurological functioning. It emphasizes the learning processes *above* the perceptual level, an important consideration when we consider the number of educators who equate learning disabilities with perceptual problems and do not stop to consider higher levels of learning.

Johnson and Myklebust would undoubtedly be among the first to note that this portion of their ideas does not represent a complete theory of learning. It is only one part of their explanation of how children learn in the verbal (language) areas of learning. It is, however, a much more complete explanation of how children learn than the conceptualizations of many teachers.*

If this explanation and conceptualization of learning is understandable and "makes sense," it may be used as a base for further learning and development on the part of teachers of the learning disabled. (For further explanation of Johnson and Myklebust views

---

*My experience in working with hundreds of teachers and teacher trainees has led me to think that many good teachers who are quite effective in the classroom teach with a variety of methods and materials (in most cases with good common sense) without having carefully thought through the learning process. However, many of these teachers have problems with certain children, problems that might be less severe if they better understood the learning process.

on teaching the learning disabled, see pp. 95-98.)

GAGNÉ'S CONDITIONS OF LEARNING

Robert Gagné is one of the leading learning theorists. He does not belong to any one of the traditional learning theory schools of thought but has developed a concept that he relates to the *conditions required for various kinds of learning.* He maintains that there are many types of learning hierarchies and gives examples of how various topics of school instruction "possess hierarchical organizations with respect to required types of learning" (Gagné, 1970). He also provides a highly interesting discussion of readiness for learning. Gagné's conceptualization of learning is one of the most interesting and potentially most valuable I have known, providing answers (for me) that no other learning theory can provide. It is not a simple theory, and my purpose in reviewing it here is to challenge the reader to study it in depth.

The descriptions of the eight basic types of learning can be of value in learning disabilities planning and programming and I hope they will be sufficiently interesting to encourage further study. The Gagné concept has the potential for resolving some of the conflicts that exist when we attempt to reconcile the better known traditional learning theories.

Gagné approaches learning by identifying situations in which learning occurs. Once the varieties of learning are identified, he analyzes the conditions that govern the learning occurrences. Gagné (1970) defines learning as "a change in human disposition or capability, which can be retained, and which is not simply ascribable to the process of growth." To him, the basic elements of a learning event are (1) the learner, (2) the stimulus situation (the event or events that stimulate the learner's senses), and (3) the response (action resulting from the stimulation).

Using this approach and definition of learning, Gagné then proceeds to attempt to identify different types of learning that may occur. Eight types of learning will be identified and certain implications for educators will be noted.

In this and all of the succeeding descriptions of learning types, we must keep in mind that *for learning to take place, the student must be capable of learning*. Unfortunately, we sometimes expect a child to learn in a way in which he is not capable (for example, a child with a serious auditory channel deficit whom we are trying to teach through a primarily auditory approach). Then we decide that the approach is generally ineffective when its ineffectiveness is actually related to the child's disability and to our lack of insight.

Signal learning

Signal learning, as described by Gagné, would be called a conditioned response by many learning theorists. In this type of learning there must be simultaneous or nearly simultaneous presentation of two forms of stimulation. For example, if a child reaches for the electrical outlet and his mother simultaneously says "no" sharply and slaps his hand, he may soon learn the signal, and when she says "no" sharply he will stop reaching for almost any object. There may be other factors in the situation (for example, the desirability of the object for which the child is reaching), but in pure signal learning the reaction becomes nearly automatic. Fear responses often are in this category, as may be a pleasure response.

Gagné points out that some signal learning may occur rapidly, while in other instances it may require many pairings of the proper stimuli.

Stimulus-response learning

Stimulus-response learning, also a response to a signal, is different from signal learning in that it requires making precise movements in response to specific stimuli or combinations of stimuli. This is the type of learning in which the learner responds *because he wants to*. Gagné uses the example of a dog learning to shake hands. In stimulus-response learning the response is a much more precise skeletal-

muscular act than in the generalized response of signal learning.

Stimulus-response learning is usually characterized by gradual learning; that is, the learner becomes better able to make the desired response through practice. It is somewhat similar to the "shaping" process in behavior modification. Still another point in stimulus-response learning is that reward or reinforcement is associated with correct responses.

A final and important difference between stimulus-response and signal learning is that in stimulus-response learning a component of the *stimulus itself* is generated by muscular movements as the process is developed. In the case of the dog the external stimulus is "shake hands," and a related proprioceptive stimulation is caused by the muscles that raise the paw.

This appears to be the form of learning involved when a child learns to vocalize a new word. In such vocalization, the "feel" of the word as it is said is part of or becomes part of the stimulus.

Chaining

A third and much used type of learning is called chaining. This is the connecting in sequence of two or more previously learned stimulus-response patterns. The building of such "chains" is the means whereby children are taught many of their early habits and is the reason that some habits or other early learning may seem to take place almost overnight. What often happens is that two stimulus-response patterns are learned over a relatively long period of time. If these have the potential of being easily connected, it can be accomplished in such fashion that the final end result (chaining) appears to have taken place very quickly.

Verbal association

Verbal association is essentially chaining, but it involves language rather than purely motor activities. Learning a word in a foreign language is one good example; this is accomplished simply by acquiring a chain between the native language and the foreign language word. An example given by Gagné is that of learning the French word for match—"alumette." This might be done in a variety of ways, but one way would be to mentally connect the syllable "lum" in alumette with the same syllable in illuminate. To do this, however, it would be necessary to have a concept of the fact that the match, when it bursts into flame, illuminates.

For verbal association to occur, what Gagné calls a coding connection must be available (previously learned). Highly verbal persons should have more coding connections readily available than those with little verbal ability; therefore, if all other factors are equal, the highly verbal person should learn more effectively through verbal association. This type of learning is limited to humans because it requires a previously learned repertoire of language.

Discrimination learning

Discrimination learning requires attention to *interference* as a factor in reducing retention (or increasing the likelihood of forgetting). Single stimulus-response learning is relatively simple, and if all learning involved highly different types of stimuli and very different responses, learning as a process and the teaching-learning procedure would be much simplified. Learning in today's complicated society is not simple; it requires the ability to respond differently to stimuli that are only slightly different. In many cases the stimuli are in fact multiple stimuli that must be integrated, compared to other multiple stimuli, and then responded to appropriately.

Gagné believes that interference between connections in newly learned chains and older chains is a major reason for forgetting. Methods to assist the learner to discover distinctive differences between stimuli are among the best ways to enhance discrimination learning and to reduce forgetting.

Concept learning

Concept learning, according to Gagné, requires an internal neural process of representation. Although some of the higher animals may be able to accomplish something

similar on a very limited basis, in humans this is accomplished through the representative capability of language. Humans not only are quite capable of concept learning, but their voluminous written and spoken efforts indicate that they enjoy or are stimulated by such representative manipulation.

In learning concepts we learn to identify specific objects with other objects that may be said to belong to the same class or category. This obviously requires internal representative manipulation and the establishment of multiple chains and interconnections. Although the objects may be concrete, the class or category is representative and abstract.

Gagné points out that although much concept learning relates to concrete objects (chairs, desks, and tables are furniture), there is also an important type of concept learning that relates to defined classifications that must be initially learned on a purely verbal basis because they are not concrete. His example is entities such as mothers, fathers, uncles, and aunts. An uncle is an uncle *by definition*.

The difference between concrete and defined concepts is also important. It is altogether possible that a learning problem in conceptualization might affect defined concepts more than concrete ones or vice versa. In the realm of conceptualization it becomes apparent why we must develop accurate, wide ability to use language. Without adequate language a child cannot conceptualize effectively.

Rule learning

Rule learning would probably be included in Johnson and Myklebust's theory as conceptualization. Rule learning is a chain of two or more concepts; in general form it can be represented by the statement "if A, then B," where both A and B are concepts. If A and B are merely words or phrases and "if A, then B" is just a verbal sequence, the learning involved is verbal association.

For rule learning to take place the concepts to be linked must have been learned previously; in other words, the concepts being chained must have already been classified.

Problem solving

Problem solving, like rule learning, would likely be included as part of conceptualization by Johnson and Myklebust. According to Gagné, it is the combining of two rules to produce a new capability, an answer to a question or a problem. For this type of learning to take place the learner must know something about the type of response that will be the solution *before* he arrives at the solution. This procedure involves many lengthy chains; many would use the more general term "thinking." It is at this level that humans arrive at new knowledge by means of combining old rules (rule learning). It seems rather ordinary to nearly all adults, but it must be learned by children. People who are characterized as logical usually tend to be individuals who accomplish this level of learning consistently.

The eight types of learning described by Gagné are much more complex than indicated here and have specific implications for teachers, particularly those who work with learning-disabled children, and a careful study of Gagné's basic writings would be of value.

Preconditions for learning

Gagné's preconditions for learning are of sufficient value and basic enough in application to be worthy of mention as a part of his learning theory. The three major preconditions are (1) attention, (2) motivation, and (3) developmental readiness. These three components of readiness to learn must be considered in planning for all children, particularly for the learning disabled. The reader is directed to Gagné's discussion of these preconditions and their implication for the teacher for more detailed information (Gagné, 1970).

SUMMARY

The learning disabilities teacher must develop a working theory of learning to most effectively develop meaningful educational activities and procedures for learning-disabled children. Such children are in need of special assistance because the normal school program is for some reason ineffective. Understanding the basic steps in the learning sequence will permit the teacher to more accurately pinpoint the step or stage at which remedial and assistive efforts should start and thus save valuable time. One concept of critical importance is that the existence of a disability at one particular stage of the learning sequence does not necessarily mean that remediation should start at that point. The inability to perform at a given level may often be the outgrowth of more basic, lower level disabilities. Knowledge of how children learn is essential if the teacher is to "track down" the real cause of the problem.

Johnson and Myklebust and Gagné have provided theoretical constructs that are of value in assessing learning problems and planning educational programs based on such assessment. Their explanations of learning make it clear that learning disabilities must not be equated with "perceptual problems," for many learning disabilities develop at a higher level in the learning sequence than perception. Johnson and Myklebust present a view of verbal learning that is particularly valuable in learning disabilities programming because of its consistency with assessment tools and with much of the available literature, particularly curriculum and methods suggestions.

One major caution must be observed in planning and implementing educational programs based on existing learning theories and assessment tools. Most of these theories and assessment tools are process oriented, and we may often find significant process disabilities. These should be remedied, but we must also make certain that the required task-oriented assistance is provided and that affective needs are considered. Learning disabilities programming can be only minimally effective if it retains process variables as its only point of focus.

REFERENCES AND SUGGESTED READINGS

Ausubel, D. *The psychology of meaningful verbal learning.* New York: Grune & Stratton, Inc., 1963.

Bruner, J., Goodnow, J., and Austin, G. *A study of thinking.* New York: John Wiley & Sons, Inc., 1956.

Gagné, R. The acquisition of knowledge. *Psychological Review,* 1962, *69,* 355-365.

Gagné, R. *The conditions of learning* (2nd ed.). New York: Holt, Rinehart & Winston, Inc., 1970.

Gearheart, B. *Learning disabilities: educational strategies.* St. Louis: The C. V. Mosby Co., 1973.

Gibson, E. *Principles of perceptual learning and development.* New York: Appleton-Century-Crofts, 1969.

Gibson, J. *The senses considered as perceptual systems.* Boston: Houghton Mifflin Co., 1966.

Guilford, J. *The nature of human intelligence.* New York: McGraw-Hill Book Co., 1967.

Johnson, D., and Myklebust, H. *Learning disabilities: educational principles and practices.* New York: Grune & Stratton, Inc., 1967.

Kleinmuntz, B. (Ed.). *Concepts and the structure of memory.* New York: John Wiley & Sons, Inc., 1967.

Lerner, J. *Children with learning disabilities.* Boston: Houghton Mifflin Co., 1971.

Wickelgren, W. Memory. In J. Swets and L. Elliot (Eds.), *Psychology and the handicapped child.* Washington, D.C.: U.S. Government Printing Office, 1974.

4 Assessment in program planning

Assessment is an all-important first step in planning individual programs for children with learning disabilities. Even in the unusual circumstance in which all known assessment provides no indication of the basic problem, this at least may avoid the type of indiscriminate general perceptual remediation that has sometimes been utilized in the past.

Since referral to a learning disabilities program usually means that a pupil is having difficulty in one or more subject areas, assessment of those basic skills or subject areas is the first type of assessment to consider. This usually includes an individual test of achieve-

ment followed by diagnostic tests in the subject areas in which the greatest difficulty appears to exist. Then tests of process to discover the existence of faulty *or poorly developed* basic process abilities should also be administered.

If any clue or hint of process difficulties may be obtained from background data or specific referral information, these should be considered first. However, it is a serious error to stop at this point, even if specific difficulties are discovered as a result of such assessment. In many cases preliminary information suggests problems related to visual processing and tests confirm this indication, but it is later discovered that there are even more serious auditory problems. The opposite can also be true.

The likelihood of the teacher focusing on one area of process remediation or development is increased by the fact that teachers become more expert with certain types of remedial efforts and accumulate tests, materials, and equipment to work in this one major area. They then look for this type of problem, and if they look long and hard enough, they tend to find it. Furthermore, once they find it they often look no farther. It is a dangerous type of self-fulfilling prophecy and is reinforced by success in cases in which the major problem *is* the one for which they look with such regularity, persistence, and expertise.

The assessment process in learning disabilities is in a state of rapid development and evolution (including some confusion), with new tests, manuals, and guides being developed regularly. Appendix D contains an annotated list of tests and assessment tools that may be of value to those who are not familiar with the variety of instruments available. The list of references at the end of this chapter will provide another source for further investigation. In most cases teachers who work as learning disabilities specialists develop assessment procedures that include tools used in nearly all cases, those used in unusual cases as dictated by special circumstances, and those that may provide results needed by the teacher but must be given by someone else because of their highly specialized nature. In some cases certain tests are administered by other specialists as a part of the initial referral and program placement procedure (for example, the Wechsler Intelligence Scale for Children [WISC or WISC-R], perhaps given by the school psychologist), or medical examination data may already have been obtained, but more and more the learning disabilities specialist is being asked to complete a major part of the assessment task.

Before proceeding into the specific assessment functions likely to be expected of the learning disabilities specialist, it will be of value to overview the sources of assessment data that should be tapped in completing the assessment process with children referred for consideration for learning disabilities programs. It must be noted that all of these sources will not necessarily be utilized in all cases, but most will be in most cases, and all represent potentially useful sources of meaningful data. These sources of data will be outlined, and then models for assessment will be suggested. Just as is the case in relation to a "learning disabilities method," there is no single assessment procedure that will fit all cases and circumstances. Part of the reason is the variety of conditions and disabilities that may fit under the learning disabilities umbrella, but a more significant reason relates to the variety of settings in which diagnostic and assessment procedures may be implemented.

For example, some school districts may employ social workers, school and clinical psychologists, psychometrists, educational diagnosticians, speech clinicians, hearing clinicians, etc. and may have the services of medical doctors, including pediatric specialists and neurologists, available for such referrals. Others may have a school psychologist, a speech therapist, and one minimally trained special education teacher whose basic training may have been in mental retardation. Some may utilize the services of a nearby university diagnostic clinic, complete with all of the medical specialties, while others have only the services of a part-time psychometrist (provided through some sort of cooperative arrangement with other school districts) who has little knowledge in this relatively new area of interest.

Another set of variables grows out of the manner in which the administrative structure of the schools lends itself to cooperative work among various divisions of the school system. If the school psychologists and other more clinically oriented personnel are under a different director than the special education classroom teachers, or if there is intrasystem controversy and misunderstanding between the director of elementary education and the director of special education, the assessment system must be "bent" to be consistent with this condition. Those experienced and familiar with the manner in which schools operate will understand this situation. Although it is highly unfortunate, unless human nature changes overnight, this product of lack of understanding and conflict of interest will continue to affect the establishment of effective assessment procedures. However, there are assessment components that are relatively constant and that, along with certain highly specialized needs in some specific cases, should be systematically pursued within the local structural framework.

HISTORICAL DATA

One major component or category of assessment data is basically historical in nature. This may include but is not limited to the following.

Health history. The health history may be obtained from the parent or guardian but should be cross-checked with any earlier information that may have been gathered, for example, at the time of entrance into kindergarten. The cross-checking is mainly for purposes of verification but may lead to the discovery of things that have been forgotten, particularly in the case of an older child.

Attendance record. In a few cases checking the attendance record (which often requires writing or telephoning schools that the child attended previously) makes the reason for poor achievement clear. In a few cases I have known the poor achievement was apparently due mainly to lack of educational opportunity. When this is the case or appears to be the case, local or state regulations regarding state-approved learning disabilities programming may prohibit inclusion of the child in such programs, but at least we then know much more about the likely cause for the problem, and this will help in planning educational alternatives.

Social history. The social history is best developed by a trained school social worker and is the source of considerable valuable data. It is, however, only one piece of evidence and should not become the basis of prediction or hard decisions about causation

except as supported by and used in conjunction with other data.

Records of past test results. Although past test results may be overemphasized, they may be quite important. For example, when such results show a consistent picture of average or above-average achievement for 2 or 3 years and then a sudden drop, the time period during which the drop occurred should be more carefully scrutinized. This may lead to critically important information about causal factors. No one test result should be viewed as a reliable indicator (of anything), but a pattern of results will generally have some meaning, particularly as related to other data.

Anecdotal records, reports of conferences, etc. Like the record of past test results, records containing other information may mean little or nothing alone but in concert with other data may help to explain factors that might otherwise be left in doubt.

CURRENT DATA

A second major assessment category or component, one that usually receives the most attention, is the variety of testing and diagnostic data gathered just prior to or immediately following referral. In most states the gathering of such data requires parent permission, which in turn requires a parent conference in which the reasons for concern, the purposes of learning disabilities programming, and related topics must be discussed. (This procedure, including the requirements of due process, is discussed on pp. 198-199.) These assessment tools may include the following.*

Psychometric and psychological tests and measures. Psychometric and psychological tests may include tests such as the Wechsler Intelligence tests (the Wechsler Preschool and Primary Scale of Intelligence [WPPSI], the

---

*This listing of types of assessment data is subcategorized in an arbitrary manner; that is, it does not follow any established assessment sequence or any particular authority's theoretical construct. Some of the types of assesment as listed may overlap others to a significant degree, but the purpose of this listing is to provide the reader with a broad conceptualization of what is involved in learning disabilities assessment, not to train or develop diagnostic experts.

Wechsler Intelligence Scale for Children [WISC], the Wechsler Adult Intelligence Scale [WAIS]), and the Stanford-Binet Intelligence Scale. Other tests such as the Slossen Intelligence Test and the Columbia Mental Maturity Scale may be given as "back-up" tests when there seems to be need for some additional verification in unusual cases.

Tests of this type are those that are more likely to be given by the school psychologist or psychometrist; however, an increasing number of individuals with local school district titles such as educational diagnostician, psychoeducational diagnostician, learning specialist, and learning disabilities specialist are fully trained and qualified to administer many, if not all, tests of this type.

Academic achievement tests. Although in most cases pupils have been referred for assistance on the basis of poor academic achievement and their educational records usually include a number of scores from academic achievement tests, it is often wise to complete some individual testing. In many cases this simply verifies the information on the referral form, but in some cases the careful observer can learn a great deal from how the individual approaches the task of reading, mathematics, or spelling. Also, past records tend to indicate a grade equivalent with no further information as to what type of problems caused the low score. For example, a low math score does not indicate what type of "finger counting" procedures or other specific behavior or methods the individual may use or exhibit. Diagnostic tests provide this type of information also, but a straightforward, individually administered test of achievement in the basic academic areas is worth giving for the information it may provide.

Subject or skill area diagnostic tests. Based on referral information and any guidance that might be provided by academic achievement tests, diagnostic tests should be given to determine the most critical problems. Diagnostic tests, particularly in reading, come in all sizes, shapes, and descriptions. Various geographical areas of the United States appear to have "favorites," perhaps relating to the training received by reading and remedial reading teachers at key universities. The only pertinent advice to be given here is that individual teachers should use tests that seem to work best for them, but at the same time (as school or personal budgets permit) try out new tests as they appear. It is *not* safe to count on the publicity given many new tests or on their alleged "representative" norm group. There are some specific problems relating to norms for minority cultural and ethnic groups, but we should not generalize any further than to advise considerable care.

Sensory acuity tests. In most cases tests of visual and auditory acuity should be given early in the referral and study procedure. Auditory acuity should be tested by an audiometer, a screening instrument that measures the child's threshold of hearing at different frequency levels. Visual acuity testing should include the traditional testing with a chart of block letters (the Snellen Chart is the most often used), plus stereoscopic test instruments such as the Keystone Telebinocular, the Ortho-Rater, and the AO Sight Screener. These provide measures of near and far-point visual acuity, depth perception, lateral and vertical muscular balance, and color perception. It is of critical importance that sensory acuity be carefully tested; if not, we may later try to remedy some assumed problem that in fact is primarily an acuity problem.

Affective domain assessment. How the child feels about himself, about his lack of success in academic areas, and about his success and lack of success in other areas of life may be major factors in any plan of remediation or skill development. Research in other areas of human endeavor has made it obvious that at times feelings are the single most essential key to success or even to continued existence.*

---

*I refer here to commonly accepted evidence that individuals who are ill may recuperate much more rapidly if they have positive feelings; to the causal effect of tension and anxiety on ulcers, even in young children; and a variety of related evidence as to the tremendous effect of feelings on achievement.

A variety of instruments may be used to obtain an indication of this important area, including standardized tests, sociometric tools, and of great importance, careful teacher observation and analysis. It is important to remember that affective problems may be masked by the child unless we deliberately review and assess in this area. It is commonly accepted that many learning-disabled children have some emotional overlay to the learning problem, and when such emotional components are obvious, we usually attend to them. In a complete assessment in learning disabilities we must deliberately and methodically look for this type of problem so that even if it is minimal, we may attend to it and thus increase the chances that our other efforts will be effective.

Tests of process. A variety of tests of process are available and, like the diagnostic tests, are not all what they purport to be. Chapter 5, which includes a discussion of the Illinois Test of Psycholinguistic Abilities and other similar tests, will expand on the potentialities and the limitations of such tests. One generalization can be made with confidence: if a single test of, for example, visual perception indicates a problem in that area, it is *not* a sufficient basis for launching an involved program of development of visual perception abilities. The same thing applies to diagnostic tests and, for that matter, any type of test that attempts to measure complex skills, processes, or behaviors in a single, short-term sample.

Speech and language evaluation. Speech and language evaluation may usually be accomplished by a competent speech clinician using a variety of tests and evaluative tools. Comencing in the early 1970's, many speech therapists were trained to evaluate and to work with both speech and language development. In many school districts they may also complete the hearing evaluation. In any case the speech and language evaluation is an essential part of the total evaluative process.

Physical examination. The physical examination, which in many cases should also include a neurological examination, is quite essential. In some cases the general practitioner has not been involved in evaluations

of the type necessary for a child with learning problems, but an increasing number of pediatricians and general practitioners in addition to most neurologists are showing an interest in the role they can play in this field. Although it would be a mistake for the educator to try to second-guess medical problems, it is helpful to the medical doctor to receive the type of behavioral hints that may assist his efforts.

Although a medical cause may not be the major factor in any large number of cases, there is sufficient evidence of learning disabilities that may be "cured" (the cause corrected) through various medical efforts that we must be alert to this are of concern. Teachers must note, however, that in most cases, even if the cause of a serious educational problem can be corrected, usually the educational lag and related personality problems that have been created earlier must receive specific educational assistance.

Evaluation of developmental level. This evaluation may have been a part of the physical examination, the psychometric or psychological evaluation, or the historical data. If this is so, then no further efforts need be made. But if this information has not been gathered or existing information has not been put together in such a manner as to permit those who must plan and implement special educational programs to see how each child's overall development compares with others of his chronological age, then this must be accomplished. We fairly often find that a 10-year-old child referred to a learning disabilities program is in almost every developmental respect perhaps only 7½ years old.* We have been viewing him as 10 years

---

*A child who is actually 10 years old but has been hospitalized for many years may have had limited opportunity to explore the environment at an early age, to develop language normally, to use muscles, etc. and may be only 7 years old for purposes of planning educational efforts. If this is the case, then it is usually fruitless and certainly frustrating to both child and teacher to try for 10-year-old goals. Learning disabilities practitioners at times forget to fully consider this possibility. In one such case the historical evidence coupled with a developmental evaluation made it clear that we should think in terms of working with a 7-year-old or at most an 8-year-old.

old and making all comparisons with this chronological age in mind, but for all practical purposes we may be dealing with a 7-year-old. If this is the case, we have a most different situation than if we have a 10-year-old who is developmentally 10 years old in most respects but only reads as well as a 7-year-old.

Classroom teacher's observation report. If the child has been with one teacher for as much as 6 to 8 weeks (in some cases less time may be sufficient), with proper guidance the teacher may complete a highly meaningful evaluation report form that systematizes the evaluation. In such a report the teacher records how the child approaches various tasks, how he follows (or cannot follow) directions, and other similar information. A number of individual school districts are apparently in the process of developing a form of this type, and most school districts with organized screening committees and several of the specialized personnel mentioned earlier (psychologists, educational diagnosticians, speech therapists, etc.) can develop a guide that is appropriate to the system and to the classroom teacher's role in this total procedure in the district.

Although overlap may occur between the historical data and the current data, it is important that the type of information that may be obtained through each of these procedures actually be obtained. It is easy and in some settings it is common to assume that certain data are not really important, but we must consider that each type of information or data may provide a significant piece in the puzzle. Seldom is the puzzle actually complete, even if we attend to each item listed with great meticulousness. In dealing with highly complex human beings we seldom can obtain all the information required to make the picture crystal clear. On the other hand, most such information is so highly interrelated that at times one clue tends to clarify many other points in question; therefore we must strive to gather all data possible, even if we think we already have the answer or that certain data will all be negative. Those with limited experience sometimes have just enough experience to reinforce the idea that an effective job of evaluation may be completed with limited data. With good luck this may be so. But those with much experience have seen the serious errors and blunders that can result from drawing conclusions based on limited data and are willing to spend the time required for comprehensive assessment. This is the only procedure I can recommend with good conscience.

It is sometimes charged that diagnosticians and assessment personnel spend much time, effort, and money completing evaluations that say little and that schools then do little more than "label" the child and return him to the classroom. This charge is warranted in some cases, and when true it is a major professional-educational crime. If the major result of assessment is labeling, then it is essentially useless and should be discontinued. The assessment procedure recommended assumes that the following conditions exist or can be made to exist: (1) assessment personnel are competent and are permitted time and conditions under which they may "do their thing"; (2) personnel are available and a structure is provided to ensure that the whole spectrum of assessment data is carefully considered and pertinent alternatives are explored; (3) a continuum of services is available, and children are provided services on the basis of programs that are most likely to be of maximum value (not what is most convenient for the school system); and (4) continual systematic observations plus regularly scheduled reevaluation are a part of the process.

Although this may appear to be idealistic to some, it is happening in a number of places and is being closely approached in many more. It is the goal for which we must continually strive; anything less is not enough.

ASSESSMENT MODELS

There are a variety of assessment models, many of which are quite similar. It is doubtful that a good case can be made for the use of any one model to the exclusion of all others, but certain components are necessary for any model to be maximally effective. As stated earlier, this is not a text on assessment and will not present all that must be considered in planning assessment but rather will present guidelines to assist in the selection or development of effective assessment approaches, techniques, and systems. Outlines of assessment approaches will be given, but each school district or evaluation center must build its own complete system, tailoring it to local goals, conditions, and capabilities.

The following questions should be asked about any assessment system or model in attempting to determine its effectiveness.

1. Does it provide for input data from all individuals who have had recent contact with the pupil? This would include teachers (including preschool contacts where this applies), parents or other adults who regularly contact the child, medical personnel, law enforcement or other juvenile authorities when applicable, and any others as the case indicates.
2. Does it provide for the kinds of information indicated on pp. 36-39?
3. Is some one individual (or small group) with the necessary competence charged with the responsibility and given the time to organize the data for most efficient utilization and consideration?
4. Does it provide for due process? (See pp. 198-199.)
5. Does it provide for group decision making in program planning, and is the group membership representative of those disciplines and interests necessary for sound decision making?
6. Does the system provide for someone in the decision making group who fully understands all possible program alternatives?
7. Does it provide for systematic, ongoing evaluation?
8. Does it provide for fast, temporary, emergency-type reassessment and program changes as necessary in unusual situations?
9. Does it provide for regular, comprehensive program review based on planned reassessment?
10. Is there a plan whereby the entire assessment system may be reviewed and modified as experience indicates is necessary?

Other questions may seem particularly pertinent in a given local situation (such as "will local funding be available for this system as federal funds are withdrawn?") and should be considered where appropriate. But whatever the unique local circumstances, the assessment system or model must be carefully planned; any individual assessment will be of no more value than is made possible by the system.

Tridimensional assessment model

The tridimensional model that follows is a "general purpose" model—one to which many school districts may relate. It provides for most variables present in the typical school district and will work most effectively only as all parts of the model can be fully implemented.

The first dimension, *needs assessment,* presumes that we can and will gather the information necessary to proceed to the second dimension, *contingency management.* The description of this assessment model may suggest certain contingencies that have been overlooked in earlier planning.

The third dimension, *resource allocation,* relates to planned, carefully coordinated use of available resources. Although the model on p. 41 may indicate more specialized personnel than many smaller school districts have readily available, the essential factor is careful consideration of the resources actually available and careful planning of their utilization. It should also be noted that sometimes, even in smaller communities, these human resources are available on a part-time or shared basis with other agencies.

TRIDIMENSIONAL MODEL FOR ANALYSIS
AND INTERPRETATION OF ASSESSMENT
INFORMATION*
Needs assessment

Some needs of a child can be assumed; others must be determined by assessment. There are at

---

*Modified slightly from Gearheart, B. R., and Willenberg, E. P. *Application of pupil assessment information: for the special education teacher* (2nd ed.). Denver: Love Publishing Co., 1974.

Tridimensional prescriptive educational model

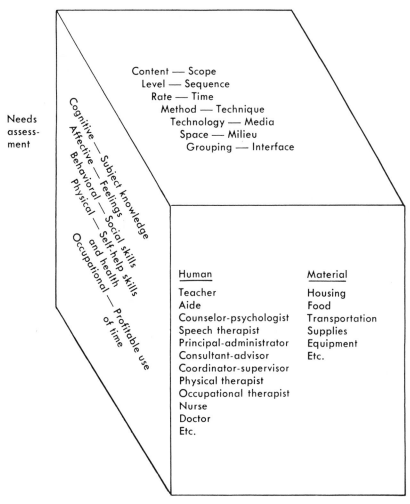

Contingency management

Needs assess- ment

Cognitive — Subject knowledge
Affective — Feelings
Behavioral — Social skills
Physical — Self-help skills
and health
Occupational — Profitable use
of time

Content — Scope
Level — Sequence
Rate — Time
Method — Technique
Technology — Media
Space — Milieu
Grouping — Interface

Human

Teacher
Aide
Counselor-psychologist
Speech therapist
Principal-administrator
Consultant-advisor
Coordinator-supervisor
Physical therapist
Occupational therapist
Nurse
Doctor
Etc.

Material

Housing
Food
Transportation
Supplies
Equipment
Etc.

Resource allocation

least three sources the teacher can use to gain more information about a child. The first is teacher observation. The others are past scholastic records and teaching—both within the classroom and by outside specialists.

Generally, pupil needs can be grouped under five major headings. It is important that each child undergo a spectral analysis to determine the relevance of a given factor in the total array of descriptors for pupil needs.

Cognitive. A child's ability to be aware of, to know, to understand, and to judge constitute forms of cognition essential to the development of subject knowledge and skills. In planning instruction it is important to know the nature and extent of his cognitive capabilities and how he is able to apply these capabilities in the achievement of specific tasks.

Affective. The way a child feels about himself constitutes a barrier or a boon to his development as a learner and vital human being. Traditionally, the dimension of "affect" has been difficult to include in the general design of curricular objectives. However, the importance of concurrent emotional development has never been more evident; the question is "How does one teach a child in order to *deliberately* enhance his affective growth?" The answer will become more evident when a complete analysis of needs has been made in the context of the educational model.

The significant thing for the teacher to recognize is that affect is learned and, therefore, can be taught.

Behavioral. As used here the behavioral dimension by definition is concerned with skills of social adaptability and relationships. Behavior can be described along two basic developmental strands: (1) skills of *independent* social behavior and (2) skills of *interdependent* social behavior. As in the case of affect, behavioral skills are acquired and can be taught as a part of the prescribed instructional plan.

Physical. Although physical education has been a part of the instructional scene for many years, its application by classroom teachers in a prescriptive teaching model has not been widely disseminated or thoroughly understood. Concern for the development of health and self-help skills can be described under five major headings.

1. Development of motor and movement skills
2. Development of playground and recreation skills
3. Development of rhythmic skills
4. Development of swimming skills
5. Development of physical fitness

Whatever the child's physical condition, the teacher can develop a remedial or developmental plan of action as the circumstance may dictate.

Occupational. Any determination of needs would be lacking without an assessment of the child's capability to use time profitably. Ordinarily described as occupational skills, this component is concerned with the potential for development of both remunerative and nonremunerative activity. As such, the occupational needs of a child not only can be assessed but also served as early as he is admitted to school. The challenge is to translate such assessment information into a meaningful educational plan. All other assessments—cognitive, affective, behavioral, and physical—are essential ingredients.

Contingency management

There are many conditions affecting learning and child development over which the teacher has little or no control. On the other hand, a number of contingencies are directly in the hands of the teacher and available as options in responding to the identified needs of pupils. The management of these contingencies in a remedial program of education is parallel to a treatment program in medicine. An examination of some of these items may serve to reassure and validate the high level professional functions still available

to the teacher in his relationship with children and in the presentation of learning opportunities.

Content. Given certain institutional restraints, the teacher is still primarily in control of *what* he teaches. The scope of learning opportunities should be directly related to identified pupil needs. For example, the relationship between content and cognitive needs is obvious. In the case of a child whose cognitive capabilities are attenuated by an intellectual deficit greater than 2 standard deviations below the mean on appropriate diagnostic instruments, one must then consider the implications for what is to be offered in the nature of valid learning opportunities. An apparent assumption is that such a child should *not* be burdened with a course of study loaded with a bias on academic performance. On the positive side, one may assume such a child *should* be offered a course of study rich in practical learnings. The search for relevant content naturally includes cues derived from the full scale needs inquiry. The child's affective condition, nature of behavioral skills, physical status, and occupational potential are all integral variables considered in the complete scope of learning experience which constitute a prescriptive educational program.

Level. At what point should a child begin instruction on content that is organized sequentially? This question is especially pertinent in conjunction with assessment of subject knowledge. Underlying the question is the assumption that certain skills and learning processes follow fundamental patterns of growth and development in the human individual. Further, it is assumed that some children may be out of phase in the order of sequential development due to unusual influences caused by grossly divergent congenital or environmental conditions. For example, it is not unusual to find that deaf children may present irregular profiles in the sequences of a developmental language program. Such findings should not thwart or confuse the teacher. Rather, the child's language program should allow for entry at the level nearest to the point at which successful performance becomes erratic.

Management of the child's entry level on a cognitive scale or subject sequence extends to similar considerations in needs associated with the affective, behavioral, physical, and occupational components of the diagnostic profile.

Rate. Management of the rate of progression on achievement provides the teacher with latitude to facilitate learning in all its dimensions.

Rate control should be viewed in a flexible time frame. The time allowed for achievement of certain language skills in the cognitive area may differ significantly from a predicted rate of motor skills achievement in the physical area. When the educational prescription notes that additional time and effort should be devoted to language skills, it follows that less time will be given to some other instructional area. Time budgeting, therefore, allows the teacher to manage (1) the distribution of instructional effort and (2) the pace of educational achievement within the limits of the child's total capabilities.

Methods. There is no known universal method by which instruction can be of maximum benefit to all children. As a matter of fact, there exists no specific method equally applicable for all children with the same educational diagnosis. On the other hand, specific techniques do work better with some children than with others, and it is the task of the teacher to find instructional approaches to which the child responds best. An open eclectic approach requires broad knowledge and skill on the part of the teacher. The needs assessment will provide clues. Obvious gross deficits such as loss of vision or hearing have directly translatable methodological implications. Generally, however, the diagnostic findings are complex and must be interpreted in the context of learning theories on which the instructional techniques should be based. When the teacher is searching for ways to meet specific cognitive, affective, behavioral, physical, and occupational needs of a given pupil, his challenge is to assure optimal benefit from appropriate learning opportunities.

Technology. Advancements in educational technology usually are associated with the "hardware" and related "software" in the delivery of instructional services. Examples include the use of television, radio, telephone, computer-assisted instruction, "teaching machines," and other support systems. As these systems are available to the teacher and would help in meeting the defined needs of a pupil, they constitute another contingency that may be considered in a comprehensive instructional plan. Especially important is the achievement of a greater degree of precision and individualization of instruction.

Teachers of visually handicapped pupils know of recent advancements made in optical aids, reprographics, audio recordings, and the like. Likewise, teachers of the hearing impaired are appreciative of improvements made in individual and group amplification equipment. Homebound children now may be taught full time in the home, participating in all classroom activities, due to technological advancements made in telephonic communication systems. When used as a means to an end, technology can serve to humanize education and enhance the artistry of teaching.

Space. Occasionally, we must remind ourselves that space can be used as an educational tool. Space can be viewed restrictively or expansively. It can be used to confine a child for security or control purposes, to provide privacy by minimizing distractions, to establish concepts of position and orientation, to create mood, etc. When a teacher considers the needs inventory of a child, he must weigh, among the various contingencies at his disposal, the values of various space usage alternatives. When movement and large muscle activity is indicated, outdoor space may be required. When the child is highly distractable, privacy or isolation may serve a useful purpose. When physical limitations restrict mobility as in the case of cerebral palsy, space modifications may be necessary to facilitate movement and body control. The blind child is taught to use spatial cues to establish orientation and independent mobility.

Grouping. Children learn from each other. The learnings can be either positive or negative. Currently, classification of pupils is often determined by negative attributes or deficits. Exemplary models of behavior, motivation, and academic performance may be seriously lacking in certain special groups of pupils with special needs. Grouping as an alternative in contingency management presupposes the achievement of beneficial results to the pupil as opposed to an institutional expediency.

When considering the needs of a pupil in relation to grouping, several questions merit consideration. How can this child be situated so that he can learn constructively from others and contribute to the learning of others in his group? How can the pupil be positioned so that he can derive support and reinforcement for positive behavior or enhancement of self-imagery and feelings of personal integrity? How can grouping promote stimulation or motivation to initiate and complete tasks or to share and enjoy the achievement of others?

Resource allocation

When needs are assessed and prescriptive plans of education devised, then one is at the point of drawing upon all of the available resources. These may be categorized as either human or material.

In looking over the prescriptive education model, one is impressed with the array of human and material resources available in a given situation. The teacher, however, should not be disappointed in his situation if some of the elements are missing. The task is to take the consolidated contingency management plan much as one would take a prescription or supply order to be filled from the stock room. In this analogy the teacher fills his order from the stock available to him. When certain essential resources are not available, the teacher either improvises or drops that particular contingency plan.

The prescriptive matrix

The tridimensional model provides for the development of numerous prescriptive matrices for the individualization of instruction. Once the teacher has sufficient information to identify significant pupil needs, knows his repertoire of contingencies, and has the resources to make them applicable, he is ready to formulate a precise educational plan. Information about a child developed in accordance with the design of the model will provide a tridimensional matrix for those elements from which a coordinated education effort may take form.

The development of prescriptive matrices may proceed from a single inquiry applied to each of the variables identified under the headings used in the model. The general question would be as follows:

"*What resources* (human or material) are available in order to provide for the contingencies (content, level, rate, etc.) required to meet the special *needs* (cognitive, affective, behavioral, etc.) of this pupil?"

When the special needs are known, the prescriptive matrix can take on specific form. For example, let us assume one element in the total array of a child's needs in the cognitive area concerns a significant remediable difficulty in expressive semantics—his ability to provide appropriate verbal, gestural, and written output of information. On an informal inventory, the child (say 6 years of age, normal in hearing and vision) failed to respond adequately at the 4-year-old level. Let's assume the child's intellectual capabilities have been established at or near the average level for his age but that he comes from

an environmentally deprived family situation. With such minimal information, one may begin to formulate at least a tentative prescriptive matrix in relation to the management of instructional content. In this case, content primarily refers to language instruction. The original general question now can be given a more precise answer that may constitute one prescriptive matrix involving specific content (what is offered) in the child's remedial program. Thus:

"The special teacher supported by the speech and hearing specialist will provide language instruction based upon the district language program starting at a point where the child can consistently function with success on a sequence of developmentally organized language activities."

An analysis of the prescriptive matrix reveals the following elements:
1. Need (cognitive area): expressive semantics
2. Contingency (content vis-a-vis expressive semantics): district language program
3. Resources (human and materials): special teachers; speech and hearing specialists; communications sequence—language

Continuing another step in the development of prescriptive matrices, one would proceed to determine how the application of the district language program (content) may help to satisfy this child's special needs in the affective area and then the behavioral, physical, and occupational needs as they would be identified in this case. The process would call for a similar analysis involving level as a contingency in the satisfaction of needs delineated under the five major headings as listed in the prescriptive model until, finally, all contingencies have been examined as viable alternatives in responding to the child's special needs. The completion of all prescriptive matrices constitutes a set—that is, the child's individualized educational program.

Diagnostic observation assessment model

Planned diagnostic observation activities are becoming more common throughout the United States. Seldom does planned observation comprise the entire assessment procedure, but it is becoming a larger component as its effectiveness is convincingly demonstrated. There are several conditions necessary to make this approach most effective, including the following.

1. *Sufficient staff to permit the necessary time to make this type of assessment effective:* For many children, half-day sessions for 2 to 3 weeks are enough time, but some may require more. A teacher plus an aide for each four to six children is the standard ratio. A larger number of children tends to seriously decrease the effectiveness of the program and thus leads to a need for longer time periods in the assessment setting.

2. *High-level qualifications for staff members:* This type of assessment setting presumes a broad range of abilities on the part of both the diagnostic teacher and the aide. This includes the ability to organize, arrange, and manipulate the setting and materials so that the required activities (and thus the desired observation) can take place. It requires the ability to accurately and objectively observe nearly all that is taking place and to record precisely. It also requires the insight to see possible causal relationships, process problems, and personality and emotional factors as they relate to learning tasks. Ability to deal effectively with parents and to work cooperatively (and nonthreateningly) with teachers and administrators is another "must"; it may often be the one factor that makes certain teachers poor candidates for this type of function.

3. *Staff and administrative assistance and support:* Unless a majority of teachers believe in the viability of such a system and administrators encourage them to refer children, supply information and assistance to the diagnostic teacher, and work with the diagnostic teacher when children are returned to the regular classroom, this is an ineffective system. In addition, administrators must provide transportation (on a schedule that is sometimes cumbersome and out of phase with other school transportation requirements), must support the system in meetings and conferences with parents, and must make it possible for the classroom teacher to have time to meet with the diagnostic teacher. Materials and space must be provided; these are not high-cost items in relation to the total school budget, but in times of tight budgets and problems with both fiscal and educational accountability, any "extra" cost may be a problem.

All concerned with the diagnostic observation assessment model must realize that it cannot work miracles, cannot be 100% effective, and like all other assessment models or systems, requires continual revision and improvement. This approach is probably more often used with young children, and the actual diagnostic setting may be called a resource room or resource unit. The teacher may be called an educational diagnostician, an educational specialist, a learning disabilities specialist, or simply a resource teacher. Usually the basic intent and purpose of such a program is for the child to be returned to the regular class along with educational materials and ideas for teaching, which are sometimes called an educational prescription. A description of an early childhood resource unit developed jointly by school district personnel in Greeley, Colorado, and personnel at the School of Special Education and Rehabilitation of the University of Northern Colorado (pp. 190-195) will permit a more accurate conceptualization of how one such unit functions.

A number of important principles are involved, but the most important is that one individual, over a longer time period and in settings that approximate those in which the child must function in school, can gain a more accurate perspective and more valuable educational insights than can be gained through the shorter time samples required to administer a standardized test battery. The use of a longer time period would cost much more than traditional assessment procedures if it were not for the fact that several children can be in such a diagnostic observation resource center at one time. In addition to the nonstandardized observational procedures used in this model, some standardized tests are often used.

SUMMARY

Assessment is a highly important first step in the initiation of learning disabilities programming. A recommendation for assistance through some type of special program means that the usual educational provisions and procedures are not effective and so dictates that we learn enough about the child to initiate a more appropriate, effective program. Some valuable data will have already been gathered as part of the referral and program placement procedure, but in most cases additional information must be obtained. In composite (including the referral data and data gathered after the placement decision is made), the following types of assessment components are essential: *historical data,* including but not limited to (1) health history, (2) attendance record, (3) social history, (4) past test results, and (5) anecdotal records, records of conferences with parents, teachers, other professionals, and so forth; and *current data,* including but not limited to (1) psychometric or psychological tests or measures, (2) academic achievement test results, (3) subject or skill area diagnostic tests, (4) sensory acuity tests, (5) affective domain assessment, (6) tests of process, (7) speech and language evaluation, (8) physical examination, (9) evaluation of developmental level, and (10) classroom teacher observation report. Some overlap will occur between these components, data gathered prior to referral, and that gathered after a program placement decision; however, this is difficult to avoid without the risk of leaving gaps in the assessment picture.

A number of assessment models exist, with the uniqueness of each relating to local goals, local capabilities, and in a few cases lack of understanding of the assessment process. A set of 10 questions were provided that may be used to determine the effectiveness of any one assessment system.

The tridimensional model for assessment was outlined and recommended as an inclusive, general purpose model. The three dimensions of this model—needs assessment, contingency management, and resource allocation—can be applied in most settings, and unlike some models, the absence of one element in one of these dimensions does not make the total model unusable.

An alternative model, the diagnostic ob-servation assessment model, provides an opportunity for planned observation by a skilled teacher-diagnostician in a setting that permits a tryout of new methods or approaches to actual learning tasks (such as reading and arithmetic).

Any assessment model requires more than lip service from the local administration. Each model requires well-trained personnel, physical space, and cooperative efforts from instructional staff and administration alike. Without an adequate assessment procedure, the learning disabilities program will be only minimally effective and may actually flounder and fail.

REFERENCES AND SUGGESTED READINGS

Anastasi, A. *Psychological testing* (3rd ed.). New York: MacMillan Publishing Co., Inc., 1968.

Bannatyne, A. Diagnosing learning disabilities and writing remedial prescriptions. *Journal of Learning Disabilities,* 1968, *1*(4), 242-248.

Beatty, J. The analysis of an instrument for screening learning disabilities. *Journal of Learning Disabilities,* 1975, 8(3), 180-186.

Beery, K. *Developmental Test of Visual-Motor Integration: administration and scoring manual.* Chicago: Follett Publishing Co., 1967.

Blackwell, R., and Joynt, R. *Learning disabilities handbook for teachers.* Springfield, Ill.: Charles C Thomas, Publisher, 1972.

Burgemeister, B., Blum, L., and Logge, I. *Columbia Mental Maturity Scale* (revised). Cleveland: William Collins & World Publishing Co., Inc.

Bush, W., and Giles, M. *Aids to psycholinguistic teaching.* Columbus, Ohio: Charles E. Merrill Publishing Co., 1969.

Dunn, L. *Peabody Picture Vocabulary Test.* Minneapolis: American Guidance Service, 1959.

Farrald, R., and Schamber, R. *Handbook I: a mainstream approach to identification, assessment and amelioration of learning disabilities.* Sioux Falls, S.D.: Adapt Press, 1973.

Frostig, M. *Frostig Developmental Test of Visual Perception.* Palo Alto, Calif.: Consulting Psychologists Press, 1963.

Gearheart, B. *Learning disabilities: educational strategies.* St. Louis: The C. V. Mosby Co., 1973.

Gearheart, B., and Willenberg, E. *Application of*

pupil assessment information: for the special education teacher (2nd ed.). Denver: Love Publishing Co., 1974.

Keele, D., et al. Role of special pediatric evaluation in the evaluation of a child with learning disabilities. *Journal of Learning Disabilities,* 1975, *8*(1), 40-45.

Kirk, S., and Kirk, W. *Psycholinguistic learning disabilities: diagnosis and remediation.* Urbana, Ill.: University of Illinois Press, 1971.

Kirk, S., McCarthy, J., and Kirk, W. *Illinois Test of Psycholinguistic Abilities: revised edition, examiners manual.* Urbana, Ill.: University of Illinois Press, 1968.

Lovitt, T. Assessment of children with learning disabilities. *Exceptional Children,* 1967, *34,* 233-240.

Paraskevopoulos, J., and Kirk, S. *The development and psychometric characteristics of the Revised Illinois Test of Psycholinguistic Abilities.* Urbana, Ill.: University of Illinois Press, 1969.

Roach, E., and Kephart, N. *The Purdue Perceptual-Motor Survey.* Columbus, Ohio: Charles E. Merrill Publishing Co., 1966.

Terman, E., and Merrill, M. *Stanford-Binet Intelligence Scale, manual for third revision.* Boston: Houghton Mifflin Co., 1961.

Valett, R. *The remediation of learning disabilities.* Palo Alto, Calif.: Fearon Publishers, 1967.

Wechsler, D. *Wechsler Adult Intelligence Scale: manual.* New York: The Psychological Corporation, 1955.

Wechsler, D. *Wechsler Intelligence Scale for Children: manual.* New York: The Psychological Corporation, 1955.

Wechsler, D. *Wechsler Preschool and Primary Scale of Intelligence: manual.* New York: The Psychological Corporation, 1967.

Wepman, J. *Auditory Discrimination Test.* Chicago: Language Research Associates, 1958.

Woodbury, C. The identification of underachieving readers. *Reading Teacher,* 1963, *16*(4), 218-233.

5 Tests and assessment: a second look

Nancy Golden Hanck

The various tests and assessment tools with which we have attempted to measure abilities and disabilities are under regular attack by a variety of critics. Some of these individuals are a part of the education profession, some are from other professions, and some are lay persons. There is little doubt that much of their criticism is valid and that a good "housecleaning" is in order. On the other hand, some of these criticisms might be better directed at those who use the tests, both the diagnosticians who administer them and the educators and others who misinterpret them or draw conclusions far beyond the intent of those who constructed the instruments.

One point that has not been properly emphasized is that many of these assessment tools can provide more information than that given by profiles, summary sheets, scores, and quotients. For this information to be available and properly used, learning disabilities diag-

nosticians must become more competent in deriving information, and learning disabilities teachers must become familiar with its scope and potential.

An adequate understanding of assessment must be developed in training and practice far beyond the scope of this volume, but it is critically important that this principle be discussed and illustrated here. I therefore sought out an individual who has considerable experience as a learning disabilities practitioner in the public schools and now works in educating learning disabilities teachers. Nancy Hanck agreed to share with readers some of the insights that I have heard her share with teachers during in-service programs and with teachers in training. It is unfortunate that her contribution here is limited to only one chapter, but I hope that this chapter might encourage teachers to look more carefully at all the practices and processes that we have called assessment, and truly take a deeper "second look."

B. R. G.

Throughout the last decade there has been accelerating interest in the various ways in which children learn, particularly as related to learning problems. Parents are bringing increasing pressure to bear on the schools to more effectively teach their children. Education has been emphasized as a means to adult goals, and today children are encouraged not only to succeed within elementary and secondary grades but also to search out meaningful postsecondary training. Various scientific, cultural, and political events have led to the movement of more and more content material down into the primary grades, which have traditionally focused on the skills of "reading, writing, and arithmetic." With increasing pressure on children to learn and succeed and with apparently less time to do either, it is not surprising that more and more children require additional educational assistance. In a time when questioning "the system" is the norm, parents now question what is being taught to their children and the manner in which it is taught.

Special education has been viewed by many as an ancillary service to the public schools, providing an adaptive rather than an innovative service. General education has rarely turned to special educators for suggestions as to how *all* pupils might be better educated. The task of special education has been to identify and classify children for the purpose of removal from the educational mainstream to facilitate education according to an individual mode or rate of learning, a role generally accepted by the professional community and by parents. More and more parents have watched their children having difficulty in school and have asked for additional services in the form of school psychologists, special teachers, special materials, and hardware in hopes that a way can be found for their children to succeed.

As this changing pupil population is designated the responsibility of special educators, diagnosticians have turned to instruments that have been developed for observably handicapped children and remedial techniques designed for their "special" education. They have developed screening scales and referral procedures and have pulled together various diagnostic instruments to form extensive batteries. Children are referred or screened and then evaluated; after evaluation, recommendations are made for special training or remedial work to take place within the resource room or the regular classroom. Special educators are then asked to provide assistance to classroom teachers to provide for adaptations to individual learning abilities and styles in the classroom.

Teachers of the deaf, retarded, or other handicapped children who have been educated in self-contained classrooms have often used a general educational curriculum as a guide to teaching but have not needed to accomplish particular academic tasks by a specific time. While these teachers have been constantly searching for new ideas and techniques to better educate handicapped children, they have not been under the gun of accountability. As they assume the role of consultants they enter an entirely different world. Not only are they required to share specific teaching techniques that have in the past been used only with more severely handicapped children, but they are now asked to "cure" whatever problems children in the regular classroom may have.

Special educators have often had to struggle with the fanciful image of "healer" when becoming involved with handicapped children; however, this struggle has been primarily an internal one. Now as they move into the role of consultant, they face the predicament of disparaging the role of healer while at the same time needing to prove their worth as educators. Classroom teachers are not easy customers. Often beset with overcrowded classrooms and insufficient time or assistance, they need help with their problem children and do not want to wait 6 to 8 months for it. Not only must they have answers right away, but they had better be correct. Special educators are quickly learning that if they serve classroom teachers promptly and effectively, they will find real supporters. Failure in this task brings prompt, often uninhibited criticism.

This new pressure on special educators has developed rapidly. It is felt as soon as specialists begin to act as consultants to the regular classroom and has a significant influence on their thinking. As they take the specialized tools and techniques from their work with handicapped children and attempt to apply them to children who are mildly handicapped (if handicapped at all) their attitudes and expectations tend to change. With more severely handicapped children they were happy with any clue to understanding; now they too want instant results from the special tests and techniques. If a diagnostic tool or teaching technique does not bring immediate, observable results, there is a strong tendency to disregard or even discard it. Not only is the specific tool or technique subject to this treatment, but it is also not unusual for specialists to condemn the entire theoretical basis for the tool in question.

It is interesting that educators whose focus has been on understanding and dealing with children who are different suddenly find themselves intolerant of inanimate objects (tests and assessment tools) that do not do their bidding. They find themselves cast in a role (willingly or unwillingly) of trying to write infallible remedial prescriptions. Too often specialists use tests for other than their intended purpose, write prescriptions based on results of these tests, and then when these prescriptions are not effective, criticize not only the specific test but also its theoretical base.

ILLINOIS TEST OF PSYCHOLINGUISTIC ABILITIES

One instrument that has fallen into this pattern of use and misuse is the Illinois Test of Psycholinguistic Abilities (ITPA). It is currently being administered by psychologists, speech pathologists, educational diagnosticians, guidance counselors, remedial reading specialists, and teachers of various types of handicapped children. It is being administered to children who are having difficulty learning in the mainstream of general education as well as children with specific handicapping conditions. Although it is not intended for use as the primary instrument for evaluation and placement of a child in a special class or program, it is often used as the major support for such placement. It is properly used to make note of relative strong points and weak points in a child's repertoire of learning strategies. It is regularly misused as the basis of some new curriculum that supersedes or supplants the academic program. Following a brief review of its history we will examine the ITPA in terms of what it is supposed to do and what it can do.

In France in the early 1900's Binet and Simon developed an intelligence scale designed to assess general intellectual ability and to screen mentally retarded children. The scale was brought to the United States, was standardized by Terman, and soon became a major evaluative instrument. Although the Stanford-Binet scale has been used extensively in evaluating intelligence, Binet's views on the educability of intelligence have not been as widely known. Psychologists in the United States treated intelligence as a fixed entity, but Binet saw it as a composite of various functions that could be specifically trained. While American psychologists viewed mental retardation as an unchangeable condition, Binet saw it as remediable in many cases (Binet, 1913).

The development of the ITPA was the result of an attempt by Samuel Kirk to follow in Binet's footsteps. Its purpose is to analyze the type of intelligence assessed on individual intelligence tests for the purpose of attempting to increase that intelligence. Kirk was interested in working with young retarded children; thus the target of analysis was of necessity the Stanford-Binet Intelligence Scale. (It should be remembered that at this time the Wechsler Intelligence Scale for Children [WISC] tested children only as young as 5 years of age. The Wechsler Preschool and Primary Scales of Intelligence [WPPSI] had not yet been published.)

Early research with the ITPA used a standard procedure in training various individuals and groups. Investigators administered the Stanford-Binet Intelligence Scale and the ITPA, selected specific areas for training on the basis of the ITPA scores, and proceeded to teach the subjects for a specified period. After the training period the subjects were again tested on the ITPA and the Stanford-Binet scale and indicated gains in both (Bateman, 1965).

Later research involved use of the ITPA in an attempt to differentiate various populations of children in terms of their learning characteristics. We also find research in its use with aphasic children, mentally retarded children, poor readers, the speech handicapped, and members of various subcultures within our society (Bateman, 1965). The purpose of this research has been to identify specific learning styles of various groups to enable

educators to teach these children more effectively.

Although Kirk's attempts to analyze verbal intelligence began in the early 1950's, they took more definite shape after being influenced by Osgood's model of communication. The experimental edition of the ITPA was developed and published in 1961; it was subsequently revised and the new edition published in 1968 (Kirk et al., 1968).

Organization

The ITPA consists of 12 subtests that tap abilities in two main channels of communication (auditory-vocal and visual-motor), three types of psycholinguistic processes (receptive, organizational, and expressive), and two levels of functioning (representational and automatic). (See Fig. 1.) The five senses provide us with channels of communication, and the various types of information we receive through each of these enables us to function in our environment. However, two of these channels of input, the auditory and the visual, are used more often in educational experiences than the other three. These auditory and visual channels are used in our schools as the major avenues for teaching and are therefore the most logical to assess. These two channels of input have also been paired with major modes of output—auditory with verbal and visual with manual. Although it would have been possible to construct a model and subtests that would have included all possible combinations of input and output, it was not considered practical.

The three psycholinguistic processes tap the three general aspects of communications: (1) reception, which involves understanding of auditory and visual stimuli; (2) expression, which involves the ability to transmit ideas either verbally or by gesture; and (3) organization, the ability to structure information so it can be more readily understood, ordered, and expressed. The two levels of functioning are the representational level and the automatic level. The former involves understanding, organization, and expression of concepts occurring at a meaningful level, a level at which the individual is actively

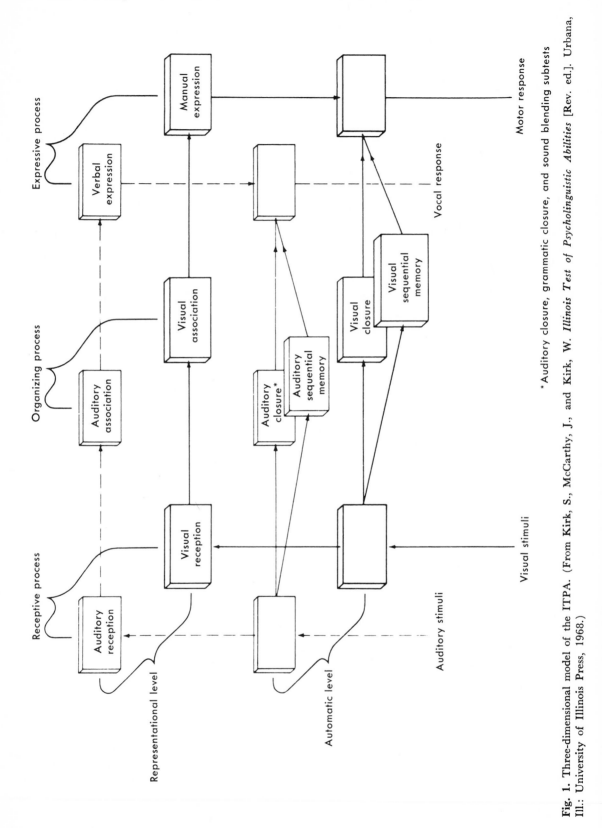

Fig. 1. Three-dimensional model of the ITPA. (From Kirk, S., McCarthy, J., and Kirk, W. *Illinois Test of Psycholinguistic Abilities* [Rev. ed.]. Urbana, Ill.: University of Illinois Press, 1968.)

*Auditory closure, grammatic closure, and sound blending subtests dealing with the communication process. In the latter there is little or no cognitive mediation taking place. Whereas an individual may need to actively deal with the understanding and association of ideas and relationships, he may be able to function somewhat involuntarily in such tasks as memory for sequences and completing sentences or words.

Each psycholinguistic ability is defined by its channel of communication, psycholinguistic process, and level of functioning. Each is described below.

Representational level functions. The representational level functions include the receptive, organizing, and expressive processes.

Receptive process. The receptive process taps the child's ability to understand the meaning of auditory and visual symbols.

1. The *auditory reception* subtest assesses the child's ability to obtain meaning from the spoken word. He is presented with up to 50 short, direct questions to which he need only respond with a yes or no answer.

2. The *visual reception* subtest assesses the child's ability to receive information from visual symbols. The child is presented with a stimulus picture (usually a photograph) for 3 seconds and is then asked to choose a functionally similar item from another page of pictures. The other choices may be associated with the stimulus picture structurally or in some other nonfunctional way.

Organizing process. The organizing process involves the child's abilities to relate, organize, and manipulate symbols in a meaningful way.

1. The *auditory association* subtest assesses the child's ability to relate concepts presented orally. It utilizes completion of verbal analogies such as "Soup is hot; ice cream is ————."

2. The *visual association* subtest assesses the child's ability to relate concepts presented visually. It utilizes a picture association technique in which the child is asked to attend to a stimulus picture on a page and then choose from accompanying pictures the one most related to the stimulus. The test is expanded at the upper level to provide visual analogies comparable to the auditory analogies on the auditory association test.

Expressive process. The expressive process involves the child's ability to transmit his ideas through symbols.

1. The purpose of the *verbal expression* subtest is to assess the child's ability to relate a number of discrete, relevant, and predominantly factual concepts about four familiar objects.

2. The *manual expression* subtest assesses the child's ability to express ideas in gestures. The child is asked to look at pictures of objects and demonstrate their use.

Automatic level functions. Two abilities are measured at the automatic level—closure (auditory and visual) and sequential memory (auditory and visual).

Closure. Closure has been defined as the ability to derive a whole concept, picture, or statement either (1) when only some of the parts are presented or (2) when all of the parts are presented but need to be integrated.

1. The *grammatic closure* subtest assesses the child's knowledge of the syntactical conventions of the English language. He is presented with sets of statements in which the first is complete and the second incomplete. Correct completion of the second statement is dependent on the child's ability to make changes in word endings and forms.

2. The *visual closure* subtest assesses the child's ability to identify a common object from an incomplete visual stimulus.

3. The *auditory closure* subtest assesses the child's ability to recognize a word presented orally with parts deleted and to produce the complete word.

4. The *sound blending* subtest assesses the child's ability to recognize a word presented orally when the sounds are produced individually and to tell what the word is.

Sequential memory. Sequential memory has been defined as the ability to reproduce a sequence of stimuli.

1. The *auditory sequential memory* subtest assesses the child's ability to reproduce from memory sequences of digits presented orally. The sequences increase in length from two to eight digits.

2. The *visual sequential memory* test assesses the child's ability to reproduce a sequence of designs from memory. The child looks at a picture of the design sequence for 5 seconds and is then required to reproduce the sequence with individual design chips.

For a more thorough discussion of the subtests, the reader is referred to Paraskevopoulos and Kirk (1969, Chapter 2).

Task analysis approach to interpretation

A great deal has been written about interpretation of the ITPA. The main thesis of the authors of the ITPA is that testing should lead to teaching and diagnosis should lead to an educational program; testing is worthless unless something is going to be done about it. There are a variety of books with teaching suggestions that are derived from the ITPA model (see the references and suggested readings at the end of this chapter). There are also commercial packages that provide educational programs designed to teach in relation to ITPA test results. However, many of these books and programs do not make full use of the ITPA as a tool of observation. Too many of them try to improve on or expand the various processes without regard for (1) the purpose of the particular diagnosis, (2) an analysis of the psychological processes required by each of the subtests, and (3) the relation that these processes have to education. They tend to encourage teaching according to the model rather than to the individual child and his educational problem.

When the history of the ITPA, its development, and its intended usage are considered, this approach to the test results is logical and beneficial. However, since the ITPA is being used increasingly to diagnose academic problems of children within the normal range of intelligence rather than to analyze children with lower levels of intelligence for the purpose of increasing their intellectual abilities, this approach is insufficient and in some cases actually inappropriate. While the former use is part of an attempt to find another way to teach a particular academic subject, the latter is related primarily to attempting

to increase general intellectual ability. While the former is attempting to increase academic achievement, the latter is attempting to increase academic aptitude.

If we teach to increase aptitude, it is possible that we will also increase academic achievement, but this does not automatically follow. Children tend to learn what they have been taught. If we expect them to learn to count or identify numerals, to identify long and short vowels, or to find information in a written passage, we need to teach them these things. It is possible to gain information as to how best to teach these things from instruments like the ITPA, but to do this we must be able to accomplish two tasks: (1) analyze the subtests in terms of psychological processes involved in the particular items and (2) analyze academic subject matter in terms of psychological processes.

Diagnostic test scores may be shown to correlate with specific academic performances, but the extent to which they correlate is dependent on the amount of similarity between the two. To find the similarity between diagnostic test scores and academic performance we need to analyze each.

The task analysis of each ITPA subtest involves (1) an analysis of the stimuli the child must process, (2) the logical steps he must take in dealing with the stimuli, and (3) an analysis of the child's response.

The following task analysis assumes (1) attention to task, (2) comprehension of directions, and (3) desire to respond appropriately. All errors may then be assumed to be cognitive and related to the task.

Auditory reception
1. Listen to a simple question involving noun-verb relationship.
2. Recognize noun-verb relationship. (Modifiers are added at the upper level.)
3. Respond with yes or no.

Visual reception
1. Perceive photograph of stimulus object.
2. Choose response object according to similarity of function or structure.
3. Avoid choosing object according to similarity of shape.

Auditory association
1. Listen to an incomplete verbal analogy.

2. Manipulate any of the following types of concepts: opposites, attributes, categories, part-whole relationships, occupation-tool-product relationships.
3. Respond with correct analogous concept.

Visual association
1. Perceive visual analogy format.
2. Understand language "goes with." (Directions state, "What goes with this? Which one of these?")
3. Manipulate any of the following concepts: categories, part-whole relationships, tool-product relationships.
4. Choose correct response item according to one of these relationships.

Verbal expression
1. Recognize an object (ball, block, envelope, button).
2. Relate to objects in terms of the following categories:
   a. Label
   b. Color
   c. Shape
   d. Composition
   e. Function or action
   f. Major parts
   g. Numerosity
   h. Other characteristics
   i. Comparison
   j. Persons, places, things associated with the object
3. Verbalize this knowledge.

Manual expression
1. Perceive photograph of object.
2. Recognize object in terms of its major parts.
3. Associate major parts of object with their particular function (action).
4. Execute action.

Grammatic closure*
1. Listen to a complete statement about a picture.
2. Complete a second statement about the picture utilizing appropriate grammatic inflections; this might involve any of the following:
   a. Plurals, regular and irregular

b. Possessives
c. Verb forms
d. Adjectives, comparative and superlative forms
e. Prepositions
f. Idiomatic expressions

Visual closure
1. Look at stimulus (line drawing of dog, fish, shoes, hammers, and saws).
2. Look at picture strip in which stimulus drawings are incorporated but partly hidden or changed in position. (The picture is designed with few aids for perceiving the third dimension—no shading, shadows, etc.; it involves figure-ground discrimination, speed of perception, and particular part-whole relationships.)
3. Point to as many as possible in 30 seconds.

Auditory closure*
1. Listen to a word when part of it is deleted but rhythm, accent, and pronunciation of remainder of word remain standard.
2. Recognize sounds as part of a whole word.
3. Produce entire word.

Sound blending*
1. Listen to group of sounds produced at half-second intervals.
2. Recognize that these sounds are parts to be made into a whole.
3. Blend these sounds to form words or syllables.

Auditory sequential memory
1. Listen to groups of two, three, four, five, six, and seven digits presented verbally at half-second intervals.
2. Repeat these digits.

Visual sequential memory
1. Look at a sequence of designs involving groups of two, three, four, five, six, and seven symbols presented for 5 seconds.
2. Reproduce from memory sequence of designs with chips.

The purpose of diagnosis is to ask the right questions—to ask what the child is not doing, what is preventing him from doing it, and if there is any way that we can facilitate his doing it. When children are referred for special help, the diagnostician *must* ask

---

*Grammatic closure scores may reflect different problems. If a child comes from a middle-class English-speaking environment, then a low score may indicate an inability to pick up inflections and nuances of language. If a child comes from a non-English-speaking environment or one that speaks a dialect of American English, then a low score may only reflect his nonexposure to these particular word forms and phrases.

---

*Although both auditory closure and sound blending are closure tasks, there is a fundamental difference between the two tasks. Auditory closure requires that the child understand the vocabulary, since he is being asked to recognize the word. Sound blending does not require the child to understand the word, since all parts are presented.

these questions and often must use specific diagnostic tests such as the ITPA. If a test such as the ITPA is used, the diagnostician must be able to interpret the results in a variety of ways. For example, when two or more ITPA subtest scores are significantly high or low, they may represent either two different abilities or disabilities or an ability or disability common to both. A child who demonstrates weakness in manual expression and sound blending may have specific disabilities in each. At the same time he may be demonstrating a difficulty in dealing with part-whole relationships. The test of manual expression requires that the child do the following.

1. Perceive a photograph of an object.
2. Recognize that the object has major parts.
3. Associate these major parts with their particular action.
4. Execute action.

The test of sound blending requires that the child do these things:

1. Listen to a group of sounds.
2. Recognize that these sounds are parts to be joined into a whole.
3. Blend these sounds to form words or syllables.

The common factor in these two subtests is the ability to deal with parts in relation to the whole.

Whether we use the task analysis approach, the more traditional approach, or a combination of the two, we are still in danger of improper diagnosis. It was stated earlier that diagnosis requires asking the right questions. Tests attempt to ask pertinent questions. However, it is up to the examiner to test and question, not according to some theory or model, but as determined by a specific problem—*why* Johnny and Mary are having problems learning and *what* they are having difficulty learning. The diagnostician must be able to relate results of tests such as the ITPA to specific school concerns. What can we do about the child who comprehends only when he reads aloud? How do we teach a child who cannot learn the multiplication facts? It is possible for us to deal with these

problems if we are able to isolate the school task, analyze it in terms of orderly steps, and match these steps to related or underlying processes.

Two examples of specific problems follow. These are provided to illustrate this principle as it relates to the ITPA. They are given in brief form for illustrative purposes.

Problem: Difficulty in memorizing multiplication facts

Task	*Ability*
Memorize series of numbers expressed as sequence such as $3 \times 5 = 15$. (Each symbol in this arithmetic problem must be considered as a separate unit requiring memorization; thus this problem is similar to memorizing five digits in sequence.)	Possess sequential memory ability for five digits or symbols.

Symbol No. $\underline{1 \quad 2 \quad 3 \quad 4 \quad 5}$
$3 \quad \times \quad 5 \quad = \quad 15$

If a child cannot remember five digits or symbols, it is of little importance that his scaled score is or is not significantly deviant or that his age score is close to his chronological age. If he cannot perform in this manner and has no means of compensating for this inability to perform, then he will likely have problems in any school task that requires this ability. *The important fact to note is his sequential memory ability.*

Problem: Read passage silently and give answers to questions presented orally by the teacher.

Task	*Process*
Decoding: Translate written word into spoken word either by sound-symbol or whole word association.	*Decoding:* Sound-symbol association for individual letters or groups of letters.
Comprehension: Recognize meaning of individual word, recall sequence of words, retain meaning.	*Comprehension:* Re-auditorize word, possess word in receptive auditory language pool, use immediate auditory sequential memory.

Task	Process
Answering questions: Recognize and respond to type of questions asked by teachers, select answer and respond.	*Answering questions:* Knowledge of specific question forms. Possess auditory expressive language, associate specific question with specific memory of written material, analyze question as to type of answer required, select proper answer from memory of read material and respond.

If reading silently and then answering questions posed by the teacher can be conceptualized as involving these processes, the teacher may be much more successful in interpreting the problem(s) and initiating appropriate training or experiences. Inasmuch as the ITPA provides information regarding some of these processes, it can be of great assistance separate from (and in addition to) results that reflect profiled strengths and weaknesses. The diagnostician must be "tuned in" to this type of thinking to be able to make such an assessment.

Other tests can provide a wealth of information beyond that provided by the reported scores alone. The amount and type of information varies from test to test but most hold at least limited potential beyond scores obtained from norm-based data. Two other tests, the Developmental Test of Visual-Motor Integration and the Test of Auditory Discrimination will be discussed later in this chapter.

Traditional scoring procedure

The traditional procedure for examining ITPA scores involves attention to the following types of scores.

Global scores. Global scores indicate the overall ability of a child and include (1) composite psycholinguistic age, (2) psycholinguistic quotient, (3) mean and median scaled scores, (4) estimated Stanford-Binet mental age, and (5) estimated Stanford-Binet IQ.

Part scores. Scores may be derived for each of the three dimensions of the ITPA (channel, level, and process) for the purpose of intraindividual comparisons. It is possible to obtain scores for (1) auditory-vocal channel, (2) visual-motor channel, (3) representational level, (4) automatic level, (5) receptive process, (6) associative process, and (7) expressive process.

Profile of abilities. There are occasions when the manipulation of scores does not definitely indicate a problem. It is therefore helpful to examine the profile of abilities and compare the scores on separate functions. The scaled score for each subtest is plotted, and the mean scaled score is indicated by a reference line. (See Fig. 2.) In examining the deviation between the scores the examiner's manual states:

1. Differences between a subtest scaled score (SS) and the mean or median scaled score of ±6 should not be considered an indication of a special ability or disability. This is the range within which over eighty percent of average children score.
2. Differences between the mean or median scaled score and a subtest scaled score of ±7, ±8, or ±9 are considered borderline discrepancies.
3. A difference between mean or median scaled score and a subtest scaled score of ±10 or greater is considered a substantial discrepancy; that is, a deviation of that magnitude is indicative of a discrepant function.*

By examining these types of scores and rearranging them in various patterns, the users of the ITPA attempt to find reasons for a child's performance or nonperformance in school. However, some examiners never move beyond the manipulation of numbers and consequently often have confusing or meaningless reports. This is unfortunate because in a relatively short time the ITPA samples many behaviors that are believed to be important in school learning.

CASE STUDY

Jim B. is a first-grade boy whose chronological age is 6 years 7 months. His ITPA scores will be reported according to (1) the traditional approach and (2) a task analysis approach.

*From Kirk, S., McCarthy, J., and Kirk, W. *Illinois Test of Psycholinguistic Abilities* (Rev. ed.). Urbana, Ill.: University of Illinois Press, 1968.

Traditional approach

The following list shows Jim's psycholinguistic age scores (PLA), his scaled scores (SS), and the differences between his overall mean scaled score and his scaled score on each subtest (difference).

	PLA	SS	Difference
Auditory reception	6-8	38	−0.7
Visual reception	9-3	45	+6.3
Auditory association	5-3	26	−12.7
Visual association	9-4	49	+10.3
Verbal expression	5-6	32	−6.7
Manual expression	9-2	44	+5.3
Grammatic closure	7-3	42	+3.3
Visual closure	7-6	41	+2.3
Auditory sequential memory	4-10	30	−8.7
Visual sequential memory	7-3	40	+1.3
Auditory closure	6-9	38	−0.7
Sound blending	7-10	46	+7.3
Composite psycho-linguistic age	6-10		
Estimated Stanford-Binet mental age	7-0		
Mean scaled score	38.7		

Global scores

Jim's performance on the ITPA yielded a composite psycholinguistic age of 6-10, a mean scaled score of 38.7, and an estimated Stanford-Binet mental age of 7-0. His composite psycholinguistic age (6-10) and his estimated Stanford-Binet mental age (7-0) suggest he is capable of performing at age and grade level. His mean scaled score (38.7) is very close to the normative group average of 36. These scores suggest that he is of average ability.

Grouped scores

Channel

	PLA	SS
Auditory-vocal channel		
Auditory reception	6-8	38
Auditory association	5-3	26
Verbal expression	5-6	32
Grammatic closure	7-3	42
Auditory sequential memory	4-10	30
Mean	5-10	33
Visual-motor channel		
Visual reception	9-3	45
Visual association	9-4	49
Manual expression	9-2	44
Visual closure	7-6	41
Visual sequential memory	7-3	40
Mean	8-6	44

Process

	PLA	SS
Reception		
Auditory	6-8	38
Visual	9-3	45
Mean	7-11	41.5
Association		
Auditory	5-3	26
Visual	9-4	49
Mean	7-3	37.5
Expression		
Verbal	5-6	32
Manual	9-2	44
Mean	7-4	38

Level

	PLA	SS
Representational		
Auditory reception	6-8	38
Visual reception	9-3	45
Auditory association	5-3	26
Visual association	9-4	49
Verbal expression	5-6	32
Manual expression	9-2	44
Mean	7-6	39
Automatic		
Grammatic closure	7-3	42
Visual closure	7-6	41
Auditory sequential memory	4-10	30
Visual sequential memory	7-3	40
Mean	6-3	38

Discussion. It is possible to examine Jim's performance on the ITPA by grouping the individual subtest scores according to (1) channels of communication (auditory or visual), (2) psycholinguistic process (reception, association, or expression), and (3) level of organization (representational or automatic).

Regrouped scores

	Mean PLA	Mean SS
Channels of communication		
Auditory-vocal	5-10	33
Visual-motor	8-6	44
Psycholinguistic process		
Reception	7-11	41.5
Association	7-3	37.5
Expression	7-4	38.0
Levels of organization		
Representational	7-6	39
Automatic	6-3	38

A cursory review of the scaled scores suggests (1) no substantial differences between the representational and automatic levels, (2) little difference among the psycholinguistic processes, although the scaled score for reception was higher than either of the other two, and (3) a substantial difference between the auditory and visual channels, the visual channel being 11 points

PROFILE OF ABILITIES

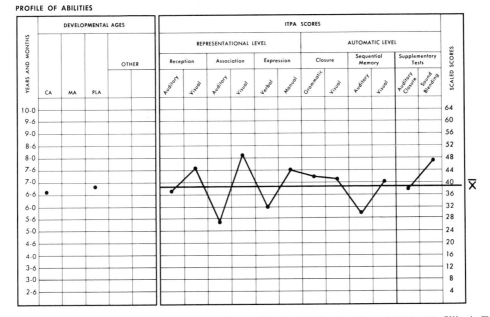

Fig. 2. Jim B.'s profile of abilities. (Record form from Kirk, S., McCarthy, J., and Kirk, W. *Illinois Test of Psycholinguistic Abilities* [Rev. ed.]. Urbana, Ill.: University of Illinois Press, 1968.)

higher. Although there is a slight variation in the differences among the grouped scores, none of the group mean scaled scores differs significantly from the mean scaled score for the whole ITPA (38.7).

Profile of abilities (Fig. 2)

The profile of abilities is plotted according to the scaled score for each subtest and the mean scaled score is indicated by a reference line. A glance at Jim's profile indicates low scores in the areas of auditory association, verbal expression, and auditory sequential memory and high scores in visual reception, visual association, and sound blending. In evaluating the significance of these scores it is necessary to compare the scaled score of each with the mean scaled score of the total test.

	SS	Difference
Auditory association	26	−12.7
Verbal expression	32	−6.7
Auditory sequential memory	30	−8.7
Visual reception	45	+6.3
Visual association	49	+10.3
Sound blending	46	+7.3

According to the criteria on p. 57, visual reception cannot be considered a strength since the difference of ±6 is within the range in which 80%

of average children score. If the difference score for verbal expression is rounded up to −7.0, then it would be considered a borderline disability along with auditory sequential memory. Sound blending would be considered a borderline strength. The scores for auditory association and visual association are indicative of substantial weaknesses and strength, respectively.

From a review of this profile many diagnosticians would conclude that Jim has a significant disability in the area of auditory association but is able to compensate for his weakness by using his strong ability in visual association. They might infer that this disability in auditory association might be influenced by a borderline weakness in auditory sequential memory and that it might in turn depress functioning in the area of verbal expression.

Common remedial recommendations

It is common for diagnosticians to make educational recommendations on the basis of this type of analysis. These recommendations might be predicated on the following analyses of disability.

Auditory association. Jim's low score in auditory association indicates an inability to draw relationships from spoken material. His problem may stem from any one or a combination of the following factors (Kirk and Kirk, 1971).

1. He may have difficulty holding two or more concepts in mind and considering them in relation to each other. Since Jim does have a borderline disability in auditory sequential memory, it may indeed be a problem for him to remember what it is he must relate. Therefore it may be necessary to guide his thinking with leading questions, to add visual clues, or to name objects that have one quality in common, two qualities in common, etc.

2. He may have difficulty identifying and verbalizing first-order relationships (directly relating two verbal concepts). In this case he would need (1) to be taught opposite concepts and (2) to identify differences and similarities in concepts with regard to function, structure, attributes, and part-whole relationships. He would need to derive relationships of cause and effect, time and space, and number and space.

3. He may have difficulty identifying and verbalizing second-order relationships (finding a specific relationship to match one already given). Jim would need to be led through verbal analogies by identifying the relationship in the first half of a statement and then finding the corresponding relationship in the second half. "Grass is green" tells the color of grass, so the answer to "Grass is green; the sky is _____" is "blue" since the relationship is color.

4. He may have difficulty learning to classify or categorize concepts. Jim would need to identify common attributes of objects and group objects by these attributes.

5. He may have difficulty finding and evaluating alternative solutions to a problem. Jim might need to develop ideational fluency, flexibility in thinking, and evaluative thinking.

Verbal expression. Jim's borderline performance in verbal expression indicates a possible difficulty in putting ideas into words. Any of the following teaching approaches may apply to his problem.

1. He may lack basic vocal skills. Although it is possible that Jim may need work in articulation, his performance in grammatic closure (PLA, 7-3; SS, 42) does not indicate that he has been prevented from learning and using highly specific elements of language and speech.

2. He may lack adequate vocabulary.

3. He may not express words spontaneously (difficulty in retrieval of words and ideas). Jim may be aided in retrieving words by teaching him specific verbal formats that will "trigger" the needed word. He may also need to learn strategies for retrieving ideas.

Auditory sequential memory. Recommendations may be derived according to each of the following.

1. He may have difficulty attending to details of auditory stimuli.

2. He may have difficulty repeating what he has heard and attended to.

3. He may have difficulty storing and retrieving information.

Most recommendations would also urge that in addition to remedying these weaknesses, time should be spent teaching the child to use his strengths (in this case, visual association and sound blending).

Task analysis approach

The traditional approach to analysis of ITPA scores requires the perusal and interrelating of global and grouped scores and a working knowledge of the ITPA model and its theoretical implications. Difficulties that arise in interpreting ITPA scores come not so much from deficiencies in these areas but instead from nonattention to the actual tasks given a child and the exact requirements of those tasks. The following discussion will look at Jim's ITPA scores according to a task analysis approach.

Auditory association. On this subtest Jim was asked to do the following.

1. Listen to an incomplete verbal analogy.
2. Manipulate any of the following types of concepts: opposites, attributes, categories, part-whole.
3. Respond verbally with the correct analogous concept.

A review of this section of the record form (Fig. 3) indicates that he made one error before the ceiling (three consecutive failures) and that the ceiling came rather quickly. If the ceiling had not occurred until later in the test with enough scattered errors to arrive at the same score, it might be inferred that he could deal with sophisticated verbal relationships but had difficulty in specific instances. In Jim's case it might be inferred from the specific questions and errors that he can deal with concrete relationships that pertain to himself and his immediate world but not to more abstract relationships. The questions (Kirk et al., 1968) and his answers follow.

Demonstration II: Grass is green; sugar is white.

+ 11. During the day we're awake; at night we're asleep.

+ 12. A rabbit is fast; a turtle is slow.

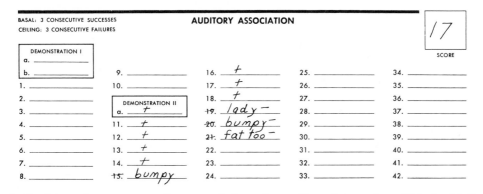

Fig. 3. Jim B.'s performance on auditory association subtest. (Record form from Kirk, S., McCarthy, J., and Kirk, W. *Illinois Test of Psycholinguistic Abilities* [Rev. ed.]. Urbana, Ill.: University of Illinois Press, 1968.)

+ 13. I cut with a saw; I pound with a <u>hammer.</u>

+ 14. On my hands I have fingers; on my feet I have <u>toes.</u>

− 15. Cotton is soft; stones are <u>bumpy</u> (acceptable answer: hard).

+ 16. A boy runs; an old man <u>walks.</u>

+ 17. A block is square; a ball is <u>round.</u>

+ 18. An explosion is loud; a whisper is <u>quiet.</u>

− 19. A man may be a king; a woman may be a <u>lady</u> (acceptable answers: queen, princess).

− 20. Mountains are high; valleys are <u>bumpy</u> (acceptable answers: low, deep).

− 21. A pickle is fat; a pencil is <u>fat too</u> (acceptable answers: skinny, thin, slim).

After reading this many first-grade teachers will quickly conjure an image of a little boy who likes to run barefoot outside in the summer and who usually writes with a primary pencil rather than the usual size. However, we need to look beyond what Jim did on this test to what he needs to do. This subtest has been analyzed on p. 54, but it might be beneficial to examine it again. To deal with verbal analogies Jim first needs to perceive the second part of the statement as separate from the first: Cotton is soft; stones are _____. He may know that cotton is white, fluffy, and soft, comes from a plant, and grows in the southern United States. He may know that stones come in many colors, are hard and heavy, may be rough or smooth, are found on or near the ground or near bodies of water, etc. However, the second step is to understand that cotton and stones are related in some way and that the clue to the relationship is found in the first part of the statement. Third, he needs to select texture as the concept being sought, and

fourth, he needs to select the descriptor that denotes texture (hard) from all other descriptors of stones.

This is a process of focus and selection that requires an ability to amass and retain relevant but isolated facts, but it also requires the child (1) to look at objects in his environment in terms of component parts and associated factors, (2) to perceive similarities between or among these parts or factors, and (3) to group and regroup objects and events on the basis of selected factors. This process is described at a more advanced level by Bloom et al. (1956) in their taxonomy of the cognitive domain.

A summary of this taxonomy of educational objectives is as follows (Bloom et al., 1956):

1. Knowledge
2. Comprehension
3. Application
4. Analysis
5. Synthesis
6. Evaluation

According to Bloom et al., analysis involves breaking concepts apart into component parts or ideas and synthesis involves putting these parts or ideas back together to form a *new* whole—a new idea or a new relationship.

Does Jim have difficulty with this process in general, and does he have difficulty attending to and dealing with specific kinds of relationships? Since his scores on the visual association subtest were high (PLA, 9-4; SS, 49; difference, +10.3), we may assume that the general process is not the problem. However, if he is able to analyze and synthesize visually, he may need to be taught to operate this way auditorily.

Verbal expression. On verbal expression, Jim was asked to do the following.

BASAL: NONE
CEILING: NONE

VERBAL EXPRESSION

18

TOTAL SCORE

DEMONSTRATION

Nail

1 Label
2 Color
3 Shape
4 Composition
5 Function

6 Major Parts
7 Numerosity
8 Other Characteristics
9 Comparison
10 Person, Place, or Thing

1. Ball

⑤ bounces
⑤ play with it
make rubber man with it
④ rubber ball
⑤ throw it
⑤ roll it

2. Block

③ Square
④ Wood
Throw it
put it on shiny for beads

⑤ make things

3. Envelope

⑤ lick it
⑤ put mail in it
hundreds of things in it
put toys in it

4. Button

It's a button ①
⑤ Sew it on a shirt ⑩
Roll it like a penny
⑤ See through it

ITEM SCORES

6	+	*3*	+	*3*	+	*6*	=	*18*
BALL		BLOCK		ENVELOPE		BUTTON		TOTAL SCORE

Fig. 4. Jim B.'s performance on verbal expression subtest. (Record form from Kirk, S., McCarthy, J., and Kirk, W. *Illinois Test of Psycholinguistic Abilities* [Rev. ed.]. Urbana, Ill.: University of Illinois Press, 1968.)

1. Recognize an object (ball, block, envelope, button).
2. Relate to the object in terms of label, color, shape, composition, function or action, major parts, numerosity, other characteristics, comparison, and persons, places, or things associated with the object.
3. Verbalize this knowledge.

A review of this section of the record form (Fig. 4) indicates that while his total score might be classified as a borderline disability, his verbal responses to the various objects were limited. The categories that he used are listed on the next page.

1. *Ball*
   Label
   Composition
   Function or action
2. *Block*
   Shape
   Composition
   Function or action
3. *Envelope*
   Function or action
   Persons, places, or things associated with the object
4. *Button*
   Label
   Comparison
   Function or action
   Persons, places, or things associated with the object

Performance on the verbal expression subtest may lead to explanations of other test behaviors. Children with disabilities in the area of verbal expression may score in an acceptable range, since the score reflects quantity. However, their responses usually fall into the categories of label, function or action, and persons, places and things, with occasional use of the other categories.

It is conceivable that a lack of diversity in verbal expression could influence the kind and amount of verbal associations made on a test such as auditory association. On such verbal tests, which require the child to analyze two different concepts into their component parts and identify areas of similarity, it is important that he have a wide variety of verbal responses from which to choose. A verbal expressive capability of limited scope could impair this ability to analyze verbal relationships.

Auditory sequential memory. On the test of auditory sequential memory Jim was asked the following.

1. Listen to groups of digits presented verbally at half-second intervals.
2. Repeat these digits verbally.

Fig. 5 portrays his performance on this subtest. One may observe that Jim was able to repeat three digits, had some difficulty with four digits, and was unable to repeat five digits correctly.

It is interesting that although auditory sequential memory is considered a borderline disability and sound blending is considered a borderline strength (PLA, 7-10; SS, 46; difference, +7.3), the two subtests are vitally related. To blend sounds to form a word we must be able to retain those sounds long enough to blend them. An examination of the record form for sound blending (Fig. 6) will indicate that although Jim received a high score on this test, the score was based on his ability to blend words of three sounds. Since the sound blending test is composed mostly of words broken into three phonemes, his auditory memory was not overtaxed.

Visual sequential memory. It is naturally assumed that since Jim's score on visual sequential memory is average for his age group (PLA, 7-3; SS, 40; difference, +1.3), problems in that area should not be considered. However, examination of his responses on that test (Fig. 7) indicate that this may not be the case. In this subtest Jim was asked to do the following.

1. Look at a sequence of designs presented for 5 seconds.
2. Reproduce the sequence from memory using individual design chips.

The ITPA record form indicates that although he did as well as his peers in the normative group, Jim still had difficulty with sequences of more than three designs. He could work with three designs, began having problems with four,

| BASAL: 3 CONSECUTIVE SUCCESSES CEILING: 2 CONSECUTIVE FAILURES | **AUDITORY SEQUENTIAL MEMORY** | | SCORE |

*DEMONSTRATION		1st	2nd		1st	2nd		1st	2nd
a. 2–2	6. 2–7–3–3	+		15. 7–4–8–3–5–5	___	___	24. 4–9–6–3–5–7–1	___	___
b. 2–1	7. 6–3–5–1	•	+	16. 2–9–6–1–8–3	___	___	25. 3–1–9–2–7–4–8–8	___	___
	8. 8–2–9–3	+		17. 5–2–4–9–3–6	___	___	26. 9–6–3–8–5–1–7–2	___	___
1st 2nd	9. 1–6–8–5	+		18. 4–7–3–8–1–5	___	___	27. 4–7–3–1–6–2–9–5	___	___
1. 9–1 ___ ___	10. 4–7–3–9–9	•		19. 6–9–5–7–2–8	___	___	28. 8–2–5–9–3–6–4–1	___	___
2. 7–9 ___ ___	11. 6–1–4–2–8	•	•	20. 3–6–1–9–2–7–7	___	___			
3. 8–1–1 + ___	12. 1–5–2–9–6	___	___	21. 5–3–6–9–7–8–2	___	___			
4. 6–4–9 + ___	13. 7–3–1–8–4	___	___	22. 8–1–6–2–5–9–3	___	___			
5. 5–2–8 + ___	14. 5–9–6–2–7	___	___	23. 2–7–4–1–8–3–6	___	___			

Fig. 5. Jim B.'s performance on auditory sequential memory subtest. (Record form from Kirk, S., McCarthy, J., and Kirk, W. *Illinois Test of Psycholinguistic Abilities* [Rev. ed.]. Urbana, Ill.: University of Illinois Press, 1968.)

BASAL: SEE DIRECTIONS
CEILING: SEE DIRECTIONS

SOUND BLENDING

SCORE: 19

Section A Words with pictures

DEMONSTRATION I: d – og

1. f – oot
2. m – an
3. sh – oe
4. c – ap
5. c – ar
6. c – u – p
7. sh – i – p

Section B Words without pictures

DEMONSTRATION II: d – og

8. ea – t +
9. e – gg +
10. u – p +
11. c – ow +
12. m – e +
13. f – i – sh +
14. c – a – t +
15. b – i – g bit –
16. s – a – d +
17. b – oa – t +
18. n – o – se nest –
19. d – i – nn – er DK –
20. f – ea – th – er DK –
21. l – i – tt – le
22. k – e – tch – u – p
23. b – a – b – ie – s
24. t – e – l – e – ph – o – ne

Section C Nonsense words

DEMONSTRATION III: ō – g, z – ē

25. l – ĕ – k +
26. ā – f – ē +
27. v – ŭ – m +
28. r – ă – s – t rest –
29. t – ē – k – ō take –
30. t – ā – p – ĭ – k tape it –
31. r – ŭ – s – ō – p
32. ō – p – ă – s – t – ō

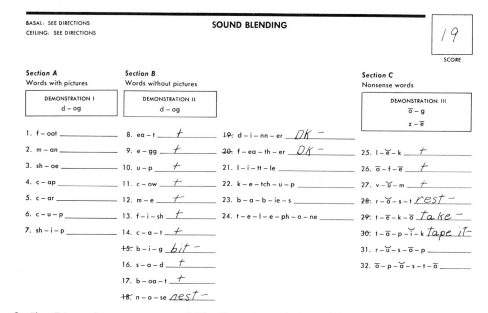

Fig. 6. Jim B.'s performance on sound blending. (Record form from Kirk, S., McCarthy, J., and Kirk, W. *Illinois Test of Psycholinguistic Abilities* [Rev. ed.]. Urbana, Ill.: University of Illinois Press, 1968.)

BASAL: 3 CONSECUTIVE SUCCESSES
CEILING: 2 CONSECUTIVE FAILURES

VISUAL SEQUENTIAL MEMORY

SCORE: 20

Item	1st	2nd	Item	1st	2nd	Item	1st	2nd	Item	1st	2nd	Item	1st	2nd	Item	1st	2nd
•DEMONSTRATION I			•DEMONSTRATION II	+		7.	+		•12.	•	+	•17.			•22.		
1.			4.			•8.	+		13.	•	•	18.			23.		
•2.			•5.	+		9.	•	+	14.	•	•	19.			24.		
3.			6.	+		10.	•	+	15.			20.			25.		
						11.	•	+	16.			21.					

Fig. 7. Jim B.'s performance on visual sequential memory subtest. (Record form from Kirk, S., McCarthy, J., and Kirk, W. *Illinois Test of Psycholinguistic Abilities* [Rev. ed.]. Urbana, Ill.: University of Illinois Press, 1968.)

and reached his ceiling at five designs. (Items 1 through 3 are two symbols, 4 through 6 are three symbols, 7 through 10 are four symbols, and 11 through 15 are five symbols.)

Anticipation of educational problems

The task here has been to discuss interpretation of the ITPA and to provide examples of such interpretation without the benefit of support of other test scores. Such isolated interpretation and later prediction of educational problems is shaky at best. Nevertheless, it is important to recognize possible correlations between tasks on the ITPA and activities in the school curriculum.

The ITPA is an instrument that evaluates communication, and since much of public school teaching involves monologues and dialogues between teacher and student, most of the areas evaluated on the ITPA are related in some respect to the classroom situation. However, it is important for diagnosticians to look beneath the obvious in formulating diagnostic hypotheses.

The subtests of association require the child to know concepts of opposites, categories, part-whole relationships, etc. They also require that the child be able to analyze two different concepts into their component parts and select one of those components on the basis of a specific relationship. According to Bloom et al. (1956), unless we are able to analyze concepts into component parts and regroup those components into a new whole, we cannot fulfill tasks that require us to compare or contrast.

The tests of expression attempt to assess a child's organization for expression rather than articulation or motor coordination. Unless the child can perceive objects and events in terms of their major parts, functions, and attributes, he will have difficulty analyzing, selecting, and synthesizing information.

The tests of sequential memory measure a very specific kind of immediate memory but are viewed as vital components to rote learning tasks. Children's sequential memory may tend to increase with age, but school tasks are not always correlated with their abilities. Although a child in the age range of 6 years 4 months to 6 years 7 months may have a visual memory for three or four designs, the teacher may ask him to read or spell words of more than three or four symbols. While the scaled score may indicate a borderline disability, inability to remember more than three digits presented orally can be a definite handicap when the child is asked to take words or sentences from dictation or to memorize number facts, which require five memory units.

The tests of auditory and visual closure require the child to identify the whole word or object when only part is given. An ability in auditory closure is needed when a child is asked to use contextual clues to decode a word. It is also necessary when decoding words in which the sound-symbol relationship is not regular. Although "said" is considered a "sight word," it is possible sound it out. However, to reconcile the strange pronunciation it is necessary to infer meaning and therefore pronunciation from context. An ability in visual closure and figure-ground selection is needed every time a student is required to scan for information in a story or in one of the content areas. When an efficient student is asked to list the factors that led up to a certain event, he does not read every word. Instead he skims, looking for key words that would indicate the location of the kind of information needed.

Conclusion

The ITPA is a multifaceted test that samples many different kinds of behaviors relevant to school performance in a relatively short time. Although other tests sample the same or additional behaviors, the ITPA forms a cogent package that can be administered in a relatively short time.

All tests sample behavior, and it is the duty of the examiner to go beyond the face value of the general results and to delve deeper into the actual behaviors elicited. It is this analysis of actual cognitive behavior that makes diagnosis meaningful.

DEVELOPMENTAL TEST OF VISUAL-MOTOR INTEGRATION

The Developmental Test of Visual-Motor Integration developed by Beery is a graded series of geometric forms to be copied with pencil and paper. The test may be administered to individuals or groups of children in the age range of 2 to 15 years, but it was intended for use with children in the preschool and primary grades (Beery, 1967).

The children are asked to look at geometric drawings and copy each one in the space provided. There is no time limit for the task, but the child is not permitted to erase. He must perceive, plan, and execute each form to the best of his ability. To copy the forms correctly the child must be able to (1) perceive the direction, position, and type of the various lines used in the geometric form, (2) identify a starting point, (3) draw each form, section by section if necessary, and (4) not be confused by intersecting forms or lines. If the test is administered individually, the examiner may discontinue testing when three consecutive items are failed. If the test is administered to a group, the students are instructed to do the best they can and attempt each item (Beery, 1967).

The test is scored by comparing the student's drawing with the model according to specific criteria. For example, when evaluating a form entitled oblique cross (commonly called an X), the examiner checks for the following.

1. There are two continuous intersecting lines.
2. The lines are angled between 20 and 70 degrees and between 110 and 160 degrees.
3. The "legs" are of fairly equal length.

Examples of student responses that have been categorized as passing or failing (with the failing drawing labeled as to the criterion failed) are provided as a guide to scoring. For each form there is also a chart containing representative selections from various age ranges to illustrate a developmental pattern of responses. It is possible, then, to look at each form and observe how children of various ages typically execute the drawing and how they eventually arrive at the correct response.

The test score is then reported as a visual-motor integration age, which is derived from separate tables for males and females.

The value of this test is twofold: (1) it is possible to arrive at an educational assessment of a child's ability to integrate visual input with motoric output and (2) it trains the examiner to structure the evaluation according to task levels and task components.

Beery provides an excellent discussion of his methodology and philosophy in the test manual. He believes that teachers are attracted to prepackaged instructional programs but that these materials are often used automatically, almost without thinking. He feels that teachers should be more than dispensers of programmed materials, especially when children have unusual educational problems. The teacher needs to be able to *observe* the needs of children and *devise* methods and materials on the basis of these observations.

Beery's philosophy is one of "testing down" and "teaching up." He does not categorize a child's problem, define the developmental steps necessary to achieve the desired goal, and then march the child through all of those steps. Instead he defines a task according to various levels and components, arranges these levels and components in a hierarchy of difficulty, and proceeds to test the child beginning from the *most difficult level*. He proceeds down the hierarchy, giving the child less difficult levels until the child reaches a level at which he is able to succeed. At this point Beery changes direction and begins remediation by working back up through the hierarchy, teaching the child to perform at each step until the highest level (which is the desired outcome) is achieved.

This principle is applied to visual-motor integration by identifying five levels of difficulty and their various components. For a more thorough discussion of these levels and ways of assessing and remedying each, see Beery (1967, pp. 68-77).

Level V: Visual-motor integration
  1. Direct reproduction
  2. Imitation
  3. Dot-to-dot
Level IV: Perception
  1. Perceptual-motor closure
  2. Recognition of similarities
  3. Recognition of differences
Level III: Tracing
Level II: Tactual-kinesthetic sense
  1. Kinesthetic control
  2. Kinesthetic recognition
  3. Tactual localization
Level I: Motor proficiency
  1. Control
  2. Speed
  3. Scribble
  4. Grasp

Children who have difficulty with test items below their age level are asked to deal with these same test items at progressively easier levels until they reach a level at which they can succeed. Teaching (or remediation) begins from that point. Note that the Developmental Test of Visual-Motor Integration assesses ability at level V step 1—direct reproduction.

This is a technique that can and should be applied to many different kinds of learning difficulties, and it is unfortunate that its description is tucked away in the back of a test manual. Beery's major contribution to assessment comes not from the test score, which is reported dutifully by examiners and then forgotten, but instead from the assessment and teaching strategy that he has applied to visual-motor skills but that is universal in application. Thus we find another example of a test that has value beyond the scores, grade-age equivalents, and profiles we so often see. In contrast to the ITPA, which requires considerable special training to administer, the Developmental Test of Visual-Motor Integration may be given by any classroom teacher. Since the regular classroom teacher seldom has much specific training in the use of tests, particularly with respect to any use beyond the use of the derived scores, much of the value of this test and many similar tests is lost. The learning disabilities teacher should make every effort to avoid this type of problem.

GOLDMAN-FRISTOE-WOODCOCK TEST OF AUDITORY DISCRIMINATION

The Goldman-Fristoe-Woodcock Test of Auditory Discrimination measures auditory discrimination under both quiet and background noise conditions for subjects ages 4 years and older. The subject is required to listen to a word and select from a group of four pictures one that represents the word. A preliminary training procedure ensures that the subject knows the word-picture associations before the actual testing, and the use of a prerecorded tape permits a standardized presentation of speech sounds. The responses are recorded for both the quiet subtest and the noise subtest and the errors analyzed.

The test measures the ability to discriminate auditorily among consonant sounds only, and the discrimination errors are grouped as follows:

1. *Voiceless or voiced*

p	b
t	d
k	g
ch	j
f	v

th	*th*		
s	z		
sh	zh		
hw	w		
h	r		
	l		
	y		

2. *Plosive*

p	t	k	ch
b	d	g	j

3. *Continuants*

m	f	s	hw
n	v	z	w
ng	th	sh	r
	th	zh	l
			y
			h

4. *Nasals*

m

n

ng

Responses are then counted and recorded in combination, that is, voiced plosives, voiceless continuants, etc. For each subtest the examiner records total errors and percentile rank.

Would-be examiners should note that although this test comprehensively assesses discrimination of specific consonant sounds, it does not test discrimination between vowel sounds, a major source of concern for teachers of beginning reading.

BEHAVIORAL OBSERVATIONS AS ASSESSMENT

Behavioral observations should be made as an important part of the assessment process. These observations may be made in the classroom, but they are often made and noted throughout testing sessions. These observations usually include some of the following factors.

1. Physical characteristics
2. Voice and speech characteristics
3. Dress and grooming
4. Gross and fine motor coordination
5. General anxiety: nervousness, blushing, blanching, jumping from one subject to another, interest in correctness or in-

correctness of response, hostility, shyness or reserve.

6. Language: fluency, choice of words, bizarre responses, echolalia

7. Work behavior: amount of effort, motivation, spontaneity, erratic or compulsive behavior, fatigue, frustration

We may also observe a child's approach to a difficult task as an *approach to problem-solving.* We may observe (1) the decision making involved in initiating problem solving, (2) the speed of response, and (3) the sequence of responses. In addition we may observe the *quality of delivery;* we may listen to vocal quality to determine whether the voice is strained, relaxed, normal, or quiet. We may observe the motor aspect and look for tension in holding the pencil; quick, abrupt movements; or hesitancy to commit oneself to an answer.

The amount and kind of observations an examiner might make are dependent on proficiency in handling testing materials, knowledge of what kind of behaviors or characteristics to look for, and the ability to recognize them when they are presented.

The diagnostic observation assessment model mentioned in Chapter 4 provides an extended time period in which to make this type of observation and may be one of the more promising of the newer approaches to assessment.

SUMMARY

The major theme of this chapter is that a variety of information may be extracted from various types of diagnostic instruments. It should be noted, however, that the amount and kind of information that may be obtained varies according to the length and scope of the particular test. A lengthy, involved diagnostic instrument such as the ITPA samples a number of different kinds of behavior. Each of its 12 subtests tests a particular kind of cognitive behavior, and within each subtest are levels of sophistication and difficulty. The Developmental Test of Visual-Motor Integration samples specific copying behavior in the visual-motor area, but may be expanded to include various levels of visual-motor processing. The Test of Auditory Discrimination measures very specific discrimination abilities and does this comprehensively within its own defined bounds. It does little more than it sets out to do, but this in no way limits its value as a diagnostic instrument.

This multiple information principle does not mean that the "traditional" types of information are of little value. Rather, it indicates that we must understand and be able to extract a wide variety of information from diagnostic and assessment instruments that are capable of providing such information. In using the ITPA both traditional analysis and task analysis approaches are essential if we are to provide maximum assistance to the children with whom we are concerned. With other tests a similar procedure should be followed if we are to obtain full benefit from an analysis of the child's test responses and behavior.

Behavioral observations were mentioned only briefly but should be considered as a highly valuable type of adjunctive assessment. This topic deserves and requires lengthy consideration and for most individuals considerable special training is necessary for behavioral observation to be of maximum value. Behavioral observation and planned attention to task analysis approaches in the use of standardized tests require the services of a specialist who is more than a well-trained test technician. They require an understanding of the learning process, of how we attempt to teach children in the public schools of this nation, and a sensitivity to something beyond scores, scales, profiles, and normative data. We truly must take a "second look" at tests and assessment instruments and how we use them.

REFERENCES AND SUGGESTED READINGS

Bateman, B. *The Illinois Test of Psycholinguistic Abilities in current research: summaries of studies.* Urbana, Ill.: Institute for Research on Exceptional Children, 1965.

Beery, K. *Developmental Test of Visual-Motor Integration.* Chicago: Follett Publishing Co., 1967.

Binet, A. *Les idées modernes sur les enfants.* Paris: Flammarion, 1913.

Bloom, B., et al. *Taxonomy of educational objectives: cognitive domain.* New York: David McKay Co., Inc., 1956.

Bush, W. J., and Giles, M. *Aids to psycholinguistic teaching.* Columbus, Ohio: Charles E. Merrill Publishing Co., 1969.

Goldman, R., Fristoe, M., and Woodcock, R. *Test of Auditory Discrimination.* Circle Pines, Minn.: American Guidance Service, Inc., 1970.

Karnes, M. *GOAL: language development.* Springfield, Mass.: Milton Bradley Co.

Karnes, M. *Helping young children develop language skills.* Washington, D.C.: Council for Exceptional Children, 1968.

Kirk, S., and Bateman, B. *Ten years of research at the Institute for Research on Exceptional Children.* Urbana, Ill.: University of Illinois Press, 1964.

Kirk, S., and Kirk, W. *Psycholinguistic learning disabilities: diagnosis and remediation.* Urbana, Ill.: University of Illinois Press, 1971.

Kirk, S., McCarthy, J., and Kirk, W. *Illinois Test of Psycholinguistic Abilities* (Rev. ed.). Urbana, Ill.: University of Illinois Press, 1968.

Minskoff, G., Wiseman, D., and Minskoff, E. *The MWM program for developing language abilities.* Ridgefield, N.J.: Educational Performance Associates, 1972.

Osgood, C. A behavioristic analysis. In J. Bruner (Ed.), *Contemporary approaches to cognition: a symposium.* Cambridge, Mass.: Harvard University Press, 1957.

Paraskevopovlos, J. N., and Kirk, S. *The development and psychometric characteristics of the revised Illinois Test of Psycholinguistic abilities.* Urbana, Ill.: University of Illinois Press, 1969.

6 Teaching reading to the learning disabled

There seems little question that, at least for the present, there is more emphasis on reading disabilities than any other subject or skill area in the various classes and programs for children with learning disabilities. Some programs may emphasize the development of visual process skills, others may relate more to auditory channel problems, and still others may claim a general perceptual-motor emphasis, but if the children in most of these programs had been reading at an acceptable level, they would not have been included in the program. We may therefore conclude that the development of reading skills and abilities commensurate with apparent intellectual potential is a primary goal for a majority of children in learning disabilities programs in the United States. Even though some programs may include stated objectives that do not indicate reading as the most important goal, the objectives are almost always those assumed to be prerequisities to reading success.

This strong position statement must not be interpreted to mean that problems in other academic areas, for example, mathematics, are unimportant or unworthy of careful attention and consideration. In fact, the strong emphasis on reading has tended to obscure the needs of children who have specific disabilities that relate primarily to mathematics, a fact that will be further explored in Chapter 7. However, the concern for reading problems that I have witnessed in every class for the learning disabled that I have ever visited is sufficient reason to believe that *every* teacher who specializes in learning disabilities must become well informed and highly competent in the teaching of reading skills.

Knowledge of how most children learn to read, the learning abilities assumed to be present and functioning normally by authors of most traditional reading series, the variety of reading methods or approaches (and their strengths and weaknesses), and a host of other related factors is essential to the teacher who specializes in learning disabilities. Therefore in this chapter I will review some of the major controversies in the field of reading, summarize and briefly describe many of the major reading approaches, and give further direction as to how to apply this information in educational planning for children with learning disabilities.

ISSUES AND CONTROVERSIES

In 1961 the Carnegie Corporation approved a grant to investigate many of the major issues involved in the question of how children may most effectively be taught to read. This study was carried out by Jeanne Chall from 1962 to 1965; like many other Carnegie studies, it ultimately resulted in the publication of a text (Chall, 1967) that is part of the Carnegie Series in American Education. I recommend it to all readers of this volume.

Its major contribution is a critical, comprehensive review of methods and philosophies in the field of reading. It is presented in an objective manner that was previously difficult, if not almost impossible, to find within the field. Although the reasons for this lack of objectivity are relatively easy to explain, they are seldom discussed; many of the discussants would be subject to the same biasing factors that they would be compelled to enumerate. The factors that lead to this situation include the following.

1. The basic research in reading has tended to be inconclusive, with ambiguous results.

2. Research results have been so subject to varied interpretation that at times the same research has been used to support opposite points of view.

3. The major authorities tend to have considerable commercial interests in specific programs, which tends to discourage serious, long-term efforts in a direction that might require them to refute their earlier work.

4. Commercial interests aside, most authorities have personal or professional interests and ideas based on strongly held philosophical or theoretical beliefs. These are often the result of long years of effort and observation and lead to basic convictions that are difficult to shake. Thus the efforts of these authorities tend to be directed toward making their earlier approaches most effective and usable rather than toward identifying new methods or approaches.

5. In terms of results achieved from efforts expended, it is undoubtedly more practical for highly experienced professionals to continue work in some avenue of present expertise rather than to switch to a new one.

The result of these factors is that many of the best minds in the professional field of reading continue in the direction they have already established, changing or modifying their attack on reading problems to only a minor degree. As long as some sizable segment of consumers (public schoolteachers, reading supervisors, etc.) uses these approaches with apparent success, this will be likely to remain the pattern.

Chall's investigation led to a number of observations, implications, and conclusions that are pertinent to all teachers of reading and particularly to learning disabilities and remedial reading teachers. They are of more interest to these two groups because they must deal with children for whom the "standard" method, whatever it may be, has been ineffective.

One of the more interesting observations made by Chall—one that is obviously subjective but certainly deserves consideration—is that there is a strong *emotional* involvement on the part of most authors, reading specialists, teachers, administrators, and even researchers in the field when they discuss reading methods. This observation could be discounted as highly subjective, but a careful study of Chall's investigation gives the impression of a high degree of objectivity, and there is little of the appeal to emotion that one may find in such historically popular critiques of reading as *Why Johnny Can't Read and What You Can Do About It* (Flesch, 1955).* In fact, it is my belief that educators, like the general public, tend to ignore many of the more valuable educational investigations because they are carefully and objectively done and are not designed to increase the blood pressure or otherwise significantly affect body chemistry.

Chall says of reading researchers, "Their language was often more characteristic of religion and politics than of science and learning." If researchers do tend to be emotionally involved, serious questions of validity must be asked about their research. To her credit, Chall indicates that neither evidence nor issues are conclusive or clear-cut and that her conclusions are mainly interpretations.

Perhaps *the* major issue in the teaching of reading (it has been restated every few years since the idea of basal readers became generally accepted in the 1920's) is whether or not the basal reader approach is really the "best" approach. Often the approach advocated by some authority who opposes the existing system is similar to it but has one facet that is quite different. During the past 25 years this difference has often related to

the use of phonics, although different authors use different modes of implementation according to what they believe to be effective. A discussion of methods that emphasize phonics will be given later in this chapter and the basal reader approach will be described in some detail.

A second issue, one discussed by Chall but not included as a basic part of her investigation, is the issue of when reading should be initiated. It should be carefully noted that although how to teach reading is the major thrust of both past and present controversy, "when" is also a part of some reading schemes. If "when" (age 4, 5, 6, or 7 years) is changed significantly, it will undoubtedly affect "how." With some writers providing instructions to parents about how to teach reading to 3- or 4-year-old children, an entirely different set of needs could exist in 6-year-olds if any large number of children learned to read before entering school.

A third issue, referred to by Chall but not given the priority that it has received recently due to increased emphasis on the needs and rights of minority students, relates to the use of modified content and the use of languages other than English in reading programs. This issue leads to a variety of questions as to the basic purposes of education, the need or lack of need for standard English, and many others. It will require different consideration in different geographical areas of the nation and in some areas is a major question.

Many other issues could be raised, but the one that is most often asked in classrooms throughout the nation is the first—how to teach. This question, relevant to all teachers of reading, is even more important to the learning disabilities teacher. This is true because (1) the child who is referred for learning disabilities program assistance usually has already demonstrated that the "regular" method is not effective for him and (2) the regular classroom teacher may be able to say, "I would use another method, but I must follow established program procedures" or "If I had only three or four children I could

---

*This text almost literally turned the world of reading upside down for several years in many parts of the nation. It was well written and appealed to a concern felt strongly by many parents because our society has equated success with a high level of education and reading skill is seen as the basic prerequisite for an adequate education. Although younger readers may not remember its impact, those who had to deal with its results in parent-teacher meetings, with members of boards of education, and in individual parent conferences remember it as an educational hydrogen bomb.

teach him," but the learning disabilities teacher usually has small groups of children and in most cases can use methods and approaches that seem most effective. The question of effective methods (not method) is of utmost importance.

Because the point of view taken in this text is that *there is no single best approach to teaching reading to the learning-disabled child* (due to the variety of causal factors and the variable effects of earlier educational efforts), we will not pursue the question of a best way to teach reading. We will consider other factors discovered by Chall as she pursued the question of how reading might be most effectively taught, factors that do have considerable relevance to selection of a reading approach for the learning-disabled student.

All of the findings that follow have some aspect of subjectivity, but they are the impressions of a highly trained and experienced observer and investigator. To the extent that each of these findings is accurate, it is relevant in planning for children with learning disabilities that result in reading retardation.

Specific findings of Chall's study*

1. *Interest in reading may be determined more by what a teacher does with a particular method than by which method is used.* What is done with the method should be interpreted to include what is done with materials, with boys and girls, and with space and time parameters. Interest appears to be highly related to pacing, to how well the teacher could sense and manipulate the time and materials so that children were challenged but not presented with impossible tasks. Children who find the basic work too easy or the pace to slow should be provided additional challenge through additional work of interest, not busywork.

2. Contrary to what has been held by

many reading specialists for years and promoted by authors and publishers, *the story— the content of what is read—does not seem to be a major factor in the child's interest.* It was observed that children were as interested in words, in spelling, and in rules for learning reading as in the stories. Basal readers were exciting to most children if they were in fact learning successfully. It was concluded that children can become interested in almost anything if the atmosphere is conducive of such interest.*

3. Although the teacher's use and presentation of materials seem to be highly important, certain hazards that relate to specific methods seem to be subject to generalizations. *Systematic phonics programs, while not necessarily inherently "dull," have a potential for such dullness if the words sounded out and defined are too abstract or too far removed from the real world of the child.* Some systematic phonics programs are so highly structured and the teacher is so strongly admonished against deviation from format that commonsense judgment may be ignored and the teacher may push ahead with the program even though children are sending clear signals that they have been "turned off." Basal reading programs have a similar problem with teacher questions to determine whether the material read has been understood. *Extended questioning about a story—a part of many basal reader programs—may be too much for many children.* As in the case of phonics, an element of common judgment should be applied to interpretation of the teachers' guides that commonly accompany basal readers.

4. *Any extended use of workbooks or teacher-made worksheets tends to produce apathy, leads to bad practice effect (copying*

---

*Chall observed more than 10 different classes and teachers for each of the many reading methods reviewed in her investigation. These numbered findings are based on her observations as abstracted from the reports of her study.

*Note that Chall is referring to children who are learning *along with other children at the same grade level*. These generalizations may not apply to, for example, 10-year-old children who are presented second-grade material to which they have already been exposed many times. Also note that the general assumption is that these children have the visual and auditory acuity and perception to learn through the methods used.

of the work of others with little or no under-standing), and has a number of other nega-tive effects. Some few children may work in-dependently for relatively long periods of time, but for most the worksheet is something to avoid. Some types of programmed ma-terials or the use of educational hardware may reduce this effect, but these should be carefully monitored.

5. *Although some success factors can be attributed to method, the most important factor seems to be whether the method is preceived as "new" or "old" by teachers using it.* It appears that at times a "new" method is thought by those using it to be solving nearly all reading problems; that is, they are reluctant to admit that it does not work with all children. However, other schools or individuals using this same method who view it as old (if it has been in use for several years) are much more likely to admit its shortcomings.

Factors other than perceived newness may be in effect in many of these settings: such factors as more workshops, more discussion with other teachers, and perhaps more self-examination as to the various other aspects of the teaching-learning process that may contribute to success with new methods. Another factor that may be in operation is some type of self-selection of teachers who are willing to innovate. Within a given school unit it may be that the more able teachers and those who are more imaginative and questioning of the system are those who become involved in new methods and ap-proaches. Differences between school units may exist because teachers may seek employ-ment in school districts on the basis of knowledge (or hearsay) regarding that dis-trict's tendency to use or permit the use of new methods.

Paradoxically, one of the factors that may limit the effectiveness of any new method is the inability of those using it to see its short-comings. Seldom is an old method discarded unless it can be demonstrated that it has serious limitations or shortcomings. These are usually analyzed and documented, and of course the new method is one that takes these problem areas into account. What is sometimes forgotten is that the old method was once new and that it is the responsibility of those initiating a new method to seriously investigate for shortcomings as well as strengths both before and after adoption. It is unlikely that the publisher who is promoting the new method will document these problem areas; therefore it is up to the searching professional educator to find them.

One additional caution must be observed carefully in the assessment of a method by those who have used it for some time. The usually accepted measure of effectiveness of any reading approach is the amount of measurable reading improvement of children using this approach. However, the manner in which this improvement is viewed is highly important. An actual case may best illustrate this point.

Case study

The following description relates to a school district that adopted a new reading approach (method N) in place of the old approach (method O). After a few years of use of method N, years in which most teachers seemed to think that it was quite effective, an undercurrent of concern devel-oped. This concern was triggered by the fact that some children achieved at a much higher level than others in their grade. Method N led to a large range between the lowest level of reading achieve-ment and the highest level of reading achieve-ment in any given grade. This led the teachers to worry about why they could not more success-fully teach some of the children who made the lower scores, and the "distance" between the highest and lowest level of achievement in each grade tended to emphasize this problem. Teachers were fully aware of the fact that the new method was very successful with many chil-dren but in an attempt to be objective noted the low scores of children at the bottom of the achievement range. They even initiated meetings at which they discussed the possible need to re-place this method because it was so ineffective with those children in the bottom quartile of achievement. Then certain facts were pointed out to them. The data below indicate the range and median reading scores (grade equivalents) for third-grade pupils with method O and method N. This was after method N had been in use for 3 years.

	Lowest score	Median score	Highest score
Method O	1.4	3.4	4.9
Method N	1.4	3.7	5.7

It must be considered that although the same standardized achievement test was used with these two third-grade classes, they were two different groups of children, and the second group may have been more capable or have had better preschool preparation for reading. Nevertheless this comparison led the teacher group to see that it was the large difference between the high and low scores that was causing their concern, a difference to which they reacted in terms of how far the low-score children were lagging behind the high-score children. When method O, now 3 years in the past, was compared to method N in this manner, it provided the needed perspective. The fact that the median score was 0.3 higher suddenly became very important, and the extended range became of less concern. Teachers remembered something that they had known but had almost forgotten: a method that really provides for individual differences tends to widen group achievement differences; it encourages the very able children toward maximum growth.

The lesson to be learned is clear. Although we must strive for objectivity and must search for and openly admit shortcomings in any educational approach, we must be careful of other effects, particularly the "extending the range of achievement" effect, which may result from any approach that really "turns on" children of high intellectual ability.

6. In some cases *teachers using a "new" method, although enthusiastic about its advantages, tend to use components of the old method that common sense indicates important but are left out of the new method.* Chall reported that several times during her observations proponents of a specific method were embarrassed to find teachers doing a number of things "not permitted" by the method. She further suggests that this may in some cases be part of the strength of many new methods.

Based on this observation and on the history of the effectiveness of new methods, an interesting theory may be postulated. If, as new methods are adopted, teachers tend to use the new method but add some of the components of the old that are missing in the new, the result may be a highly viable combination of old and new applied in a manner that is compatible with observed success on the part of children. This combination of methods developed by practitioners who actually work with children may provide the best of both approaches. After many years of theoretical acceptance of the new method, as children grow up through more and more "pure" application of the new approach and teachers come into the field who have never used the old approach, the method becomes more pure and perhaps less effective. This could explain the apparently greater effectiveness of the initial move away from phonics programs in the late 1920's and the 1930's, with the new program receiving more and more criticism until in the mid-1950's (just prior to Chall's investigation) when a countermovement back to phonics began.

7. As a result, *the mingling of old and new approaches often carried out by the teacher when the classroom door is closed makes the results of any large-scale research efforts highly suspect.* This is a factor to consider carefully when attempting to interpret research results.

8. *As time passes, the innovators who helped initiate the presently used approach become the greatest force against change.* This is due to a combination of many of the factors outlined above and is a situation to reckon with.

9. As a broad generalization, it could be stated that *reading programs that emphasize a more systematic teaching of the sound-symbol relationship tend to achieve better results.* This for the most part means systems that used such programs in addition to the basal reading program. It must be noted that this was more than 10 years ago, and there is every indication that the authors of basal reading series have moved in the direction of more planned inclusion of some sort of phonic component in all or nearly all of the major basal reading series published since that time.

10. Many school programs were observed

as a part of this broad-scope, comprehensive investigation. This included low-income districts, high-income districts, and some private schools with very low teacher-pupil ratios and children from backgrounds that should have provided optimum preparation and readiness for school. *In all programs there were children who did not read with success; that is, no system, regardless of optimistic promise, was totally successful.* In even the best programs the need for a remedial program remained.

This conclusion, apparently still valid, is the reason for present-day programs of remediation. I believe the major reason is that despite sufficient evidence that one approach will not work with all children, the problems of large class size and the high rate of attrition among primary teachers have left most public and private schools with but one major methodological approach in most classrooms. Talk of real individualization continues but is seldom factual. Different learning styles, varying preschool experiences, and differing rates of growth and development in addition to specific learning problems relating to identifiable process disabilities are facts of life. One role of the learning disabilities teacher is to assist children who do not succeed in reading, regardless of which reason or reasons apply.

APPROACHES FOR GENERAL USE

If the facts presented and the assumptions made thus far are accepted as true, the learning disabilities teacher must be familiar with how most children learn to read and what abilities and skills are required, with a number of different approaches to reading, and with the strengths and weaknesses of each. A variety of reading approaches will be discussed, and because each is the subject of one or several separate texts, the reader is encouraged to pursue additional information and insight through further investigation of the specific methods that are of most interest. (The references and suggested readings will provide a good starting point for such pursuit. Additional references in Appendix D should be of further assistance.)

As a part of the basis for discussion of reading approaches, it would be well to review skills thought to be necessary for inclusion in the developmental reading sequence. The following is an overview of these skills. Others may classify them differently, but it is less important to remember their classification than to make certain they are included in the reading program. (Some of these skills may not be within the grasp of some learning-disabled students; however, many such children will learn them if they are taught with understanding and with a firm knowledge of each child's needs.) The following classification is offered by Karlin (1971).

Classification of reading skills*
1. Word recognition skills
   a. Contextual clues
   b. Phonic analysis
   c. Structural analysis
   d. Dictionary
   e. Sight vocabulary
2. Word meaning skills
   a. Contextual clues
   b. Structural clues
   c. Dictionary
   d. Multiple meanings
   e. Figurative language
3. Comprehension skills
   a. Literal meaning
   b. Inferred meaning
   c. Critical evaluation
   d. Assimilation
4. Study skills
   a. Location of information
   b. Selection of information
   c. Organization and retention of information
   d. Graphic and typographical aids
   e. Previewing
   f. Flexibility
5. Appreciation skills
   a. Language of literature
   b. Forms of literature

Although there is some agreement regarding the basic components of reading, the

---

*If the learning disabilities teacher becomes involved in attempting to develop skills such as comprehension skills in children who are reading at the upper elementary grade levels or above, a more detailed guide must be obtained. This may be found in several of the reading texts listed at the end of this chapter.

further one investigates this area, the more one realizes that we are not absolutely certain just how we can best describe the process of reading. Not only is there disagreement among the learning theorists as to how children learn, but there is disagreement among reading specialists as to how to define reading. For example, Spache and Spache (1973), acknowledged to be among the leaders in their field, outline seven ways in which reading may be defined and provide at least limited support for each of these definitions.

The one conclusion that may be drawn with certainty is that reading is a highly complex process and that due to a variety of factors, certain children learn better through an approach other than the ap-

CLASSIFICATIONS OF READING APPROACHES

George D. Spache (1972)	*NEA bulletin (Mackintosh, 1967)*	*Jeanne Chall (1967)*	*Robert C. Aukerman (1971)*
Basal reader system	Basal reading series	Conventional basal approach	
Decoding or phonic approaches	Phonic approach	Phonics (complete program)	Basic phonemic approaches
	Words in Color	Phonics (supplemental)	Phonemic-pronunciation approaches
			Phonemics-reading approaches
Linguistic approach	Linguistics	Linguistic approach	Linguistics-phonemics approaches
New alphabets (Initial Teaching Alphabet and others)	Initial Teaching Alphabet	Initial Teaching Alphabet	One-to-one sound-symbol approaches
Language experience approach	Language experience approach	Language experience approach	Language experience approach
Individualized reading	Individualized approach	Individualized reading	Individualized reading approach
	Multilevel reading instruction	Programmed learning Responsive Environment	"Total" language arts approaches Perceptual discrimination approaches Early reading approaches

NOTE: Approaches listed above the line tend to be similar as described by the four authorities. There are differences; for example, Aukerman's category of one-to-one sound-symbol approaches includes more than the Initial Teaching Alphabet, but it is a major part of his more inclusive category. Approaches listed below the line are of relatively less importance than the six major approach categories above the line except in Aukerman's categories. In his system approaches that others would have called basal reader approaches are included in two of the three categories below the line.

proach generally used, no matter what that approach may be. A related conclusion is that the nature of the reading process changes from one developmental stage to the next. If we proceed with these facts in mind, we will be more likely to appreciate the need to understand the basic processes involved in reading and the major approaches that may be used to facilitate the acquisition of reading skills.

Analysis of reading approaches

Since the late 1950's and undoubtedly partly as a result of the large-scale criticism of programs that existed then, approaches other than basal reader programs have received renewed attention. A number of authors have provided overviews and analyses of the various reading approaches in use in the nation. Differences exist as to the major categories used for such analyses; some authors apparently thought a particular approach was worthy of mention while others did not. Other differences related to the times at which they were written, to different basic purposes, or to differences in intended readership. We will consider four of these analyses.

The first authority is George D. Spache (1972), an internationally recognized reading authority and author of numerous books and journal articles on reading. Spache prepared a simple, concise review of reading methods written for persons who are not reading specialists that clearly indicates the state of the art from the vantage point of his long experience. It is perhaps the most general of the four sources.

The second source is a National Education Association (NEA) bulletin, *Current Approaches to Teaching Reading* (Mackintosh, 1965), a collection of descriptions of eight approaches to teaching reading written by individuals who are closely associated with the method or approach. These approaches were selected by the executive committee of the Department of Elementary-Kindergarten-Nursery Education of the NEA as representative of the range of current thinking and discussion in the field of teaching reading.

The third authority is Jeanne Chall (1967). We should remember that Chall was not trying to develop a system of categories into which all reading approaches might be placed; she was trying to investigate representative samples of those approaches she considered pertinent to "the debate." In so doing she provided a classification system.

The fourth source is Robert C. Aukerman (1971). Aukerman, like Spache and the NEA committee, was deliberately trying to provide an overview of approaches to reading. In his case the topic was limited to beginning reading, but within this limitation Aukerman attempted to describe nearly every approach actually in use anywhere in the United States that was identifiable as a specific approach. In other words, he attempted to find diversity where Spache and the NEA executive committee were interested in simplification within a limited number of major categories. Aukerman identifies his work as a compendium of approaches that includes information about origins, background of authors, and descriptions of each method. In the preface he indicates that "one hundred or more approaches to beginning reading have arbitrarily been classified under ten categories." Actually, slightly more than 50 approaches are discussed in some detail, with others very briefly mentioned. Aukerman's system of categories is more different from the other three than any one of the others is different from the remaining two. In fact, his placement of approaches within the 10 major categories he has established is even more different than the chart on p. 77 indicates, a fact that can be fully appreciated only by reading his book.

Although there are differences in the manner in which various authorities categorize existing approaches to teaching reading, there is near consensus on the existence of at least six major categories: (1) basal reader approaches, (2) phonic approaches, both supplemental and complete, (3) linguistic approaches, (4) new alphabet approaches, (5) language experience approaches, and (6) individualized reading approaches. Furthermore, we know that all of these approaches are effective with some children some of the time and that no one approach is effective with all children all of the time.

Basal reader approach

The basal reader approach has been accepted by a majority of elementary school educators since the late 1920's. Although there have been variations, the following features seem to be common to most of the major basal reading series.

1. Reading is defined broadly to include word recognition, comprehension, interpretation, and application of what is read.

2. Children should go through a readiness period, and those who are not ready for reading after the prescribed length of time (usually as determined by a standardized readiness test) should spend more time in the readiness program.

3. Reading begins with the reading of whole words—words that are meaningful in the life of the reader. Reading should be related to both the experiences and interests of the reader whenever possible. Silent reading is stressed from the start, with discussion and teacher's questions the means of checking for understanding.

4. When the child is able to recognize at sight (without pausing to analyze, sound, etc.) a given number of words (different series recommend different numbers, but 50 to 80 is the usual range), he then begins to learn the basic elements of phonetic analysis. At about the same time, although sometimes earlier, he learns to identify new words by picture or context (meaning) clues. Structural analysis such as separating compound words or using a knowledge of prefixes and suffixes begins at about the same time.

5. Word attack skills, although introduced in the first grade, are presented throughout the first 3 or 4 years of schooling, or in some cases throughout the first six grades.

6. Use of phonics in isolation, particularly phonics drills, is not recommended. Phonics skills are taught and may be used as one of several word attack skills. (It should be noted that basal readers of the 1970's have considerably more phonetic analysis as a planned

part of the program than basal readers of the 1930's and 1940's. Those of the 1930's and 1940's were in part a reaction to the emphasis on phonics that existed prior to about 1920. Today's inclusion of more early phonics may be related more to criticism of the 1950's and 1960's than to the existence of new research.)

7. Words appearing in basal readers are presented often, and it is expected that children will learn to recognize them on sight through such repetition. They are related to the theoretical speaking, usage, and listening vocabulary for children at various ages. Except for the names of characters in stories, the words at the beginning levels tend to be short and the sentences short and simple in structure.

8. Although much is said about individualization, most series are based on the idea that the teacher will teach the class in three or four small groups with children grouped according to reading progress. (This has been called by some the "Redbirds, Bluebirds, Robins syndrome," although today the groups may be named for astronauts, football teams, or other such "innovative" interests.)

9. Nearly all basal readers are accompanied by workbooks in which children are expected to find the planned opportunity for additional practice with words introduced in the readers. All have teachers' manuals in which precise instructions are provided.

This characterization of basal readers was adapted from a description provided by Chall (1967) with some additions reflecting my observations of basal readers in more recent years. Chall's description related to the mid-1960's, and there have been some notable changes since that time, including a reduction in the almost total reliance on basal readers that existed from 1930 to 1960. However, many school systems still rely on an adopted basal reader series, sometimes with another series approved for use in unusual cases or as supplementary material. Durkin (1974) comments on pre-1970 and post-1970 basal readers and notes certain identifiable changes.

1. Stories and illustrations have been

changed to reflect the concerns of those in the civil rights movement. The first changes were inclusion of pictures and story content recognizing that all children were not middle-class white children living in suburban communities. Multiracial stories and pictures and recognition of urban settings were the typical publisher reaction to the challenge. Some publishers operated for a time with two or more basal series, but most have modified their major series to attempt to appeal to all populations of users.

2. Many basal readers have evolved in the direction of more and earlier use of phonics. This had an effect on vocabulary selection and control because it injected a new selection factor that was particularly noticeable at the primer and first reader level.

3. Teacher manuals, the subject of a variety of criticism, now tend to admonish the teacher not to simply follow the manual instructions step by step, but rather to use it as an idea book, a starting point for more effective teaching. *Selectivity* in the use of materials rather than the total adherence to a specific, rigid program is at last being actively promoted by those who develop basal reading programs.

In addition to these and other changes in the basal readers, an increasing number of schools use the basal reader plus planned elements of other types of reading approaches. A few have moved almost entirely away from basal readers and use another approach. On the following pages we will consider some alternate approaches.

Phonic approaches

Phonic approaches, sometimes called decoding approaches, undoubtedly represent the oldest of the modern methods of teaching reading. Spache indicates the existence of only two major types: "analytic, in which letter sounds are taught as integral parts of words, and synthetic, in which the isolated letter sounds are stressed before any great experience with words" (Spache, 1972). Aukerman (1971) emphasizes two psychological bases that relate to and undergird phonic (he calls them phonemic) systems. The first is

that phonic systems require rote memorization, the memorization of which sounds relate to which letters. This sort of memorization requires good auditory and visual memory, a particularly important fact in dealing with children with learning disabilities. The second psychological base is that of "part learning," learning through individual elements and then assembling these elements into a whole. The synthetic approach depends more totally on the part learning principle, although both do to a considerable extent.

One element of phonic systems may be viewed as both a strength and a weakness. Advocates note that the normal American child has already learned (developed oral vocabulary) thousands of words by the time he enters school. If a system can be used that maximizes this learning, certainly it will be advantageous. Phonic system enthusiasts believe that once the child learns to recognize the letters of the alphabet and to respond to the visual stimulus of these letters with the sound that they represent, he has mastered the one most efficient way to enter the world of reading. Because children already have a comparatively large oral vocabulary, comprehension (of what is on the printed page) will automatically come as a result of pronunciation. The one serious problem to this simple theorem is the irregularity of the English language.*

As noted, the element of oral vocabulary is a strength, but it may also be a weakness. Although it is a strength in early reading, it is of little value later (if our interest is in comprehension) when the older child is faced with an increasing number of words that he has never heard before. Spache (1972) indicates that phonic and decoding systems tend to produce better oral word pronunciation and silent word recognition than

---

*Note that this irregularity, the inconsistency in the relationship between visual symbols (letters of the English alphabet) and the sounds they represent, is the precise reason for the development of the Initial Teaching Alphabet and the other new alphabet systems, which are essentially phonic approaches with built-in compensation for irregularities of the English language.

many other systems. He believes that they tend to produce inferior silent reading comprehension and accuracy and rate of oral reading. These generalizations are what might be expected "on the average" from large groups of children with approximately identical intelligence, sensory abilities, and cultural and readiness background. The learning disabilities teacher is often working with children who may not be considered part of the "average."

Literally hundreds of texts have been written about phonics. Aukerman (1971) describes dozens of phonics approaches. Dechant (1969) and Aukerman talk of linguistic phonics, thus combining these two major categories. Spache (1972) indicates that some basal readers series have abandoned the idea that a certain number of sight vocabulary words must be learned before phonic approaches are used and that available research seems to support this practice. He notes that what was "second-grade-level" phonics now is introduced in the first grade in many instances.

Although a number of allegedly "pure" or total phonics approaches are in use, it appears that the 1970's will be the decade of increased use of phonics as a *support system* with basal reader series, in conjunction with linguistic approaches, or as one of the primary word attack skills. Phonics will probably be used most in the first three grades. Dechant (1969) states, "Phonics is no longer a real issue in reading. All systematized approaches to reading teach phonics in one way or another." Phonics, or phonetic analysis, is not reading. It is simply one major means of developing reading skills and abilities.

An important lesson may be learned in reviewing the historical development of reading instruction and the controversies surrounding the use of phonics since the turn of the century. At the start, some type of phonic approach was the base for most beginning reading instruction in the United States. Then research evidence indicated the potential benefit of whole-word, sight-recognition approaches, which were soon adopted wholesale. These approaches seemed to be quite effective at first, perhaps because teachers still remembered and used some of the phonic approach even though it was not a part of the prescribed program. Before long, reading was in trouble again, with too many children having serious difficulties. Numerous remedial reading systems appeared, many with highly structured phonetic elements.

Reading specialists in universities and in public schools were so involved in attempting to make the whole-word, sight-recognition methods work that they were for the most part unable to see anything else. It took writers from outside the field of reading to shake the foundations sufficiently to get the attention of reading specialists. Then the problem was to keep the pendulum from swinging too far the other way. *We surely will eventually learn that all children do not learn in precisely the same way, that most can benefit from a variety of approaches, and that different children need different "mixes" of existing approaches. A "pure" method will be appropriate only when all children come in "pure" types.*

Linguistic approaches

Linguistic approaches are generally recognized as one of the major types of approach. However, according to Spache (1972), "Although quasi-linguistic programs have been in existence for well over a century, teaching methods and materials labeled as such are a new phenomenon, dating from about 1964." Spache then states that there really is no such thing as a linguistics program for beginning reading because linguists (linguistic scientists) have not really attempted to develop a total reading program. Aukerman (1971) claims that "few, if any, true linguistics scholars claim to be reading specialists, yet a number of methods by so-called linguists have appeared in the last few years." He notes that since the increase in popular interest in linguistics as related to reading, some basal readers and supplementary materials have suddenly become "linguistically oriented" without even the benefit of a revision. Aukerman thinks that the present popularity of so-called linguistic reading approaches got its start in 1961, with the publication of *Let's Read* (Bloomfield and Barnhart, 1961). This book is the work of Bloomfield, a well-known linguistic scientist who left at his death some unpublished work relating linguistics to reading. Barnhart, a friend of Bloomfield, felt an obligation to get these ideas published; the resulting text gave the first strong impetus to what was to become a popularly acclaimed movement.

In 1963 Fries published his book *Linguistics and Reading*. This book and a variety of other influences that tended to focus attention on the possible role of linguistics in reading started the movement toward linguistic approaches. The NEA pamphlet that is one of the sources for the comparative chart on p. 77 recognizes linguistic approaches as a major type, and Fries was the person the NEA committee selected to describe this point of view.

Some authorities would liken linguistic approaches to phonic approaches, although a number of linguists who have commented on the topic are opposed to phonics methods just as much as they are opposed to the sight method. If we were to search diligently for an acceptable definition for a linguistic approach, we would probably conclude that *a linguistic approach is one that applies the science of linguistics and the knowledge held by linguistic scholars to the problems of teaching reading.* The difficulty is that even if we could obtain agreement as to a given set of linguistic knowledge, it has been demonstrated that various linguistic scholars would interpret and apply this knowledge to reading in different ways.

According to Chall (1967), although most early published writings in which linguistic science was applied to beginning reading were as critical of phonics approaches as they were of sight-recognition approaches, it appears that linguistics approaches (or those named that) and phonics approaches have grown closer together. She found at least three widely accepted reading series that she thought could have been classified as either phonic or linguistic approaches depending on the interpretation of some minor points.

One of the early linguistics-related theses was that sounding and blending (as recommended by many phonics enthusiasts) should not be taught. Early authorities such as Bloomfield believed that words should be learned as wholes, although he did believe that the "code" (the alphabet) had to be learned very early. He would suggest spelling (not sounding) a word that a child could not learn as a whole. Linguists who comment on beginning reading recommend starting with words that have regular spelling and leaving the irregularities of the English language until later. Most of them also have suggestions as to the use of word families (for example, ran, fan, and man), but the child is to discover for himself the relationship between these words *as whole words,* not to sound them out letter by letter.

Matthes (1972) suggests that the ideas of linguists as related to teaching of beginning reading may be condensed to a few basic statements of recommended procedure.

1. Initiate the formal teaching of reading by teaching children all of the letters of the alphabet by name (not by sound).
2. Start with simple, three-letter words that follow the consonant-vowel-consonant pattern. At the beginning use only words in which each letter represents just one phoneme (phonetic value). Avoid words with silent letters.
3. Use word families, those in which only one letter is changed, such as fan, ran, man.
4. Do *not* teach letter-sound correspondence rules. Allow the children to develop the correct responses as a natural outgrowth of the regularity of the words used.
5. Use words in sentences after they are learned.
6. At all times teach words only as wholes. Spell out the entire word, speak of it as a word, and emphasize the wholeness of words in reading to build recognition that reading is "talk" written down.

Like others who have reviewed reading approaches, Matthes indicates that it is difficult to describe "the" linguistic approach because linguists do not agree on how to teach reading. She thinks that a major advantage to the emphasis or popularization of approaches called linguistic is that teachers have been encouraged to explore the science of linguistics and to place more emphasis on language activities.

In conclusion, there are a number of approaches to reading that are called linguistic and that have been influenced considerably by the ideas of various linguists. The authors of many of these approaches speak as negatively about phonic approaches as they do about sight-recognition approaches, but linguistics and phonics apear to be growing closer together. However, linguistics advocates strongly prefer that children learn words as a whole; in this respect they are somewhat closer to the sight-recognition approach of most basal reader series.

More eclectic authorities in reading are now beginning to say what the reader must have concluded: there are many elements that basal sight-reading approaches, phonics approaches, and linguistics approaches have in common, and these systems, although often featured by publishers as opposing and highly different, could be modified and manipulated sufficiently to fit into the same framework if that framework were sufficiently flexible.

Modified alphabet systems

Modified alphabet systems may also be condered a major approach to teaching reading. Although acceptance and usage of these systems in the United States have not been as extensive as in England, they are important in this text because such methods are used with learning-disabled children. The most popular type of modified alphabet is the expanded alphabet system. The Initial Teaching Alphabet (ita) is the outgrowth of efforts on the part of Sir Isaac Pitman to develop a workable shorthand method for the transcription of the sounds of the English language. The 44-letter phonetic alphabet has many advocates in England including Sir James Pitman (grandson of Sir Isaac Pit-

man) and various individuals associated with the ita Foundation in England and a parallel foundation, the ita Foundation in New York City.

The ita was introduced in the United States when the superintendent of schools of Lompoc Unified School District (California) invited Professor John Downing to discuss the use of the ita in his school district. The ita was introduced in the Lompoc School District in the fall of 1965 and has gained considerable national publicity since that time. The ita is considered by its supporters to be a valuable approach for all children; in more recent years it has received attention in use with learning-disabled children. Although it has not been widely used with the learning disabled, some encouraging results have been reported, such as those summarized by Lane (1974) in a pilot study of 14 sixth-grade children with severe reading disabilities.

Most American educators associate the ita with Downing, who has lectured extensively in the United States. In the NEA pamphlet *Current Approaches to Teaching Reading* (Mackintosh, 1965) Sir James Pitman states, "Since it is a *medium,* not a *method,* ita can be used with any method of reading instruction." From this point of view, ita should not be included in this discussion as a method or approach, but because of its impact and because of the importance it has been accorded by various authors who have reviewed methods of reading, it has been included.

In support of Pitman's statement we should note that several American basal readers have been published in ita, a number of trade book classics have been printed in ita, and some test companies have published standardized reading tests in ita. We must recognize its impact, whether it is a method or a medium, and on the basis of this impact and recognition we will further discuss the what and why of ita.

At its simplest level the ita is nothing more than a phonemically based alphabet in which the inconsistent character-to-symbol relationship of the English language has been largely eliminated. It was, according to its origina-

Fig. 8. The ita alphabet. (Courtesy the Initial Teaching Alphabet Foundation, New York, N.Y.)

tors, designed to facilitate transition to the regular English alphabet *after* reading and language fluency are accomplished (Mackintosh, 1965). The ita alphabet is made up of 24 of the 26 standard, lowercase Roman letters (q and x are omitted) plus 20 new characters (Fig. 8). Its proponents point out that this eliminates many hundreds of confusing irregularities in spelling. Although there are 44 symbols to learn, traditional English has 26 lowercase letters, 26 uppercase letters, and a parallel total of 52 cursive letters. Therefore learning 44 symbols may be more simple than learning 52 or 104, and there are no irregularities to learn. (Note that Aukerman calls this a one-to-one sound-symbol approach.)

The ita symbols are taught as sounds, not as symbol names, an approach more consistent with phonic than with linguistic philosophy. On the other hand, linguists call our attention to the sounds, the phonemic nature of the language—precisely what the ita attempts to do.

The ita has received considerable research attention, but research results are difficult to generalize. We must remember, however, that this difficulty in interpretation of effectiveness of reading methods is characteristic of reading as a whole and of the complexity of the process we call reading. Considerable long-range research was initiated in England in 1960 and was supported by research efforts carried out through the University of London. In 1964 the London research effort was further supported by a Ford Foundation grant at about the same time as the Ford Foundation's Fund for the Advancement of Education announced support for an American ita center at Lehigh University.

Aukerman, in commenting on research findings on the ita experiments in both England the United States, states that "the results so far are impressive, to say the least" (Aukerman, 1971). Spache is more critical of some ita research but concludes that early reading is simplified for some children when a more consistent phonetic alphabet is used. He concludes his discussion of ita by indicating that since the British government has withdrawn its support of the ita experiment and American publishers see no reason to improve ita materials, "apparently we are not going to find the true answers to ita's worth" (Spache, 1972). Let us hope that this is not true, for there is sufficient evidence to indicate that the ita or some system similar to the ita is of value at least to some children.

A number of other less used approaches that may be characterized as modified or simplified alphabet systems could be reviewed, but the intent of most such systems is similar to that of the ita. A somewhat different approach was discussed by Aukerman (1971) in his category of one-to-one sound-symbol approaches. This approach, Words in Color, was included as a recognized approach in the 1965 NEA pamphlet but would not generally be considered a separate teaching system. Words in Color will be further discussed in the last part of this chapter as an approach to consider for use with learning-disabled children.

Language experience approach

The language experience approach is one in which reading is considered only one part of the total communication development spectrum; it is thoroughly integrated with listening, speaking, writing, and spelling. In fact, reading grows out of what the child is thinking and talking about rather than following a set pattern of development designed for all children. Allen was mentioned as the major originator of present-day language experience approaches by all of the sources used as a basis for the chart on p. 77. There appears to be more agreement (in terms of what it is and is not) about this approach than any other major recognized approaches. According to Aukerman (1971), the language experience approach is built on the belief that a child can most effectively learn to read if reading is presented so that the child goes through the following thinking process.

1. What I am thinking, I can talk about.
2. What I talk about, I can write (or someone else can write).

3. What is written, I can read, and so can others.
4. I can read what I have written and what others have written for me to read.

Thus through logical steps the child views reading as just another language activity, an extension of what is thought and what is talked about.

The language experience approach is highly individualized, with each child reading what he wants to talk about or read about. This means that the experiential background of the child is a major determinant of his reading material, and some would note that this may also be a limiting factor.

The role of the teacher is to broaden and enrich the child's experiences so that he will have a broad base from which to think, speak, and read. Organized language experience programs include such daily activities as painting and artwork, the experiencing (by the teacher reading to the class) of children's literature, practice in printing, discussion of interest topics (including those that develop as a part of the evolution of the day), and practice in developing sight vocabulary (a specified common core of words). During the course of the week the activities may include films, planned sensory experiences (tasting, smelling, feeling things, etc.), field trips, and other similar experiences.

In summarizing the results of available research on the effectiveness of the language experience approach as compared to the basal reader approach, Spache (1972) notes that in at least some of the studies the language experience approach was equal or superior to the basal reader approach in general reading performance. Although results were mixed in many areas, quality of writing was definitely superior in children taught by the language experience method. An unexpected result was a definite trend toward better performances in other academic areas by children in the language experience group. All writings about the language experience approach, both by proponents and opponents, agree that it requires a less structured, more individualized classroom atmosphere.

Certain generalizations about the language experience approach may be made.

1. The teacher who feels secure with the planned, sequential activities and detailed instructions of the basal reader may be confused and insecure with the language experience approach.

2. The innovative teacher, one who is personally secure, is certain enough about reading goals to attempt to achieve them through an unstructured vehicle, and believes in the inherent inseparability of the various communication skills, will probably be effective with the language experience approach.

3. Because the language experience approach has the potential to personalize reading for each child, some components of this approach should be considered for inclusion as a part of the primary reading program no matter which basic approach is used.

Individualized reading approach

The individualized reading approach, like the language experience approach, requires a teacher with a comprehensive knowledge of reading goals and objectives who is able to teach without the step-by-step structure of the basal reader or structured phonics program. Most programs that are identified as individualized reading programs are, in fact, a combination of programs; they include some basal readers and some planned phonics instruction. Individualized reading may not be started in some cases until after 6 months or a year of the more traditional basal reading program.

In all cases it requires a large supply of books of varied reading levels with many areas of interest represented at each level of difficulty. The cost of such a collection of books may be a significant inhibiting factor in considering the possible adoption of such a program. The individualized reading approach attempts to provide for a variety of levels and types of readiness, reading ability, and interest. However, rather than eliciting reading material from the children, it provides for such differences through a wide variety of reading material and permits self-selection of reading material. Almost always there are a number of group activities, the teacher is provided with a checklist of skills, and there may be grouping for certain types of planning and interaction.

Spache (1972) notes that a wide variety of programs have been described as individualized reading and that this situation makes it extremely difficult to comment on researched effectiveness. In fact, it is fairly safe to say that although the principles of individualized reading may be stated in such a manner as to find agreement among authorities who support it, actual public school classes that are allegedly individualized reading classes may be highly dissimilar.

It is expected that individualized reading programs will promote wide differences in achievement in children, as will any truly individualized system. Thus our more traditional attitudes toward group achievement goals, standardized testing, and accountability may have to be revised if we use individualized reading.

Individualized reading, like the language experience approach, is not likely to take the nation by storm, but each has significant contributions that may be made as a part of the overall program of teaching reading to girls and boys.

We may conclude this brief overview of major reading approaches by noting that in the 1970's a "pure" approach is used in few school systems. Even if it were, it is almost certain that some teachers in the system would use their own combinations of methods in spite of school district policy. However, most children have been initiated into the mysteries of reading in some manner that is determinable and describable, and this information may be of significant value in planning alternate approaches to remedy or compensate for reading difficulties.

SUGGESTED APPROACHES FOR THE LEARNING DISABLED

As should be apparent from the preceding discussion of reading approaches, there is continuing disagreement as to how to most effectively teach the child who is learning "normally" in accordance with his age, abil-

ity, experiences in life, and all the other factors that we know contribute to reading success. It would be all the more ridiculous to indicate that we know how all learning-disabled children should be taught, even though some reviewers of the learning disabilities literature are critical of the lack of provision of a generally accepted method for children with learning disabilities.

In this section I will suggest a variety of approaches and techniques that have been effective in certain cases. One of the major tasks of the learning disabilities practitioner is to develop a viable way to determine which of these approaches to use with any given child. Guidelines have been presented that should serve to assist in making this determination (pp. 12-18), and additional suggestions will be included with each of the methods or approaches mentioned.

As a long-time educator, I have consistently been critical of educational "gimmicks." I have retained this aversion, and think that gimmicks will not bring about remediation of process disabilities that have their origin in the nervous system, but I have learned that some of the more mildly learning disabled and those who have outgrown their earlier basic process problems may sometimes be *motivated* through approaches that appear questionable to some. This is *not* a plea for acceptance of gimmicks but rather a suggestion that sometimes we may find unusual or unorthodox procedures of value simply because they provide the feel of a new start—the motivation to try just once more.

We must remember that our goal is to provide assistance that will lead to success in the regular class without continued assistance or the continuation of special educational methods or techniques. For many children this will be a matter of a few months of extra help; for others it may take a full year. In a few cases supportive help to the student in the regular class may be required for several years, and for a few a separate special class may be required. These two latter possibilities should be considered exceptions to the general rule.

Thus as we consider alternative methods and strategies in our attempt to educationally "turn on" a particular student, we must keep in mind the fact that he must sooner or later be able to achieve in the regular class without extra help. This should not be the *major* consideration in selecting methods or strategies, but is certainly one important factor to keep in mind. An example of an actual case might help make this principle clear.

Case study

John S. was an 8-year-old with slightly above average mental ability. John had been retained 1 year in the first grade because he could not recognize and remember even one word. After 3 years in school he could recognize 11 words on sight, although three of these he missed occasionally. John could discuss many topics as well as other 8-year-old children and was superior in this ability to many 7-year-olds with whom he was placed in school. He had always been in large classes and had received little special help.

At age 8, John was taken to a clinic in a large city several hundred miles away for an evaluation. The clinic report indicated that John had average mental ability, that his spoken vocabulary was within the normal range for his age, and that his inability to read was due to unusually severe visual perception problems including visual discrimination, visual memory, and others. Certain suggestions as to visual perception training were made, but the report noted that the severity of John's problems required a trained, experienced specialist to give him much of a chance to improve his visual perception in time to avoid more serious emotional problems. It was suggested that John might be able to keep up in content if reading material were taped so that he could listen and learn through his intact auditory abilities while others were reading.

On receiving the report, school officials, who wanted to help but had no specialized personnel in their small rural town, decided that they could do little about the visual perception problems. (The report emphasized the need for a trained, experienced specialist.) They did arrange a way to provide much of the subject matter content through tapes prepared by a group looking for a community service project. Thus John was able to proceed through the next few years with fair success as long as new materials discussed in class were those that he could learn through use of tapes. He slowly fell farther and farther behind others in his grade because it took longer to listen to a taped lesson, and he might therefore still be listening to tapes when others were in the library or doing other reading. This all worked out pretty well in terms of scheduling because he could not have read in the library anyway. School personnel felt satisfied with their provision for this boy with "severe dyslexia." They even made special provisions when giving tests and used a different grading scale when computing his grades.

The future problems that John will certainly experience are obvious, and most educators today would not make any such piecemeal educational adaptations and then feel satisfied with them (or would they?). The efforts of this school system as regards the taped lessons are commendable, but these efforts gave them an excuse for not attending to John's basic need to learn to read. Most of us would not be likely to go to this extreme in providing an alternative educational approach and then ignore our responsibility to assist the student to succeed in the normal way, but what we do may have some similar elements of inadequacy unless we are constantly alert to this possibility. Success in an alternative system or approach is often the best first step, but success in the educational mainstream is the final goal.

How to select a reading approach

The guiding principles for planning and programming for learning-disabled children (Chapter 2) are a major part of the basis for selecting an initial strategy. Also, some procedure for obtaining maximum utilization of assessment data should be followed. The tridimensional model discussed on pp. 40-44 is suggested as one such model, but it is certainly not the only one. In considering reading disabilities we must also keep in mind the basic abilities that are presumed to be intact and normally operational (in the child) for any specific reading approach to be effective. If reading includes accuracy in word recognition, ability to comprehend series of words in sequence, and ability to apply what is read in personal, practical situations, then certain basic abiilties and previous learnings are presumed by most reading approaches.*

Some of these abilities are required to a greater extent by some approaches than others (auditory discrimination is needed for all approaches but is more critical to the more totally phonic systems), and relating the child's apparent abilities and disabilities to the approach or system is absolutely required. An example of the different degrees of previous learning that may be required by various approaches may be illustrated by considering the development of vocabulary with which the child is familiar. A pure language experience reading approach would theoretically be able to take whatever limited language the child had and (if all other abilities and learning factors permitted) build his reading program on present language. A basal reader approach and some phonic approaches might assume too much language ability and thus be ineffective. The list that follows is not presumed to be all-inclusive but it does include most of the basic abilities and learnings (including experiences) that must be considered in planning a reading approach.

1. Gross motor development
2. Gross motor experience (usually consistent with No. 1 but not always)
3. Fine motor development
4. Experience (practice) in using fine motor skills
5. Sensory-motor integration (directionality, laterality, etc.)
6. Visual acuity
7. Auditory acuity
8. Visual perception
   a. Discrimination
   b. Figure-ground perception
   c. Closure
9. Auditory perception
   a. Discrimination
   b. Figure-ground perception
   c. Closure

---

*This definition of reading is greatly oversimplified but will provide a starting point for discussion of abilities that are prerequisites to most reading programs.

10. Visual memory
11. Auditory memory
12. Experience in *using* visual perception skills (Usually this is consistent with developed ability, but if it is not—for example, if a child has much experience but little ability —then knowledge of the amount of experience is essential.)
13. Experience in *using* auditory perception skills
14. Language development
    a. Opportunity to have learned English
    b. Opportunity to have learned another language (where applicable)
    c. Articulation
    d. Spoken vocabulary (both in English and and in any other language)
    e. Words and phrases understood even if if not in spoken vocabulary
15. Motivation to succeed (in this case to read) in school
    a. Parental attitude
    b. Other early environmental data
16. Health and nutritional status (Does condition of health contribute or detract from readiness or motivation to learn?)
17. Attention to task (Several of these factors contribute to attention to task, but it must be considered carefully and in many cases separately from other factors.)

Many of the abilities and factors listed are required to about the same degree in most reading approaches, but some are required to a greater degree by certain approaches. All should be considered when completing individual planning for a child with a reading disability. Any one of these abilities and factors may have an important bearing on where to start, how to proceed, and which methods hold the greatest promise.

Tactile and kinesthetic approaches

Children learn through all of the sensory modalities, but for the majority of students most learning in school is through the visual and auditory learning channels. This has proved to be the most effective general procedure, and usually the questions that relate to sensory modalities in planning the teaching of reading have to do with the balance between the use of auditory and visual channels. Most educators agree that children *must* be able to discriminate between visual symbols (letters) to be able to learn to read. Similarly, the role of adequate auditory abilities in the development of effective language is well known to educators and agreed to be essential to the normal development of reading skills. But the role of tactile, kinesthetic, gustatory, and olfactory modalities are for the most part ignored.

An exception to this may be seen in the education of the blind and visually disabled. For students who cannot see, the sense of touch, the ability to feel shapes, forms, and configurations, provides an effective substitute for sight in developing the ability to read. Certainly braille is different from the letters of the Roman alphabet, but the process is similar except that the incoming signals are through the fingers rather than through the eyes.

This strength of the tactile and kinesthetic learning channels can be utilized to assist some learning-disabled students to learn to read. It may be used in a number of different ways, some of which will be outlined here.

Activities in which the young child learns to differentiate between two similar but different solid objects without looking at them appear to assist in the development of better visual discrimination. This may be accomplished in a variety of ways, many of which are outlined in the wide range of learning activity books presently on the market (see the references and suggested readings). Simple examples include the use of solid objects in a cloth bag and the use of a blindfold so that objects placed in front of the child cannot be seen. Sandpaper letters or geometric configurations provide another variety of this same principle. With 5- and 6-year-olds these activities can be accomplished in a game format.

In each of these examples the major purpose is to provide tactile and/or kinesthetic support for the visual modality, either to assist in developing skills that have been slow in developing or in an attempt to "straighten out" previously scrambled reception and interpretation of visual signals. In some cases it may be well to have children feel a letter or word while also looking at it, thus providing simultaneous signal reception through the visual and tactile senses. In other cases it may prove to be more effective to cut off the visual signal and to be certain that the student is 100% accurate in tactile sensing alone before adding the visual. In all of these *the important thing to understand is the principle of utilizing additional sensory modalities to assist in the development of other modalities.* The most common use of this principle is in the use of the tactile to support or assist the visual.

A somewhat different application of this same principle involves the teacher or a helping student tracing out letters, or sometimes words, on the arm or back of the student who needs help. This is significantly different in that the student receives no kinesthetic input, only the tactile. He may be looking at letter cards on his desk, attempting to find one that matches the letter he feels traced out on his back, or he may have his eyes closed, concentrating on feeling the letter or word accurately. In any event, a whole variety of games or activities may be developed with this type of assistance when the evidence indicates that this is in fact a need of the child. This type of activity can be misused or overdone if not carefully monitored.

These activities and approaches are most appropriate with primary-age children who give evidence of developmental or remedial needs in the visual perception abilities required for reading.

Simultaneous visual-auditory-kinesthetic-tactile approach (Fernald)

During the early 1920's Grace Fernald began the development of a simultaneous visual-auditory-kinesthetic-tactile (VAKT) approach designed to assist children with severe reading disabilities. The account of her methodology (1943) is detailed in a full-length text that has been used with various adaptations to this day. Reports of her work indicate a high degree of effectiveness, particularly with children of normal or above-normal mental ability who have been in school at least 2 or 3 years.

Her approach has variously been called multisensory, a tracing approach, and a kinesthetic method. The terms "tracing" and "kinesthetic" have been applied because those are unique features of the approach, but the most accurately descriptive title is simultaneous VAKT, which indicates the manner in which her methods are different from most others that have been called multisensory or VAKT. Much of the description that follows is taken from *Learning Disabilities: Educational Strategies* (Gearheart, 1973).

In 1921 the University of California at Los Angeles officially established a clinic school to replace an individual case study–oriented clinic in which children with a wide variety of learning problems had been served. The clinic school started with a similar wide variety of students but gradually evolved into a school for children of normal or above-normal intelligence with specific, severe educational problems—usually those closely allied to reading and/or spelling disabilities.

Although Fernald worked with the local public schools and with other universities, the UCLA Clinic School was the site of her major efforts, and the following account will relate mainly to her work there. At the time Fernald published the account of her methodology (1943), the clinic school was a full-day, 8-month school in which all subjects were taught to approximately 20 students (at any one time) in small groups. A summer program attended by 60 to 80 students was also a part of the clinic school operation, but this required a modified program. University personnel and graduate students under Fernald's supervision staffed the program.

Prior to actually starting a remedial program, the Fernald procedure requires "positive reconditioning." This is based on the assumption that almost all children who have experienced school failure have developed a poor self-concept, particularly in relation to anything connected with school or formal education. Four conditions are viewed as ones to be carefully avoided in initiating and carrying through the remedial program.

1. *Avoid calling attention to emotionally loaded situations.* Attempts by teachers or parents to urge the child to do better generally have negative effects. Reminding the child of the future importance of academic success or telling him how important it is to his family should be avoided. If the child is already a failure and knows it, these admonitions or urgings are at best useless and sometimes result in a nearly complete emotional block.

2. *Avoid using methods that previous experience suggests are likely to be ineffective.* This is important both during remediation and during the time of reentry to the regular class. If the child is experiencing success in a temporary, out-of-class remedial setting (after school or for a set time period each day) and then must return to class and to methods by which he was earlier unable to learn, the remedial program may be negated. Or, if after a period in which he has been out of class on a full-day basis and has found success in a new method, he must make an immediate return to the former methods with no planned transition, he may return to his old inability to learn.

3. *Avoid conditions that may cause embarrassment.* Sometimes a new method used in the new setting is effective and satisfactory, whereas in the old setting it may seem childish or silly unless some special provisions are made. For example, the tracing involved in the Fernald approach may seem so unusual as to be absurd back in the regular classroom. The reward, that is, the learning, may not be worth the feelings of conspicuousness and embarrassment.

4. *Avoid directing attention to what the child cannot do.* This is just a special kind of problem that might be included as a part of condition 1.

Regardless of what is required, attempting to bring about positive reconditioning and avoiding emotional reversal after the reconditioning has taken place are of prime importance.

Procedure. The first step in each remedial

case in the actual classroom or clinic procedure with the child is to explain that there is a new way of learning words that really works. The child is told that others have had the same problem he is having and have learned easily through this new method.

The second step is to ask the child to select any word he wants to learn, regardless of length, and then to teach him to write and recognize (read) it, using the method that will now be explained in some detail.

1. The word chosen by the child is written for him, usually with a crayon in plain, blackboard-size cursive writing. In most cases, regardless of age, cursive writing is used rather than manuscript. This is because the child will then tend to see and "feel" the word as a single entity rather than a group of separate letters.

2. The child traces the word with his fingers in contact with the paper, saying the word as he traces it. This is repeated as many times as necessary until he can write the word without looking at the copy.

3. He writes the word on scrap paper, demonstrating to himself that it is now "his" word. Several words are taught in this manner, and as much time as necessary is taken to completely master them.

4. When the child has internalized the fact that he can write and recognize words, he is encouraged to start writing stories. His stories are whatever he wishes them to be at first, and the instructor gives him any words (in addition to those he has mastered) he needs to complete the story.

5. After the story is written, it is typed and the child reads it in typed form while it is still fresh in his mind. It is important that this be done immediately.

6. After the story is completed and the new word has been used in a meaningful way, the new word is written by the child on a card that he files alphabetically in his own individual word file. This word file is used as a meaningful way to teach the alphabet without undue emphasis on rote memory.

This procedure is often called the Fernald tracing method because the tracing is an added feature in contrast to the usual methods of teaching reading or word recognition. However, it should be noted that the child is simultaneously *feeling, seeing, saying,* and *hearing* the word. Thus it is truly a multi-sensory approach.

There are several points to be carefully observed and followed for maximum success.

1. *The word should be selected by the student.* If it is, motivation is maximized, and the likelihood of interest in using the word in a story is greater than with a teacher-selected word. In Fernald's case studies and in cases that I have known personally, children are able to master long, complicated words and in fact may be able to do so more easily than they may learn short words in some instances.

2. *Finger contact is essential,* using either one or two fingers.

3. *The child should write the word, after tracing it several times, without looking at the copy.* Looking back and forth tends to break the word into small and sometimes meaningless units. He must learn to see, think, and feel the word as a total unit.

4. Because the word must be seen as a unit, *in case of error or interruption in writing, the word should be crossed out and a new start made.* If necessary, the child should go back to the tracing stage, but correcting the word through erasures is not permitted.

5. *Words should be used in context.* If the word the child wants to use is unfamiliar, a different one should be encouraged, or at least he should learn the meaning of the word before going through this procedure. He must learn that the group of alphabetic symbols called a word really means something.

6. *The child must always say the word aloud or to himself as he traces it and as he writes it.*

Although many additional details could be given, this is the essence of the Fernald approach. Addition of the tactile and kinesthetic avenues, or channels, to the visual and auditory ones deserves the major credit for any success this method has over more traditional approaches. After a period of tracing, stage 1, which may vary in time from a few weeks to a few months, the child will be able to enter what Fernald calls stage 2. In stage 2, tracing is no longer required. The child simply looks at the new word in cursive writing, says it to himself as he looks at it, and then writes it without looking at the copy. He proceeds in the same manner as in stage 1 except that he does not trace. In theory the child is now "tracing" the word mentally.

If the child encounters difficulty with any particular word during stage 2, he should go back to actual tracing until he masters that word. As soon as tracing is no longer necessary (except rarely), the large box used as a word file for the large, cursive words is exchanged for a smaller one for typed words.

In stage 3 the child is able to study new words directly from a book or other printed copy. He should now be able to pronounce words to himself and write them from memory. Books are provided that are consistent with his developing ability and interests. He is told words that he cannot decode by himself, and they are recorded, reviewed, and written from memory after he finishes each section of the book. He no longer keeps a file on each new word.

Stage 4 involves decoding new words from their resemblance to words previously learned. He is not "told" words but is helped to learn to figure them out through a sequence of structural analysis skills. As he is about to read difficult material, particularly any that includes technical terms (such as in science), he is encouraged to look over each paragraph in advance to find new words. These are mastered ahead of time to permit reading with comprehension.

This approach has been used with children with a variety of problems, including problems in the auditory channel. However, it is probably most beneficial for children with visual channel problems, particularly visual sequential memory and visual imagery.

There are a number of methods and materials on the commerical market that are advertised as multisensory. Technically speaking, they may be multisensory, but few are of the total, balanced, simultaneously multisensory nature of the Fernald approach. Some approaches are initially visual and then become multisensory. Others are initially phonetic, evolving into multisensory. These may be more or less effective than the Fernald approach, but the alert practitioner will do well to look carefully into what takes place in a given method and the order in which it takes place when analyzing it for possible use.

The simultaneous VAKT approach is likely to be most effective with children who have spent at least 2 years in school and thus have been rather thoroughly exposed to reading. It is one of a few approaches that my experience has indicated to be effective with secondary school students. Because much of its effectiveness depends on the ability to receive kinesthetic and tactile signals accurately, it will obviously have greatly reduced effectiveness with students in whom these channels are poorly developed. One other caution: it is believed by some that certain types of neurological dysfunction may lead to a tendency for the receptive mechanisms of the brain to "short-circuit" if there are too many signals arriving simultaneously. This is not an established fact, but the possibility of this type of reaction to multiple stimuli should be kept in mind, particularly when dealing with hyperactive children.

Phonic-visual-auditory-kinesthetic system (Gillingham and Stillman)

Gillingham and Stillman (1946) developed a highly structured, phonetically oriented, visual-auditory-kinesthetic system that has been in popular usage in various parts of the United States since the 1940's. It is highly structured, has a heavy phonetic emphasis, and has some of the elements of the Fernald approach. The major target population for the Gillingham-Stillman efforts has been children in the third through sixth grades, but the approach can be adapted for older students.

The theoretical thrust of this system is to associate visual, auditory, and kinesthetic input to learn new words. Gillingham and

Stillman stress that no spelling or reading should be done except with the remedial teacher since rigid adherence to the program sequence is necessary.

The system is for students who cannot learn by the sight-word approach and may not be the most beneficial technique to use with children who have difficulty in auditory learning. Two possible weaknesses are that comprehension is not emphasized in the early stages of remediation and that the method is very time-consuming. In fact, students commonly require a minimum of 2 years of training.

The Gillingham-Stillman method begins with the introduction of a few short vowels and consonants having only one sound. Vowels are printed on salmon-colored cards; consonants are on white cards. Letters are introduced with key words such as "apple" for "a" and "hat" for "h." Two elements of the reading program, reading and spelling with phonetic words and words that are phonetic for reading but not for spelling, will be reviewed briefly to demonstrate this approach.

The procedure for reading and spelling with phonetic words consists of the following steps.

1. The name and sound of the letter are associated with the printed symbol. The teacher shows the child a printed letter and says the name of the letter, and the child repeats it. Then the sound of the letter is made by the teacher and repeated by the student. At this stage the child is made aware of how his speech organs feel as he says the sound. When a card is exposed and the pupil is asked, "What sound does this letter say?" he gives the sound of the letter.

2. The sound of the letter is associated with the name of the letter. Without exposing the card, the teacher makes the sound and the child says the name of the letter having that sound. This is the beginning of oral spelling.

3. The letter is written by the teacher (usually in cursive writing), and its form is explained to the student. Next the pupil traces the letter, copies it, and writes it from

memory. Finally he must write the letter with eyes averted. Then the teacher says a sound and asks the student to write the letter having that sound. The child's hand may be moved to form the letter if necessary. The student says the letter's name as he writes it. This is called simultaneous oral spelling, or SOS.

4. After 10 letters are learned and their associations are known, the pupil is taught to blend sounds into two- or three-letter phonetic words. These words are written on yellow cards and placed in the child's phonetic word box.

5. Next the child is taught to read words. Cards with individual letters are laid out to form a word, and the student says the sounds as rapidly as possible to aid in recognition. Then the teacher exposes the yellow cards one by one and the child is asked to read them as rapidly as possible.

6. Spelling is introduced a few days after blending is begun. The procedure followed is called the four-point program. In this program the teacher says a word, then says it again very slowly, sound by sound. As the student recognizes each sound, its corresponding letter is placed on the table until the word is complete. The teacher pronounces the word again, and the child repeats it, names the letters, writes the word naming each letter as it is formed, and finally reads the word he has written. Simultaneous oral spelling is used as a link between sound and letter form.

7. After the student has learned to read and write the phonetic words, sentence and story writing are introduced. The stories are not for entertainment or content but are steps in the development of reading skill. The same stories are used for oral dictation exercises.

After the preceding steps for teaching words that are purely phonetic (each phonogram has only one sound and each sound is represented by only one symbol), a different procedure is used for the ambiguities of the English language. Spelling words that contain phonograms for which there is more than one possible sound are presented along with certain "rules" and "generalizations," and a brief history of the development of language (which helps explain the ambiguities) is given.

The four-point program is continued for words that are phonetic for spelling, and a reading book is chosen by the teacher to use in conjunction with the child's expanding skill in word recognition. Drill on sight words is begun, but no guessing of a word from sentence context is permitted. Finally the student is encouraged to read other books in the classroom and is allowed to take books home to read.

The Gillingham-Stillman approach is an example of one that is highly organized and structured. It was developed and became accepted at a time in the history of reading programs when whole-word, sight-recognition systems were used in most of the nation, and the teachers were admonished to never use phonics in beginning reading. As more and more phonetic teaching elements are added to basal programs, there may be less need for approaches that were brought into existence mainly because of the absence of such elements. *To benefit from this approach, a child should have or must develop a normal range of auditory discrimination.*

Language development approach (Johnson and Myklebust)

A number of different approaches might be called language development approaches because they take the factor of language development into consideration in some manner. However, those that have popularly been called language development approaches have for the most part been those that have developed out of approaches designed to teach reading to the hard of hearing or aphasic. Myklebust is one authority who moved into learning disabilities through this route, and the basic learning theory on which his work is based has already been discussed on pp. 25-29. The comments that follow are intended to provide an expanded view of Johnson and Myklebust's approach to teaching the learning disabled. Part of the description that follows is from Gearheart (1973).

Johnson and Myklebust are definite in their approach to educational planning and believe that the most important single factor is the completion of an intensive diagnostic study. This diagnosis should lead to an evaluation of the disability with five multidimensional considerations.

1. Is the disability within a single modality, does it extend to more than one modality, and does it include intersensory functions? This assists both in planning remedial processes (for the defective functions) and in planning which sensory channels to use to provide content input (the intact modalities).

2. What is the level of the involvement within the hierarchy of experience? Is it experienced first at the perceptual, imagery, symbolic, or conceptual level?

3. Is the deficiency one in which the sensations reaching the brain are meaningful or nonmeaningful? Is the problem basically verbal or nonverbal? For example, is the basic problem in auditory reception or visual imagery? Is it one of abstracting and conceptualizing, that is, of gaining meaning?

4. Which of the subject matter areas does this disability affect most? Is it primarily a reading or an arithmetic problem, or does it also show up in art and physical education? This is important both in remediation planning and in guidance regarding course work, life planning, etc.

5. What are the effects, both present and potential, of the disability on the development of social maturity? If the goal of education includes development of independent, responsible, self-supporting citizens, this dimension is of prime importance.

An educational or remedial plan that does not take all the foregoing considerations into account and does not coordinate the efforts of all who deal with the child cannot be maximally effective.

A second important part of the educational plan is a determination of the child's state of readiness, in terms of various subaspects of total readiness. For example, a child might be ready in terms of auditory, visual, and integrative functions but unable or unready to learn in the normal class setting due to social unreadiness and/or hyperactivity problems. He may be ready and able to function in class discussions at his chronological age level but be 3 years retarded in readiness for reading. The child must be approached and taught not at his *level* of readiness, but at his *levels* of readiness. Teaching that follows and takes into consideration obtaining complete knowledge of the child—information regarding his various levels of functioning and understanding of the material to be taught—is what they call *clinical teaching.* This, they believe, is the only acceptable procedure with the learning-disabled child.

In addition to the five multidimensional considerations for teaching the learning-disabled child, 13 principles for remediation are provided (Johnson and Myklebust, 1967). These principles are derived from the five multidimensional considerations, plus long experience with deaf and aphasic children. Although developed for a language approach system and more auditorily than visually oriented, these principles are applicable to the methodology of many of the other systems.

Major principles for remediation

1. *Individualize the problem.* The teacher must formulate an educational plan for *each specific child* and should be aware of his deficits, his integrities, and his levels of language function, including reading, spoken, and written language. The teacher should know the child—his intelligence, his emotional status, and his educational history. The program must be *his* program, not *a* program.

2. *Teach to the level of involvement.* Teaching must be aimed at the lowest level of involvement—perception, imagery, symbolization, or conceptualization.

3. *Teach to the type of involvement.* Does the disability involve intrasensory or intersensory learning? Does it involve verbal or nonverbal factors? Does it primarily relate to integrative functions? Whatever the case, teach appropriately for that type of involvement.

4. *Teach according to readiness.* Follow the principle of multiple readiness levels as presented in the preceding section.

5. *Remember that input precedes output.* Consider the fact that either, or both, input and output disabilities could be involved in the problem. Remember that output difficulties may actually reflect input problems.

6. *Consider tolerance levels.* Overloading is always a possibility. Certain types of stimulation may be distracting, either by themselves or by interfering with other modalities. The possibility that both psychological and neurological tolerance levels may be grossly abnormal in a learning disabled child must be carefully considered.

7. *Consider the multisensory approach.* The multisensory approach—teaching through several or perhaps all sensory channels—is always a possible alternative but must be approached with tolerance level and overloading potential in mind.

8. *Teaching to deficits alone is limited.* Teaching only to and through the deficient areas is restricted, unitary approach and is unacceptable in the light of available evidence.

9. *Teaching only to and through integrities is limited.* This approach is insufficient when used alone. It presumes interneurosensory learning, which is not an acceptable assumption in many instances.

10. *Do not assume the need for perceptual training.* Perceptual training alone may be most inadequate. To stress perceptual training, except as diagnostic information so dictates, can be a waste of time or in some cases detrimental.

11. *Control important variables.* This principle calls for teacher control of variables such as attention (control elements that lead to distractions), proximity (to the teacher or to other children), rate (as in rate of presentation of materials), and size (of writing, objects, etc.).

12. *Emphasize both verbal and nonverbal learning.* Deliberately attend to both the verbal and nonverbal components of the learning problem with planned efforts to interrelate the two. Johnson and Myklebust recommend interweaving verbal and nonverbal components.

13. *Keep psychoneurological considerations in mind.* The educator must attend to remedial needs in view of the behavioral components of the problem but should also consider the physical findings that indicate the status of the neurological system. The two must be incorporated into a single plan of educational remediation.

Specific application in reading. Johnson and Myklebust believe that remediation of learning disabilities should circumvent the major deficit but must include simultaneous work on areas of weakness. For example, children with a visual deficit usually have difficulty in learning to read through a sight-word approach since they cannot hold a sequence of letters in mind. However, many of these children can learn sounds and sound blending. In contrast, youngsters with auditory deficits may have difficulty in learning to read through phonics but may be able to learn by the sight-word approach.

Johnson and Myklebust believe that both auditory and visual learners can acquire a sight vocabulary and phonetic skills through training. Consequently the focus of initial training is on the acquisition of a systematic approach for decoding words.

Auditory learners. The remedial procedure used with auditory learners is somewhat similar to that of Gillingham and Stillman. It involves teaching isolated sounds and then blending them into meaningful words. Before initiating this approach, the teacher must evaluate the student's ability to blend sounds. If the child cannot blend sounds, the sight-word method should be used with emphasis on touch and kinesthesis. Briefly, the following guidelines are used.

1. Teaching of letter sounds begins with consonants that are different in appearance as well as sound.

2. The child is asked to think of words beginning with each sound.

3. The child is taught to associate the sound with the letter having that sound. At first the youngster should be taught only one sound with each letter or letter combination.

4. One or two vowel sounds are presented after three or four consonants have been learned.

5. The child is taught to blend sounds into meaningful words. He then must tell what each word means and use it in a sentence.

6. Word families are taught (such as it, hit, sit, mit). The pupil learns how to change the initial and final consonants to form new words.

7. Two-letter consonant blends are introduced.

8. Long vowel combinations and consonant groupings representing a single sound are taught.

9. The teacher writes simple sentences, paragraphs, and stories using the child's reading vocabulary. Sentence structure should be similar to the pupil's spoken vocabulary.

Visual learners. Visual learners are taught to read by the sight-work approach since they generally have difficulty learning by phonetic methods. Therefore a student is taught to make a direct association between the printed symbol and experience, or each new word is said for him. The auditory learner is taught from the part to the whole, whereas the visual learner works from the whole to the part. The procedures for visual learners follow.

1. The auditory-visual correspondence is taught by demonstrating to the student that words we say also can be written.

2. Nouns are selected that are in the child's spoken vocabulary and that are different in both auditory and visual configuration. The pupil matches the printed word with the corresponding object.

3. The printed word is matched with experience through labeling objects in the room such as flag, chalk, and pencil. Action verbs also are associated with experience. First the child is asked to hop, walk, or run and then he is shown the printed symbol representing each action verb.

4. The child is introduced to simple phrases and sentences within his reading vocabulary. Prepositions and adjec-

tives are presented at the same time. Pictures are used to illustrate the reading material.

5. As the child progresses, experience stories are integrated into the reading activities. Frequently a picture representing a new word is drawn below that word to aid the reading process.

Children with deficits in both auditory and visual modalities. Johnson and Myklebust recommend a version of the Fernald approach for use with children having both deficits. Modifications should be made according to the child's pattern of strengths and weaknesses. Modifications include the following.

1. Selection of a controlled vocabulary, emphasizing meaningful nouns and verbs that are relatively phonetic

2. Maintenance of a balance of sensory stimulation, depending on the child's needs (For instance, some children profit from looking, saying, and tracing; others learn better by only looking and tracing.)

A major strength of the Johnson and Myklebust approach is that there are provisions for different types of learning disabilities. These provisions take into account the strong and weak modalities, building on one and attempting to strengthen the other. The Johnson and Myklebust text and the methods advocated provide a meaningful source of suggestions for learning disabilities teachers.

Color-coded phonetic approaches

A number of reading methods use color cues to asist the reader in identifying phonetic elements in words. Two such methods will be discussed here; one, Words in Color, has received considerable international attention due in part to the early claims and unusual promotional ability of its author, Caleb Gattegno (1962). The second, the Psycholinguistic Color System, was developed by Dr. Alex Bannatyne (1971), known for his work in learning disabilities and for the Bannatyne Children's Learning Center in Miami.

Words in Color. Words in Color received

almost instant recognition following unusual success reported in connection with a UNESCO project in Ethiopa. In this project it was reported that adult pupils were taught to read Amharic (the official language of Ethiopia) in 10 hours of instruction, whereas it ordinarily required up to 18 months (Aukerman, 1971). Much of the research has been questioned, but individual reports of unusual success in the hands of highly qualified teachers hint that this may be a most valuable tool in special cases such as might be found in learning disabilities programs.

An advantage of Words in Color as compared to systems such as the ita is that it retains English spelling patterns, therefore requiring no transfer from one system to another. In this program the 47 sounds of the English language (as identified by Gattegno) are represented by 47 different colors or shades of color. Each *sound* is represented by the same color, regardless of its spelling.

In this system children learn the short vowel sounds and are then introduced to consonants. Letter names are not taught but are designated by color. Students are acquainted with spelling and writing through copying words in black and white from the chalkboard or through visual dictation in which the teacher and children point out successions of sounds from written sequences. In this manner pupils learn to associate the spatial sequence of letters with their temporal sounds.

Other features of the program include practice in enunciating the separate sounds in each word, learning to write all vowels by varying the shape of "a," and the teaching of cursive writing only. As children learn to use words in black and white, color is discontinued.

Included in the series are three introductory books, a book of stories, worksheets, word cards, and eight charts composed of the systematic order of spellings occurring in English. These materials are accompanied by 21 colored charts presenting the 20 vowel sounds and 27 consonant sounds.

This approach has been questioned because of the necessity to make a transition from color to black and white because the system does not supply a sizable amount of reading material using colored letters. Some authorities believe that the system may promote word calling without comprehension.

Since Words in Color is a phonics system, a child who has difficulty with auditory learning may encounter problems with this approach. In addition, color discrimination may be troublesome for some youngsters.

The system should be considered primarily for use at beginning reading levels; however, it has been used with illiterate or near-illiterate adults as well as children.

Psycholinguistic Color System. A second structured color system, also a phonic color-coding approach, is called the Psycholinguistic Color System. This system is called psycholinguistic because it involves planned sensory input and motor output, sequencing of phonemes and graphemes, and the use of words sequenced in meaningful context.

The Psycholinguistic Color System is a phonetic system in which the child learns the shape of each individual letter as a phoneme, with the color names serving as cues to the sounds that the colors represent. The core of the color-coding aspect is the use of the 17 vowel phonemes that are color coded. The set of materials includes 24 wall charts in color, flash cards, workbooks, and colored pencils. Bannatyne believes that traditional orthography must be used. Thus all symbols are the traditional letters; only the color coding is different from what the child may see in any usual reading material.

The whole program includes four major stages that are to take the student from the introduction to color-coded letters to reading and writing in black and white. The steps or stages are as follows:

Stage 1: The student must learn the shapes of the letters of the alphabet *as phonemes.*

Stage 2: The student must learn the sounds of both consonants and vowels. (Bannatyne believes in "overlearning" the color coding. This is emphasized in this stage.) Cursive writing is started during stage 2.

Stage 3: The program is extended to phonetically irregular words, and the child builds his own stories. Blending and syllabication are begun at this stage. Rhyming plays an important role at this level.

Stage 4: The student starts (or restarts) the use of vowels in black and white. A set of rules to assist in spelling is taught at this stage. Entrance to this stage is based on the assumption that the child has learned the various vowel sounds represented by the color coding and therefore no longer needs color.

The Bannatyne system was developed for dyslexic children and thus is undoubtedly most applicable where considerable visual perception problems exist. For such children or for those who have adequate visual perception abilities but are having significant problems in sorting out the various phonetic possibilities of the vowels, this would be a system to consider.

Informal color-coding system. A third possibility that deserves mention is the use of an informal color-coding system. Master teachers have used color coding to varying degrees for years, and Frostig indicates that although a number of specific color-coding systems are advocated, her experience at the Frostig Center has shown that "a relatively informal, flexible system is often best for teacher and child" (Frostig, 1973). Frostig suggests, for example, that short vowels might be colored red (for *stop* short) and long vowels colored green (for *go* long). She notes that this color coding directs the child's attention to sound–graphic symbol relationships and may assist in recognition and learning of phonetic rules. She points out that this type of word analysis should always be followed by word synthesis (the child should see the word that was written in color also written in black and white).

A suggestion for use of color coding with more advanced readers is the use of different colors for prefixes, root words, and suffixes. Another idea is writing syllables in different colors.

Programmed and instructional management systems

Programmed and instructional management systems have been used to varying degrees since the middle 1960's, but added interest has been stimulated by recent attention to behavioral objectives and the concept of accountability. A number of programs can be included under this general title.

Programmed Reading approach. Programmed Reading, the outgrowth of efforts of Cynthia Buchanan and M. W. Sullivan, is a sequenced linguistic-phonics approach in which students experience a sequence of learnings in which they must write their responses; this allegedly reinforces what is learned. In this particular series, as in most programmed reading approaches, certain prerequisite learning must take place so that each child in the class is at a given starting point. For these materials children must know and recognize the alphabet and be able to print both lower- and uppercase letters.

In the first books of the first series the child must read simple sentences and respond with a "yes" or "no." The teacher works through this procedure, instructing the children in the manner in which they are to read, enter their responses, and slide the "slider" into position so that they may see the correct answer. This positive reinforcement of correct answers and immediate knowledge of wrong answers is a major feature of programmed material.

Regular testing is provided to correct or compensate for the possibility (or likelihood) that some children may determine the correct answer *before* they record their choice of answers and to make certain learning is taking place.* This type of material is supposed to be self-pacing, which means (at least theoretically) that 30 different children in a given class can proceed at 30 different speeds according to their own readiness, ability, and motivation. Programmed Reading and other similar programmed materials have been used with entire classes, with subgroups within classes, or with just one or two children with whom the teacher cannot effectively work

in existing class reading groups. The immediate feedback system, the small, planned sequential steps, and the fact that this system frees the teacher from most "paper correcting" are featured advantages of this and other programmed systems.

Disadvantages include the fact that this type of programming assumes that required content and skills can be learned effectively by being broken down into small segments. There is also a question as to how well this system provides for higher level integrative and conceptual skills. Still another problem is the reduction and sometimes near elimination of class interaction when skills or topics are learned in this manner.

This type of programming lends itself to use of various types of educational hardware, the so-called teaching machines. These too are organized to provide immediate feedback and to permit the student to proceed at his own pace.

The major value of this type of reading system for children with learning problems may be in the newness of the approach. It is necessary before attempting to place a child in such a program to make certain he has the necessary process abilities to utilize the system and that there is sufficient motivation to keep him going once he starts. Proceeding through such a program may be valuable to the teacher in determining the areas in which learning, in effect, breaks down. This will require close observing and monitoring of the child and his performance with the materials.

Individually Prescribed Instruction. A second system that may be considered in this section is Individually Prescribed Instruction (IPI). IPI, introduced in the early 1960's at the Oak Leaf School in Pittsburgh by Glaser and Bolvin (Dallmann et al., 1974), is a highly individualized program. From the outset emphasis is placed on the use of comprehensive diagnostic tests to assess the learning abilities of each child at each instructional level. As soon as the student demonstrates a satisfactory degree of competency in a particular skill, he progresses to a more difficult instructional level. Master files composed of

---

*A potential problem with any programmed reading approach, particulary for use with a learning-disabled child who is likely to be anxious and eager to have the "right answer," is the difficulty in controlling the child's "peeking" at answers to be right. This must be carefully monitored.

materials collected from commercial sources, teacher's files, and newly constructed materials are set up for the entire program. These files are used to write reading prescriptions for each child based on diagnostic test results and daily progress.

This system is similar to Programmed Reading in providing for self-pacing and individual modes of problem solving. At least part of the program has the immediate feedback provision of programmed material. In addition, there is provision for supplementary materials, experiences, and learnings as indicated by the teacher's assessment of work completed. This is in contrast with some other programmed materials in which each child goes through the same steps as every other child. This system has about the same advantages and disadvantages as other programmed materials except as specifically noted.

Computer-assisted instruction. Computer-assisted instruction is a computerized version of programmed instruction in which the computer is programmed to respond to the learner, providing correction, corrective exercises, and records of progress. These systems are often advertised for use with minimal teacher participation, but most experience with such schemes indicates that the teacher remains a critical factor in the teaching-learning process. The novelty of some of the so-called teaching machines may be the most important single factor in their effectiveness.

Rebus approaches

A rebus is a picture that stands for a word. Rebus reading approaches are picture-word systems in which pictures are substituted for the traditional orthography. To the extent that a picture has only one obvious meaning, reading is quite easy; the child does not have to learn to interpret symbols that are at the start quite abstract and meaningless but rather can "read" a much nearer representation of the real thing. For example, "horse" is simply a picture of a horse.

Some type of picture-word stories have been around since cavemen used this method to record events of their day. There has been some limited use of pictures to substitute for letters in the kind of storybooks designed for parents to read to children (and for them to "read" at ages 2 and 3 years) for many years. But the first systematic application of this principle that led to commercial publication and wide use was that made by Woodcock in 1967, an effort that produced the *Peabody Rebus Reading Program*. This program, in addition to its carefully planned use of rebuses, includes the advantages of a programmed text format.

The Peabody Rebus Program includes three programmed workbooks and two readers. The content and emphasis of these five books are as follows:

Introducing Reading: Book One includes a rebus vocabulary of 35 words and introduces the child to the basic skills required in the reading process. There is an emphasis on the use of context clues in identifying new words.

Introducing Reading: Book Two extends the rebus vocabulary to 68 words. Structural analysis skills are introduced, and experience and practice with use of context clues and general skills of the reading process are continued. (See Fig. 9 for a sample of vocabulary and sentences.)

Introducing Reading: Book Three is correlated with the two rebus readers. There is further extension of comprehension skills and introduction of phonic skills for six consonants and for 10 vowel-consonant combinations.

Red and Blue Are On Me: Rebus Reader One and *Can You See A Little Flea: Rebus Reader Two* are used with *Introducing Reading: Book Three*. The reading vocabulary is extended to 172 words; 122 of these are known as spelled words. Twenty-nine of these words are taught through phonic approaches presented in *Introducing Reading: Book Three*.

Without going into detail as to the specific procedure used in the Peabody Rebus Reading Program, it may be noted that such basic reading skills as left-to-right, down-the-page, and page-to-page progression as well as use of pictorial and textual context clues are taught effectively by rebus reading. Children develop an understanding of

Fig. 9. A, Sample of vocabulary and, **B,** sample sentences from *Introducing Reading: Book Two* of the Peabody Rebus Program. (From American Guidance Service, Inc., Circle Pines, Minn.)

the facts that written language is made up of words combined to make sentences and that there is variety in sentence structure.

The Peabody Rebus Program may be used as a complete program of beginning reading; children may be started at any level (consistent with individual needs), and the program may be terminated at any level. The teacher's guide is well done, and the program has been used enough to demonstrate its usefulness for a variety of purposes.

For beginning readers who have not been successful in the more traditional approaches, the rebus approach may bring success and motivation to learn to read. With the exception of mentally retarded or bilingual children who have never read in any language, the rebus system is primarily for younger children. Certain older learning-disabled children who need immediate success to provide a stepping-stone to other methods may also benefit.

Open Court Correlated Language Arts Program

The Open Court basic readers provide an alternative to other basal reader programs and, in fact, are considerably different from many of the other basal reader series. This approach might have been listed later in this chapter under the general heading of eclectic approaches, but it is perhaps better considered as a separate program. The Open Court program has a strong phonic element and has more kinesthetic-tactile emphasis than any other of the major basal reader series. It provides one viable alternative for teachers who feel the need for this kinesthetic-tactile input but find the Fernald approach too unstructured.

The Open Court Correlated Language Arts Program has three main components or program goals. The first is to teach children to read and write independently by the end of the first grade. The second is to provide reading selections of "literary quality and rewarding content." The third is to provide a total, correlated language arts program for use through the sixth grade. Our focus here will be on the first two components.

Much of the first half of the first-grade program is multisensory, with more kinesthetic-tactile emphasis than many programs that are advertised as multisensory. The entry to this multisensory emphasis is through sounds, and in learning the sound the child hears, says, sees, and writes the letters being learned. Much of this can be accomplished in large groups, an advantage over Fernald-related approaches, which require a one-to-one setting. The intent of the program is for the child to discover inductively the basic relationships of the English language. Writing at the board, proofreading, and listening activities are all used from the start. Anagram cards and games, poems, and songs are a part of this comprehensive program.

The teacher's guide to the foundation program is very detailed and comprehensive and provides suggestions for children who are moving more slowly than the rest of the group. Aukerman (1971) suggests that the teacher's guide provided with this program is "probably the most complete teacher's guide available for any system outside of the traditional basal reader series."

The Open Court program features a "workshop" concept that is unique among the various approaches. Workshop is the term for all activities in the Open Court program in which children participate independently. The teacher guides these activities discreetly and indirectly, provides instructions, and establishes limits. Although no set time is regularly allotted for workshop, the teacher is admonished to see that time is available in

which the children are to pursue independent reading activities. In some respects this aspect of the Open Court program is an individualized reading program. A separate guide for *Reading Activities in Workshop* is provided, complete with many illustrations, materials lists, general suggestions, and detailed instructions.

Significant parts of the Open Court series were initially supported in part by the Hegeler Foundation, and research reports relating to this support sound favorable, but reports provided for public consumption do not provide sufficient data to permit careful evaluation. The literature provided with this series includes stories such as "The Little Red Hen" and others in which perseverance, self-sacrifice, and other traditional American virtues are promoted.

Although some may not wish to use the entire program, there are many strengths to this approach to early reading, and the teacher's manual and the suggested activities for workshop contain many ideas and specific suggestions that will be valuable for some children with learning disabilities. The flexibility of the program, the inclusion of specific suggestions for a multisensory approach, and the provision for a variety of individualized work make it a program to investigate.

DISTAR program

DISTAR, an acronym for Direct Instruction Systems for Teaching Arithmetic and Reading, is difficult to characterize as anything but what the name implies. This program was developed as an outgrowth of work carried out at the Institute for Research on Exceptional Children at the University of Illinois. Carl Bereiter and Siegfried Engelmann provided the original thrust for this program, which was established primarily as a compensatory effort to prepare disadvantaged black children for entrance into the traditional middle-class white–oriented school program. Engelmann continued these efforts, which culminated in the DISTAR program.

The DISTAR program has received considerable criticism from more child-centered early childhood authorities because it is admittedly very fast paced and seems (to some at least) to ignore the interests and feelings of the child (Moskovitz, 1968).

The authors admit that theirs is not a child-centered method in the usual sense of the term but rather a method whereby a good teacher can help children be ready to compete who would not otherwise succeed in school. They call their program highly structured and intensive and make no apologies. They think that such fast-paced, directive programming is essential to the children for whom this program was designed.

Teachers are given a detailed guide as to what to teach and the order in which it should be taught. No readiness assumptions are made; the program is designed to develop the skills necessary for reading. The teacher is very much in charge and children learn this quickly. DISTAR includes a special alphabet (used in initial teaching only) and practice in sequencing, blending, rhyming, and most important, in following instructions implicitly. Training in what might be called visual perception skills and auditory skills is included—all in a specific sequence. A training film is provided for in-service or preservice training. Unless teachers have seen a DISTAR teacher in action, this film is quite important if the materials are to be used in the most effective manner.

Reading I (the beginning level) starts with sound-symbol identification, left-to-right sequencing, and oral sound blending. Children learn to read by sounding words, then to read groups of words as complete thoughts. Reading I provides a highly structured, fast-paced approach to the skills usually developed in the first grade.

The DISTAR system includes take-home stories and exercises, recycling lessons, and highly specific teacher instructions. Reading II is an expansion of the skills emphasized in Reading I, and each level comes in a teacher's kit that contains all necessary materials. Student sets of materials for Reading I and Reading II come in sets of five.

Reading III is advertised as a basal reading program for grade three or for use as a remedial reading program. It is designed to teach reading skills within the framework of factual material and to provide new concepts and concept applications. Like Reading I and II it may be purchased in a complete teacher kit, but unlike Reading I and II much of Reading III is designed for use with 30 children at one time. (Beginning DISTAR program materials can be used for an entire class, but the materials are designed for use with small groups [five children] at a time.)

DISTAR must be experienced to be understood and appreciated and is sometimes "too much" for some teachers. Unusually high rates of progress in reading are reported in a variety of DISTAR literature, and teachers who try DISTAR appear to have fairly strong feelings one way or the other as to its value.

The DISTAR Reading Program is one of three components of the DISTAR Instructional System. The other two, DISTAR Arithmetic and DISTAR Language, are similar to the reading program in philosophy. Words used in the DISTAR sales literature—"disciplined," "fast-paced," "immediate feedback," and "logical sequence"—may well be used to characterize and summarize the DISTAR approach.

Montessori-related approaches

A number of approaches, often carried out on a limited basis and requiring tuition payment, have been called Montessori-like or Montessori-related. We should know of these and be aware that although many are relatively consistent with Montessori's theoretical constructs, others apparently use the name because of its popularity and have only surface adherence to most of Montessori's ideas and practices. There is, of course, nothing professionally wrong with using components of various teaching-learning approaches, but the extent to which we use a particular approach should be clearly defined and carefully followed, particularly if the program in question is one that requires the payment of tuition.

Montessori's ideas would seem to have potential value to those who work with learning disabilities because of the nature of the children with whom she originally worked and the indication that such approaches have been of value in developing reading skills in children who were not learning effectively in the regular school program. There is little research in which children specifically identified as learning disabled have been taught through this approach, but the fact that it has been recognized for many years and has usually enjoyed a good reputation makes it an approach about which parents often inquire. We will therefore consider it briefly.

Montessori's original educational efforts were directed toward teaching the mentally retarded. Historical accounts indicate that she was so successful with some children who were thought to be mentally retarded that they were able to pass national examinations that entitled them to primary certificates. Her early work with the retarded (who were likely pseudoretarded who had been denied an opportunity to normal environmental stimulation and learning) led to efforts with children in some of the worst slum areas of Rome. Here she experienced more remarkable success, which led to the formal development of the method that now carries her name, a method known and used to varying degrees all over the world. There are many components of the Montessori method; only a few will be described here. (For an interesting account of an American approach to the Montessori method, see Rambusch [1962].)

Montessori often refers to preparing children for learning, a reference to her version of readiness for reading. One of the ways in which children are prepared for reading is through use of sandpaper letters written in script. The child is directed to look carefully at the letters and then to trace them with his eyes closed. Later a stick is used to trace the letters as preparation for use of the pencil (in earlier times, a pen). The purpose of the first tracing of sandpaper letters is to reinforce the visual image and, of course, as early training for writing. As Montessori saw it, reading is preceded by writing, and writing is preceded by preparation for writing. Montessori believed that if a child could write, he could read.

Another activity in which children participate in preparation for reading is matching letters of the alphabet that can be picked up, handled, and compared with exact copies of these letters in a partitioned box. The child manipulates these letters (although they are not learned as letters of the alphabet but as sounds) and in so doing receives additional reinforcement. Vowels and consonants are separated, and children learn to recognize them all before they start to read. In the initial tracing stage, children trace and say the sound of the letter. In the next stage the teacher asks the child to "give me an i" (using the short vowel sound for the i) and the child responds by finding and handing the teacher an "i." In the third stage the teacher holds up a letter (in this case it is more properly called a phonogram) and asks, "What is this?" The child then gives the letter sound.

Montessori used an earlier version of this multisensory initial approach to teach the Italian slum children and achieved excellent results. Her observations there and in later application of her evolving method led her to believe that children can write if they are prepared in three areas: (1) how the letter feels (kinesthetically), (2) how it is pronounced, and (3) how to move a pencil to properly form the letter. Then, following her educational logic, they will be able to read.

In Montessori's work with Italian children the development of ability to write and the transition to reading came very quickly in many cases, but we must remember two things in comparing her results and efforts in the United States. Many of the children in Italy were older than children we have attempted to teach through Montessori methods in the United States; thus they had more fully developed fine motor ability. In addition, the Italian language is more phonetic in nature and has less irregularities than English, so more rapid learning might be expected.

The transition to reading is accomplished by the teacher preparing slips of paper on which the names of toys (toys available in the room) have been written; by various means the children take the slips, read the name of the toy, and get to play with it. For underprivileged slum children this undoubtedly had high motivational value; for some more privileged children this might have little motivational impact.

After words are learned through word games, phrases and sentences are learned. The sentences direct the children to perform some action such as "go to the door and close it." As soon as children are able to read the more simple directions, sentences are lengthened and made to include directions that require sequential compliance. The emphasis on active gamelike teaching is an important part of much of the Montessori method.

Original Montessori methods did not proceed through a reading aloud stage. Montessori thought that, except for the game periods, which did include activity and oral participation on the part of children, much of the day should be spent with the child working alone and in silence. American Montessori schools have modified this concept in practice over the past 20 or 30 years.

The educational continuum, according to Montessori, does not require a timetable— children will learn when they are ready. If properly prepared, the child will soon begin composing words with his movable alphabet letters, and that is the start of reading. Although some work can be done in small groups, much is individual in nature, and rate of progress is the most individual of all.

Rambusch is one of several spokespersons for the Montessori method as adapted in the United States. In *Learning How to Learn* (1962) she provides more specific suggestions on using an adapted Montessori approach. Although Montessori started with the retarded and with underprivileged children, Montessori Schools in the United States tend to enroll children from the other end of the social and intellectual spectrum. Montessori materials provide a good source of ideas and techniques for teachers searching for new or modified approaches. The emphasis on kinesthetic skills and learning to precede formal reading is similar to ideas we have seen in several other systems and might be re-

viewed by those looking for more ideas in this area. One type of learning-disabled child who might have difficulty with Montessori approaches as they are often used is the hyperkinetic or Strauss syndrome child. Although the Montessori approach is structured, it leaves the child free to proceed by providing many materials from which he may choose. This abundance of materials is just what the Strauss syndrome child should not have.

Responsive Environment approach

This approach has also been called an automated typewriter or a talking typewriter approach because of its use of such equipment. This particular approach developed from the work of Omar Moore and Alan Anderson (1967) and is often thought of as an early education approach. The term "responsive environment" means a self-pacing environment with free exploration that provides immediate feedback as to consequences of actions and is conducive to interrelated discoveries about the physical, cultural, and social aspects of the world. Moore and Anderson have attempted to establish such an environment for the teaching of reading.

The Responsive Environment approach has four parts: (1) free exploration, (2) search and match, (3) word construction, and (4) reading, writing, and handwriting. In the free exploration phase the child enters a booth where he faces an array of interesting machinery. The child knows that he can leave when he wants to without explaining to anyone where he is going or why. His only restrictions are that if he wants to enter a booth, he must use the one assigned to him, and his allotted time in the booth is a maximum time—when time is up he *must* leave.

Before he enters the booth the child's fingernails are painted with nontoxic watercolors. He is not told why, but if he explores after he enters the booth, he will discover that the watercolors match key banks on the talking typewriter. He is watched by lab assistants and is expected to experiment with the typewriter. When he does he finds that it "talks" to him when he depresses the keys. It also prints the letters and, of course, can be programmed to do a number of other things. After the staff thinks he has explored enough to be ready to enter phase 2, it is initiated.

Phase 2 is a program in which the child matches letter symbols in a workbook with those on the machine. A number of interesting variations are implemented with the talking typewriter. In a space above the carriage there may be a letter or a word that the child soon learns he must match to get the typewriter to talk. When several letters appear in this "window," an arrow points to the one that must be duplicated on the keyboard. Unless the child presses the key that corresponds to the letter to which the arrow points, the typewriter will not respond. In this manner the child learns to follow the "instructions" of the typewriter.

Phase 3 has two subphases, reading and writing. In the reading part, different words appear in the window. The child must type out the word in the right order for the machine to respond as he wants it to. After he types a word properly while the machine says it letter by letter, the machine respells the entire word, then pronounces it. Thus a basic reading vocabulary is developed in phase 3.

For the writing part of phase 3 the child dictates a story that is then played back to him. He then types his story. The machine is not used in this phase except as a typewriter. To maintain interest in phase 3 the reading and writing subphases are conducted on alternate days.

Phase 4 is reading and writing. In this phase the Responsive Environment machine asks questions, reads sentences, and expects answers (to be typed by the child) to the questions. The child must type the sentences for the sequence to continue.

A large number of variations of nearly all of these activities are possible. Less expensive, semiautomated machinery may be used; the teacher enters the booth with the child and does part of the work that would be accomplished by the fully automated typewriter. Even when the fully automated equipment is used, much assistance is required in this approach.

The Responsive Environment approach to the teaching-learning process has been supported over the years by funds from Westinghouse, the Office of Naval Research, and at one point by the Office of Economic Opportunity. From the beginning it has attracted attention because it involved machines teaching 3- and 4-year-old children to read and write. It obviously has an extremely high cost per pupil in the fully automated form but may contribute to our general knowledge about the reading process.

In addition to being an interesting experiment, these efforts have led to ones in which ordinary typewriters have been used to provide motivation to underprivileged or disabled readers. For the most part these have been efforts of limited scope, but the use of the typewriter may have some applications with children with reading problems.

Comprehension and the cloze procedure

At times we may become so concerned about a child's ability to decode accurately that we lose sight of the fact that the purpose of decoding (or word recognition) is to facilitate understanding or meaning. Deriving meaning from the printed word is a higher level skill than the decoding process, and some learning-disabled children can decode words but do not understand their meaning. Most of the methods that have been developed for the learning disabled, including most reviewed in this chapter, focus heavily on decoding.

For years reading authorities have focused attention on reading methods to teach the decoding process. In a review of current texts on reading it appears that, in general, less than 10% of any given text is devoted to comprehension skills and methods. Admittedly, methods for teaching comprehension skills are included within the developmental reading sequence; however, there does appear to be a paucity of remedial methods that relate directly to teaching or improving comprehension.

As Spache and Spache (1973) point out, one reason for this may be the lack of a basic definition of comprehension skills. Nevertheless, there does seem to be general agreement that comprehension in reading involves perceiving meaning from what is written.

In addition to the need to be aware that some children's learning problems may *start* at the comprehension level (that is, they may decode effectively, but comprehend poorly), we must be alert to the fact that we may have success with word recognition in remediation and forget to check carefully to see that this accurate word recognition results in good comprehension. This may be all the more likely to occur when we have had serious difficulties in getting over the decoding hurdle. When we finally do, we may give a sigh of relief and send the child back to the classroom teacher, "cured" and ready to achieve. This is somewhat similar to remedying process disabilities and not providing assistance in the carryover to task performance. Obviously it is a skill with which we must be concerned and to which we must give more attention.

Comprehension skills can be classified in a variety of ways. Dallmann et al. (1974) classify these skills according to the reading purpose and the nature and length of the reading unit. The skills presented here differ semantically from the ones introduced earlier; however, the reader should be able to determine which skills deal with literal or inferred meaning and which deal with critical evaluation and assimilation. For a description of detailed procedures for teaching comprehension, see Dallmann et al. (1974). In addition, the references and suggested readings at the end of this chapter include a number of texts containing suggestions for teaching reading comprehension.

Classification of comprehension skills
1. Skills classified according to purpose of reader
   a. Reading to find the main idea
   b. Reading to select significant details
   c. Reading to follow directions
   d. Reading to answer questions
   e. Reading to summarize and organize
   f. Reading to arrive at generalizations
   g. Reading to predict outcomes
   h. Reading to evaluate critically
2. Skills classified according to structure or length of reading unit

a. Phrase meaning
b. Sentence meaning
c. Paragraph meaning
d. Comprehension of longer selections

Recently the cloze procedure has received attention as a technique for developing comprehension skills. Bloomer (1962), among others, believes that the procedure provides practice in reading to note details, to determine the main idea, to make inferences, and to draw conclusions. He also states that knowledge of word meanings may be taught by this technique. In the past the procedure has been used chiefly for testing purposes and for determining the readability of material.

The term "cloze" comes from the word "clozure" (closure), which denotes determining a whole from its parts. The procedure is a deletion method in which certain words are taken out of the reading material. Teachers may create their own materials or use stories from basal readers or other commercially printed reading books. One common application is to delete every nth word. Perhaps the teacher may choose to delete only nouns or the first letter of certain words. The position and frequency of the deleted material is determined by the needs of the learner.

The following is an example of how the technique is used; every tenth word has been deleted.

I pledge allegiance to the flag of the United _____ of America and to the republic for which it _____, one nation, under God, indivisible, with liberty and justice _____ all.

The cloze procedure is more fully explained by Zintz (1972) and in sources published by the International Reading Association such as those by Jongsman (1971) and Robinson (1971).

The cloze procedure is only one of many possible ways in which a teacher may attempt to build comprehension skills in reading. I will not try to suggest methods other than the cloze procedure, but I strongly urge all learning disabilities teachers to remember that *after success with decoding we must attend to comprehension or at least make certain the classroom teacher understands that it remains to be done.*

Eclectic systems and models

We will conclude our review of approaches and systems by considering the so-called eclectic models that are beginning to appear and may hold more promise than many of the more highly publicized approaches. In considering such models it should be specifically noted that even if some of these should be generally more effective than many of the rest, there is a likelihood that they will never be utilized in proportion to their effectiveness. This is due to the nature of the educational system. Although it is not (inherently) a commercial type of profit and loss system, unless an approach lends itself to commercial reproduction and dissemination, its value may never be known by a majority of the teachers who might well become more effective if they used it. The other factor that mitigates against the wide dissemination of some approaches or models is how easily they can be used, that is, whether they can be "cookbooked" or whether they require a large degree of teacher resourcefulness and ingenuity. This factor interrelates with the commercial potential; approaches and models that require less resourcefulness tend to be more attractive to many educators, thus more commercial and more likely to be widely disseminated.

This point of view is fairly widely accepted but infrequently expressed. However, I think that the point must be made in this text because it is more likely that teachers who specialize in working with unusual educational problems are sufficiently dedicated to go the extra mile and utilize methods and approaches that require more thought, effort, and innovativeness. It is with this hope that I will review one eclectic approach.

Integrated Skills Method. The Integrated Skills Method (ISM) is one of a number of approaches that are being developed by research or demonstration units in various places in the nation. Too many of these, despite highly valuable potential for contribu-

tion, will never be utilized outside of a small geographical area. The ISM will be described in some detail, both as an example of this type of method and as a method that deserves consideration in its own right.

ISM is a method for teaching reading that is independent of any specific traditional instructional program or approach. It uses some components of many reading approaches and a variety of instructional materials. It provides for the integration of pupil needs and teacher knowledge, skills, and teaching styles. It was developed through a series of research efforts, starting with work with the talking typewriter, and has been reported by Richardson and Bradley (1974) of the New York State Department of Mental Hygiene Learning Disabilities Laboratory.

ISM is theoretically based on the relationship of reading to the whole learning situation—the interaction of pupils, materials, teacher behavior, and the manner in which these establish the classroom environment. It attempts to provide a framework that is general enough to be effective and applicable in most settings but flexible enough to be consistent with the wide range of needs in the spectrum of learning disabilities programming. According to its developers, it includes provisions for teaching the basic skills that appear to be most generally agreed on as needed for recognition of sight words and for effective phonetic decoding. It is a guide and framework, not an approach that dictates specific materials, teacher actions, and lockstep methodological instructions.

ISM is composed of three major components: a beginning skills unit, integrated skills lessons, and applied reading. The beginning skills unit includes a specific sequence of skill development with the emphasis in each part of the sequence dependent on the needs of each individual child. The ISM would be difficult to apply in its highly individualized nature with a class of 30 to 40 children but rather is designed for use with children with reading handicaps.

The first level of the beginning skills unit is the *response skills* level. At this level children are taught to name pictures rapidly in preparation for the teaching of words and phoneme-grapheme correspondence. As soon as they can respond rapidly to the picture-naming activity, they are taught to name pictures from left to right in preparation for the reading of sentences in this order. The beginnings of sound blending are introduced at the response level, with the teacher sounding a word such as "/b/, /ike/" and the children responding with "bike."

The second level of the beginning skills unit is *beginning reading.* Beginning reading in ISM means recognition of eight words selected for their motivational value on an individual basis. In cases in which, for example, the teacher plans to use a basal reader (for some combination of reasons), the first words may be from the basal reader; for many older children who have experienced failure in basal readers this probably would not be done. As a limited number of sight words are introduced, a continuation of the sound blending takes place. Sight words are selected to make possible the construction of simple sentences, thus promoting the concept that written words tell a story.

A third level, *beginning phonics,* is begun by teaching the sound of two consonants that may be used in connection with rhyming (for example, the letters "f" and "r" to be used with "un"). Sound blending is expanded (the children have already learned through practice to operate effectively with sound blending as a response skill) to include the blending of these sounds. Thus the children learn that /f/, /un/ equals /fun/ and /r/, /un/ equals run. After becoming comfortable with this phonetic concept in practice the children learn to recognize fun and run as sight words. More letters and word elements of this type are presented, pursued through sound blending, and related to sight words. The use of simple sentences, originated at the second level, continues with words that have been learned in this phonetic sequence.

When children become familiar with the three levels of the beginning skills unit they have a foundation and have built simple concepts in letter sounds, sound blending, the process of sounding out new words, and the learning of sight words. They have learned through practice that some words may be initially learned by how they look (sight recognition) and others by a phonetic approach. They have learned to "read" pictures in a left-to-right direction, then to read simple abstract symbols (words) in this same manner.

The second major component of the ISM is called *integrated skills lessons;* it involves the integrated use of the beginning skills learned earlier. If the teacher feels comfortable with the synthetic approach to teaching sound code, the work started in the beginning skills unit is continued. The teacher attempts to make words and stories as meaningful as possible, extend the sound blending to phonic decoding, and expand sight vocabulary in the way that seems most effective.

The developers of this approach note that a teacher who is *not* comfortable with the synthetic phonetic approach and prefers an approach used more often in linguistic methods may use such an approach. In this case the procedure involves experience with words that have common phonic elements. However, the words are taught as whole words with the expectation that the children will learn about phonic elements in their response generalization.

The third major component of the ISM is *applied reading.* At this level it becomes obvious that *teachers who use this approach must be well-trained teachers who understand all the basic skills fundamental to the reading process.* The ISM does not give the step-by-step structure ("teacher says this; teacher says that") of some other approaches. It is based on an assumption that the teacher knows and appreciates the relative value of the many skills involved in reading. At the applied reading level the teacher makes available a selection of books with content geared to what has been taught in the integrated skills lessons. In fact, the potential choices available for applied reading must be kept in mind when planning the steps of the integrated skills lessons so that the child's first attempts to read a book are successful.

Selection of content with which to work is most important. In the basal series this is done *for* the teacher; in the ISM it is done *by* the teacher. It is suggested that pictures for the first "picture reading" steps may be selected by the children and will work best if they are simple, one-word objects that promote rapid responses. At the sight-recognition level children's names and a few nouns with high motivational impact should be used (for example, cake and bicycle). These nouns coupled with the right verbs (eats and rides) permit the construction of sentences as soon as the individual words are learned in isolation.

Word selection for sound blending may be easiest if the teacher selects from one of the existing beginning phonics programs. They provide a source of readily developed material, and most will have taken into account such factors as avoidance of visual similarity and ease of pronunciation in first pairs of words used.

The combination of learning through use of phonic and sight approaches is a very deliberate part of the ISM. This permits the teacher to observe the child's reaction and ability to use each approach and to tailor the learning of reading skills to the approach that is best or most effective for him. It also provides the basis for remedially oriented efforts that may be carried out separate from the development of reading skills or, at times along with such development. Once the "best" procedure is found, the teacher will teach that child through that approach. Once again it must be noted that the total ISM procedure is based on the assumption that the teacher has a good understanding of the reading process and has the sequence of basic skills firmly in mind at all times.

Basic teaching techniques in the basic skills unit and the integrated skills lessons are essentially the same. Similar drill routines are used in picture naming, sight-word recognition, and in teaching the phonic sounds of the letters. Although the teacher may make a number of variations based on pupil interest and unique pupil needs, the essential sequence is carefully outlined and not really difficult to follow once it is conceptualized. Features such as using content to teach skills

(rather than the opposite) should be quite effective for children who are experiencing reading difficulties.

The ISM has certain fundamental principles that remain even if specific techniques and materials are varied considerably. Simplicity of presentation and brief lessons conducted several time a day are the rule. Mastery of old content before starting the new and the use of content to teach skills are among the more important. The basic ideas and principles are for most part those that have been generally accepted for many years. The new and unique aspect of ISM is the way these ideas are sequenced and the flexible role given the teacher.

The ISM has been reviewed in somewhat more detail than many of the other approaches, not necessarily because of relative value, but because it represents a whole variety of eclectic approaches that tend to receive too little attention. I frequently hear that a certain teacher is highly successful simply because he or she understands the reading process and is effective in dealing with children's behavior. If all learning disabilities teachers were as competent and knowledgeable as these unusually successful ones, we would not need to talk about methods and approaches. But most teachers, even skilled ones, benefit from guidelines that serve as checkpoints within which to operate. Approaches such as the ISM provide some of the more effective ways in which educational efforts may be planned in accordance with sound learning principles, permit flexibility, provide for individuality on the part of teachers, and still be sufficiently simple that most good teachers can learn to use them. With identifiable elements of many more specific approaches, ISM certainly qualifies as eclectic, and initial reports indicate considerable success with children with reading disabilities.

READING TESTS

Before bringing this chapter to a close, we should consider the function of certain reading measurement tools in planning in learning disabilities. Commercially available reading tests may be divided into three categories: written reading survey tests, oral reading tests, and reading diagnostic tests. A listing of some of the more common tests in each of these categories is included in Appendix D. Nearly all survey tests provide measures of comprehension and vocabulary. Some measure such items as skills in phonetic analysis and ability to locate information in written materials. Reading survey tests provide a general measure of these abilities and indicate whether a child scores unusually low in one area as compared to another. Depending on which definition of learning disabilities is used, they might be used along with other measures of reading level to indicate that significant reading retardation exists, thus making a particular child eligible for learning disabilities programming and services. They are not particularly useful in planning the type of approach to use or where to start in remediation.

Oral reading tests provide information as to speed and comprehension and supplementary information as to reading level and speed. Because they are given individually, they can sometimes provide important information about reading deficiencies, but their usefulness varies with the type of problem under consideration and the clinical competence of the person giving the test. If a diagnostic test is to be given, oral reading tests may not be required since most diagnostic tests include an oral test section.

Diagnostic reading tests are the most valuable in planning educational approaches. They are more comprehensive and provide specific information in a number of important subskills in reading. The list of reading difficulties that follows is a generalized composite indicating the types of difficulties measured by a number of diagnostic reading tests.

Areas of reading difficulty measured by diagnostic reading tests

1. Oral reading
   a. Omissions
   b. Additions
   c. Repetitions
   d. Pointing to words
   e. Losing place frequently
   f. Tenseness (of body position)
   g. Mispronunciations (reversals, wrong beginnings, wrong endings, wrong middles)
   h. Voice (notation of pitch, volume, etc.)
2. Word recognition and analysis
   a. Letter naming (lowercase, capital letters)
   b. Words (flash presentation, untimed)
   c. Phonics (letter at a time, syllables, overall rating)
   d. Blending (general)
   e. Consonants
   f. Consonant blends
   g. Vowels
3. Supplementary subtests as indicated in specific cases
   a. Syllabication
   b. Auditory discrimination
   c. Spelling

SUMMARY

Reading skills or skills that are prerequisites to effective reading are among the major objectives in most learning disabilities programs. How to most effectively teach beginning reading to children who are learning normally has been the subject of controversy for years, and no final resolution of this debate has been achieved. In the various efforts that have been launched to research this question, a number of interesting observations have been made; among them is the fact that all programs, no matter how effective they are alleged to be, are ineffective for certain children. This observation and a variety of related ones lead to the conclusion that there is no "best" program for all children and there is no "best" method for all children with learning disabilities.

An alternative to the concept of the best program, particularly for the learning disabilities teacher, is to be familiar with the reading process, the skills required for success in reading, and a number of varied approaches to teaching reading. Then, if strengths and weaknesses of children can be determined, a program can be developed that is appropriate to these strengths and weaknesses.

Reviews of reading programs in existence in the United States today indicate that there are at least six generally recognized approaches plus a variety of methods used less widely. The six major approaches are (1) basal readers, (2) phonic approaches, (3) linguistic approaches, (4) modified alphabets, (5) language experience approaches, and (6) individualized reading approaches. Often these approaches are used in combination, and the basal reader approach, the most popular one, tends to include elements of other approaches.

In addition to these six, there are a number of more specialized approaches, most of which have been used in learning disabilities programming. Those considered in this chapter were tactile and kinesthetic approaches, Fernald's simultaneous visual-auditory-kinesthetic-tactile approach, Gillingham and Stillman's phonic visual-auditory-kinesthetic approach, Johnson and Myklebust's language development approach, Words in Color, the Psycholinguistic Color System, Programmed Reading, Individually Prescribed Instruction (IPI), computer-assisted instruction, rhebus approaches, DISTAR, Montessori-related approaches, and the Responsive Environment (talking typewriter) approach. Each of these approaches has some potential for use with learning-disabled children, some limited and narrow, others fairly broad and generally applicable.

The cloze procedure is a promising avenue to the development of better comprehension. With much of the emphasis of learning disabilities programs on decoding, comprehension is sometimes overlooked, a situation that must be corrected. Another promising possibility that is not sufficiently publicized is the variety of eclectic approaches that have been developed at specialized research and demonstration facilities throughout the nation. An approach called the Integrated Skills Method developed at a state-sponsored learning disabilities laboratory in New York is representative of the best of these eclectic approaches.

There are no pat answers to the question, "How should we teach learning-disabled children to read?" There are a number of promising approaches, but all have limitations. The variety of children in learning disabilities programs is so great it appears that there will be no single applicable reading program for the learning-disabled child unless that program is so flexible and so subject to variation and modification that it is, in fact, not one program but an almost infinite number of programs arranged to fit into one loosely tied package.

REFERENCES AND SUGGESTED READINGS

Aukerman, R. *Approaches to beginning reading.* New York: John Wiley & Sons, Inc., 1971.

Bannatyne, A. *Language, reading, and learning disabilities.* Springfield, Ill.: Charles C Thomas, Publisher, 1971.

Bereiter, C., and Hughes, A. *Teacher's guide to the Open Court kindergarten program.* LaSalle, Ill.: Open Court Publishing Co., 1970.

Blau, H., and Blau, H. A theory of learning to read. *The Reading Teacher,* 1968, *22,* 126-129.

Bloomer, R. The cloze procedure as a remedial reading exercise. *Journal of Developmental Reading,* 1962, *5,* 173-181.

Bloomfield, L., and Barnhart, C. *Let's read.* Detroit: Wayne State University Press, 1961.

Bond, G. and Tinker, M. *Reading difficulties: their diagnosis and correction* (2nd ed.). New York: Appleton-Century-Crofts, 1968.

Carter, H., and McGinnis, D. *Diagnosis and treatment of the disabled reader.* New York: Macmillan Publishing Co., Inc., 1970.

Cazden, C. *Child language and education.* New York: Holt, Rinehart & Winston, Inc., 1972.

Chall, J. *Learning to read: the great debate.* New York: McGraw-Hill Book Co., 1967.

Cooper, J. A procedure for teaching non-readers. *Education,* 1947, May, 494-499.

Dallmann, M., Rouch, R., Chang, L., and DeBoer, J. *The teaching of reading* (4th ed.). New York: Holt, Rinehart & Winston, Inc., 1974.

Dechant, E. *Diagnosis and remediation of reading disability.* Engelwood Cliffs, N.J.: Parker Publishing Co., 1968.

Dechant, E. *Improving the teaching of reading* (2nd ed.). Englewood Cliffs, N.J.: Prentice Hall, Inc., 1970.

Dechant, E. *Linguistics, phonics, and the teaching of reading.* Springfield, Ill.: Charles C Thomas, Publisher, 1969.

Downing, J. The Initial Teaching Alphabet. In J. Downing (Ed.), *The first international reading symposium.* New York: The John Day Co., Inc., 1966.

Downing, J. *The Initial Teaching Alphabet reading experiment.* Chicago: Scott, Foresman and Co., 1965.

Durkin, D. *Teaching them to read* (2nd ed.). Boston: Allyn & Bacon, Inc., 1974.

Ellson, W. Programmed tutoring: a teaching aid and a research tool. *Reading Research Quarterly.* 1965, *1,* 77-127.

Fernald, G. *Remedial techniques in basic school subjects.* New York: McGraw-Hill Book Co., 1943.

Flesch, R. *Why Johnny can't read and what you can do about it.* New York: Harper & Brothers, 1955.

Fries, C. *Linguistics and reading.* New York: Holt, Rinehart & Winston, Inc., 1963.

Fries, C. *Merrill linguistic readers: a basic program.* Columbus, Ohio: Charles E. Merrill Publishing Co., 1962.

Frostig, M. *Selection and adaptation of reading methods.* San Rafael, Calif.: Academic Therapy Publications, 1973.

Gagné, R. *The conditions of learning* (2nd ed.). New York: Holt, Rinehart & Winston, Inc., 1970.

Gattegno, C. *Words in Color.* Chicago: Encyclopedia Britannica, Inc., 1962.

Gearheart, B. *Learning disabilities: educational strategies.* St. Louis: The C. V. Mosby, Co., 1973.

Gillingham, A., and Stillman, B. *Remedial work for reading, spelling, and penmanship* (6th ed.). New York: Hackett & Wilhelms, 1946.

Goodman, D. (Ed.). *The psycholinguistic nature of the reading process.* Detroit: Wayne State University Press, 1968.

Guszak, F. *Diagnostic reading instruction in the elementary school.* New York: Harper & Row, Publishers 1972.

Harris, A. *How to increase reading ability* (5th ed.). New York: David McKay Co., Inc., 1970.

Johnson, D., and Myklebust, H. *Learning disabilities: educational principles and practices.* New York: Grune & Stratton, Inc., 1967.

Jongsman, E. *The cloze procedure as a teaching technique.* Newark, Del.: International Reading Association, 1971.

Kaluger, G., and Kolson, C. *Reading and learning disabilities.* Columbus, Ohio: Charles E. Merrill Publishing Co., 1969.

Karlin, R. *Teaching elementary reading.* New York: Harcourt Brace Jovanovich, Inc., 1971.

Lane, A. Severe reading disability and the initial teaching alphabet. *Journal of Learning Disabilities,* 1974, *7(8),* 23-27.

Lerner, J. *Children with learning disabilities: theories, diagnosis, and teaching strategies.* Boston: Houghton Mifflin Co., 1971.

Mackintosh, H. (Ed.). *Current approaches to teaching reading* (pamphlet). Washington, D.C.: National Education Association, 1965.

Matthes, C. *How children are taught to read.* Lincoln, Neb.: Professional Educators Publications, Inc., 1972.

Money, J. (Ed.). *The disabled reader: education of the dyslexic child.* Baltimore: The John Hopkins University Press, 1966.

Monroe, M. *Children who cannot read.* Chicago: University of Chicago Press, 1932.

Montessori, M. *The Montessori method.* New York: Schocken Books, 1964.

Moore, O., and Anderson, A. The responsive environments project. In R. Hess and R. Bear (Eds.), *The challenge of early education.* Chicago: Aldine Publishing Co., 1967.

Moskovitz, S. Some assumptions underlying the Bereiter approach. *Young Children,* 1968, *24*(1) October, 24-31.

Myers, P., and Hammill, D. *Methods for learning disorders.* New York: John Wiley & Sons, Inc., 1969.

Pitman, J. *Evidence submitted to the Bullock committee of inquiry into reading and the use of English* (Foundation Publication No. 18). New York: The ita Foundation, 1973.

Rambusch, N. *Learning how to learn—an American approach to Montessori.* Baltimore: Helicon Press, Inc., 1962.

Richardson, E., and Bradley, C. ISM: A teacher-oriented method of reading instruction for the child-oriented teacher. *Journal of Learning Disabilities,* 1974, 7(6), 19-27.

Robins, D. *Special education guide to the Open Court program.* LaSalle, Ill.: Open Court Publishing Co., 1970.

Robinson, R. *An introduction to the cloze procedure, an annotated bibliography.* Newark, Del.: International Reading Association, 1971.

Schubert, D., and Torgerson, T. *Improving the reading program* (3rd ed.). Dubuque, Iowa: William C. Brown Co., Publishers, 1972.

Spache, G. *The teaching of reading: methods and results.* Bloomington, Ind.: The Phi Delta Kappa Educational Foundation, 1972.

Spache, G., and Spache, E. *Reading in the elementary school* (3rd ed.). Boston: Allyn & Bacon, Inc., 1973.

Strang, R. *Diagnostic teaching of reading* (2nd ed.). New York: McGraw-Hill Book Co., 1969.

Woodcock, R. *Peabody Rebus Reading Program.* Circle Pines, Minn.: American Guidance Service, Inc., 1967.

Zintz, M. V. *Corrective reading* (2nd ed.). Dubuque, Iowa: William C. Brown Co., Publishers 1972.

7 Teaching arithmetic and mathematics to the learning disabled

George E. Marsh II

For many years instructional programs in mathematics were designed with an emphasis on the utility of mathematics in daily living activities. Until the middle of this century, teaching techniques stressed rote memorization of facts and processes. The formats of many texts were composed of successive pages of "practical" problems. Remedial education received little attention.

Federal funds were made available by the National Defense Education Act in 1958, which was a result of congressional concern that the United States was lagging behind the Soviet Union in the initial stages of the "space race." Mathematics instantly became a primary concern in relation to national defense and national pride.

The years since 1958 have witnessed the growth of "new math," an issue that provokes a variety of emotional reactions in both parents and teachers. The significant reason for such a change in mathematics has been a shift in the professional attitude of many educators. Mathematics is no longer viewed as a unitary, simple subject. It is now regarded as an expansive subject to be studied for its theoretical content as well as to serve as a foundation for the sciences and branches of advanced mathematics. Young children are being introduced to very abstract concepts in the primary grades. This practice has not been implemented without creating pressures for some children who might have achieved satisfactorily in another time.

These changes were not necessarily founded on sound research conclusions. Spitzer (1970) indicates that the purpose of all new programs had been to experiment with untried procedures and to vary the content in an effort to improve the programs. New math programs were constructed on principles leading to the development of concepts and processes that were far removed from concrete or practical reference. The result of this approach, which stressed deductive reasoning and oral instruction, was that children were incapable of performing with the same degree of computational skill as children who had been instructed in traditional programs. As a consequence many schools are eliminating the new programs, and the field is in a state of vacillation. Meanwhile the mathematics curriculum is decidedly more difficult for children with learning disabilities because of the level of abstraction.

For various reasons a distinction must be made between arithmetic and mathematics, according to Chalfant and Scheffelin (1969). Arithmetic is the science of numbers and computation with numbers, more specifically, addition, subtraction, multiplication, and division. Mathematics is the abstract science and study of quantity, form, arrangement, and magnitude. It can be reasoned that arithmetic is a branch of mathematics, although historically it may have been the mother of mathematics.

Arithmetic is concrete in nature; little abstraction is superimposed. It deals with concrete entities, and the symbol system of arithmetic is not far removed from actual manipulation of objects. Barakat (1951) concludes

that mathematics is abstract and does not deal with concrete factors. It is possible for a child to develop rather complex concepts but be unable to recognize, reproduce, or calculate numbers. It is well known, on the other hand, that some children who experience difficulty in virtually every school subject have unusual ability in arithmetic.

ARITHMETIC-MATHEMATICS AND LEARNING DISABILITIES

As attention is being drawn to the problems children experience in this field, the teacher who must assist them is faced with a challenge that is frustrating and at times disheartening. Reisman (1972) concurs with many authors who state that there are few guides to follow in planning remediation. In fact, the actual incidence of learning disabilities in arithmetic is unknown, and syndromes related to arithmetic disability are unclear and vaguely described.

Chalfant and Scheffelin (1969) provide a discussion of correlates to quantitative thinking that is worthy of review and consideration. Their discussion is probably the most extensive and comprehensive summary of research through 1968. Certain of these plus additional factors and correlates will be considered in the following discussion.

Spatial ability

Although research concerned with spatial ability is equivocal, it appears that this trait is more closely related to success in mathematics than to arithmetic. The trait is not fully understood, and Chalfant and Scheffelin indicate that it may not be a single, discrete factor but one that is related to other skills. It seems that this ability is important to the development of arithmetic skill, but because it is not fully understood, specific training directed at improving spatial ability is based on questionable assumptions.

Verbal ability

Inferior verbal ability is undeniably a causative factor in poor achievement. Kelley (1928), Mitchell (1938), Barakat (1951), and Kaliski (1962) have demonstrated a clear relationship between verbal ability and achievement at all levels of education. Because it is clear that there is an emergence of quantitative concepts with concomitant development of language and mental age, it is interesting that a negative relationship exists between verbal ability and spatial relations, according to Stafford (1972). This is explained as a result of the complex development of asymmetrical specialization of the two hemispheres of the brain and their cognitive processes.

Neurophysiological correlates and heredity

Barakat (1951), Gerstmann (1957), and Kosc (1974) have described a developmental condition, dyscalculia, that has been described as impairing the acquisition of arithmetic skills as a result of either neurological factors or heredity. Some children do seem to inherit an inferior aptitude for arithmetic skills, but the condition has not been related to any specific genetic aberration and has been disputed as a sex-linked characteristic because both sexes are affected. The definitions of this disorder are frequently only descriptive, and corrective procedures are not implicit in the descriptions.

Extensive studies of brain-damaged and aphasic adults have clearly shown the effects of lesions on quantitative thinking and computational skills, but caution must be used when making direct applications of such research results to children. To date the status of research in brain pathology cannot serve as a foundation for treatment of arithmetic disorders in children with any degree of confidence.

Emotional disorders

Emotional disorders have long been thought to be critical in the disruption of learning. The difficulty has often been to determine if emotional disorders are causative or the result of arithmetic failure. Many teachers report excellent achievement by children with emotional problems.

Memory

Short-term memory, long-term memory, and initial learning have been studied by many researchers (Zeaman and House, 1963; Ellis, 1963). Memory has been defined in a variety of ways, and there is confusion as to whether it is memory or attention with which we must be concerned. In any event, there have been few reports of improvement of poor memory. Cratty (1969) has claimed success in lengthening the attention span of children by perceptual-motor training. The effects of poor memory are well known.

Visual perception

There is little doubt that visual perception is important in the development of arithmetic. If the child inefficiently perceives or reproduces figures, his achievement will certainly be impaired. Disruptions of visual-motor integration can account for the difficulty some children have in counting or manipulating objects. This can also be manifested in poor handwriting in the form of what appears to be bizarre reproductions of numbers and designs.

Laterality

Laterality and directionality are particularly sensitive in arithmetic computation. The process of many operations in arithmetic is from right to left, unlike reading.

Poor teaching

Poor teaching is undoubtedly a factor in school failure. Providing the child has no other problems, corrective measures should be fruitful. If the child has learning disorders, poor teaching is devastating. The school should be in a position to eliminate this factor.

Many causes for learning disabilities in arithmetic have been postulated, and with the exception of neurophysiological factors, these causes approximate the etiological factors found in reading disorders. Because less is known about the causes of arithmetic disorders, relating corrective measures to certain syndromes and emphasizing remediation of hypothetical correlates not actually involved in learning tasks would seem to be an example of specious logic. Therefore *a more defensible approach is to emphasize the de-*

velopmental process in the acquisition of skill in arithmetic, the diagnosis of explicit problems, and the application of existing teaching strategies that are known to be effective.

PIAGET AND THE DEVELOPMENTAL PROCESS

Teachers who are frustrated by the failure of their students often search in desperation for the best method or the latest program that may make exaggerated claims of success. Time and again this is repeated until it is learned that there is no panacea.

It is mandatory that the teacher thoroughly understand the developmental process by which the child acquires skill in arithmetic and concepts of mathematics. With this knowledge as a framework, the teacher is in a position to develop expertise in the diagnosis of various learning disorders that cannot be identified by formal testing alone. The teacher must assume a role in diagnosis, determine what the child can learn, and use appropriate techniques and materials.

An important beginning point for the study of the developmental process is the work of Jean Piaget (1958, 1963, 1965, 1974). Piaget's theoretical position on cognitive development of children is basically concerned with the structures of cognition. Piaget has consistently been interested in how the mind of the child operates rather than its products. The process of development unfolds some answers and gives clues to the child's conception of number, time, and space.

Piaget's theoretical formulations and descriptive terminology are most difficult to grasp on first reading because of his writing style, the use of symbols to describe human behavior, and perhaps because of the added factor of translation from French to English. It is not expected that the reader will find it possible to acquire a true understanding of his work from this brief summary, but additional reading (see references and suggested readings) should lead to further insight and understanding.

From information and observations assembled over many years of investigations, Piaget has described periods of intellectual development. These periods are associated with chronological ages and have been found to coincide with mental age as well. Many replications of Piagetian experiments have been conducted, and the Piagetian developmental stages have been found to exist in the same sequences and the same approximate ages in various cultures. The periods actually consist of several substages; this discussion will pertain to the sensorimotor period, the preoperational subperiod, the concrete operations subperiod, and the formal operations period.

Sensorimotor period

The sensorimotor period is composed of six successive and overlapping stages of development. The initial activity of this period is the development or organization of perceptual units that are the result of the child's interaction with his environment. By tasting, mouthing, feeling, manipulating, seeing, and hearing objects and their activities in the environment, the child gradually incorporates perceptions that become the bases for higher cognitive processes. Logical development is initiated as the child learns that objects can be represented by signs. At the end of this period the normally developing child is able to imitate the movement of living and inanimate objects, including those that are not present. This is the beginning of the concept of time, symbolic thinking, and cause-effect relationships.

Preoperational subperiod

The essential feature of the preoperational subperiod (ages 2 to 7 years) is that the child begins to use symbolism to represent his world, whereas previously he had been limited to dealing with the world in terms of immediate interaction in individual instances of activity. The child becomes able to separate symbols from what they represent and rapidly acquires a more complex symbol system.

The child is able to deal with the past as well as the future, and his ability to do this is the distinctive sign of symbolism. He becomes capable of mentally relating symbols rather than simply handling objects about him. Mental processes at this stage have been linked to mentally performing actions as if with the hands. In a sense the child "handles" objects through thinking. Language takes on significance because it serves in large measure as the processor of internal representation.

An understanding of certain Piagetian concepts is essential to further consideration of this subperiod. These concepts are egocentrism, reversibility, and concreteness.

The child is egocentric in the sense that he is incapable of seeing or understanding the world from any vantage point but his own. He has one point of view that is unique to him, and it is impossible to view the world in a manner foreign to his insulated awareness. Conversations of children of this age reveal interesting and sometimes amusing non-sequiturs that result from egocentric thinking. True communication cannot exist because it is necessary to appreciate another person's position. Children of this age are unsuccessful in participating in games that require understanding several roles.

Reversibility is related to egocentrism in that the child cannot reverse mental operations to a point of origin during the preoperational subperiod. In arithmetic, for example, the child is unable to reverse the operation $4 + 3 = 7$ to $7 - 3 = 4$. Classical tests used by Piaget can easily demonstrate this behavior.

One experiment uses balls made of equal amounts of clay or Plasticine; they are formed into identical shapes. The balls are presented to the child in this manner:

One is then changed in shape:

The child is asked if they are still equivalent. Typically, a preoperational child will state that the elongated shape is larger. The problem is related to the inability of a child to conserve, a concept that will be described later.

Concreteness, which describes the whole period, refers to the child being one step removed from the actual process of physical manipulation of objects. He performs the same tasks mentally that he could with his hands. He is not yet capable of making sophisticated judgments and seems to be tied to the concrete world; he is stimulus bound. Although his thinking is now symbolic, it is not truly abstract.

Concrete operations subperiod

In the concrete operations subperiod (ages 7 to 11 years) the elementary teacher can readily recognize features of the child's thinking as described by Piaget, especially since he employed school-related tasks to tap thinking processes. The child develops the concept of set and equivalence of sets, or one-to-one relations, and is not led to error by the perceptual arrangement of objects (for example, the clay balls) as previously.

In another experiment checkers or counters may be placed in one-to-one correspondence in two rows of equal numbers. The preoperational thinker will agree that both rows are equivalent. If one row is expanded to take up more space, the preoperational thinker will most generally give an intuitive response on examination and believe that there are more checkers in one or the other of the rows. (Remember, only the arrangement has been altered.) This is typical; the child is responding to spatial perceptions. The concrete operational thinker will not be confused by this. He is not controlled by perceptual factors; he has the ability to conserve. The child of this stage is less egocentric, begins to understand other points of view, and can participate in games that require the understanding of various roles.

The ability to conserve is evident when the child knows that number is not lost or changed when objects or groups of objects are rearranged or divided into subsets or when the form of an object is apportioned differently. This is a landmark in a child's thinking.

Formal operations period

The final period is very different from the other periods. The child emerges from the formal operations period with thinking processes that are characterized by abstract qualities. The formal thinker is able to remove himself from the world of real objects, to hypothesize, and to relate mental operations to one another without concrete referents. This is abstract thinking.

Piagetian theory has stimulated a reexamination of traditional theories of intelligence and intellectual development. As many theories have maintained that it is an accumulation and refinement of knowledge in the growing child, Piaget contends that the very nature of operations and structures changes during each period. Traditional theorists would quantify intelligence in terms of measured scores; Piaget would examine it in terms of qualitative differences.

The child in the sensorimotor period is limited in his concept of time, space, and object reality. The child in the concrete operational period is able to enjoy more freedom from the world of concrete objects, but his thinking is intimately tied to it. The formal thinker can disengage himself from the concrete world, perform mental operations of an abstract nature, deal with things that do not exist, think in the past or the future, or leave time constraints altogether.

This ability can apparently improve throughout a lifetime. Consider the philosophical concept of existentialism of which Satré is the most famous proponent. The qualitative differences, not measurable differences, of the three types of thinkers allow only the formal thinker to begin to grapple with such an abstraction, which entails nothing present or tangible and cannot be considered with concrete referents.

The student of child development will appreciate the unique abilities and limitations of a child in any given period of development. The type of thinking dictates what can be expected of the child in the arithmetic curriculum. Children pass through the various stages at varying rates. "Meeting the child where he is" or "teaching at his level"

takes on meaning when one can determine where the child is in his development.

As children enter school they have already progressed through many stages of development, but they do so at varying rates. Children between the ages of 5 and 8 years develop the ability to conserve. When the child can conserve, then he is in a position to effectively deal with the demands of the arithmetic curriculum. The teacher who thinks of each child in terms of these stages will understand teaching sequences. If a child is preceptually bound, a preoperational thinker, he will not be able to compare and contrast sets of objects. If the child cannot establish one-to-one correspondence, he is not ready to manage any of the basic arithmetic operations.

Summary

In *Science of Education and the Psychology of the Child* (1974), Piaget directly addresses the problem of instruction in mathematics. He asserts that mathematics is a direct extension of logic itself, so much so that it is impossible to separate the two. It seems paradoxical that there are students who are well endowed with logical thinking but unable to perform adequately in mathematics. Piaget explains that the operational structures of intelligence, being of logico-mathematical nature, are not consciously present in the child's mind. Rather they are structures of actions or operations that direct a child's thinking but are not objects of conscious reflection. Piaget compares this with being able to sing a tune without developing a theory of singing a tune or even reading music. Another useful comparison is that of a child who can use precise, traditional grammatical forms in spoken language without being able to identify grammatical rules. The process is automatic.

The use of mathematics, however, requires a child to consciously think about the structures that he uses through the medium of symbolism and abstraction. A child may generate immediate speech that conforms with conventional grammatical rules while using operational structures of intelligence automatically. In mathematics the child must make a transition from natural, nonreflective structures to conscious awareness of those structures. If the products of spoken language required the same processes as mathematics, the child would have to be consciously aware of internal operations of thinking as well as the rules of morphology, semantics, phonology, and syntax prior to the utterance of a lucid sentence.

The work of Piaget has been stressed to serve as a guide for instruction, not as a basis for a curriculum. The teacher who is familiar with the stages of development as described by Piaget will at least know what *not* to teach. If this is not an ideal strategy, at least the child will not be expected to perform in areas and at times when he is incapable of such performance. This would contribute to better teaching methods and eliminate useless, unnecessary feelings of failure experienced by many children.

ASSESSMENT PRACTICES

All school systems employ some method of assessment; achievement testing is often the major component. Achievement testing in arithmetic generally reflects a "frustration" level (a procedure similar to that used in reading) and caution must be used in interpreting results and determining instructional levels. The spread of scores, limited numbers of items, and basic design of achievement tests make these instruments of dubious value as they are sometimes employed.

Consider two children, both 8 years of age and in the same third-grade classroom. One child earns a grade achievement score of 4.9 and the other 2.3. Who is the underachiever? Perhaps neither is underachieving. Children in any class (as we may readily admit, but frequently forget) seldom have the same intellectual abilities. Test scores that are not properly used by the teacher or diagnostician can sometimes obscure the nature of a child's performance.

A procedure used by many practitioners (Johnson and Myklebust, 1967; Kolstoe, 1972) is helpful. Essentially it involves the determination of an expected learning quotient or grade expectancy. The formula used for this determination is as follows:

GRADE EXPECTANCY CHART

	IQ									
	85	*90*	*95*	*100*	*105*	*110*	*115*	*120*	*125*	*130*
CA										
6-0	0.1	0.4	0.7	1.0	1.3	1.6	1.9	2.2	2.5	2.8
6-6	0.5	0.8	1.1	1.5	1.8	2.1	2.4	2.8	3.1	3.4
7-0	0.9	1.3	1.6	2.0	2.3	2.7	3.0	3.4	3.7	4.1
7-6	1.4	1.7	2.1	2.5	2.9	3.2	3.6	4.0	4.4	4.7
8-0	1.8	2.2	2.6	3.0	3.4	3.8	4.2	4.6	5.0	5.4
8-6	2.3	2.7	3.1	3.5	3.9	4.3	4.8	5.2	5.6	6.0
9-0	2.6	3.1	3.5	4.0	4.4	4.9	5.3	5.8	6.2	6.7
9-6	3.1	3.5	4.0	4.5	4.9	5.4	5.9	6.4	6.8	7.3
10-0	3.5	4.0	4.5	5.0	5.5	6.0	6.5	7.0	7.5	8.0
10-6	3.9	4.4	4.9	5.5	6.0	6.5	7.0	7.5	8.0	8.5
11-0	4.3	4.9	5.3	6.0	6.5	7.1	7.6	8.2	8.7	9.3
11-6	4.8	5.3	5.9	6.5	7.1	7.6	8.2	8.8	9.4	9.9
12-0	5.2	5.8	6.4	7.0	7.6	8.2	8.8	9.4	10.0	10.6
12-6	5.6	6.2	6.9	7.5	8.1	8.7	9.4	10.0	10.6	11.2
13-0	6.0	6.7	7.3	8.0	8.6	9.3	9.9	10.6	11.2	11.9
13-6	6.5	7.1	7.8	8.5	9.2	9.8	10.5	11.2	11.9	12.5
14-0	6.9	7.6	8.3	9.0	9.7	10.4	11.1	11.8	12.5	13.2
14-6	7.3	8.0	8.7	9.5	10.2	10.9	11.7	12.4	13.1	13.8
15-0	7.7	8.5	9.2	10.0	10.7	11.5	12.2	13.0	13.7	14.5

$$\frac{IQ \times CA}{100} - 5 = \text{Grade expectancy.}$$

The teacher who uses this formula is in a position to more meaningfully evaluate children and interpret test information. If the formula indicates a grade expectancy of 2.3 and the child's achievement is actually within a reasonable range* of deviation from this score, then he should not be considered an underachiever regardless of his grade placement. Intraindividual differences are of utmost importance, and comparison of children with chronological age peers is unrealistic.

For quick reference the practitioner may use the grade expectancy chart on p. 122, which lists grade expectancies for children with IQ scores between 85 and 130 whose ages range between 6 and 15 years. The equivalencies are reported for each half year. To use the chart, enter the chronological age (CA) row (for example 7-6) and follow it across until the appropriate column is found for the IQ (for example, 110). The grade expectancy is located where the row and column intersect (3.2). Grade expectancy for a child with a discrepancy of 10 or more points between verbal and nonverbal IQ scores determined by tests such as the WISC should be determined by using the nonverbal score. This is especially true for children in grades one through four.

This simple technique should not be used without caution. There are many factors that should be considered in the diagnosis and educational preparation for children with learning disabilities. Therefore these grade expectancies are only estimations, and use of this technique must be combined with diagnostic information from other disciplines.

Arithmetic readiness

Readiness is a term that has been used by educators for many years. It is applied as a descriptive term in characterizing the behavior of children as they approach instruction in any of various subjects in the school curriculum. Textbooks, especially in reading, invariably include a section on readiness activities. The question must be asked, "Readiness for what?" Readiness is frequently viewed in terms of the student's ability to initiate processes or problem-solving activities. An evaluation of structures or thinking processes within the child is not usually attempted. Rather the child is introduced to certain problems and asked to perform; readiness is determined by the child's responses. Failure is seen as behavior that is below certain criteria. How far below? What does he actually do? What does he do incorrectly? These are questions that are not usually asked. Readiness activities are initiated by giving the child practice in tasks that he seems unable to perform.

Readiness should be determined by the teacher's evaluation of the student, a process that should be continuous and deliberate. Understanding of each child's learning characteristics accumulates from daily observations. This is not a task that can be satisfied by occasional formal testing. Knowledge of developmental milestones will assist the teacher to make such determinations.

Effective teaching strategies are implicit in the knowledge of cognitive development and the nature of arithmetic skills that can be managed by the child at any level of cognitive growth. The requirement of the arithmetic task and the nature of the child's thinking processes must be considered simultaneously. A grade equivalency score of 3.2 derived from an achievement test reveals only the most restricted information. Two children in the same class, each with the same achievement score, may vary greatly in learning styles, specific knowledge of arithmetic facts, and operations mastered. It is essential that the teacher know how the child is mentally equipped in a learning situation. Informal methods of assessment will help the teacher in this task.

Formal and informal methods

Assessment in mathematics includes both formal and informal methods. Formal assessment, often the responsibility of special personnel, utilizes standardized achievement and

*The "reasonable range" may be defined by state regulations governing eligibility for special programming.

diagnostic tests. Achievement tests usually provide the examiner with a grade equivalent to indicate the highest level of attainment by the child. A diagnostic test, which also yields a grade equivalent score, provides the teacher with information about the areas of strength and weakness underlying the various processes considered important to achievement.

Informal methods are not standardized but focus on elements of computation and attempt to uncover the nature of the child's thinking. Informal methods have not been widely used in arithmetic.

Formal methods are widely used in school districts across the nation. Teachers are familiar with most of the popular tests that are used. Many educational publishers have at least one such test. These tend to be similar, although some are more popular for a variety of reasons. However, all have limitations and teachers must not rely upon them inappropriately. Informal methods of assessment such as teacher-constructed tests can isolate behaviors and learning styles that are not sensitive to detection by most standardized achievement tests.

Many teachers are perplexed by the divergent scores a child might receive on different tests in arithmetic. This is sometimes a reflection of test error but is often a result of reading problems. Some tests present arithmetic problems with the simple requirement of computation. Other tests require considerable reading prior to problem solution. It is not uncommon for one child to have extremely different scores when comparisons are made between two such tests.

When considering the nature of learning activities, it is clear that some are related to language and some to nonverbal abilities. If the child has a language disorder, he will experience considerable difficulty in academic subjects. If a child's disorder can be assigned to known causes of reading failure or language disability, then the nature of instruction must be altered. If, however, the child experiences no serious problems in language and reading development, how should we view his difficulty with computation? Owing to the lack of definitive syndromes in arithmetic

disorders, the most tenable procedure seems to be examination of the child's logical development in terms of Piaget's developmental stages and in the actual processes of computation.

Mentally retarded children seem to perform at higher levels of achievement in arithmetic computation than in reading (Dunn, 1954). The reasons for this phenomenon are not so clearly established. Could it be hypothesized that retarded children, who do not develop abstract levels of thinking, find that these skills are not required in computation? Again, it is important to separate the functions of arithmetic and mathematics when considering the learning styles of children and how they process information.

It is difficult to establish a basis on which to delineate the separate activities of arithmetic and mathematics. Nonetheless, such a dichotomy must be established. In diagnostic efforts the teacher or diagnostician must determine if the child is failing because of inability to grasp abstract concepts or if the problem resides in processing and manipulation of concrete objects or symbols representing concrete objects.

Informal methods of assessment can be thought of as useful in analyzing the process by which a child solves a problem. This does not concern itself so much with the final response as with the nature of the computational process. In-depth analysis should reveal what the child does and how he does it. Such information is essential before planning intervention.

Formal tests. KeyMath is a diagnostic test developed by Connolly et al. (1971) that is unique because of the nature of its construction. It is being highlighted here because of its excellence.

> *Title:* KeyMath Diagnostic Arithmetic Test
> *Publisher:* American Guidance Service, Inc. Circle Pines, Minn. 55014
> *Description:* This test is based on the developmental sequence of skill acquisition and logical thinking of children and thus obviates the problems encountered in norm-referenced tests as applied to children with learning disorders. Most

such tests include about seven or eight items that are appropriate for such children, are timed, rely on reading skill, and are introduced in a multiple-choice format. Moreover, there is much emphasis on the computational process with pencil in hand. If the child is experiencing difficulty because of these reasons, little confidence can be placed in the results, which may be spurious for a variety of reasons.

Features of KeyMath include individual administration, virtual elimination of the reading and writing requirement, and open-ended problems. There are 14 subtests categorized into three areas. KeyMath includes an appendix that lists each subtest item with a description of the content sampled by each item. The examiner is able to record the items that the child fails, turn to the appendix, and find a written description of the process involved. In other words, rather than mere scores, the teacher is provided with a written analysis of the child's behaviors that can in turn be related to other diagnostic information.

Standardized achievement and diagnostic tests are used in most schools to determine functioning levels of students. Although most such tests are of value to determine approximate academic level, many do not lend themselves to diagnostic interpretation. A list of commonly used tests follows.

Title: Peabody Individual Achievement Test
Publisher: American Guidance Service, Inc.
Circle Pines, Minn. 55014
Description: This test measures achievement in several areas, including mathematics. It yields grade equivalents, age equivalents, standard scores, and percentile ranks.

Title: SRA Achievement Series
Publisher: Science Research Associates, Inc.
259 East Erie St.
Chicago, Ill. 60611
Description: This achievement test is useful for testing children in grades two through six. It measures skills in the areas of concepts, reasoning, and computation.

Title: Stanford Diagnostic Arithmetic Test
Publisher: Harcourt Brace Jovanovich, Inc.
Test Department
757 Third Ave.
New York, N.Y. 10017
Description: This test is provided in two forms that overlap and cover the second through the

eighth grades. The test gives information in the form of stanines, percentiles, and grade level equivalents. Also this test can be scored by a computer with a programmed readout for interpretation and recommendations.

Title: Metropolitan Achievement Tests
Publisher: Harcourt Brace Jovanovich, Inc.
Test Department
757 Third Ave.
New York, N.Y. 10017
Description: This test is given to children in the third through the ninth grades and offers two scores: computation and problem-solving concepts.

Title: California Achievement Tests
Publisher: California Test Bureau
McGraw-Hill Division
Del Monte Research Park
Monterey, Calif. 93940
Description: The subtest for arithmetic gives three scores: reasoning, fundamentals, and total test. It may be used in grades one through nine.

Title: Wide Range Achievement Test
Publisher: Western Psychological Services
12031 Wilshire Blvd.
Los Angeles, Calif. 90025
Description: The WRAT is provided in two forms; the range is from kindergarten to college level. The arithmetic sections on both forms are designed to virtually eliminate reading. The test is individually administered and can be completed within 10 minutes.

Title: Los Angeles Diagnostic Tests
Publisher: California Test Bureau
McGraw-Hill Division
Del Monte Research Park
Monterey, Calif. 93940
Description: These tests are used with children in grades two through nine and measure skill in the four basic computational areas and in reasoning.

Title: Diagnostic Arithmetic Tests
Publisher: California Test Bureau
McGraw-Hill Division
Del Monte Research Park
Monterey, Calif. 93940
Description: This test measures skill development in the four computational areas: weights, percentage, measures, and fractions.

Title: Pattern Recognition Skills Inventory
Publisher: Hubbard Press
2855 Shermer Road
Northbrook, Ill. 60062

Description: This instrument is for use with children between the ages of 5 and 10 years. It analyzes the development of pattern recognition ability and the relationship of this ability to the development of other cognitive concepts. The inventory enables teachers to understand why students display knowledge of certain concepts and not others.

There are a number of additional tests or parts of test batteries in use throughout the United States, but the preceding are among the more commonly used and represent the variety of tests available.

Informal assessment. Techniques in the informal assessment of arithmetic errors are becoming more refined. This type of assessment can be implemented by the teacher and can yield satisfying results. In the past the errors were seen as resulting from inability to grasp the "idea" of an arithmetic process, and the remedy was practice. It is clear that the learning styles of children and the nature of various learning disorders vary from one child to another. It is as important to devote time to the assessment of arithmetic processes as well as to characteristics of the learner.

Two recent books might be considered when developing informal assessment strategies. The *Handbook in Diagnostic Teaching: A Learning Disabilities Approach* by Mann and Suiter (1974) contains a section on arithmetic that includes the sequence of grade level arithmetic and a very complete arithmetic inventory that can be used by the teacher for informal assessment. *A Guide to the Diagnostic Teaching of Arithmetic* by Reisman (1972) is useful in developing an informal diagnosis of arithmetic; however, its use should not be restricted to this area. The guides outlined are useful in directing attention to the nature of learning difficulty, methods of diagnosing mathematics problems, and diagnostic teaching.

Reisman (1972) has developed an analysis chart that is pertinent to any informal strategy. Inclusion of the chart is for reference in informal assessment by the teacher. The chart includes examples of common errors in elementary school mathematics and anal-

ysis of the reasoning for them to serve as a diagnostic aid when the child is in need of reteaching.

TEACHING ARITHMETIC SKILLS

Piaget demonstrates that the origination of the concept of number is interrelated with the development of logic. Prior to the development of numerical concepts, the child's thinking is called prelogical. As the child is able to deal with the conservation of objects he is similarly developing processes of classification on the basis of likenesses and ordering on the basis of differences. Childhood is a time in which the child organizes and categorizes his environment while developing language and logical thinking as a result of his direct encounters with the objects and activities of his world.

In his investigation of these interactions Piaget identified the development of logical thinking and the child's ability to consider, and later conserve, continuous and discontinuous quantities, ordinality and cardinality, and the basic computational processes derived from logical thinking. To Piaget the concept of number is the synthesis of class and asymmetrical relations.

Piagetian "tests" or experiments, replicated many times, have been used to study these operations. The conservation of continuous quantities may be examined by having equal amounts of water in identical glass containers. These are presented to the child and he is allowed to satisfy himself that the quantities are equivalent. The quantity of one is poured into a container of a different shape and size and the child is requested to determine if the amounts are still equivalent. A child who cannot conserve, generally younger than 7 years old but sometimes older, will be confused by the perceptual change and often believes that the amount in the container with the highest water level is greater.

The child is bound by the perceptual configuration; he does not conserve. The process of developing conservation passes through gradual stages; sometimes the child is accurate, sometimes he is not. As the child is able to take into account two factors, height and

Text continued on p. 131.

ERROR ANALYSIS CHART*

Analysis	*Example*

1. Lacks mastery of basic addition combinations

$$\begin{array}{r} 32 \\ +43 \\ \hline 74 \end{array}$$

2. Lacks mastery of basic subtraction combinations

$$\begin{array}{r} 38 \\ -25 \\ \hline 12 \end{array}$$

3. Lacks mastery of basic multiplication combinations

$$\begin{array}{r} 32 \\ \times 3 \\ \hline 86 \end{array}$$

4. Lacks mastery of basic division combinations

$$35 \div 5 = 6$$

$$\begin{array}{r} 6 \\ 9\overline{)56} \\ -56 \\ \hline 0 \end{array}$$

5. Subtracts incorrectly within the division algorithm

$$\begin{array}{r} 3)\quad 73\ R1 \\ 70) \\ 3\overline{)230} \\ -21 \\ \hline 10 \leftarrow \\ -9 \\ \hline 1 \end{array}$$

6. Error in addition of partial product

$$\begin{array}{r} 432 \\ \times 57 \end{array}$$

3	0	24
21	6	0
24	0	24

7. Does not complete addition
   a. Does not write regrouped number

$$\begin{array}{r} 85 \\ +43 \\ \hline 28 \end{array}$$

   b. Leaves out numbers in column addition

$$\begin{array}{r} 4 \\ 8 \\ 2 \leftarrow \\ + 3 \\ \hline 15 \end{array}$$

8. Rewrites a numeral without computing

$$\begin{array}{r} 72 \\ +15 \\ \hline \rightarrow 77 \end{array}$$

$$\begin{array}{r} \rightarrow 32 \\ \times 3 \\ \hline \rightarrow 36 \end{array}$$

9. Does not complete subtraction

$$\begin{array}{r} 582 \\ - 35 \\ \hline 47 \end{array}$$

ERROR ANALYSIS CHART—cont'd

10. Does not complete division because of incompleted subtraction

$$
\begin{array}{r}
1)\ 41 \\
40) \\
7\,\overline{)\,397} \\
-280 \\
\hline
7 \\
7 \\
\hline
\end{array}
$$

11. Fails to complete division; stops at first partial quotient

$$
\begin{array}{r}
50 \\
7\,\overline{)\,370} \\
350 \\
\hline
\end{array}
$$

12. Fails to complete division; leaves remainder greater than divisor

$$
\begin{array}{r}
80\ R9 \\
9\,\overline{)\,729} \\
720 \\
\hline
9 \\
\hline
\end{array}
$$

13. Does not complete multiplication within division algorithm

$$
\begin{array}{r}
1)\ 201\ R3 \\
200 \\
3\,\overline{)\,603} \\
600 \\
\hline
3 \\
\hline
\end{array}
$$

14. Does not add by bridging endings; should think 5 + 9 = 14, so 35 + 9 = 44

$$
\begin{array}{r}
35 \\
+\ 9 \\
\hline
33 \\
\end{array}
$$

15. Lacks additive concept in addition

$$
\begin{array}{r}
35 \\
+\ 20 \\
\hline
50 \\
\end{array}
$$

16. Confuses multiplicative identity within addition operation

$$
\begin{array}{r}
71 \\
+\ 13 \\
\hline
73 \\
\end{array}
$$

17. Lacks additive identity concept in subtraction

$$
\begin{array}{r}
43 \\
-\ 20 \\
\hline
20 \\
\end{array}
$$

18. Confuses role of zero in subtraction with role of zero in multiplication

$$
\begin{array}{r}
37 \\
-\ 20 \\
\hline
10 \\
\end{array}
$$

19. Subtracts top digit from bottom digit whenever regrouping is involved with zero in minuend

$$
\begin{array}{r}
30 \\
-\ 18 \\
\hline
28 \\
\end{array}
$$

20. Confuses role of zero in multiplication with multiplicative identity

$$7 \times 0 = 7$$

21. Confuses place value of quotient by adding extra zero

$$
\begin{array}{r}
20 \\
30\,\overline{)\,60} \\
\end{array}
$$

22. Omits zero in quotient

$$
\begin{array}{r}
30\ R3 \\
4\,\overline{)\,1203} \\
1200 \\
\hline
3 \\
\hline
\end{array}
$$

ERROR ANALYSIS CHART—cont'd

23. Lacks facility with addition algorithm.

    a. Adds ones to ones *and* tens

    $$\begin{array}{r} 37 \\ +\ 2 \\ \hline 59 \end{array}$$

    b. Adds tens to tens *and* hundreds

    $$\begin{array}{r} 342 \\ +\ 36 \\ \hline 678 \end{array}$$

    c. Adds ones to tens *and* hundreds

    $$\begin{array}{r} 132 \\ +\ 6 \\ \hline 798 \end{array}$$

    d. Is unable to add horizontally $345 + 7 + 13 = 185$

    Thinks: $3 + 7 + 1 = 11$; writes 1 $\begin{array}{r} 8 \\ 5 \\ \hline 185 \end{array}$
           $4 + 3 \quad = 7 \quad (+\ 1\ \text{carried})$
           $5 \quad = 5$

24. Does not regroup ones to tens

    $$\begin{array}{r} 37 \\ +\ 25 \\ \hline 52 \end{array}$$

25. Does not regroup tens to hundreds
    (or hundreds to thousands)

    $$\begin{array}{r} 973 \\ +\ 862 \\ \hline 735 \end{array}$$

26. Regroups when unnecessary

    $$\begin{array}{r} 43 \\ +\ 24 \\ \hline 77 \end{array}$$

27. Writes regrouped tens digit in ones place; carries one
    digit (writes the 1 and carries 2 from "12")

    $$\begin{array}{r} ② \\ 35 \\ +\ 7 \\ \hline 51 \end{array}$$

28. When there are fewer digits in subtrahend:

    a. Subtracts ones from ones *and* from tens (*and* hundreds)

    $$\begin{array}{r} 783 \\ -\ 2 \\ \hline 561 \end{array}$$

    b. Substracts tens from tens *and* hundreds

    $$\begin{array}{r} 783 \\ -\ 23 \\ \hline 560 \end{array}$$

29. Does not rename tens digit after regrouping

    $$\begin{array}{r} 54 \\ -\ 9 \\ \hline 55 \end{array}$$

30. Does not rename hundreds digit after regrouping

    $$\begin{array}{r} 532 \\ -\ 181 \\ \hline 451 \end{array}$$

31. Does not rename hundreds or tens when renaming ones

    $$\begin{array}{r} 906 \\ -\ 238 \\ \hline 778 \end{array}$$

ERROR ANALYSIS CHART—cont'd

32. Does not rename tens when zero is in tens place, although hundreds are renamed

$$\begin{array}{r} 803 \\ -\ 478 \\ \hline 335 \end{array}$$

33. When there are two zeros in the minuend, renames hundreds twice but does not rename tens

$$\begin{array}{r} 5 \\ \cancel{6}11 \\ \cancel{7}00 \\ 326 \\ \hline 248 \end{array}$$

34. Decreases hundreds digit by one when unnecessary

$$\begin{array}{r} \boxed{3}\,7\ 1 \\ -\ \boxed{1}\,3\ 4 \\ \hline \boxed{1}\,3\ 7 \end{array}$$

35. Uses ones place factor as addend

$$\begin{array}{r} 32 \\ \times\ 4 \\ \hline 126 \end{array}$$

36. Adds regrouped number to tens but does not multiply $(7 \times 5 = 35; 30 + 30 = 60)$

$$\begin{array}{r} 35 \\ \times\ 7 \\ \hline 65 \end{array}$$

37. Multiplies digits within one factor $(4 \times 1 = 4; 1 \times 30 = 30)$

$$\begin{array}{r} 31 \\ \times\ 4 \\ \hline 34 \end{array}$$

38. Multiplies by only one number

$$\begin{array}{r} 457 \\ \times\ 12 \\ \hline 914 \end{array}$$

39. Carries wrong number

$$\begin{array}{r} 8 \\ 67 \\ \times\ 40 \\ \hline 3220 \end{array}$$

40. Does not multiply one times tens

$$\begin{array}{r} 32 \\ \times\ 24 \\ \hline 648 \end{array}$$

41. Reverses divisor with dividend (thinks 6 + 3 instead of 30 + 6)

$$6\ \overline{\smash{\big)}\ 30}\ \ {}^{2}$$

42. Does not regroup; treats each column as separate addition example

$$\begin{array}{r} 23 \\ +\ 8 \\ \hline 211 \end{array}$$

43. Substracts smaller digit from larger at all times to avoid renaming

$$\begin{array}{r} 273 \\ -\ 639 \\ \hline 446 \end{array}$$

44. Does not add regrouped number

$$\begin{array}{r} 37 \\ \times\ 7 \\ \hline 219 \end{array}$$

ERROR ANALYSIS CHART—cont'd

45. Confuses place value in division

    $$1)$$
    $$200)\ 201$$
    $$3\overline{\smash{\big)}\,6003}$$
    $$6000$$
    $$\overline{3}$$
    $$3$$

    a. Considers thousands divided by ones as hundreds divided by ones

    b. Records partial quotient as tens instead of ones

    $$50)$$
    $$100)\ 150$$
    $$7\overline{\smash{\big)}\,735}$$
    $$-\ 700$$
    $$\overline{35}$$
    $$35$$

    c. Omits zero needed to show no ones in quotient

    $$2\ R1$$
    $$3\overline{\smash{\big)}\,61}$$
    $$6$$
    $$\overline{1}$$

46. Ignores remainder because:
    a. Does not complete subtraction
    b. Does not see need for further computation
    c. Does not know what to do with "2" if subtraction occurs, so does not complete further

    $$80$$
    $$7\overline{\smash{\big)}\,562}$$
    $$560$$
    $$\overline{}$$

---

width, then he can disregard the perceptual factors leading to his confusion and respond correctly.

Conservation of discontinuous quantity is tested by placing equivalent numbers of marbles or beads into containers that are identical. This is similar to the method just described. The marbles are manipulated from one container to another, and the child is asked about the equivalency of marbles in differently shaped containers. If he succeeds in not being confused by the perceptual change, he is a conserver of number.

Investigations of one-to-one correspondence proceed along the lines of establishing equivalent sets. The child is presented with the task of matching two sets of objects of different classes such as bottles and caps or eggs and cups. There are three noticeable stages of development. Initially the child is bound by perceptual considerations impinging on his reasoning. The objects that occupy more space are thought to be more in number. In the second stage the child can establish equivalency by matching but is confused if the spatial arrangement is disrupted. Finally, as in other developments noted, he is able to disregard perceptual inconsistencies and know that arrangement does not affect the number.

It can be seen that the practice of counting, which is taught by rote to very young children, has little meaning in the development of the concept of equivalence. It is useful in later development as language begins to facilitate the learning process, but Piaget makes it clear that motor activity precedes language development. The importance of this to the teacher is that the child should be given as much freedom as possible to interact with his environment in order to understand and to learn. The child will not learn effectively through strict verbal instruction; he must use his hands.

Through his senses the child learns that objects are simultaneously equivalent but quite different in color, substance, shape, and density. This learning is reflected in logical and conceptual development by evidence that the child can group, classify, and order objects. To know the number system the child must satisfactorily develop two mental operations. The child must be capable of intellectually considering cardination and ordination simultaneously. The number "5" is symbolic of a group or set that represents a class, and it also may be representative of serial order or position. The child does not really understand numbers until he can use these two systems. When he can, the door to mathematical operations is opened.

Another example of the caution necessary in using published programs is the fact that many recent texts introduce cardination prior to ordination. Brainerd (1973) has shown that children first become aware of number in terms of ordered sequences and later in terms of quantity. The sequence of conceptual thinking is ordination first, the number second, and then cardination. The practice of many programs of reversing this process runs counter to normal development in children and underscores the need for teachers to adapt any book or materials to the child's ability and sequences of cognitive growth.

Manipulation of objects

A rich world exists for the child and the teacher if freedom is allowed and confinement to the desk or table is avoided. The teacher should provide the child an opportunity to interact with the environment in as many ways as possible. This is sound practice if the needs of children in an active learning environment are considered. To put children into chairs in rows and talk about arithmetic and mathematics is not a satisfactory approach to teaching. Children must have every exciting and active experience possible to discover, touch, and incorporate sensations into a repertoire of gradual achievement. Learning by doing, at least as old as the philosophy of John Dewey, is reiterated in the findings of Piaget and other contemporary theorists.

Discrimination

The world of concrete objects is filled with things that are interesting to feel, smell, taste, push, roll, kick, toss, spin, bounce, catch, pull, and hide. The child can discover characteristics of objects and thus develop concepts of smoothness, roughness, hardness, softness, and much more. By involvement in such experiences the child learns to categorize objects by commonalities of texture, color, size, and shape. This inevitably leads to determination of distinctiveness or discrimination. If discrimination can be made, then differences can be enumerated, and this culminates in more abstract concepts of classification. A classification is a set.

Sets

A set is a number of real or symbolic objects that can be grouped according to a defined characteristic. This is a difficult concept that emerges with the development of logical thought.

Piaget describes a child who, as a preoperational thinker, experiences difficulty in thinking of a set of wooden beads being composed of subsets of colored beads. For example, if there are 20 wooden beads that can be divided into three groups according to their colors (5 red, 5 blue, and 10 yellow), the preoperational thinker cannot simultaneously think of a total set of wooden beads and the three subsets of wooden beads grouped by colors. As he attends to the quality of color, he forgets that the beads are also wooden. If he thinks about them being made of wood, he cannot retain the color distinctions. This is a function of the type of thinking associated with mental development. The concrete thinker is able to simultaneously attend to more than one variable and to reverse objects into sets and subsets using various permutations. The only way to develop this ability is through experience.

Classifying objects by likenesses and differences in terms of many characteristics is a goal. Attribute blocks or any physical, tangible objects can be used for this purpose. Beads, blocks, cans—anything—can be brought into the classroom and presented to the children, who are asked to think of ways in which to compare and contrast the objects. The variety of concrete materials for use in the development of set concepts is virtually unlimited. When children are able to identify the qualifications for membership in a set, they are ready for a new stage of instruction.

Set comparisons

Set comparison is much more complex than the activities just described. The child is now required to associate sets, which may be different or similar, in one-to-one correspondence. Essentially the child is presented with the task of matching sets that contain equal numbers of different objects. Young children are able to establish equivalence but are confused by the perceptual or spatial factor if one row of objects is spread across a wider field. Children of the age of 6 to 7 years begin to conserve and will be able to understand that the equivalence remains regardless of the different spaces between objects in two rows. One-to-one correspondence is essential to an understanding of fundamental arithmetic.

Ordination and natural numbers

As explained earlier, the research of Brainerd (1973) indicates that ordination seems to appear before cardination (sets). In fact, elements of both may appear simultaneously, with ordination taking the lead. In its simplest explanation ordination is the concept of order in a sequence. The child is required to learn that the status of an object in a row from one end or the other is first, second, third, to the nth position. Identification of the ordinal position of an object is represented by ordinal numbers (1st, 2nd, 3rd . . . nth).

Counting is used as an activity that attempts to center attention and learning on ordinal concepts. A child who counts from rote or "parrots" counting is not truly learning ordinal concepts, and he shows naïveté if he is asked to identify a position that is reversed. (See the earlier discussion of reversibility.) Counting can proceed on the basis of twos, threes, and so on until facility is developed with counting behavior.

Ultimately *the child will need to fuse ordination and cardination into a single ability.* The two systems do not serve the child if they remain independent. It is important to recognize that training and experience with ordination will facilitate the use of natural numbers by children in simple computational problems. It appears that working with sets exclusively (cardination) will not facilitate the development and use of natural numbers. Perhaps the teacher should stress ordination in young children because it seems to develop first, and children need this skill to perform satisfactorily in the solution of addition and subtraction problems.

If the child has reached a level of intuitive thought, he will have such concepts as "more than" and "greater than" and have ideas about objects in terms of perceived relationships. Younger children are stimulus bound and will regard any person as older if he is taller than another. Cause and effect are also viewed intuitively.

When the child is able to classify and categorize by sets, his experience leads to knowledge of equivalency of sets and one-to-one correspondence. This is related to concepts of quantity. As ordinality develops, objects can be placed into sequences according to some characteristic such as short to tall.

Next the child must learn the commutative and associative properties of addition. With the development of conservation, the child is able to reverse processes and can regroup. Addition facts will be at a higher level, and the child can deal with subtraction problems. Reversibility allows the child to complete an addition problem or subtraction problem and reverse the operations. Teachers will recognize that a child may be able to add $\frac{3}{+2}$ accurately, but he may have difficulty with $\frac{3}{+\Box}$. However, this problem is much simpler than adding $\frac{\Box}{+\ 3}$. Knowledge of the functions of reversibility and conservation adds a dimension of clarity to the process of logical thought explored by the child as he attacks such problems.

Subtraction is intrinsically related to addition. It is virtually impossible to compute simple subtraction without being able to perform addition operations. Subtraction is a process rooted in reversibility. A child should not be expected to perform these problems until he has reached the level of thinking that makes problem solution possible.

Multiplicative and additive compositions are related, and according to Piaget, mastery of one implies mastery of the other. Because multiplication stands at an upper level in the hierarchy of skills, difficulty with it may mean that addition was not truly mastered.

It is rather simple to provide concrete problems that are typical of addition, subtraction, and even division, but this is not true of multiplication. Therefore multiplication may be introduced to a child in the following manner:

$$2 + 2 = \ \ 4 \rightarrow 2 \times 2 = \ \ 4$$
$$4 + 4 = \ \ 8 \rightarrow 2 \times 4 = \ \ 8$$
$$8 + 8 = 16 \rightarrow 2 \times 8 = 16$$

This uses the foundation of additive properties as a springboard for multiplication rather than using the traditional tables.

In all of the operations of addition, subtraction, and multiplication the teacher might consider the perceptual demands of the activity. If addition is taught in rows, it should always be introduced in rows; if in columns, then it should remain constant until the child is able to demonstrate he can switch without confusion.

Division is often thought of as the reverse process of multiplication. Piaget contradicts this with the suggestion that it is more closely associated with additive composition. In addition the child grasps the concept that the sum of parts is equivalent to the whole. Distributing the parts of the whole is the reverse process of addition; it is not subtraction and certainly not multiplication—it is division. Addition is association; division is dissociation.

The quality and quantity of educational research into the teaching of arithmetic is low. This is a serious problem, but it should not deter us from making applications of theories and teaching strategies that show promise. It should not be surprising to find that many problems will yield to the intervention of competent teaching. Such strategies would, by definition, have to be based on the current knowledge of cognitive development, arithmetic skills, analysis of errors, assessment of cognitive development, and application of appropriate techniques in concert with well-designed materials. Children cannot wait until research efforts are expanded nor can they be expected to make significant gains in arithmetic achievement by concentrating on noneducational training.

Certain factors must be considered in this regard. The use of drills has been attacked by many authors in the last decade. However, the research indicates that many children with learning problems must have an opportunity to overlearn. In perhaps a simplistic definition, overlearning is the result of drills. Each individual must then have an opportunity to apply what he learns for it to remain intact within the secondary retrieval system, or long-term memory. This has a bearing on the use of arithmetic skills and knowledge in solving computational problems. *The emphasis of many new programs has been on the more abstract processes underlying practical application. This approach directs training toward definite weaknesses in many learning-disabled children.* Therefore it is postulated that drills may be necessary for children to be equipped with the necessary, memorized information to be used in solving problems. If the child is familiar with the process of multiplication, understands the operations, and can verbalize the functions of the process but is not able to instantly state the product of 6×6, he is at a disadvantage.

It is not suggested that the curriculum should be primarily memorization, but it should be recognized that drills are necessary. Creative ways should be developed in which to disguise drills in the form of stimulating activities. *Sufficient and varied practice in the basic operations of addition, subtraction, multiplication, and division is mandatory.*

Teachers should not think that they are committing professional heresy if they deviate markedly from basic textbook approaches and curriculum guides. As pointed out earlier, many of the approaches are not well constructed in that they ignore important developmental considerations. The teacher who recognizes this, who develops an understanding of child growth, and who develops personal expertise can make appropriate educational decisions.

Language and math

Many problems in mathematics and arithmetic are related to language disorders of children. Johnson and Myklebust (1967) have addressed themselves to this and other causes of failure. Language disorders must be remedied by the teacher. However, if achievement in arithmetic and mathematics is desired, the teacher must conceive of methods to circumvent the language hurdle. An interesting technique has been used by Furth (1966), who has experimented with symbolic and logical development of deaf children through the visual channel. Although this method was used by Furth as a teaching demonstration of logical thinking with deaf children, I have employed a modified system to teach arithmetic in a classroom of learning-disabled children.

The technique requires that the children remain silent and that all operations stem from visual imagery as initiated in blackboard exercises. Training can involve approximately 1 hour of the class day. In resource and itinerant programs the technique would have to be adapted for use within the time constraints, but could be extended into the regular class by the classroom teacher.

The teacher begins the exercise by having the children reproduce activities on the board or on paper. A few symbols are placed on the board:

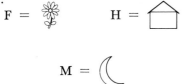

Then the children are asked to complete missing symbols.

They rapidly respond with "S."

For a while at this early stage the teacher can continue to introduce many pictures of objects on the board and require the children to fill in the appropriate symbol. Anything can be used, but the simplest objects requiring only quick, simple artistic skill are desirable. Stars, stick people, houses, trees, and cars are excellent examples.

After the children become comfortable with this activity, it is possible to introduce the concept of a negative by placing a straight line above a symbol and shaking the head or saying "no" to communicate the negative concept:

or

Then the teacher can deliberately place problems on the board and have children correct errors or make the problems equivalent, depending on the task. The following problem may be presented:

This problem can be solved in at least two ways:

or

It can be seen that the children can process increasingly difficult concepts requiring logical, although nonverbal, thinking. This is the goal—to diminish oral instruction.

It is surprising how children, even very young ones, can easily process some difficult concepts that they would otherwise not be able to understand or express if restricted to spoken language for instruction and response modes. This technique, which emphasizes arithmetic concepts, can incorporate all of the symbols of arithmetic that are popularly used in modern texts: $+$, $-$, $=$, $\times$, $\therefore$, $\because$, $>$, $<$, $\rightarrow$, etc. It is important to remember that oral instruction is not used, with few exceptions. Examples with other symbols are:

Sets can be represented by classification of many objects on one side of the operation while changing the order on the other. Children learn that there is still equivalency regardless of the arrangement. For example: $F + F + F + S + S =$

The nature of these activities can become increasingly more complex and the children can be guided into a transition from pictographs to the use of arithmetic symbols and algorithms exclusively, with virtual elimination of spoken language. This approach is in keeping with Piagetian principles and the nature of language disabilities.

Money concepts

The use of money in developing concepts is essential. Children need to handle it and use it in practical situations. Using pictures of money in a workbook is just not as practical. Any number of games and types of "classroom economies" can promote the development of skill in this area. They key is practice. The primary prerequisites of the child's ability are that he understand addition, subtraction, and place values.

Measurements and fractions

Introduction of measurement requires a strategy to get children to see a need for standard measuring units. As will be explained, this is accomplished by having children measure objects in the class by means of nonstandard units such as books or chalk sticks and comparing the number of items required in each instance.

Fractions should be introduced by using a variety of concrete objects that can be sectioned or separated into subgroups. A fraction represents subparts of one object or subsets of larger sets that are classified by common characteristics.

Time: a digital system*

The problems involved in teaching time concepts and the use of a clock are well known. The learning process requires the use of a different number base, and directional confusion and language deficiencies pose formidable barriers when traditional prepositions and fractional words are employed (to, from, till, before, after, half-past, etc.).

To facilitate learning it is necessary to circumvent these barriers. An ability to count by fives to 55 and to recognize the numerals 1 through 12 are essential prerequisites. This approach will not necessarily lead to an understanding of time *concepts*, which requires a higher level of cognitive development. Children who learn to read a clock face by any method do not necessarily comprehend time concepts until late childhood, and a child must be 8 to 9 years of age before he is able to read a two-hand placement by 1-minute intervals. Until that time a normal child relies on rote learning. In a digital system the child is taught to read the minute hand by counting by fives in a clockwise direction until he reaches the placement of the minute hand. The child does not count a

*I wish to express my gratitude to Ted Montemurro for his assistance with this section.

unit of five until the hand has crossed the plane of the next numeral. For example:

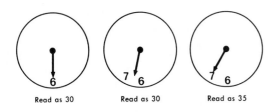

Read as 30   Read as 30   Read as 35

The same procedure is used for the hour hand. The child is taught to read the hour hand at the numeral it has passed and not to read the next numeral until the hour hand crosses the plane of the next numeral. For example:

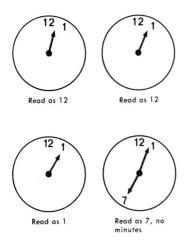

Read as 12   Read as 12

Read as 1   Read as 7, no
                             minutes

The problem that may be encountered here is that the child must be able to visually discriminate the accurate placement of the hour hand between numerals. The use of large learning models and clear plastic overlays in the shape of pie wedges to center attention on the discriminable elements are of value. As the child learns to make accurate discriminations, he can read a clock by the hour and by 5-minute intervals. This system should be successful with many learning-disabled children.

INSTRUCTIONAL PROGRAMS

As noted previously, few programs have been specifically designed for use with children who have learning disabilities. Many programs that have been developed are not based on empirical evidence or sound theory. It is encouraging to note that this is changing. New programs are being developed by authors who take into account the thinking processes of children rather than assemble materials that are based on a priori opinion.

The important task is to fuse theory and practical application. This is not an easy task, and an understanding of theory is a prerequisite. Theory guides instruction, and instruction without theory will continue to flounder. Therefore there is no emphasis on gimmicks, games, or suggested "cookbook" activities. (Most teachers are aware of such activities anyway.) The task is one of directing attention to factors that have too long been ignored but that hold promise for improving instructional techniques. Games, activities, and highly developed programs may be effectively used after considering the principles of assessment, abilities of the child, analysis of errors, and knowledge of the teaching process.

Historical attempts in the development of corrective approaches are few. Fernald (1943), who is most noted for her widely used technique in reading, was of the opinion that there is no such thing as a normal child who cannot learn to do arithmetic. Primary emphasis in the Fernald technique is placed on considerable practice with computational problems.

Strauss and Lehtinen (1947) viewed arithmetic development as an expression of inherent organizational tendencies and the capacity for abstraction. Largely influenced by the Gestalt school of psychology, Strauss and Lehtinen believed that brain-injured children were incapable of this organizational capacity. They advocated an approach to develop a scheme of visual spatial organization with emphasis on the relatedness of parts of the scheme. This was considered important because difficulties in arithmetic were attributed to general disturbances of perception and behavior or specific perceptual disturbances that prevent organization of meanings and development of an adequate perceptual scheme.

Jansky (1965), writing in one of the first volumes devoted to the new field of learning disabilities a decade ago, contributed a seven-page article dealing with arithmetic disorders that were caused by what was termed plasticity in two children. Since that time few authoritative articles or methods have been developed, and certainly the research has been limited.

Due to the recent controversies involving noneducational therapies thought to improve academic achievement, the status of research in arithmetic and mathematics dictates that initial attention begin at the content level rather than emphasizing training directed at peripheral skills. It is obvious that visual perception, auditory perception, motor skills, and other similar factors should receive attention. However, the relationship of these processes to arithmetic achievement is ill-defined, and the teacher would be advised to refrain from expecting improvement in arithmetic and mathematics solely from training exercises rooted in noneducational therapies until these processes are clarified.

KeyMath Instruction

A promising instructional program is currently being developed by Connolly et al., authors of KeyMath. They have drawn on the contributions of Piaget, Bruner, Dienes, Benoit, Guilford, and Gagné to develop Key-Math Instruction (KMI) in arithmetic under the auspices of the American Guidance Service, Inc. Field testing is being completed and instructional materials should be marketed in the near future. Its development should be a welcome and significant contribution to the instruction of children with learning disorders.

Weaving together the various elements of theory and practical application of instructions, the KMI sequence will incorporate the following principles that could be the framework of any sound mathematics program.

1. Learning is based on self-experience and moves from concrete to abstract.
2. Learning should be preceded by participation of the learner, even at the abstract level.
3. Learning is enhanced by verbalization.
4. Learning should incorporate various thought processes involved in problem solving.
5. Learning is most efficient when the difficulty of the content is precisely sequenced and new tasks are related to mastery at lower levels of learning.
6. The learner should have exposure to a multiplicity of concepts under investigation.
7. Learning is a process that demands a variety of practice modes and confirmation by the learner.
8. Although learning is an experience that is an individual process, it can be effected in group instruction.

The program content of KMI is developed in strands; the sequence of the instruction being developed merges the child's level of functioning with appropriate materials. Lessons are developed with an objective, a prerequisite of learner behavior; for example, "The child can match objects through one-to-one correspondence." Lessons will include concept presentation instructions, a method of concept exploration activities, student discussion guides, and seatwork exercises. If the teacher determines that a child does not have the prerequisite skills such as one-to-one correspondence of objects, this activity would not be introduced.

An integral part of the KMI approach is careful consideration of instructional activity. For example, fractions will be introduced with part-to-whole representation of unitary fractions before part-to-group representation of unitary fractions. Then the program leads from part-to-whole nonunitary fractions and finally to part-to-group nonunitary fractions. Many other programs include pages of activities that mix the various operations rather than following the instructional sequence as outlined by the KMI method.

Another area of concern is measurement. Too often children are introduced to the use of a ruler or yardstick without preliminary training. The KMI approach will begin with measurement of ordinary environmental objects such as tables with nonstandard measurement. This could be measurement with books of the same size, then pencils, paper clips, or crayons. After witnessing and participating in these activities, children should more quickly recognize the need for standard units of measurement.

Other instructional programs

Title: Diagnostic and Learning Activities in Mathematics for Children
Publisher: Macmillan Publishing Co., Inc.
866 Third Ave.
New York, N.Y. 10022

Description: This book is a companion to a text designed by Copeland to assist the teacher in mathematics instruction. It is based on Piaget's theories. There are 32 activities arranged under four groupings: space, number, logical classification, and measurement. These activities are associated with approximate ages at which children develop certain kinds of thinking. It is possible for the teacher to use the activities to investigate the abilities of a child and in planning an instructional program.

Title: DISTAR Arithmetic I, II, and III
Publisher: Science Research Associates, Inc.
259 East Erie St.
Chicago, Ill. 60611

Description: Arithmetic I, originally published in 1969, has been revised. There are now two more levels of the program, II and III. The program is highly structured for use with small groups of children. The format is organized for the teacher to rigorously involve students in the sequential activities. Emphasis is placed on students working independently. Students are taught the basic operations of addition, subtraction, signs, ordinal counting, multiplication, money concepts, operations with problems in columns and with fractions, factoring, analogies and methods for solving story problems, and algebraic addition.

Title: Intermediate Math Program
Publisher: Special Education Materials, Inc.
484 South Broadway
Yonkers, N.Y. 10705

Description: This individualized program of basic instruction consists of 40 tapes and student response booklets aimed at developing skill in addition, subtraction, place value, renaming, multiplication, and division.

Title: Math Readiness and Level I Mathematics

Publisher: McGraw-Hill Instructo Division
Paoli, Penn. 19301

Description: These programs, which are also offered in Spanish, are designed to provide individualized instruction for children in the range of preschool to first grade. Using tapes and correlated activity sheets, children are directed through activities involving readiness activities and basic skills and facts.

Title: Programmed Math 2/e
Publisher: Special Education Services
McGraw-Hill Book Co.
1221 Avenue of the Americas
New York, N.Y. 10020

Description: The programmed series, a basic program for intermediate and older students, is divided into lesson units for individualized instruction in 11 books. The sequence covers addition, subtraction, multiplication, division, fractions, decimals, measurements, and consumer and personal math.

Title: Cuisenaire Rods
Publisher: Cuisenaire Co. of America, Inc.
9 Elm Ave.
Mount Vernon, N.Y. 10550

Description: Cuisenaire rods utilize a size- and color-coding system to develop concepts by providing the child with manipulative devices. The rods have long been popular with teachers of the mentally retarded, and experience shows that the activities can be related to computational tasks and their prerequisites.

Title: Structural Arithmetic
Publisher: Houghton Mifflin Co.
110 Tremont St.
Boston, Mass. 02107

Description: This is a structured program that provides the child with activities through the use of blocks and cubes that have numerical properties associated with them. The program emphasizes problem-solving tasks that develop from the child's encounters with concrete objects.

SUMMARY

Unusual learning difficulties in mathematics have become more obvious in recent years, a fact that may be related to the increase in approaches concerned with the theoretical content of mathematics and its importance as a foundation for the sciences. The move away from the practical, computational emphasis may have been particularly problematic for children with learning disabilities.

In the learning disabilities literature there is a serious lack of attention to learning disabilities in mathematics; thus there is no well-defined approach or approaches to which we may refer. The suggestions provided in this chapter are based heavily on an understanding of Piagetian developmental principles that may serve as a guide for instruction. Until a better approach is found, it is suggested that the teacher may at least know that a given child may not be able to perform satisfactorily at certain levels in the mathematics program because he is not ready or not able to do so due to his present developmental level.

Various types of assessment instruments and procedures were presented, and at least one program that appears to have much promise (still under development) has been reviewed. Suggestions for further reading and a number of suggestions of instructional approaches that have been effective within limited areas of mathematics were provided. The entire learning disabilities field is relatively new, but the area of learning disabilities in mathematics is almost untouched as compared, for example, with reading. Those searching for fields in which to pioneer would do well to look carefully here.

REFERENCES AND SUGGESTED READINGS

Barakat, M. A factorial study of mathematical abilities, *British Journal of Psychology,* 1951, *4,* 137-156.

Brainerd, C. The origins of number concepts. *Scientific American,* 1973, *228*(3), 101-109.

Chalfant, J., and Scheffelin, M. *Central processing dysfunction in children: a review of research* (NINDS Monograph No. 9). Washington, D.C.: U.S. Government Printing Office, 1969.

Connolly, A., Nachtman, W., and Pritchett, E. *Manual: KeyMath Diagnostic Arithmetic Test.* Circle Pines, Minn.: American Guidance Service, Inc., 1971.

Copeland, R. *Diagnostic and learning activities in mathematics for children.* New York: Macmillan Publishing Co., Inc., 1974.

Copeland, R. *How children learn mathematics —teaching implications of Piaget's research* (2nd ed.). New York: Macmillan Publishing Co., Inc., 1974.

Cratty, B. *Perceptual-motor behavior and educational processes.* Springfield, Ill.: Charles C Thomas, Publisher, 1969.

Dunn, L. A comparison of the reading processes of mentally retarded boys of the same mental age. In L. Dunn and R. Capobianco (Eds.), *Studies of reading and arithmetic in mentally retarded boys.* Lafayette, Ind.: Child Development Publications, 1954.

Ellis, R. The stimulus trace and behavioral inadequacy. In N. Ellis (Ed.), *Handbook of mental deficiency.* New York: McGraw-Hill Book Co., 1963.

Fernald, G. *Remedial techniques in basic school subjects.* New York: McGraw-Hill Book Co. 1943.

Furth, H. *Thinking without language.* New York: The Free Press, 1966.

Gerstmann, J. Some notes on the Gerstmann syndrome. *Neurology,* 1957, *7,* 866-869.

Jansky, J. The phenomenon of plasticity in relation to manipulating numbers and early learning of arithmetic. In J. Hellmoth (Ed.), *Learning disorders* (Vol. 1). Seattle, Wash.: Special Child Publications, 1965.

Johnson, D., and Myklebust, H. *Learning disabilities: educational principles and practices.* New York: Grune & Stratton, Inc., 1967.

Kaliski, L. Arithmetic and the brain-injured child. *The Arithmetic Teacher,* 1962, *9,* 245-251.

Kelley, T. *Crossroads in the mind of man.* Stanford, Calif: Stanford University Press, 1928.

Kolstoe, O. P. *Mental retardation: an educational viewpoint.* New York: Holt, Rinehart & Winston, Inc., 1972.

Kosc, L. Developmental dyscalculia. *Journal of Learning Disabilities,* 1974, *7*(3), 46-59.

Mann, P., and Suiter, P. *Handbook in diagnostic teaching: a learning disabilities approach.* Boston: Allyn & Bacon, Inc., 1974.

Mitchell, F. *The nature of mathematical thinking.* Melbourne: Melbourne University Press, 1938.

Piaget, J. *Play, dreams and imitation in childhood.* New York: W. W. Norton & Co., Inc., 1951.

Piaget, J. *The growth of logical thinking in the child.* New York: Basic Books, Inc., Publishers, 1958.

Piaget, J. *The origins of intelligence in children.*

New York: W. W. Norton & Co., Inc., 1963.

Piaget, J. *The child's conception of number.* New York: W. W. Norton & Co., Inc., 1965.

Piaget, J. *The language and thought of the child.* New York: World Publishing Co., 1967.

Piaget, J. *Science of education and the psychology of the child.* New York: Grossman Publishers, 1974.

Reisman, F. *A guide to the diagnostic teaching of arithmetic.* Columbus, Ohio: Charles E. Merrill Publishing Co., 1972.

Sptizer, H. *Teaching elementary school mathematics,* Washington, D.C.: National Education Association, 1970.

Stafford, R. Negative relationship between ability to visualize space and grades in specific courses. *The Journal of Learning Disabilities,* 1972, *5*(1), 38-40.

Stern, C. *Children discover arithmetic.* New York: Harper & Row, Publishers, 1949.

Strauss, A., and Lehtinen, L. *Psychopathology and education of the brain-injured child.* New York: Grune & Stratton, Inc., 1947.

Wolinsky, G. The application of some of J. Piaget's observations to the instruction of children. *Teaching Exceptional Children,* 1970, *2*(4), 189-196.

Zeaman, D., and House, B. The role of attention in retardate discrimination learning. In N. Ellis (Ed.), *Handbook of mental deficiency.* New York: McGraw-Hill Book Co., 1963.

8 Nonverbal disorders

This consideration of nonverbal disorders was not presented earlier for two main reasons. First, there appears to be a growing conviction that many learning disabilities programs have focused too heavily on nonverbal disorders and have emphasized the remediation of such disorders without sufficient attention to the learning tasks, that is, reading, arithmetic, and so forth. This point of view is a significant part of the basic rationale of this book. Second, it can be demonstrated that minor nonverbal disabilities do not always lead to recognizable learning problems in other areas of functioning. Apparently some children compensate for some types of nonverbal disorders, and remedial programs based on the assumption that nonverbal disabilities will *always* lead to academic disabilities cannot be given total credibility.

I do not want to emphasize or encourage major efforts in the area of nonverbal disorders on behalf of all learning-disabled children, but such disorders are real, are sometimes the cause or part of the cause for academic learning disabilities, and should be considered for specialized programs in some cases. It is important that such assistance be provided for children who really need it, and it may be the most practical, if not always the only, way to approach learning disabilities remediation for such children.

Johnson and Myklebust (1967) are among the authorities in learning disabilities who discuss nonverbal disorders and use that specific terminology in their discussion. Their recognition of nonverbal disorders is all the more important in that their primary emphasis has been on verbal disorders (pp. 25-29 and 96-97). There are some differences in the disabilities that are called nonverbal disabilities by various authors, just as there are differences in definitions of perception, memory, and so forth. We will consider as nonverbal functions all those in Johnson and Myklebust's verbal learning sequence (see chart on p. 24) that fall below the level of symbolization. Thus we are primarily concerned with disabilities at the level of perception and imagery. These are properly considered as highly important in the verbal learning sequence below the level of verbal learning; thus they may be classified as nonverbal.

In their discussion of nonverbal disorders of learning Johnson and Myklebust (1967) consider a number of major topics, including learning through pictures, gesture, nonverbal motor learning, body image, spatial orientation, right-left orientation, social imperception, distractibility, perseveration, and disinhibition. Other authorities had been writing and researching a variety of problems in this area for some time, but for many the nonverbal area was their major area of concern.*

Some of the basic underlying beliefs of the perceptual-motor theorists and those who work primarily with hyperactive, brain-dam-

---

*I refer here to the perceptual-motor authorities and those who worked almost exclusively with the brain-damaged or highly hyperactive. For a review of the work of major authorities and theorists in these two areas, see Gearheart (1973, Chapters 3, 4, and 10) or the writings of Kephart, Getman, Barsch, Cratty, Cruickshank, and Strauss as listed in the references and suggested readings at the end of this chapter.

aged children will be reviewed and suggestions for assisting children who require either or both of these emphases will be the primary concern of the remainder of this chapter.

PERCEPTUAL-MOTOR THEORY

Perceptual-motor or motor-learning theorists base much of their system of remediation on solid, generally accepted hypotheses. They believe (and are supported by the preponderance of child development research) that children learn first through a series of basic motor explorations. Kephart (1971) states that "it is logical to assume that all behavior is basically motor, that the prerequisites of any kind of behavior are muscular and motor responses." Another principle of perceptual-motor theory is the assumption that higher forms of behavior (learning) grow out of these early motor responses and are dependent on the accuracy, degree of completeness, and sequential correctness of early motor and perceptual-motor learning. Observations and research with children and related research with lower primates (in which animals such as apes are subjected to conditions and controls that could not be applied to humans) clearly indicate the importance of early motor development and the relationship to later learning. We know how most children learn, and we generally accept the importance of the learning steps on which the perceptual-motor theorists concentrate.

A variety of efforts, many of which could be best characterized as clinical observations (rather than carefully constructed research efforts), indicate that an unusually high number of children with severe learning problems also have underdeveloped motor skills or specific perceptual-motor problems. In some cases this is generalized underdevelopment, but more often it is "spotty" or variable development—normal in some areas, but unusually and unexplainably low in others. It thus seems logical to assume that if unusually low perceptual-motor skills are often found in learning-disabled children and the development of such skills is highly important for normal learning, there may be a cause-effect relationship. Most perceptual-motor theorists' remedial programs are based on this assumption of cause-effect relationship and a related assumption that if a child has learning problems and poor perceptual-motor skills, the learning problems may be remediated through improving perceptual-motor skills.

Common sense also indicates that, for example, a child who has not developed normal visual discrimination skills by age 6 years is not likely to have much success when asked to discriminate between letters and words in the process of learning to read. Therefore visual perception exercises seem to be a logical course to permit the child to have the basic skills assumed by those who construct first-grade curricula.

A similar type of logic would apply with regard to ability to focus and move the eyes across the printed page in the manner required to be able to read; activities that promote this type of ability or skill would seem to be a logical program to follow.

It will be apparent to those who read the work of perceptual-motor theorists in any depth that *visual* abilities are emphasized to a much greater degree than auditory abilities. In fact, some perceptual-motor authorities are actually visual-motor authorities, although in recent years there has been some increase in attention to the auditory component. This emphasis on visually related problems is another shortcoming to the adoption of perceptual-motor theory as the only base for learning disabilities programming, but where visual problems do exist there may be considerable value to this approach.

In summary, then, the perceptual-motor theorists believe that a child's first learning is through muscular and motor responses. Through physical exploration the child gains experience with his surroundings and thus learns about the world. Through practice he develops both motor patterns and motor skills. (Motor skills are specific, precise motor acts; motor patterns are more broad and may lead to motor generalizations.) If the child proceeds in the development path as he should, he will develop a series of motor patterns that are prerequisites to the next step in the sequence. These include posture, laterality, directionality, and body image.

Motor generalizations are the next concern of most perceptual-motor authorities.* These are combinations of motor patterns and are thus more general than the motor patterns. Balance and posture, locomotion, contact, and receipt and propulsion are the four motor generalizations believed (by Kephart) to be most important.

Perhaps the most important single concept in relation to later academic learning is perceptual-motor match. In brief, this means that the child can match, or process and interpret as the same, incoming signals through the motor and visual channels. Although the young child almost always *feels* an object (such as velvet cloth) to determine what it is that he is seeing, he will later be satisfied that it is velvet cloth just by seeing it. His earliest mode of learning was tactile-kinesthetic, but it is later replaced in many cases by visual learning. This is much more efficient than having to go over to an object to feel it, and in the case of objects overhead or otherwise out of reach, it may make interpretation possible when otherwise it would not be possible. This also permits the child to interpret various objects when viewed from different angles even though they look somewhat different from these different vantage points. The carryover to academic tasks is obvious if we think of the various ways in which a letter, for example, an A, may be written; yet we expect the child to always know it is an A.

If we recall an earlier quotation, "It is logical to assume that all behavior is basically motor, that the prerequisites of any kind of behavior are muscular and motor responses" (Kephart, 1971), and add, "Behavior develops out of muscular activity, and so-called higher forms of behavior are dependent upon lower forms of behavior, thus making even these higher activities dependent upon the

---

*The basic ideas and the resulting remedial outcomes of most of the perceptual-motor theorists are quite similar, but they use somewhat different language to describe their ideas. Because his work represents a sort of "middle ground," we will use the terminology of Kephart for the most part.

basic structure of the muscular activity upon which they are built" (Kephart, 1971), we have the fundamental premise on which most perceptual-motor theory is based. These two statements and the implications that may be logically developed from them provide a fitting close to this summary. The ideas, activities, and suggestions that will be given later in this chapter are for consideration for use with children who appear to have significant problems in this perceptual-motor area. Other ideas may be obtained from the references and suggested readings.

THE HYPERACTIVE BRAIN-INJURED CHILD

There is little question that brain injury exists and that many brain-injured children exhibit severe and sometimes bizarre symptoms that lead to or may be classified as learning disorders. The major reason that the term "brain injury" is avoided by some is that it has been overused, misused, and misapplied so often. A second reason is that absolute, clear-cut cases of brain injury are found relatively infrequently among the school-age learning-disabled population. The term "cerebral dysfunction" is found with more frequency in educational literature, and to the extent that a child's functioning in one of the basic processes (those processes requisite to normal learning) is greatly inconsistent with other processes, it may be reasoned that there is some sort of dysfunction or malfunction. For the most part, those who support the perceptual-motor theories deal with either minimal dysfunctions or underdeveloped functions, but the hyperactive or brain-injured child to be considered in this discussion is conceptualized as having much more severe dysfunctions and some obvious medical indication of brain damage.

It is probably safe to say that there is no basic agreement as to precisely why the brain-injured child acts as he does (other than the fact of brain injury), for there is still much to be learned about how the brain functions when it is functioning normally. (See Chapter 11 for further discussion of brain functioning.) In an extensive review of research on central processing dysfunctions in children, Chalfant and Scheffelin (1969) categorized dysfunctions as (1) dysfunctions in the analysis of sensory information, (2) dysfunctions in the synthesis of sensory information, and (3) dysfunctions in symbolic operations. Their third major area of dysfunction is obviously verbal and thus not applicable to this chapter; however, it must be noted that examples of the manner in which dysfunctions in nonverbal areas contribute to verbal area dysfunctions are not difficult to find. The first two areas of the Chalfant and Scheffelin review are concerned with nonverbal dysfunctions and include consideration of auditory, visual, and haptic processing dysfunctions, dysfunctions in multiple stimulus integration, and in short-term memory. These areas of concern may be defined to include most types of problems with which we must work if we are to assist the brain injured, most of whom are also hyperactive.

Rather than attempt to review what theorists believe may be happening neurologically in terms of, for example, the excitation of brain cells due to the firing of neural axons, thus leading to synaptic knobs, additional neurological integration, and so forth (Hebb, 1949), we will consider how the receipt and processing of incoming sensory signals appear to be different in brain-injured children and normal children. This difference will then be the basis for curriculum modifications as they are necessary.

For practical purposes let us consider that most of the classic hyperactive brain-injured children have their greatest educational difficulties because they cannot (they are literally unable to) receive, process, and integrate visual, auditory, or haptic signals in the same manner as other children of the same approximate chronological age. The "why" is something about which educators can do little in terms of treating dysfunction. Some such children are greatly assisted by medication and some eventually learn in a more normal manner, but the teacher is faced with the immediate problem of dealing with specific behavior, and assisting the child to learn acceptable social-behavioral patterns, build academic skills, and develop necessary concepts.

Dysfunctions in analysis of sensory information

In relation to sensory processing we may assume that any of the following problems may occur in brain-injured children. (Simple acuity problems will not be reviewed.)

Auditory processing dysfunctions

1. Inability to accurately locate the source of a sound
2. Inability to discriminate between sounds that vary in any of a variety of acoustic dimensions, single or multiple ability
3. Ability to sense that sounds are different but inability to tell how
4. Inability to make auditory discriminations consistently
5. Inability to attend to major, meaningful auditory input in the presence of even slightly conflicting or competing sounds from other sources
6. Inability to attend to major auditory input in the presence of competing visual signals
7. Inability to synthesize basic speech sounds
8. Inability to tell the relevant from the irrelevant in many cases (auditory figure-ground difficulties)

These eight auditory problems are among those commonly found among the brain injured, and many are interrelated. A child who exhibits several of these behaviors may be called distractible, confused, inattentive, immature, hyperactive, or any of a variety of other similar adjectives.

Visual processing dysfunctions

1. Difficulties with binocular fusion (This should receive final diagnosis and treatment by the medical profession, but teachers must be alert to this possibility, which is not discovered by use of the Snellen chart or similar screening methods.)
2. Difficulties with muscular imbalance (There is continuing debate as to the value of eye exercises, which we cannot hope to settle here.)
3. Inefficient visual scanning ability in (a) random, or back-and-forth scanning (as in familiarizing oneself with a new area), (b) tracking a moving object, and (c) systematic scanning, as in reading

4. Inability to discriminate between two actual objects that are quite similar in configuration
5. Inability to see the essential differences between pictures of two objects or between symbols (letter, numbers, etc.) when the differences are minimal but of varied nature or when one is the reverse, or mirror image, of the other
6. Inability to attend to written material in the presence of competing or conflicting written material (that is, pictures of great interest on the same page with reading material, as in many primers and first readers)
7. Inability to attend to written material in the presence of competing auditory signals
8. Inability to accurately receive and process visual symbols in sequence and differentiate between slightly different sequences
9. Inability to use normal visual closure skills
10. Inability to recognize common objects that have been seen, discussed, etc., many times before
11. Inability to tell the relevant from the irrelevant in many cases (visual figure-ground difficulties)

This is only a partial listing of visual processing difficulties. Many of these problems are interrelated, and the child who demonstrates them is likely to become confused and distressed when faced with academic tasks that presume normal functioning in these areas. He may be viewed as inattentive, a trouble maker or mentally slow, or many other inaccurate conclusions may be drawn.

Haptic (tactile and kinesthetic) processing dysfunctions

1. Inability to accurately reproduce movements of lip, tongue, and face
2. Inability to reach in a given direction or move in a given manner on instruction to do so
3. Inability to reach or move as appropriate in imitation of movements of others
4. Inability to inhibit one set of muscle groups while activating others
5. Inability to "feel" the difference between two radically different movement configurations (as in two different letters), even if manually moved through these configurations
6. Inability to differentiate between touch sensations in two different parts of the body if touch is simultaneous

7. Inability to imitate with one limb the movements of the other, even extremely simple movements

Haptic processing problems have been researched even less than visual or auditory processing problems, and the need for more research is great. Problems in such areas as spelling may result from haptic process disabilities, and if the tactile and kinesthetic modalities are to be used to support the visual and auditory in some cases (as in simultaneous VAKT methods of teaching reading, p. 90), we must make certain that these modalities are functioning adequately. In addition, as pointed out by Cratty (1971), inability in this area may be particularly devastating to children who are concerned about athletic prowess, and resulting self-concept problems may greatly affect academic learning.

In each of these three areas (auditory, visual, and haptic) there is considerable evidence of a direct connection between the processing ability and brain function or dysfunction as indicated by research conducted with children with brain lesions. A similar brain trauma causation applies in many documented cases of dysfunctions in the synthesis of sensory information, which will be discussed next.

Dysfunctions in synthesis of sensory information

Stimulus integration is a relatively complex procedure, and intersensory systems probably develop after the successful development of intrasensory systems (Birch, 1954, 1965). Integration of multiple stimuli may mean either the matching of stimuli from two different modalities or matching multiple stimuli received through a single modality. Many of the problems outlined previously may also result from dysfunctions in multiple stimulus integrative ability, and in all likelihood a combination of dysfunctions may exist. In specific cases of brain lesions or brain surgery some differences might be determined, but for practical purposes (for the educator) dysfunctions in the sythesis of sensory information lead to many of the same problems as dysfunctions in the analysis of sensory information.

The implications for the normal teaching-learning process may be different, however. Most of our educational efforts as carried out with normal children in a typical curriculum call for the ability to match or integrate multiple stimuli. Even if, for example, the child can receive and analyze sensory information through all modalities as required for a certain task, he may have difficulty when multiple stimulus integration is required for information provided in simple units one unit at a time. Thus, although the outward manifestations of dysfunction in simple sensory processing and in synthesis (integration) of sensory information may be the same, these two phenomena are different and the educator may need to use a trial and error procedure to determine guidelines for remedial teaching efforts.

A dysfunction in short-term memory (or storage and retrieval) is another common dysfunction in brain-injured children. The symptoms may be almost as simple as the process is complex. If a child cannot store and retrieve effectively, he may apparently know (recognize) a word or letter and be able to recognize it as different from all others but be unable to duplicate the task the next day or next week. Another symptom is inability to repeat a series of three or four words in a sequence.

Luria (1966), one of the more quoted authorities in theory and research in neurological functioning, speaks of memory traces of four kinds: visual traces, acoustic traces, kinesthetic traces, and verbal traces. Most research has been concerned with visual traces because they are the easiest to assess, but all types of problems of retention and recall fit under the learning disabilities "umbrella" and are commonly found in children who are brain damaged.

BRAIN DAMAGE OR LEARNING DISABILITIES?

The confusion that may exist between those who speak of children with brain damage, minimal brain damage, or cerebral dysfunction and those who speak of learning-disabled children may be related to many factors. In some areas of the nation the terms are used synonymously; in others it may be unusual to hear one or the other of these terms. Special education for children with brain damage came before the idea of special education for children with learning disabilities, and associations of parents of children with brain damage predated those for parents of children with learning disabilities. Why are these terms so often confused? Several reasons stand out.

1. In some cases two different professional disciplines have referred to the same children in different ways: "children with minimal brain damage" and "learning-disabled children." This was especially confusing when the Department of Health, Education and Welfare sponsored concurrent studies using these two different terms. Some of the studies were under the auspices of the medical discipline (health), and the disability was thus called minimal brain damage. Others were under the direction of education, and the problem was called learning disabilities.

2. In some instances special classes or special education services for brain-injured or Strauss syndrome* children were authorized by state regulations before the term "learning disabilities" became accepted. These were the forerunners of present-day programs for the learning disabled, and where this was the wording of state reimbursement regulations, there was a tendency to expand the interpretation, permitting more mildly disabled children to be served under this category, rather than to change the wording as the concept of learning disabilities grew in acceptance. Thus in some states children were called brain injured on official state class lists but were called "learning disabled" for all other purposes.

3. As mentioned earlier, if a child cannot

effectively relate to and process incoming sensory data in the same manner as other children, particularly if he has obvious difficulties, it may be inferred that the brain or some facet of the neurological system is not working properly. Because it is known that there are a variety of ways in which the brain can be damaged (blows to the head, high temperatures leading to anoxia, and others), it is no great stretch of the imagination to reason that "not working properly" means "brain dysfunction" and that brain dysfunction *may* mean "brain damage."

4. Given this reasoning, the "clinching" factor for some is the fact that many children for whom there are no causal factors suggesting brain damage exhibit a pattern of problems—many of which are nonverbal disorders—just like the brain injured.

This last factor is also the reason that some of the methods used for the brain injured during the 1950's and 1960's were used with the learning disabled in the late 1960's and the 1970's. In many cases the major differences between the nonverbal disorders of the known brain injured and the learning disabled was a matter of degree. The dysfunctions in the analysis and synthesis of sensory information may apply either to children we would call brain injured or those we would be more likely to call learning disabled. For most of the discussion of nonverbal disorders we will consider learning problems below the level of verbal learning and make no attempt to differentiate whether or not the children experiencing these problems are brain injured. Rather we will be concerned with what children can or cannot do, how they act, and what we can do about it.

HYPERACTIVITY AND BEHAVIOR CONTROL PROBLEMS IN CHILDREN WHO ARE NOT PRIMARILY EMOTIONALLY DISTURBED

The determination of whether a child is primarily emotionally disturbed or whether his unusual or unacceptable behavior is a result of neurological dysfunction or brain

---

*Strauss syndrome has been commonly used to indicate the composite behavioral symptoms of the very hyperactive child others might call brain injured. This syndrome is named for Alfred Strauss, who pioneered efforts for the brain injured.

trauma must be left to specialists other than the learning disabilities teacher. Often this decision is a matter of professional consensus based on the diagnostic efforts of a physician (sometimes but not always a neurologist), a psychologist, and when needed, a psychiatrist. The psychiatrist may be called into the deliberations if it appears that the primary cause may be emotional disturbance.

We must remember that children and their learning problems do not come in "pure" types. Therefore a combination of factors may be involved, but our primary consideration in this discussion is the child who is unable to control his reactions to normal classroom environment stimuli and thus is unable to learn effectively. In a majority of cases such a child also has significantly negative effect on the learning of others.

In times past, particularly in some large cities, there were separate, self-contained classes for highly distractible, hyperactive children. Such classes still exist, but the trend is toward maintaining all children in the regular class for at least part of the day. The existence of more effective learning disabilities resource room programs and better medical control through drug therapy have made this a feasible alternative. The learning disabilities resource room teacher or itinerant teacher may therefore have children who exhibit these characteristics and must be ready to assist them in the specialized setting as well as to assist and advise the regular class teacher regarding management in the regular class.

The most basic single fact to remember about the hyperactive child is that he may process and respond to environmental signals in a manner that is different from that of the majority of children in the class. A sound that goes almost unnoticed by most of the class may cause a violent reaction in the hyperactive child. We must understand and must help the regular class teacher understand that he is not being "bad" or "belligerent" or trying to disrupt the class. It is just that he is different.

We might use the example of the effect experienced when a person puts on glasses that cause extreme distortions of visual images. If he knows what things really look like, he can handle the different image, but what would happen if he had never seen things as other people see them or if he saw them normally at times and distorted at others with no control over when the image changed?

In addition to being abnormally responsive to various environmental stimuli (visual, auditory, and haptic) such a child may also tend to perseverate in his responses. This, too, can cause a problem in a class of 30 children. The child may be able to discriminate between two different letters of the alphabet at some times and be absolutely unable to do so at other times. The variability of his responses, which leads to inability to predict what he may say or do next, is a major problem. The obvious question—"What do we do with him?"—must be answered.

Most authorities in this field provide a series of suggestions that add up to one basic admonition—*control the environment* (Cruickshank, 1961, 1966, 1967; Strauss and Kephart, 1955; Strauss and Lehtinen, 1947). If the school environment is too confusing or too stimulating, then we must modify it. In the regular class this may be accomplished by arranging for an "office" for the hyperactive child. This may be done with room dividers or with any device that effectively reduces visual and auditory input. (I have seen rooms in which large packing boxes were used effectively.)

In all cases the parents must be contacted and the situation explained so that there will be no chance that the parent will think that the child is being treated unfairly. Usually if a child requires this much additional assistance, the parent is well aware of his problems and happy with anything that may work. Other children in the class may be told that "John has real trouble learning as long as he can see and hear everybody else, so this is a way to help him learn."

A way to assist in reducing auditory input is through the use of headsets (not connected to any sound source). This produces the same effect as earplugs but is more acceptable. (Earplugs should not be used, even though they might be effective, because problems may arise from putting objects in the ears.) We must keep in mind that the objective is to reduce incoming sensory signals so that the child may attend to his assignment.

These suggestions will be helpful when the child is doing seatwork, but other provisions must be made for class discussion. Seating (for class discussions only) might be arranged so that the child is near the front of the room in a position that minimizes eye contact with other children. Children who tend to tease or do things that might trigger misbehavior in others should be seated as far as possible from the hyperactive child. The application of a generous supply of common sense and logical thinking, keeping in mind the fact that we need to control the environment and reduce environmental stimuli, is the general rule of thumb. The knowledge that the resource room teacher will be taking the child out of class for special help may also help the regular class teacher over some of the "rough spots" in the day.

Certain environmental components are recognized as possible problem sources and should be carefully monitored with any unusually hyperactive child. These are *not* necessarily to be automatically avoided, but rather they are factors to watch, to make certain they are not a problem. Many of these are positive factors for most children and must not be changed except as observation indicates them to be a problem.

The following are factors and settings to observe and to modify or control if they are a problem.

1. Learning materials that are multicolored, particularly if they are bright colors, may cause problems. Some highly distractible children are so attracted by pictures that accompany primary grade primers and readers that they have difficulty attending to the written material they are supposed to read.

2. Classroom interest centers such as science tables; a particulticularly attractive aquarium; bright, colorful bulletin boards; and the like may demand so much attention that the child cannot effectively attend to class discussion or instructions from the teacher.

3. Background auditory clutter may prevent the child from hearing what is being said. This may be a particular problem in an open classroom.

4. Bright clothing and glittering jewelry worn by the teacher may hold the child's attention when the teacher attempts to provide one-to-one assistance.

5. More than one object on the child's desk at one time may make it difficult to stay with one task.

6. The availability of a number of items at the student's desk (such as pencils, erasers, tablets, library books, and rulers), even if these materials are in the desk, may be a problem. All such materials may have to be stored in a tote tray away from the desk, with only those items required for the immediate task provided at the desk.

7. A desk with a hinged top may lead to problems. The child may unconsciously move it up and down almost continuously, thus distracting from other efforts.

8. Proximity to areas such as the pencil sharpener may be a problem. There may be several factors in operation here—the movement of the pencil sharpener, the noise of the sharpener, and the student activity as children go to and from the pencil sharpener.

This list could be expanded almost indefinitely, but the eight examples should adequately illustrate the point. In the most extreme cases of brain damage–related hyperactivity nearly all of the kinds of classroom activities that we have traditionally linked with a "good" or interesting classroom are wrong.

One caution must be carefully observed: we must not remove too many of these attractive distractors because our goal is to assist the child to slowly learn to contend with these factors. Otherwise we are training the child to function in a setting that does not exist in the real world.

The unusually hyperactive, distractible child requires structure and order. Too many choices are difficult for him to handle, and free-play periods and free-form art emphasis may not be appropriate. A learning cubicle or "office" may be one answer to provide the freedom from competing noise and visual stimuli that is required for work to be accomplished. The environment should be controlled, but the child must eventually be taught to cope with these distracting factors. Slow exposure to normal noises, materials, etc. should be a part of the plan. Of the various references included at the end of the chapter, *The Brain-Injured Child in the Home, School, and Community,* by Cruickshank (1967), a commonsense guide, is highly recommended for further reading. It contains a minimum of theory and many helpful suggestions.

NONVERBAL DISORDERS OTHER THAN HYPERACTIVITY

Nonverbal disorders other than those that are a part of the hyperactivity syndrome may relate to all learning channels and are so varied that they are difficult to discuss in terms of a simple basic rationale to guide programming. The discussion of perceptual-motor theory presented earlier in this chapter provides the general underlying theoretical base but will be of limited help in directing the teacher as to where to start and how to proceed. Specific assessment must be used as the base for programming, and use of tests and assessment instruments will be a part of a separate course in the training program of most learning disabilities teachers. A number of texts attend primarily to the problem of nonverbal disorders. Sections of others are unusually good as resource material. Some of this information could be condensed and presented here, but it would be of much more value for the teacher to actually use these books and materials. The following are suggested as primary references for this purpose. (There will be some overlap in these materials, but there are unique sections that

make each worthy of a separate recommendation.)

Chaney, C. and Kephart, N. *Motoric aids in perceptual training.* Columbus, Ohio: Charles E. Merrill Publishing Co., 1968.

Cratty, B. *Active learning: games to enhance academic abilities.* Englewood Cliffs, N.J.: Prentice-Hall, Inc., 1971.

Ebersole, M., Kephart, N., and Ebersole, J. *Steps to achievement for the slow learner.* Columbus, Ohio: Charles E. Merrill Publishing Co., 1968.

Getman, G., Kane, E., Halgren, M., and McKee, G. *Developing learning readiness.* New York: McGraw-Hill Book Co., 1968.

Johnson, D., and Myklebust, H. *Learning disabilities: educational principles and practices* (Chapter 8). New York: Grune & Stratton, Inc. 1967.

Kephart, N. *The slow learner in the classroom.* Columbus, Ohio: Charles E. Merrill Publishing Co., 1971.

There are many other texts and parts of texts that may be of value, but these six will provide a good selection of methods specifically designed for nonverbal disorders. In addition, there are many tests to assess specific nonverbal abilities, and in many cases helpful suggestions are provided in the test manuals. In some cases specific remedial programs are associated with the tests. (See p. 66 for an example of teaching ideas presented in test manuals.)

SUMMARY

Nonverbal disorders as considered in this chapter include all learning disorders that occur below the level of symbolization. These disorders include all that occur at the perceptual or imagery level, including specific disorders that grow out of faulty perception or imagery. In more commonly used learning disabilities terminology, this includes children who may be called brain injured, hyperactive, or highly distractible; the child with minimal cerebral dysfunction; and the "Strauss syndrome" child. Although some authorities would insist that some of these terms are specifically and inherently discrete, in practice they are often used interchangeably. These children are labeled according to their behavior or to the assumed cause of this behavior, but they consistently exhibit severe disabilities at the perceptual or imagery level of learning.

Also included in this nonverbal disorder category is the child who has one or more of the problems on which the perceptual-motor authorities concentrate: spatial orientation problems, right-left confusion, body image difficulties, and the like. Social imperception as viewed by Johnson and Myklebust (1967) would also be included.

A generalized basis for working with the type of problems caused by hyperactivity or the Strauss syndrome was presented. This involves understanding the type of problems that may be associated with inability to handle normal environmental signals (the primary problem areas are visual and auditory). The technique employed is careful monitoring of sources of distraction or conflicting signals and control of the environment. The goal of such a program is building (in the child) the ability to handle his environment, a goal that must be accomplished in slow steps. In the meantime the classroom setting must be controlled to permit learning to continue and to minimize the negative effect that such behavior may impose on others. Six major sources for methods and ideas for work with other nonverbal disorders were given.

REFERENCES AND SUGGESTED READINGS

Ayres, J. *Southern California Perceptual Motor Tests.* Los Angeles: Western Psychological Services, 1969.

Balow, B. Perceptual-motor activities in the treatment of severe reading disability. *Reading Teacher,* 1971, *24,* 513-525.

Barsch, R. *Achieving perceptual-motor efficiency.* Seattle: Special Child Publications, 1967.

Birch, H. Comparative psychology. In F. Moreuse (Ed.), *Areas of psychology.* New York: Harper & Row, Publishers, 1954.

Birch, H., and Belmont, I. Auditory-visual integration in brain-damaged and normal children. *Developmental Medicine and Child Neurology,* 1965, *7,* 135-144.

Bush, W., and Giles, M. *Aids to psycholinguistic Teaching.* Columbus, Ohio: Charles E. Merrill Publishing Co., 1969.

Chalfant, J., and Scheffelin, M. *Central processing dysfunctions in children* (NINDS Monograph No. 9). Washington, D.C.: U.S. Government Printing Office, 1969.

Chaney, C., and Kephart, N. *Motoric aids in perceptual training.* Columbus, Ohio: Charles E. Merrill Publishing Co., 1969.

Cratty, B. *Active learning: games to enhance academic abilities.* Englewood Cliffs, N.J.: Prentice-Hall, Inc., 1971.

Cruickshank, W. *The brain-injured child in home, school, and community.* Syracuse: Syracuse University Press, 1967.

Cruickshank, W. (Ed.). *The teacher of brain-injured children.* Syracuse: Syracuse University Press, 1966.

Cruickshank, W., et al. *A teaching method for brain-injured and hyperactive children.* Syracuse: University Press, 1961.

Ebersole, M., Kephart, N., and Ebersole, J. *Steps to achievement for the slow learner.* Columbus, Ohio: Charles E. Merrill Publishing Co., 1968.

Frostig, M. *Movement education: theory and practice.* Chicago: Follett Publishing Co., 1970.

Getman, G. *Pathway school program.* Boston: Teaching Resources Corp., 1969.

Getman, G., Kane, E., Halgren, M., and McKee, G. *Developing learning readiness.* New York: McGraw-Hill Book Co., 1968.

Hebb, D. *The organization of behavior: a neuropsychological theory.* New York: John Wiley & Sons, Inc., 1949.

Johnson, D., and Myklebust, H. *Learning disabilities: educational principles and practices.* New York: Grune & Stratton, Inc., 1967.

Kephart, N. *The slow learner in the classroom.* Columbus, Ohio: Charles E. Merrill Publishing Co., 1971.

Luria, A. *Higher cortical functions in man.* New York: Basic Books, Inc., Publishers, 1966.

Roach, E., and Kephart, N. *The Purdue Perceptual-Motor Survey.* Columbus, Ohio: Charles E. Merrill Publishing Co., 1966.

Strauss, A., and Kephart, N. *Psychopathology and education of the brain-injured child* (Vol. 2). New York: Grune & Stratton, Inc., 1955.

Strauss, A., and Lehtinen, L. *Psychopathology and education of the brain-injured child.* New York: Grune & Stratton, Inc., 1947.

9 Motivational techniques and the positive reinforcement

The primary emphasis of learning disabilities programming has tended to be determination of strengths and weaknesses in psycholinguistic abilities, perceptual-motor skills, specific reading or arithmetic skills, or some combination of specific skills and abilities. Some authorities place more emphasis on remediation of disabilities or deficits; others focus on effective utilization of strengths. Some combination of these two emphases is commonly used. Each of these approaches or combinations has been successful for some children; therefore each has advocates who can attest to its value. The popularity of such approaches is further enhanced by the exis-

tence of a multitude of diagnostic tools that purport to measure abilities and disabilities and thus provide guidance as to what type of effort is required and where to start.

Except when a particular teacher or diagnostician is so enamored of one approach, test, or type of disability that he or she is unable to recognize the existence of other needs, this can be an effective general avenue of approach to learning disabilities planning and programming. However, one other dimension to successful planning for the learning disabled should be considered and applied where appropriate.

As indicated in the principles for program-

153

ming in Chapter 2, *high motivation is a prerequisite to success.* This is applicable to nearly all children, and for those who are learning successfully the act of learning often becomes a prime source of motivation. For the learning disabled the opposite effect occurs; difficulties in learning provide a vector of discouragement, a force that must be overcome if the child is to succeed. Although success may come eventually if we implement the right approaches with the right children, overcoming the failure syndrome at the beginning is highly important. Motivational and reinforcement systems provide one means whereby we may be able to overcome this initial problem and continue to provide the needed encouragement toward success.

Motivational systems and positive reinforcement techniques are unlike most learning disabilities approaches because they are not based on a diagnostic-prescriptive model. Rather than focusing on the child's learning strengths and weaknesses, they ask how we can make the child feel more confident and self-assured or how we can reinforce the kinds of behavior we want the child to exhibit.

MOTIVATIONAL SYSTEMS AND POSITIVE RECONDITIONING

Fernald (1943) and Gillingham and Stillman (1965) used positive reconditioning in the 1920's and 1930's with excellent results. (Their approaches were reviewed in Chapter 6 and will not be detailed here.) The thrust of their reconditioning efforts was to help the child who had failed repeatedly to feel that the failure was as much or more a fault of the system (the methods used and the teachers' lack of knowledge) than his fault. The purpose was to counteract the failure syndrome so that the child could respond to a new learning approach more successfully. This type of effort to promote initial motivation to learn is important for the learning-disabled child; in general we may assume it becomes more essential the longer the child has experienced learning problems.

Once the initial stages of attempting a new learning approach are past, there is a strong likelihood that the child may become discouraged as he comes face to face with new, more difficult learning tasks. Most of us have experienced the discouragement that comes when we are confronted by new, more complicated learning processes and find that we cannot understand or are unable to accomplish what we are supposed to do next. The learning disabilities teacher must be alert to the likelihood of this happening in the learning-disabled youngster. Even though the child may have overcome initial feelings of inadequacy, his long experience with failure makes it easy for him to slip back into the conviction that he cannot learn.

The principle of motivational systems requires planned initial motivation, planned motivation at various stages along the learning path, plus emergency plans for the time when normal motivational efforts are not enough. Getting over these "emergency hurdles" may in some cases be the most important of all techniques with learning-disabled children particularly older, teenage students.

POSITIVE REINFORCEMENT TECHNIQUES

Reinforcement techniques gained increased attention with the popularization of behavior modification in special education programs. Although there is continuing debate as to the propriety of wide use of behavior modification techniques, the concept of planned, systematic reinforcement seems to be generally accepted, exept by those who think that the reinforcement of social approval should be sufficient to promote learning. Some appear to believe that anything more than social approval is improper, if not downright immoral. I believe that we must stretch our imagination and ingenuity to find a way to motivate children who have for some reason not "turned on" to academic learning. This includes using various reinforcement techniques with the hope that we can develop the built-in motivational system that many children experience from the beginning of their school career.

Master teachers have used a variety of types of reinforcement techniques since schools were first organized. Special privileges in the classroom or on the playground are effective for some children. Gold stars are effective—for children who recognize gold stars as important or of value. Words of praise and encouragement or a pat on the shoulder are commonly used reinforcement techniques, but for many learning-disabled children these are insufficient. This is not because they are "spoiled" or think they are better than other children. It is because they have more difficulty in learning than others, have had some usually unrewarding school experiences, or perhaps have had no home reinforcement for academic success. It is the *magnitude* of their learning problems that brings about the need for unusual tactics, and positive reinforcement techniques represent one potentially valuable avenue of approach.

As noted, reinforcement techniques or reward systems are not new; what is new is the organization and systemization of such techniques that has led to more consistency and thus more effectiveness. Stephens (1970) uses the terms "reward" and "positive reinforcement" synonymously, a procedure that will be followed here. Rewards may be classified into three main groups: (1) primitive rewards, (2) interim rewards, and (3) social rewards (Stephens, 1970).

Primitive rewards include such things as candy, ice cream, and other foods. Toys and other concrete objects that have high value to the child are included in this general classification. If candy, other foods, or toys are used, the parents must be consulted and an ample amount of common sense must be exercised. For example, it would be the height of absurdity to use candy as a reward for a child with hypoglycemia. Even if this did increase his motivation to learn, it would contribute to a physiological reduction in his ability to learn. The purpose of any positive reinforcement program must be viewed as twofold: (1) to provide immediate, high motivation to learn new facts or develop new skills and (2) to work toward

the development of inner motivation in which the feeling of accomplishment involved in successful learning becomes the primary motivating force.

An *interim reward* is a symbol or token that represents something of value. Good grades or good reports to parents may serve as interim rewards, and where this is the case it is a desirable system. Unfortunately it is not a sufficient reward for many learning-disabled children, at least at the start of remedial programming. The most common type of interim reward is a point or token system in which the child may earn real objects that are of value to him (a yo-yo, a small transistor radio, candy, or some other primitive reward). Money is also commonly used, but both parents and teachers tend to object more to the use of money than to use of tokens that represent monetary value. In either event, token systems are of value because they are one step away from primitive rewards and thus may provide a bridge to the use of other reinforcers.

Social rewards are those that the typical middle-class American parent (and teacher) seem to think are totally acceptable. These are the smile, the look of approval, the pat on the shoulder, recognition in class, and the other methods of saying "you did a good job." If a reward is not tangible, does not in any way lead directly to a primary reward, and could be classified as secondary in nature, it is properly called a social reward (Stephens, 1970).

Before continuing with the discussion of reward or positive reinforcement techniques, it may be of value to consider philosophical issues that are sometimes raised with regard to behavioral approaches. Perhaps this is not necessary for the teacher who is seriously considering the use of such approaches, but it may be of value to have in mind for use with parents, administrators, or other critics or skeptics. Please note that our concern here is with the use of *positive* reinforcers and will not include recommendations of other behavior modification procedures, although this should not be interpreted to mean that others are unacceptable.

Worell and Nelson (1974) approached the philosophical objections to behavioral approaches through an enumeration of common misconceptions regarding behavioral approaches. The following listing of misconceptions and the discussion of why they are misconceptions should provide further insight into the present status of behavioral approaches as they may be used with the learning-disabled child.

MISCONCEPTIONS ABOUT BEHAVIORAL APPROACHES*
Misconception No. 1

Teachers should teach, not play psychologist or provide therapy.

This statement as it stands may be true, but it is not necessarily applicable to most behavioral approaches if they are properly utilized by the teacher. Research indicates that behavior is learned. This includes responses to environmental factors such as demands of the classroom and the academic setting. Even if teachers view their work as almost solely that of academic learning (an outdated view), it can be demonstrated that behavioral approaches can increase academic learning.

Research into the skills that appear to be commonly required for academic success has led to the use of the term "survival skills." These may be viewed as parallel to survival skills taught to wilderness hikers and backpackers, except that these apply to survival (successful performance) in the academic wilderness. Perhaps the school should not be likened to a wilderness, but to some learning-disabled children it is precisely that.

Cobb (1970) indicates that the essential survival skills for children in grades one through four are (1) attending to the academic task or to the teacher, (2) ability to comply with instructions given by the teacher, and (3) volunteering answers. Cobb's study indicated that children with lower achievement levels in arithmetic and reading

*Modified from Worell, J., and Nelson, M. *Managing instructional problems: a case study workbook.* New York: McGraw-Hill Book Co., 1974.

had deficits in these competencies. Those who were most successful were competent in these three skills. It could be argued that children should be able to learn without these skills, but in the existing academic setting they appear to be essential. *Therefore the learning disabilities teacher should observe these skills in the class setting. If a child's survival skills are considerably less well developed than those of his peers, efforts should be initiated to promote and assist the child to develop them.* Behavioral approaches appear to be among the most effective in promoting these skills, particularly attending skills, which must be developed before the other two can have much meaning. Behavior modification techniques are widely reported as successful with the learning disabled. (For three illustrative case studies, see Gearheart [1973, pp. 121-126].)

Misconception No. 2

Inappropriate behavior indicates an underlying cause, and you cannot really change the behavior until you find the cause.

This misconception is based on a misapplication of the medical model, and some educators have difficulty operating within any framework but this. However, it should not be assumed that behaviorists believe that behavior does not have causes. Certainly behavior is caused, but at times it is very difficult to discover it, and knowledge of the cause may provide little worthwhile guidance as to what to do next. A further problem is the existence of multiple causes, which is the rule rather than the exception. At times it would be beneficial to know the origin(s) of a given behavior, but often we can do little about it even if we do discover these origins.

The behaviorist thinks that if we can make it sufficiently important to the individual for him to change behavior, he will do so. When dealing with learning disabilities in adolescents it is possible, perhaps even likely, that the academic retardation was caused by an earlier process disability. In many such cases the specific disability, the original cause of present academic problems, is now gone. Even if we could discover precisely what was wrong 6 years ago, it would have little importance now as far as providing direction for remediation. What presently exists is more likely to be a combination of failure syndrome (as regards academic tasks) and some sort of substitute coping mechanism (perhaps resulting in antisocial behavior). A tendency to regard anything relating to formal learning tasks with suspicion is also common. *These are the behaviors we must work with, not the earlier problem that does not exist as a present cause.*

Misconception No. 3

If a child has an unusually poor home environment, there is no point in trying to change the child unless we can change the home.

This is little more than a convenient cop-out. It is true that the influence of parents and home environment is strong, but not all of the successful people in the world have come from homes where all was joy and light. Children will eventually leave their homes, and one of the major goals of education is to prepare children to be happy, well-adjusted, effective adult citizens of a democratic society. We will not be successful in educational efforts with all children, but to *give up* because of a poor home environment is inexcusable. To understand that the role of education is much more difficult in such cases is only realistic, but to equate difficulty with certain failure cannot be accepted.

Misconception No. 4

Some children cannot be changed.

This misconception, emphasized separately by Worell and Nelson (1971), is an extension of No. 3. However, instead of using parental and environmental influence as a reason for giving up on a particular child, teachers may use a label as the reason. Labels such as "hyperactive," "dyslexic," and "mentally retarded" are commonly used to *explain* behavior rather than to *describe* it.

Even the more severely mentally retarded have been helped through behavioral ap-

proaches to accomplish such tasks as toilet training after years of previous effort has led to no success. Limitations (when in fact they do exist) have great importance in relation to what and how much can be learned, but they do not indicate that the child cannot learn. A good example is the blind child. His blindness dictates that he cannot be effectively taught to read the printed word in its normal form. Braille makes it possible for him to be taught to read, but it changes the "how." In learning disabilities we must be particularly careful as we deal with medically related labels and syndromes; the word of the physician tends to become absolute and final. Physicians may speak of brain injury and not have in mind what others think of when they see that the brain-injured child cannot read. The ramifications are many, but the principle is simple: children's behavior can be changed and it is the educator's task to change it.

Misconception No. 5

Children should do schoolwork because they enjoy it; we cannot accept a system that involves bribery.

This idea is fairly common among teachers, if one is to believe the comments heard in teachers' lounges and in college classes. Every behaviorist I have known would like for children to do their schoolwork because they enjoy it, and they want children to find success. The problem is that children come to school as kindergartners or first graders with widely varying degrees of ability, readiness, and built-in motivation. *They do not all start "equal"; therefore we cannot expect equal performance from them.* It would be great for all children to enjoy the teacher's efforts to teach phonetic approaches to word recognition, but if they cannot discriminate between the sounds (as the teacher may assume they can), it is difficult to enjoy this type of schoolwork. There are many examples of how we may assume abilities that are not yet developed and then blame the child for not doing and enjoying his schoolwork.

Another type of entry-to-school variation that may have equal importance as a reason why some children do not automatically enjoy schoolwork relates to preschool *practice* in enjoying schoolwork. It is common in many homes to "play school" to show the child how he should feel and to make it clear that school performance is important to the parents and will be rewarded at home. In truth, some children enjoy schoolwork, particularly school success, primarily because it brings rewards at home. In other homes school is given no positive emphasis, school officials are part of "the system" that the child has learned he should dislike and distrust, and there is little chance that the child will automatically do schoolwork for the joy of doing it.

The extreme variation in children's general ability, specific abilities, readiness, and socially and culturally based motivation makes the idea that all children should do schoolwork because they like it ridiculous.

The belief that all reward systems are bribery is unfortunate and is based on narrow thinking and emotional reaction. Bribery means something immoral or illegal; thus when we use the word the whole idea takes on negative connotations, and rational thinking becomes difficult. Perhaps it is the suggestion that we might use money in a reward system that causes the most problems, but let us examine the educational system as it now works. If a child is really good in athletics, we spend additional money to help him become even more proficient. We spend money for travel costs for him to go to athletic events; then we buy a trophy to present to him if he is unusually successful. We may not directly pay him for setting a new record, but we provide things that only money can buy. I am not suggesting that we change our policy of supporting athletic competition. I am pointing out that we do use money to promote better performance and that it is effective. I am also suggesting that it is *not* immoral.

The use of positive rewards, whether they are extra field trips, free time, primitive rewards, or whatever works, is designed to get the student *started*. The goal is the same in all cases. It is to help the child with learning problems to experience success in learning and to eventually find enough motivation in successful learning (something he has not experienced) to make him want to learn for the sake of learning.

Misconception No. 6

"I tried behavior modification methods once, and they didn't work—that's proof enough for me."

If this principle were valid, anything that did not work out the first time it was tried would be abandoned forever. The fact is that nearly all teachers use some behavioral approaches, find success in some, and thus repeat them. Often a teacher who tries to change a child's acting out behavior may be taking on a relatively involved case. Without guidance in both planning and implementation it is easy to make errors, and the end result is not what was planned. This does not mean that behavioral approaches will not work. When behavioral approaches do not work it often means that the techniques and procedures were not well planned or were not well implemented. *The principles are sound.* The implementation is often difficult.

• • •

These six misconceptions are fairly common, but *they are misconceptions.* They were presented because teachers who work with learning-disabled children will undoubtedly need to use some techniques based on behavioral theory and should be ready to deal with these misconceptions. They also provided an effective vehicle for review of some major principles of behavioral theory. In the section that follows we will consider two cases in which behavioral approaches have been effective. These are studies in which I have had some personal involvement and, as will be seen, all did not proceed exactly as planned.

ANECDOTAL STUDIES OF REINFORCEMENT APPLICATIONS
Positive reinforcement with a teenage Navajo population

This study involved 24 Navajo children from 14 to 16 years of age. There were 18 boys and 6 girls; all might have been "diagnosed" or "labeled" in a variety of ways. They performed at a low level in both reading and mathematics (midfirst-grade level to low third-grade level in reading; midfirst-grade level to upper second-grade level in mathematics), and all had been in school less time than their chronological age would suggest. Their primary language was Navajo; English was their second language. As best could be measured through a variety of instruments, they were within the normal range of intelligence. They would not fit the definition of learning disabilities used by some, but they were considered learning disabled because they were learning considerably less than their peers, many of whom had received no more formal education than they, and because they did not have sensory acuity deficits or significantly low intellectual ability.

The children were divided into four groups, and each group attended a resource room for 90 minutes per day. During this 90-minute period they were given special assistance by a resource room teacher (a white male) and an aide (a Navajo female) in developing arithmetic skills. Extensive achievement testing and diagnostic work-ups had been completed before the project began. Special materials with an appropriate achievement level but a higher interest level were obtained. An effort had been made to obtain materials closely related to American Indian culture, but such materials are not in great supply.

Sufficient standardized data and personal-social information had been gathered to lead to the belief that the following general description fit all 24 students.

Intellectual level: Normal range or above.
Visual and auditory acuity: Normal.
Achievement level: Very low, even as compared to peers who had no more known opportunities to learn than they.
Attendance record: Very low for the past 2 years, even though this was a boarding school; some known truancy.
Known process disabilities: None that could be established definitely except low auditory discrimination in some.

Interest in extracurricular activities sponsored by school: Very low.
General motivation in school: Very low.
Known interests: Some had an obvious interest in members of the opposite sex; some boys had an interest in sports; all were interested in Western music; all appreciated the value of money; most (particularly the older ones) were interested in quitting school, and several had tried at least once.

There were limited guides to remediation; few were provided by diagnostic tests, and there were indications that some students did not have normal auditory discrimination.* It was decided to attempt to utilize materials with as much inherent interest as possible and to provide strong positive incentives for the students to attend to the learning task. Because they showed an interest in music and having their own radio, a system of points was established. Students could earn credits toward some fairly significant prizes, including radios and record players. Boots and other rewards selected by the students were also included, thus following the principle that rewards must be true rewards in the eyes of the subjects.

A system was established in which points were awarded for work completed, with the likelihood that many students could earn a significant reward in 3 to 4 months. In addition, when work was completed each period students were permitted to listen to Western music tapes of their own choosing through headsets that enabled them to listen without leaving class. Leaving students in the class where others could see that they were listening seemed to provide motivation for others to finish their work so that they too could listen.

Budget arrangements were made to cover the costs of the incentives, and the system apparently worked well for 2 to 3 weeks. The aide indicated that there was genuine interest

---

*With younger Navajo children we thought that results of auditory discrimination tests were meaningful. With these older, very unmotivated children we were not certain whether the results indicated auditory discrimination problems or "I don't care" problems.

in earning enough points to get the rewards, and the students were apparently motivated by the Western music. Teachers who had worked with the children before were impressed. It appeared we had found the "key" to improved achievement.

Then the project began to fall apart. The music still provided some incentive, but students completed barely enough to get to listen to the music, then slipped back into their nonattending, nonachieving ways. The desire to gain points toward prizes in which they had seemed so interested melted away. A series of conferences were held to try to save the project; university consultants who earlier had felt so smug were baffled.*

Project personnel turned to the aide for help. She was a most insightful individual and had been invaluable in assisting with the learning tasks, so she was now asked to help discover what was wrong, which she did.

It seems that the class members jointly decided that it was too much work just to earn points. They felt that they might receive prizes, but what if they quit school? Or what if the prizes were not available later? They had little faith in school authorities and (as we knew, but had not been sufficiently sensitive to) were not very future oriented. They wanted rewards *now*. (This lack of future orientation had been discussed, but after initial conversations with the class the aide thought that they did understand the longer term reward system and liked the plan. Perhaps they did, but it took less than 3 weeks for this type of motivation to become ineffective.)

In further discussions as to what might prove a meaningful reward, the aide suggested *big* chocolate candy bars to be given on Friday according to points earned during the week. Parents were contacted by school personnel and all agreed.

It is important to remember that one principle of establishing an effective reward

system is that the rewards should be personalized; they should fit individual desires because what is a reward to one student may not be to another. In this case our desire to personalize led us to overlook the principle that we should not establish a system in which rewards are too far in the future.

This story does have a happy ending. Our major emphasis in this program was mathematics, and the combination of Western music (daily) and oversize candy bars (on "payday"—Friday) apparently was the major contributing factor to growth in arithmetic achievement. The average improvement was almost two grade levels, and three boys progressed more than three grade levels. Methods and materials used to teach arithmetic concepts were undoubtedly a part of the reason, but some of these same methods and materials had been used earlier to no avail. The low teacher-pupil ratio was also undoubtedly a factor, but a low teacher-pupil ratio had not been the answer in other similar efforts. All connected with the project thought that the main two factors were the Western music and the big chocolate candy bars. We did a great deal of planning and theorizing, then stumbled onto the right combination. *The students were motivated to achieve in school in a way they had not been for years, perhaps never had been.*

In this case success came only after a reassessment of earlier plans that did not proceed as planned, but this may happen with behavioral techniques just as it does with other educational efforts. The important fact is that excellent results were obtained when we eventually arranged a set of circumstances in which these students felt real motivation to try to learn. Behavioral approaches cannot assist children to do something for which they do not have the ability, nor can it cause them to skip over large segments or steps in the learning process. Blind children cannot be made to see, and the severely retarded cannot be taught to read at the grade level of their normal peers. Children can be effectively encouraged to attend to academic tasks and to try much harder than they ever have before if we give them a reason that is im-

---

*I played a major role in this project and must take responsibility for the miscalculation. We tried to combine immediate rewards (the music) and long-term rewards (the radios, boots, etc.) and thought this would work. It did not!

portant to them. Carefully planned and implemented positive reinforcement can be a powerful tool in the hands of learning disabilities teachers.

Sam R.

Sam R., an 8-year-old of above-average mental ability, had what could be called a mild learning disability. He had a varied set of reading problems that the teacher freely admitted she could not understand. He scored only one grade level below average on achievement tests—not enough to consider referral for learning disabilities assistance in this particular school district. However, the learning disabilities resource room teacher had an open period during the last 6 weeks of the school year with no one on a waiting list (an unusual situation) and decided to try to help with Sam. His parents agreed to this help, but Sam was never listed as an "official" part of the learning disabilities program. The principal encouraged the arrangement, and a program was initiated.

In many ways, for example, in class discussions, Sam seemed to do as well or better than many other children in the class. Sometimes when he read silently and then was tested on comprehension, he would do near grade-level work. At other times he was considerably below grade level. When reading aloud he missed a large number of words, and there was no apparent rhyme or reason for the type of mistakes he made. The school psychologist reported his IQ to be between 110 and 120.

The learning disabilities teacher determined that there was no sign of visual acuity problems, and his hearing had been tested recently and found to be normal. The teacher's check of visual and auditory perception abilities indicated normalcy.

When asked to read Sam would attempt to read rapidly and make many errors; apparently he was unable to effectively use word attack skills. Sam "read" various words as something entirely different from what context clues, length of word, and beginning and ending sounds would indicate. When

shown these same words *one at a time* he recognized many of them.

A number of assumptions as to possible causation might have been made at this time, but with only a few weeks of the school year left the teacher started to try to get Sam to slow down and to look at each word carefully. Sam did not seem too concerned about the whole thing until the teacher started making a mark every time Sam made an error. Then he said, "Don't do that. I don't like it." The teacher replied, "But I have to; it's part of my job, and I'm supposed to help you make less errors." As Sam continued to try to read aloud, all errors were recorded. Although this was not an unusual procedure, the negative feelings that Sam indicated about all those "miss marks" were stronger than the teacher had ever seen.

A positive reward system for reducing the number of errors was implemented, but Sam initiated his own system. He said, "You said you were supposed to help me—now let's see if you can." He attended to the reading task and he listened and tried to apply word attack skills in a manner that other teachers could not remember having seen in him. His reward was reducing the "miss marks" **rather** than the free time that he was to have earned by reducing the number of misread words.

Over the weekend following the first full week of the program Sam made out his own schedule for reducing missed words. His parents may have assisted in home motivation, but the major motivation was apparently from within. He charted his goals and met and exceeded them, but to do so he had to read slowly and use a place marker. By the end of the second week (the resource room teacher worked with him 45 minutes a day) he had reduced his errors significantly and showed signs of beginning to use a variety of word attack skills. It is certainly likely that he progressed so rapidly because he had been "exposed" to these skills over and over, but for some reason he had not fully integrated them to the point of successful implementation.

When he returned for the start of the third

week, he said he wanted to do something like the marking of missed words to help him increase his speed. Sam and the teacher worked out a method of timing how long it took to read 100 words. This, too, became a chart, and he began to increase his speed. By the end of the school year, after only 6 weeks of special help, he scored 1.3 grade levels above where he had tested on the reading achievement test in January. Tests given at the end of the year often reflect a lack of interest that educators have tended to relate to the summer vacation spirit, but in this case the test was given because Sam was very motivated and wanted to know how well he was doing. The regular class teacher was delighted and amazed, as were the parents. They had watched the almost miraculous improvement but, as is often the case, they wanted to see the test results.

In this instance a combination of factors was involved. The one-to-one attention from a special teacher who was really "special" was undoubtedly one factor. (The fact of *asking* to take on additional work with only 6 weeks left rather than using the time for reports, conferences, coffee periods, or some other such need indicated that the teacher was either inexperienced or very special.) The matter-of-fact response to Sam's dislike for the recording of errors and the encouragement of his plans were just the right thing in this case. The slowing down worked well, and the methodicalness of the recording, permitting a record of how he was improving, apparently was effective.

It seems likely that Sam was ready to improve for reasons that remain unknown, but the positive reward that worked best in this instance was not the free time (which often is quite effective) but Sam's own motivation to reduce errors and then to increase reading speed. It is true that this was a very mild case of learning disabilities, but it was one that had not responded to earlier efforts and did respond to this system. It cannot be determined with certainty, but it seems likely that good remedial methods alone would not have accomplished what this system accomplished. At the very least it was unusually

rapid improvement in reading skill, a skill that carried over into the next school year.

CONTRACTING AS A MOTIVATIONAL TECHNIQUE

Contracts have been used with success in a variety of school settings and may more often be applicable to unacceptable behavior than to academic performance. They can be of value in academic application and are simply another form of systematic reinforcement. A manual for teachers, *How to Use Contingency Contracting in the Classroom,* by Lloyd Homme (1971) provides a programmed source for teachers who wish to learn more about this topic than will be presented here. A comprehensive discussion by Coloroso (1976) may also be of value. (The discussion and sample weekly academic contract that follow are adapted from Coloroso's discussion.)

Contracts are a joint agreement between student and teacher concerning the accomplishment of a specific objective. Contracts may be drawn up to include many phases of academic performance; they commit both the student and the teacher to specific, responsible performance. If the student agrees to and signs the contract, it represents an outward admission that the stated objectives are realistic and that they should be accomplished. The teacher's signature means something similar—that the objectives are the ones to be accomplished and that they are fair and reasonable for the student under consideration.

Contracts should permit each student to progress at his own speed, they should assist toward the goal of self-control and independence, and they should result in a feeling of self-importance and increased willingness to learn. Contracts may be the ultimate in individualization, although with improper use they may be something less. Contracting forces the teacher to become organized. According to Homme (1970), contingency management in the classroom requires the teacher to accomplish four basic steps:

1. Identify and describe the subject areas

2. Break down the subject area objectives into daily task units
3. Collect materials for subject areas
4. Divide materials into task units

In general, these basic steps must be taken if meaningful contracts are to be written; contracts must be *specific* so that no misunderstanding is possible. One type of contract, the weekly academic contract, will be discussed in more detail.

Weekly academic contract

The weekly academic contract (shown below) may be drawn up for an individual student or an entire class. If it is done for an individual student, the student and teacher should discuss the student's academic level in a specific area, his goal for the quarter (or semester), his goal for the week, and his daily goal. Each week the student and teacher review what the student has accomplished that week in relation to his goal for the quarter.

The purpose for determining goals for all three time intervals is to permit the student to see realistically where he is in a given subject area, where he is going, and how he can reach his goal—step by step. For a student who is behind in school this is most important. If he is 3 years behind in math at the beginning of the semester and $2\frac{1}{2}$ years behind at the end of the semester, he might not be able to see any improvement without the step-by-step goals. Without the specific goals

---

WEEKLY ACADEMIC CONTRACT

	DATE	ASSIGNMENT	COMMENTS
MATH	MONDAY		
	TUESDAY		
	WEDNESDAY		
	THURSDAY		
	FRIDAY		
CONSEQUENCES:____			

STUDENT: _____

TEACHER: _____

DATES: _____

ADDITIONAL COMMENTS:

he is just "still behind." With the goals he is moving ahead.

Directions for use. The teacher and student plan the activities for the week. (Mathematics will be used as an example.) The assignments are written in the second column. Several variations can be used in this column.

1. *Green circles:* Write down the number of the problems a student is expected to complete. If a student chooses to do more problems, write the additional numbers down and circle these numbers in green. A student often tries to do more than what is expected of him, especially if the type of material is geared to his abilities. The problems circled ing green serve as a message to the student's parents that the student did more than was assigned.

2. *Free day:* Write "free day" in one square. The student may use any mathematics materials that are available in the room or that he can bring from home. The only rule is that the student must spend the entire period on the assignment of his choice.

3. *Listening day:* Some class activities do not require a written assignment. The student needs to learn to listen in an active responsible manner. Discuss with the student the general rules for acceptable listening behavior during the class session. Write "listening day" in the second column.

The third column is perhaps the most important and profitable part of the contract. It is a space for *positive* evaluation of the student's work habits and attitudes—*not* his grades. At the end of each class assess with the student his performance for that class period. Place a "smile face" or positive comment in the column.

If the student did not do well that day, no comment is placed in the column. If a negative comment is written, the student may become frustrated, tear the contract up, or refuse to continue with the plan. Accent the positive, and put it in writing. Remember that this is not a grade report. It reflects work habits and attitudes. The slow learner and the underachieving student have a chance to be successful. Inform parents that they, too, can accent the positive and assume that a blank space indicates that the student

had a problem that day and that the problem was handled adequately at school. It need not be further elaborated at home.

A specific space is provided for recording consequences. These consequences should be stated positively if at all possible. There should be a joint effort by the student and teacher to determine relevant consequences.

The student and teacher sign the contract on the appropriate lines. The signing respects the integrity of the student and teacher and establishes a written commitment on the part of both parties.

Once the contract is signed, the two parties agree to be responsible for it. This can often be more difficult for the teacher than the student. For example, a student draws during math period. You remind him of the contract. (Don't nag—just remind and offer him your help.) You and he agreed to the consequences beforehand. When the class is over his work is not completed. It is a beautiful day and his friends are getting up a basketball game. He comes up to you with crocodile tears and begs, "Please let me go out today. I promise to do my math tomorrow." If you let him go out, you are doing him an injustice. A more appropriate response would be, "We agreed to the contract and I want to help you be responsible. Today you chose not to complete your math during the class period and the consequence of your choice is to stay in and complete your math during break." Then walk away and do not argue with him. It was his choice; you are not punishing him. You offered your help, you reminded him of the contract, now you must let him accept the consequences of his own behavior.

If you really care and the student knows this, he will respect you for your resistance to his pleading or arguments. He will also move one step more toward being a more responsible individual. If you give in to the tears today, the student may indeed get his work done tomorrow. However, the next time he feels like not working, the same thing will happen. The student is allowed to be irresponsible and does not grow. At best he refines his game, enabling him to manipulate and control more easily.

The contract can also be "dressed up" with cartoons or written in legal terms. Be creative and invite the student to be responsible.

SUMMARY

Motivation is essential to learning, and the learning-disabled child may have lost much of the normal motivation that educators too often assume is "built in" to all children. For the child who is learning normally the act of successful learning may produce a circular effect in which learning produces motivation for more learning. For the learning-disabled child the opposite effect may occur. Learning difficulties may lead to a negative force that must be overcome for learning to take place.

Several types of motivation should be planned: (1) motivation to overcome the failure syndrome, (2) motivation that may be applied when the learning-disabled child faces temporary but unusually strong learning roadblocks, and (3) general, ongoing motivation that may be provided through planned, positive reinforcement. Positive reconditioning as suggested and implemented by both Fernald (1943) and Gillingham and Stillman (1965) provides one excellent way to overcome the failure syndrome. Unusual and especially rewarding emergency measures may be necessary to overcome problems that arise when the student has just begun to feel success and then faces what he perceives as an impossible task. Primary reinforcement, including the possible use of money incentives, may be required here. Longer term planned behavior management techniques that emphasize positive reinforcement should be considered to maintain momentum in learning. This may include a variety of plans, including contracting systems.

In planning for the learning disabled, careful analysis of learning strengths and weaknesses is the best way to start. However, particularly with older students, such analysis sometimes provides little guidance for programming. In such cases the use of high-interest materials and careful attention to motivational techniques, including the use of positive reinforcement as part of a planned behavior management system, may be the best available program. Even when the learning strengths and weaknesses assessment provides meaningful direction for programming, motivational techniques may be required to achieve initial success. The inertia that almost always develops after months or years of failure in academic tasks is a formidable opponent that must be conquered before continuing success may be realized. The student must overcome this strong negative force, but the role of the teacher is to provide every possible assistance in this effort.

REFERENCES AND SUGGESTED READINGS

Buckley, N., and Walker, H. *Modifying classroom behavior* (Rev. ed.). Champaign, Ill.: Research Press, 1970.

Burns, R. *New approaches to behavioral objectives.* Dubuque, Iowa: William C. Brown Co., Publishers, 1972.

Cobb, J. *Survival skills and first grade achievement* (Report No. 1). Eugene, Ore.: Center for Research and Demonstration in the Early Education of Handicapped Children, University of Oregon, 1970.

Coloroso, B. Strategies for working with troubled students. In Gearheart, B., and Weishahn, M., *The handicapped child in the regular classroom.* St. Louis: The C. V. Mosby Co., 1976.

Fernald, G. *Remedial techniques in basic school subjects.* New York: McGraw-Hill Book Co., 1943.

Gearheart, B. *Learning disabilities: educational strategies.* St. Louis: The C. V. Mosby Co., 1973.

Gillingham, A., and Stillman, B. *Remedial training for children with specific disability in reading, spelling, and penmanship* (7th ed.). Cambridge, Mass.: Educators Publishing Service, Inc., 1965.

Haring, N. *Attending and responding.* San Rafael, Calif.: Dimensions Publishing Co., 1968.

Homme, L. *How to use contingency contracting in the classroom.* Champaign, Ill.: Research Press, 1971.

Stephens, T. *Directive teaching of children with learning and behavioral handicaps.* Columbus, Ohio: Charles E. Merrill Publishing Co., 1970.

Worell, J., and Nelson, M. *Managing instructional problems: a case study workbook.* New York: McGraw-Hill Book Co., 1974.

10 Services for children: alternatives and models

Even if we are fairly certain of how to determine the type of assistance each child needs and are able to tell when we have provided sufficient service, one question that must ultimately be answered is how to provide or deliver that service. Unlike regular school programs that have certain well-established teacher-pupil ratios and historical precedents for service delivery models, programs for the learning disabled are provided through a variety of models and structures. In this chapter we will examine a generalized, composite model and then consider four actual programs that are applicable in many settings, even those with very limited enrollments. The "how to do it" question is a most important one in establishing new programs, and in my experience smaller school units have had the most questions. Much of their concern has related to the fact that they cannot emulate the more complex organizational patterns of larger school districts and have difficulty in "reducing" the larger district plans to meet their needs and their limitations.

Before discussing these specific plans and models, we will review the terminology to be used in describing these services. Some differences exist in the way these terms are used, and in many instances state guidelines dictate the use of certain terminology to be consistent with approval and reimbursement regulations. I will attempt to use generalized descriptions that should be consistent with most of the existing literature.

RESOURCE ROOM PROGRAM

Resource rooms are in common use in learning disabilities programs. The resource room may be staffed by only one resource room teacher, but a trend in the direction of some type of team effort, either two teachers or a teacher and an aide, seems to be developing.

In describing a resource room program, Reger (1973) elected to approach the description from the point of view of (1) mission, (2) administrative structure, and (3) advantages. I will follow a somewhat similar pattern in describing resource rooms.

The role and function of the resource room teacher is to provide assistance to children who are having sufficient educational difficulties to cause the regular class teacher to ask for help. Usually this means more than just temporary, minor difficulties with some new process in arithmetic or a new word attack skill in reading. In most school systems a placement or program planning committee reviews a variety of information about any child referred for possible assistance in the resource room, and programming is initiated only as this committee has indicated its feasibility (for the child) and its consistency with local district policies. In all cases the parents should be involved in such placement or planning committee deliberations and give express permission for the type of educational intervention chosen.

It should be noted that in "real life" the resource room teacher who is well accepted by the local school staff can provide a great deal of highly valuable "unofficial" assistance to various teachers, sometimes in terms of general instructional ideas but often for a specific child. This is one of the more effective functions of resource room teachers, but in many states it must be done unofficially because of state reimbursement guidelines and restrictions.

State officials usually know what is happening, and if it is beneficial educationally, they ignore it on an official basis so as to not be compelled to intervene. Such state level restrictions are necessary in some cases to keep the local district administration from using personnel in a manner that would lead to proliferation of services and weakening of the entire program. Ideas and suggestions received in the halls or the coffee room continue to be effective in many settings, and materials loaned out—even if the child who will use them has not been approved for the learning disabilities program—may be benefits of a resource room program that are never publicized.

Resource room teachers should have the time, the materials, and the training to find effective ways to teach children with special needs. Their function then becomes a dual one: (1) to initiate remediation and help the child find success in the resource room and (2) to provide suggestions to the regular class teacher that may help the child find success in that setting so that the momentum toward remediation begun in the resource room is not lost.

Sometimes it is assumed that a teacher who is one of the best classroom teachers (in a given school) will be a good resource room teacher. This *may* be so, but it is not a good assumption. Too often teachers who are quite successful in the regular classroom tend to rely heavily on "the" method that they find successful and in which they have invested much time and effort. In addition, teachers who are quite effective when left to teach "their own" children with little or no outside observation and interference sometimes have real difficulty when they must spend much of their time dealing with other teachers, serving as a helping teacher, having to consider the feelings and ego needs of other teachers first, and needing to deal with care and diplomacy with other teachers (including some who are not doing a very good job of teaching). However, to be successful in the resource room setting and to attain the desired educational goals for children who spend most of their school day in another teacher's classroom, it is essential to have this sensitivity, diplomacy, and ability to place one's own ego needs second.

Reger (1973) believes that the primary mission of the resource room teacher has to do with changing the *attitude*, not the competence, of other teachers. He cites the fact that many teachers think of the child who is not achieving as not responding to "my" reading program, thus making the child's lack of success a personal affront to the teacher. When this is the case the efforts in the resource room may be successful, but the overall mission of the resource room may be a failure without a change in attitude on the part of the regular classroom teacher.

Where local conditions permit, the resource room teacher should provide some in-service training for other teachers. Although much of this may be carried out by resource room teachers, it is a good procedure to obtain outside assistance part of the time so that resource room teachers are not placed in too much of an "expert" role. When all formalized in-service efforts are ineffective due to reasons that cannot be readily overcome, alert resource room teachers will find ways to accomplish many of the same goals on an informal basis.

Reger (1973) makes a number of specific points about administrative guidelines for the resource room program. Many of the following points of emphasis are consistent with his ideas, but some are not. (These inconsistencies will not be specifically or systematically indicated; they are matters of opinion and are difficult to support with any type of objective data. This fact of minor inconsistency is mentioned only because it should not be assumed that all points that follow are from Reger's discussion or are totally consistent with his ideas.)

1. Resource rooms should be established in all buildings, and teachers should be assigned to only one building. If this cannot be done, the next best choice (and it is definitely a second choice) is to have the teacher assigned to two buildings with a specific room in each. The rooms should not be used for other purposes during the half day when the teacher is not at the building. Although this may seem like ineffective space utilization, it is extremely difficult to maintain control of room materials, records, etc., if the space is used by others.

2. Time should be set aside each week for interaction between the resource room teacher and teachers who send children to the resource room. This is sometimes opposed by those who want the resource room teacher to be "tutoring" children during all available time. However, if this is to be a resource room and not an office for a tutor, then the time must be set aside. One-half day per week for the teacher who is in one building all week should be sufficient.

3. A total pupil load of 15 to 20 should be the specified maximum. The variation (between 15 and 20) may be determined by age of the children, severity of problems, and

other such factors. It should be carefully spelled out.

4. No more than three, or in usual situations four, children should be in the resource room at one time with one teacher. If an aide is available on a full-time basis, this may be increased to as many as six *after* the aide is trained.

5. Each child should be expected to spend 60 to 90 minutes per day in the resource room. If a child requires less than 1 hour per day, it is likely that he could remain in the regular class with consultative and materials assistance. If he requires much more than 2 hours, he should perhaps be in a self-contained program. There are exceptions to these generalizations, but too many exceptions mean that the program should be re-planned.

6. Resource room teachers may be asked to participate in placement, a role that Roger (1973) believes they should not be asked to play. His reasoning is that if they do, they may be accused of favoritism toward certain other teachers or perhaps of not wanting the real problem children. I agree that placement is an administrative function and responsibility, but in many cases a resource room teacher is indispensable in providing information as to how a particular child may be helped, which other children (already in the program) he can be effectively grouped with, and a variety of related input.

In most school settings there is a way to permit the teacher to provide information about placement variables (which may include being a part of some screening and placement deliberations) without running the risk of bad feelings about favoritism. We should keep the problem in mind but not permit it to reduce the ability of resource room teachers to provide essential information when needed—and it may be needed during placement deliberations.

7. Parental understanding and cooperation with program efforts are important for all children, but particularly for children who are having educational difficulties. The role of the resource room teacher in parent conferences and in initiating parent-teacher co-operative efforts as special problems arise must be carefully delineated. The regular classroom teacher has the primary responsibility for the child's program and should coordinate parent contacts for purposes of special conferences.

As a general rule the regular class teacher should be present at all such conferences and, if not, should have had every opportunity to be involved. In other words, the regular class teacher should be the primary initiator of conferences, and such conferences should be scheduled at a time when both the regular class teacher and the resource room teacher can attend. Then if last-minute conflicts arise and the regular class teacher asks the resource room teacher to "go ahead," there is little question about conflict of interest. This whole matter may seem overemphasized, and in settings where there is complete mutual trust and total cooperation such specific administrative regulations are seldom necessary. However, such an ideal situation is seldom completely realized, and all efforts must be directed toward minimizing sources of potential conflict between the two teachers, who must work closely together for the benefit of the child.*

---

*An actual situation may best illustrate the reason for emphasizing this point. In an elementary school setting that I observed a new resource room teacher and regular class teacher were just beginning to develop a good working relationship when the regular class teacher suddenly stopped communicating. She was not negative but avoided any type of meaningful conversation, even though she was known as a cooperative person, had good standing among other teachers in the building, and had often gone out of her way to provided needed special programs for children. She was not a person who tended to complain or gossip, and it was some time before it was discovered that a parent whom she trusted told her that in a conference with the resource room teacher the parent understood that she (the regular class teacher) did not know how to teach the child in question. Eventually the problem was worked out, but it could have been avoided if the parent conference had been a joint conference. This and similar situations have been repeated many times, and if the classroom teacher in this situation had been at all malicious or had tended to gossip, she might have alienated much of the staff before the situation was worked out.

8. The parent-teacher conference relationship between the resource room teacher and other teachers is just one part of a larger consideration—the resource room teacher's professional relationships with and responsibilities to all personnel in the building, central office consultants, and supervisors. This relationship must be carefully spelled out and articulated to all concerned so that children are not shortchanged due to conflicts or misunderstandings.

This relationship includes other school district specialists (speech clinicians, remedial reading teachers, counselors, psychologists, and curriculum supervisors), building administrators (principal, vice principal, and others who may have such responsibility), and all other teachers, both those who have children in the resource room and those who do not. Such considerations as the types of diagnostic and evaluative services that the resource room teacher can provide, how they must be obtained, and the types of materials and equipment available and how they must be accounted for must be carefully spelled out. The building principal is in charge of the building and thus responsible for the resource room but may need guidance on these matters, which should come from the local director of special education.

If the resource room teacher must provide services to two buildings (not a good practice, but it does happen), then this too must be spelled out. In instances in which the services of the resource room teacher are provided through some sort of larger, cooperative service district the lines of authority and responsibility become even more complex; there is even more to be carefully delineated.

9. The resource room should normally be the same size as any other classroom. Because of the need to store a variety of materials and to provide for the possibility of an aide, a room of about two-thirds the size of a normal classroom must be considered the absolute minimum size in which a meaningful program may be provided. Although many programs will not require space for motor activities, a full-size classroom is essential if motor activities are required.

A teacher desk, chair, and four-drawer file (plus another desk and chair if an aide is employed), student desks of various sizes, and at least two small worktables with chairs of various heights are required. Although different children use the same desk at different times of the day, there must be large storage spaces for the materials required for each child in the program. Shelves with large, individual "tote boxes" may adequately fill this need in most instances. Reger (1973) indicates that at least $1,500 is required to equip a newly established resource room, with $1,000 per year to maintain the program. I believe his estimates to be adequate *if* certain audiovisual equipment is available from an existing school inventory and if the program does not include some of the more expensive programmed material I have often seen in use. Otherwise the funds required might be doubled.

The resource room appears to be the most commonly used service delivery vehicle at the present and will likely remain so for the immediate future. Two other service delivery alternatives will be mentioned: the itinerant teacher program and the consultative and special materials program. These will be discussed as though each were a distinct entity, but in many cases a combination of programs is used and the same teacher provides assistance through some combination of all three arrangements. Some theorists maintain that if the teacher is not in a single resource room at one specific school for all of every day, it is not a resource room program. This may be, if they define the resource room in this manner, but in practical application we often hear of a part-time resource room.

ITINERANT TEACHER PROGRAM

The itinerant teacher pattern with which educators are most familiar is that followed by many public school speech clinicians. Although there are variations in the manner in which this is implemented, a large number of speech clinicians work with each child two or three times each week for 30 to 40 minutes each day. Some itinerant teachers of learning-disabled children follow a similar pattern, but I believe this tends to be too little time to be of much value to most learning-disabled children. A minimum period of direct service to each child of 1 hour per day for 3, 4, or 5 days a week is the least that is likely to be of significant value. This is a *minimum;* many children serviced by an itinerant teacher should be seen for longer periods of time, dependent on the type and severity of the problem.

Itinerant teachers usually do many of the same things that resource room teachers do, but they are limited by time constraints and the difficulties involved in moving equipment and materials. (Some itinerant teachers use a van or station wagon, filling much of the cargo space with equipment and materials, but this should certainly not be a requirement for the position. For the most part, it is a matter of limiting what can be done in relation to what can be carried from school to school and attempting to obtain adequate storage at the various schools to keep certain materials, in addition to children's work, protected but readily available.)

This is not to say that itinerant teacher program cannot be effective, but rather to indicate that if direct service to children is the major thrust of the program, the resource room program is usually more effective than the itinerant program because the latter has physical limitations. One other disadvantage must be cited; there is limited contact with the faculty of the various schools served by itinerant teachers. This factor, with the added consideration of personnel time lost in travel, makes an itinerant program the second choice when either an itinerant or a resource program may be chosen for a given setting.

Certain conditions lead to adoption of the itinerant program, and in some of these situations it appears to be the best method of service delivery. In sparsely populated areas of the country, where schools tend to be quite small in total pupil enrollment, it is difficult to justify a full-time resource room program at one school. Because of long distances between schools, it is equally difficult to justify busing children into a specific school to en-

large the population of children requiring learning disabilities programming. (It is not difficult to justify busing if we are considering only the most severe cases, but there are even fewer of these children and it would take an even larger geographical area to find enough children who require such services.) Therefore the itinerant program may be the most effective in sparsely populated areas. In larger population centers a combination of resource room and itinerant programs may be used, with the itinerant service reserved for very mild cases. A third possibility is that of a part-time itinerant service in combination with consultative and materials assistance. One learning disabilities teacher may work part of the day providing direct service to children in an itinerant program and during the same day, perhaps even in the same school, serve a consultative role. The adoption of this combination service model may be related to a whole variety of needs or to space variables.

In summary, the itinerant program is useful, it may be used in combination with other service delivery models, and it appears to be in more common use in sparsely populated states. It requires that a good deal of valuable personnel time be spent in travel and is inefficient to this extent. Compared to a resource room program it is less effective, both on a time-cost basis and on the basis of achievement of educational goals with children; however, where conditions dictate its use it is certainly much better than no program at all, and innovative, dedicated practitioners have found ways to increase its effectiveness through careful planning and spending some very long days on the road.

CONSULTATIVE AND SPECIAL MATERIALS PROGRAMS

The consultative program and the special materials program represent less service to the regular class teacher and to the learning-disabled child than either the resource room or the itinerant program. Consultative and materials program service is usually called indirect because specialized personnel limit their activities to contact with the teacher.

In contrast, resource room and itinerant programs provide direct contact with children. Specialized personnel are required for this type of service, and it seems to take a special type of personality to be highly successful in either of these programs. Although it would be theoretically possible to have either the consultative or special materials program alone, in practice there are usually components of each in any program that carries either name.

For example, when the emphasis is on special instructional materials housed in some central facility there must be someone to "check out" such materials. It would be possible to make this a purely clerical, record-keeping task, but often a well-qualified specialist is selected so that assistance may be given teachers who come looking for ideas or help. This then becomes a combination special materials and consultative program. When the consultative facet is the major emphasis and the specialist goes from school to school (usually on a request basis) teachers almost invariably ask for assistance with materials. Even if it is not a part of the original plan, the program usually serves a combined consultative and special materials function. In essence, we have found through practice that consultative asssitance without help with materials is relatively ineffective, and a supply of materials without assistance in how to use them is equally ineffective. In fact, the official name given such a combined program usually is a result of how the project was sold to the public and the board of education, what title is required to obtain federal funds, or both.

We should recognize that any of these service delivery alternatives could be organized and implemented in such a way that children other than learning-disabled children are served. This is likely to be the case with the special materials and consultative program, for school districts often choose to place materials for all types of handicapping conditions in one center. At times this may be combined with a materials center established to serve all children (handicapped and nonhandicapped) in the district.

Special materials and/or consultative assistance is probably most useful in dealing with mild problems or as an additional support system for the teacher who has considerable experience with children with unique learning problems but limited time and must have this minimal amount of extra help. Generally speaking, it is not sufficient for many children with moderate learning disabilities, and it is seldom sufficient for those with severe learning disabilities.

MULTITHRUST PROGRAMS

Several types of what might be called multithrust programs exist. The most common is one in which a planned combination of resource room, itinerant service, and consultative service is provided; all are backed up by a special materials and media center. At times various individuals provide "pure" services; that is, they serve only as a resource room teacher or only on an itinerant basis. At other times learning disabilities specialists may wear one hat in the morning and another in the afternoon.

Another multithrust program is one in which diagnostic efforts are conducted in a half-day (or whole-day) program that lasts for 2 to 4 weeks. This is not just "testing," but assessment of learning abilities and learning needs in the teaching-learning setting. After trying out new methods or materials, the child is sent back to the regular classroom with new ideas and teaching materials. This, then, is a combination assessment–resource room–materials approach with consultative help and in some cases continued itinerant services as a follow-up. (See pp. 190-194.) Adding the assessment facet provides an almost endless variety of programming in combination with the resource room, itinerant program, and the consultative and materials approaches. Local interest (with funds to support it), local need, and the ability to find and employ qualified personnel are the major determinants of this variety, with no set rule or pattern as to what will be best for any given community.

Any of these program approaches may be ineffective if children requiring a certain level of service are placed in a program that is not appropriate for their unique needs. Any can be ineffective if the teachers who provide the services are poorly trained or are insufficiently flexible and believe that there is "a method" through which all learning-disabled children learn. A number of additional factors are known to be potentially dangerous to successful program implementation and should be carefully monitored. These include the following factors. (1) Because these are additional service programs (children in these programs all have a home room, a desk, and a teacher somewhere else in the system), they can be cut from the budget without increasing class size. They thus become prime targets for the attention of budget trimmers. (2) Learning disabilities programs have often led to territorial conflicts with other specialists both within the school and in the community. (3) Leadership at the policy-making and budget-construction levels may not wish to admit ignorance of this relatively new program and inadvertently wreak havoc through unfortunate decisions based on faulty or inadequate data. (4) Expectations of miracles, often unwittingly promoted when the program is "sold" to a board of education, always lead to disappointment. (5) Effectiveness of program provision can be seriously reduced by inadequate assessment and placement procedures and decisions.

Learning-disabled children may be served in a variety of ways, with some demonstrated success for all major service delivery modes. The major determinants of which is best in a given setting are severity of disability and a variety of physical and geographical considerations such as school size, density of population, and available space in buildings. Other considerations include funding, other services available in the community or school, and readiness and philosophical attitude of the educational community. Any combination of service delivery systems should be considered acceptable if it is effective.

The last half of this chapter will consist of descriptions of five program models. The first is a composite model that includes many of the promising practices in several school districts with pupil enrollments in the range of 50,000 to 100,000. The last four are descriptions of actual programs and will provide guidelines for implementation in much smaller districts or for development as one part of a larger system.

MIDVILLE PROGRAM

Midville is a hypothetical city with a population of 260,000 and a public school enrollment (kindergarten through grade twelve) of 53,000. The program description that follows is taken from actual programs now in operation in communities of this approximate size. Most of these programs could be used in communities with pupil enrollments of 25,000 or more, although we cannot always count on scaling down or multiplying numbers of personnel in exact proportion to enrollment. Factors such as other pupil services, flexibility of the elementary reading program, and size and effectiveness of the remedial reading program must also be considered.

Midville has had a comprehensive special education program for many years and is usually considered a leader in the state in educational planning and programming. Its basic economy is good, its tax base is strong, and education in Midville is well funded.

The backbone of the Midville learning disabilities program is generally considered to be the elementary school resource room program. There are 51 elementary schools, and elementary school enrollments range from approximately 400 pupils in the smallest school to more than 900 in the largest. The median elementary school enrollment is 610 pupils, and the total elementary school enrollment is 29,400. The larger elementary schools made it relatively easy to sell the idea of a resource room in each school, and although it took a span of 6 years to accomplish, there is now one resource room in each building. There are full-time aides in all buildings with more than 700 students, part-time aides (usually one-half time at each of two schools) in schools with 500 to 700 students, and only the resource room teacher in schools with less than 500 students.

All the resource room teachers (51 in the elementary program) are endorsed to teach in this specialty area; nearly 90% of them have a master's degree in learning disabilities. About one third of the aides have at least one college degree, but many of these degrees are in an area other than education. The other two thirds of the aides range in formal education from high school graduates to 3 years of college. All aides receive 1 week of special training in the fall of the year in which they are first employed, and there are at least 4 all-day in-service training sessions during the school year for all aides, new or returning.

Midville special educators plan on the basis of an estimate that 2% to 3% of the elementary age children have sufficiently serious learning disabilities to require resource room assistance (2% to 3% at any one time—this means that the program serves 7% to 10% of the children at some time during their school years). With 51 resource rooms this population can be served adequately. By state regulation resource room teachers at the elementary level can serve only 15 children at one time without an aide. With an aide they may serve 20 children. Midville conforms with state regulations; reimbursement of 60% of the salaries of both teachers and aides is an important incentive for this program.

In addition to this basic resource room program, two other direct classroom services to learning-disabled children are provided at the elementary level. The first is a self-contained class program for children with severe learning problems. Children are considered for this program only as a last resort, and usually the resource room program is given an extensive tryout first. If all other efforts fail, after careful consideration and parent approval, children may be placed in self-contained classes; the goal is return to the resource program and then to the regular classroom at the earliest possible date.

Midville has four such self-contained classes, three of them for extremely hyperactive children (most are on medication and under continuing medical care), and one that is admittedly a sort of "miscellaneous" class of children with a variety of problems in addition to basic, severe learning disabilities. No one is particularly happy about this last class, but without it these children would be really lost educationally. Each of these four classes is limited to eight children and is staffed by a teacher and an aide. The three classes for hyperactive children represent three different age ranges, and children are transported by special minibus to these self-contained settings.

The other direct classroom service at the elementary level is a system of high-risk classes established in about half of the elementary schools for children whose apparent lack of readiness for academic performance and other related behavior (at the kindergarten level) indicate they may be likely to have learning disabilities. In the larger elementary schools a staffing formula is used that permits one first-grade class of only 15 to 18 pupils as compared to other classes, which average 26 to 28 pupils. At present this is not called a learning disabilities program, does not receive special state reimbursement, and does not exist at all elementary schools. Some principals think they can accomplish the same goals in another manner, but an increasing number adopt this program after observing it in action in other schools.

Children are grouped in this small class after screening by the kindergarten teacher, the educational diagnostician, and the speech clinician. Parents are fully informed about the program, and children are placed in this class only with parental approval. The class is just another first-grade class as far as any official records are concerned, but it is much smaller and the teachers have received special training (a combination of in-service and university credit courses, planned jointly with the local state university) in how to identify potential learning problems and how to promote learning abilities.

The small class size permits much more individual attention, and many children move on to the second grade in the normal manner. Others may be kept another year in the first grade, but if so, they go to another nonhigh-risk class and teacher. Still others may go on to second grade with referral to the learning disabilities resource room program. Some children are moved out of these classes after a few weeks in the fall, after teacher observation indicates they are ready for regular first-grade classes.

At successively higher grade levels a lower and lower percentage of children is served in the learning disabilities program. At the secondary level there are 11 large junior high schools and 6 high schools. Two of the junior high schools have three learning disabilities staff members; the other nine have two each. In each school these teachers work as a team to assist students with academic inadequacy stemming from learning problems. Each high school has a team of two teachers who work in a similar manner.

Administrative and supervisory support for the learning disabilities programs is provided by a coordinator of learning disabilities programs, who reports to the director of special education, and a consultant in learning disabilities, who works with the coordinator. Officially the consultant is responsible to the coordinator, but in practice they work as a team, with the coordinator providing consultative assistance at the secondary level and also serving as primary consultant for learning disabilities programs in 12 of the elementary schools. The consultant serves the other 39 elementary schools.

Curriculum development at the elementary level is the primary responsibility of the consultant, while curriculum development at the secondary level is the responsibility of the coordinator. (It should be noted that this specific division of responsibility is *not* related to the titles of consultant and coordinator but rather to the interests and expertise of these two individuals.) For most purposes these two operate as a team with equal responsibility and authority. In the final analysis, however, because the director of special education wants one person to hold responsible for learning disabilities program development, evaluation, personnel recruit-

ment, and related responsibilities, the coordinator is officially responsible for decisions that involve difficult choices likely to be ultimately defended to the superintendent or the board of education.

Midville has an above-average number of support personnel for all special programs: school psychologists, social workers, speech clinicians, school nurses, and academic area consultants. Midville also has a special group of diagnostic personnel called educational diagnosticians who work almost exclusively with the learning disabilities program. The 12 diagnosticians (there is one "head diagnostician," a title that inspires numerous bad jokes but simply means one person must plan and coordinate their efforts) are each assigned to five or six schools; they provide specialized assistance to resource room teachers and do specified diagnostic work at the time of referral. They also provide support to the high-risk first-grade classes. They do only educational assessment, and their work is carefully coordinated with that of the school psychologists. They are experienced learning disabilities teachers who have received additional training (at the postmaster's level) in educational diagnostic assessment procedures.

When a recent time analysis of their efforts was completed it was discovered that they spent approximately 40% of their time in diagnostic procedures and meetings relating to possible placement, 40% with teachers in the resource rooms or self-contained rooms, 10% in the high-risk first-grade program, and the remainder in conferences with parents, teachers, and administrators. In many ways they are used as additional consultants by the learning disabilities teachers, but their critical importance is in assisting the teachers to better develop their own skills in determining pupil needs and strengths and in more precise evaluation of pupil progress. They have also relieved the psychologists' case loads to some extent; in fact, they were first added to the staff as an alternative to adding additional school psychologists.

Midville operates a central diagnostic and assessment center staffed by a director, a part-time medical (M.D.) consultant, and individuals from the existing staff of school psychologists and educational diagnosticians. (Psychologists and diagnosticians provide service to the center as part of their regular assignment.) In addition, one of the best trained of the district speech clinicians is assigned to the center on a full-time basis and provides speech, language, and audiological evaluations.

This center provides diagnostic service for children who appear to require more thorough or complete evaluation than can be arranged at the schools. In addition, because of a state law that permits such services to children starting at age 3 years, the center provides preschool evaluation if it appears to be justified by the referring agency or individual (usually a pediatrician). The purpose is evaluation of suspected learning disabilities, and the center usually does not become involved in evaluations when a clear etiology of mental retardation or severe emotional disturbance exists. Although individuals in the community, including a group of influential physicians, have suggested that the center should expand its services, for the present the board of education has defined its responsibilities in such a manner that learning disabilities must remain the primary focus.

As the learning disabilities program has grown rapidly over the past few years there have been some problems of interdisciplinary rivalry because this program ended the planned expansion of school psychological and remedial reading services. Whether this should have happened is debatable. The fact is that it happened, and after a few years most professionals decided to act professionally. The coordinator of the remedial reading program is helpful in planning joint services, and many in-service meetings of remedial reading and learning disabilities teachers are now held jointly. Planning of cooperative efforts tends to be on a school-by-school basis, reflecting the strengths of the two individuals assigned to the schools and the unique problems of the school rather than a specific,

district-wide plan. In general, however, it appears that (1) if the academic problems seem to have a significant carryover into areas other than reading, the learning disabilities program is likely to be considered first and (2) because a relatively small learning disabilities pupil load is established by reimbursement regulations, children with more severe problems are usually assigned to learning disabilities and the remedial reading program serves larger numbers of children with milder problems.

Most program referrals of school-age children are made by classroom teachers. Some referrals of school-age children and most referrals at the preschool level (for the diagnostic and assessment center) come from physicians. At both preschool and school-age levels referrals may come from parents, but these are unusual.

The procedure for planning and programming follows the sequence outlined in the chart on p. 21, and the programming could best be described as eclectic. Because of the close cooperation between learning disabilities and remedial reading personnel, the program focus reflects a true combined task-process approach. New methods or materials are regularly considered and evaluated by the coordinator and the consultant along with a small, standing committee of teachers who have volunteered to evaluate such new ideas. This does not indicate that teachers cannot try out new ideas, methods, or materials without permission but rather that they are encouraged to ask this committee to evaluate them and to share the results of evaluation with all staff members. There is a specific budgeted amount for purchase of such materials, which makes it possible for teachers to have the benefit of looking over items in which they have an interest without personal expenditure.

A wide variety of evaluation instruments is used in the Midville program, but every attempt is always made to verify an area of deficit before initiating remedial programming based on the existence of that deficit. In Midville verification means the use of at least two standardized instruments (which measure the same or closely related skill or process areas) and additional corroboration through informal measurements and observations in the learning-teaching setting. Educational diagnosticians play an important role along with the learning disabilities teachers in this verification.

Evaluation instruments, a supplementary supply of kits, materials, and equipment, and a well-stocked professional library are maintained at the diagnostic and assessment center. This center is located in a small school building that became impractical to use as an attendance center when the downtown Midville business area expanded. There was more room in this setting for materials and books than in the school administration building, so the entire curriculum materials and media center (for all subjects and all grades) was moved from the administration building to the diagnostic and evaluation center. This move brought important fringe benefits as regular classroom teachers visited to get books and materials and stayed to observe evaluation procedures through the one-way observation windows.

A great deal more might be said about the Midville program, but details as to teaching procedures might soon become inaccurate (or at least partially so) because Midville teachers are busy developing new methods and participating in the evolution of the learning disabilities field. Many communities are not as fortunate as Midville, but an increasing number are approaching this level of service. Taking a careful look at the most promising aspects or components of a number of good programs remains one of the best ways to obtain new ideas in any area of education. Midville educators continue to follow this procedure and it is highly recommended to readers of this text. (As indicated at the beginning of the Midville description, this is a composite of features of a number of learning disabilities programs. For descriptions of 11 actual school district programs, see Gearheart [1973, pp. 159-185].)

DIAGNOSTIC-PRESCRIPTIVE CENTER FOR CHILDREN WITH LEARNING DISABILITIES

PITT COUNTY SCHOOLS

Robinson Primary School
Winterville, North Carolina

The state of North Carolina has made commendable efforts to promote the training of learning disabilities teachers through a learning disabilities staff development program carried out jointly between state universities and local public school districts. Some of the staff development centers provide a good example of what might be called a single unit model, that is, a model that can be applied in a single school without extensive administrative or supervisory structure. In North Carolina these staff development centers serve two specific purposes: (1) to provide a demonstration and training center to assist in the training of learning disabilities teachers and (2) to assist children with learning disabilities. The educational assistance to children with learning disabilities will be the focus of this description.

There is little doubt that these centers, because they are a part of a staff development program, receive more attention from special consultants than an isolated center of the same type. However, the training function requires additional time and effort on the part of those who actually conduct the program. With a well-trained teacher, sufficient space and materials, and the will to provide such a program most schools could provide a program nearly as effective as the one at the Robinson Primary School.

The descriptive outline that follows includes the features that are most essential to understanding the general program operation. As with any such program, all of the materials, structure, and outward appearance of effectiveness would be only a facade without the support of the principal and building staff and acceptance by the parents. The Robinson School program has all of these. Last, and certainly not least, the program must have a good, knowledgeable teacher who can provide special assistance to children and work harmoniously with the building staff. The Robinson School has a teacher who meets these qualifications who is assisted by a competent aide.

For additional information about the diagnostic-prescriptive center and forms used in the program, see Appendix C.

Teacher referral

At the beginning of the school year classroom teachers are given a brief overview of the learning disabilities program, a list of the characteristics of learning-disabled children, and referral forms. They are instructed to complete a referral form for each child with average or above-average intelligence who seems to possess those characteristics displayed by children with learning disabilities. These forms are turned in to the school principal, who may add comments as appropriate. The principal then gives them to the learning disabilities teacher.

Screening and assessment

The following instruments are used in the screening and assessment process.

1. Peabody Picture Vocabulary Test
2. Slosson Intelligence Test
3. Slosson Drawing Coordination Test
4. Wide Range Achievement Test
5. Peabody Individual Achievement Test
6. Wepman Auditory Discrimination Test
7. Slosson Oral Reading Test
8. Draw-A-Man Test

Informal assessment is a vital part of the screening process. The following are some of the activities used.

1. Writing complete name
2. Writing alphabet (small letters)
3. Writing numbers (1 to 10)
4. Distinguishing between b, d, p, g, q
5. Distinguishing between "saw" and "was"
6. Visual discrimination activity
7. Writing a sentence
8. Eye dominance test
9. Informal reading inventory

The following questions are considered in identifying children with learning disabilities.

1. Is the child average or above average in intelligence?
2. Is his achievement 2 years or more behind his current grade placement?
3. Does he appear to have visual-motor problems that could affect reading, writing, or spelling?
4. Does he have a distorted conception of the human figure and interrelationship of its parts?

The parents of those children whose test results indicate possible learning disabilities are sent a letter requesting their permission for psychological testing. When the permission slips are received, the children are given the Wechsler Intelligence Scale for Children and other tests as required to determine their level of intelligence.

Parent conferences

Individual parent conferences are held with the parents of the children identified as having learning disabilities. The learning disabilities program is explained and permission is obtained to place the child in a resource class to work on areas in which deficits have been indicated if the placement committee so recommends.

Placement committee

The test results and information obtained about each child are presented to a placement committee for consideration for placement in the resource class. The committee may consist of the learning disabilities teacher, the principal, the medical-social counselor, the special education supervisor, the classroom teacher, and others as may be necessary in an individual case. The committee must reach substantial agreement on the need for placement before such placement is made.

Diagnosis and prescription

The following diagnostic instruments are commonly used to prescribe for the individual needs of each child. Others are used as required.

1. Illinois Test of Psycholinguistic Abilities

2. Basic Education Skills Inventory—Math and Reading
3. Frostig Developmental Test of Visual Perception
4. KeyMath
5. Slingerland Screening Test
6. Goldman-Fristoe-Woodcock Test of Auditory Discrimination
7. Woodcock Reading Mastery Test
8. Sucher-Allred Reading Placement Inventory

Learning lab

The learning lab is a diagnostic-prescriptive center designed to meet the individual needs of each child. Assets, deficits, and long-range prescriptions are recorded in individual folders for each child.

As each child enters the learning lab each day, he picks up his tote tray containing his *daily task folder* and other materials he keeps in his tray. The prescription centers (reading and language, writing, math, auditory perception, visual perception, kinesthetic-tactile) are identified by Walt Disney characters. The child goes to the centers in the order of arrangement of the picture cards in the pockets of his task folder. Once the child is in the center to which he has been assigned, the teacher or aide assists him in getting the appropriate materials, understanding the instructions, and beginning the assigned task. The teacher then leaves the child to work independently and goes to other children in much the same manner. "Help Please" signs are available at each center as a means of letting the teacher know that the child requires help in completing a task or is ready to have his work checked.

The children may work in two or three centers each day in the learning lab. Constant monitoring and individual assistance are paramount in the individualized approach. Incomplete tasks or unfinished center activities are ordinarily assigned for the next class period in an orderly, sequential manner throughout the week. At the close of each day individual daily prescriptions are written for the following day.

The center activities and tasks consist of commercial programmed materials, teacher-made games, laminated task cards, record players, cassette tape players, books, puppets, and assorted activity folders. Although most of the tasks are individually oriented, there is planned opportunity for social development through games, peer teaching, puppetry, and group activities.

Approximately 20 children are served in the learning lab on a daily basis under the supervision of the resource teacher. The resource teacher also serves as a consulting teacher for a limited number of children who do not come to the resource room. The maximum number of children the teacher can serve is 25 as specified by state regulations.

The children served in the learning lab range in age from 7 to 10 years. The majority of the children are in the second and third grades, and IQ's range from 90 to 130. The most significant academic discrepancy is in the area of reading. The perceptual area causing the greatest difficulty is auditory learning.

The learning lab serves five or six children at a time for 1 to 1½ hour each day Monday through Thursday. Friday is designated as a day for individual evaluations and testing, teacher and parent conferences, classroom observations, and follow-up activities in the regular classroom.

Learning disabilities staff development center

The learning disabilities staff development center is located next door to the learning disabilities resource room. The purpose of the center is as follows:

1. To train learning disabilities teachers in diagnostic-prescriptive techniques
2. To familiarize regular classroom teachers with identification and remediation procedures
3. To provide administrators some insight into the problems involved in establishing learning disabilities programs in their own school systems
4. To assist parents of learning-disabled

children in becoming involved with their child's education

An observation window between the two rooms permits the participants in the staff development center to observe various techniques and innovative materials being utilized with children with learning disabilities.

Training in the center is accomplished through the use of modules. These modules consist of a pretest and posttest, objectives, activities, take-home contracts, and an evaluation. The following modules are being used in the center.

1. Introduction to and organizational plans for learning disabilities programs
2. Diagnosis and prescription
3. Methodology of prevention and remediation
4. Selection and evaluation of curriculum materials
5. Training of administrators, principals, and supervisors for planning and implementing learning disabilities programs
6. Reading techniques in learning disabilities
7. Parental awareness and involvement

Other modules are under development.

Students in internship training in the field of learning disabilities at East Carolina University work closely with the Pitt County learning lab. The following are among the objectives to be met in this setting.

1. Design a screening procedure to be used with any school unit.
2. Evaluate and prescribe for a specific learning disability.
3. Use evaluation data to establish type and level of discrepancies.
4. Write a prescription in behavioral terms, specifying instructional objectives that are appropriate to needs and levels of the child.
5. Implement the prescription.
6. Design and implement prescription centers for academic and perceptual disorders.

The university provides consultive assistance in planning to the resource teacher and to the coordinator of the staff development center.

Summary

The learning-disabled child is provided an opportunity to improve his self-concept through success-oriented tasks. Since each child works at his own level, at his own rate, and with materials designed to remedy his specific problems, the program is truly individualized. Teaching the child to work independently in the resource room and to continue to do so in his regular classroom is of prime concern. The ultimate goal is to enable the child to function well within his regular classroom, thereby phasing him out of the resource room as soon as the necessary remediation has been completed.

Although individual pupil growth and progress are observable to the resource teacher, specific test data must be recorded as a means of verifying pupil progress. Examples of individual pupil progress in academic areas are determined from pretest and posttest scores on the Peabody Individual Achievement Tests. One child repeating the second grade made the following gains during the period from October to May: in math, from 1.9 to 3.5; in reading word recognition, from 2.2 to 3.3; in reading comprehension from a level too low for a grade equivalent to 2.9; and in spelling, from 1.1 to 2.7. Another second-grade pupil showed significant gains in reading word recognition from 1.6 to 2.6, reading comprehension from too low for a grade equivalent to 3.4, and spelling from 1.5 to 3.4.

Other school districts may choose to pursue slightly different emphases in the learning lab but the manner in which children are selected for this program, evaluated, and placed provides a good model. The use of long-range prescriptions based on assets and deficits and daily prescriptions that are made each day for the following day is an excellent model. The daily prescriptive folder with pockets directing the child to appropriate learning centers by use of Walt Disney characters is simple but highly effective and unusually motivating—frosting on an already good cake.

LEARNING DISABILITIES PROGRAMMING IN AN OPEN SETTING

MOORE COUNTY SCHOOLS

Pinehurst Middle School
Pinehurst, North Carolina

A second learning disabilities program in North Carolina that deserves special mention is quite different from the Robinson Primary School but is also connected with a staff development center. This program is located in the Pinehurst Middle School in Pinehurst, North Carolina, and is perhaps not as likely to be readily emulated as the Robinson School program due to a variety of factors.

The open class model program at Pinehurst was established as a demonstration classroom in 1972 to promote a child advocacy approach to teaching. More recently a learning disabilities component was added, including the related staff development center. As a demonstration center it has undoubtedly received the benefit of unusually adequate supplies and materials and certainly has the advantage of an excellent staff and strong administrative support.

The program involves a fifth-grade classroom with between 50 and 60 children housed in a room that is approximately two and one-half times the size of a normal classroom. Two teachers and a project assistant are in the class full time; the coordinator of the staff development center assists at times but is primarily responsible for the training of learning disability teachers. The learning disabilities resource teacher is not limited to helping exceptional children only; the staff views this as a procedure that would lead to "labeling." Although they are not labeled as such for most purposes, there are, in fact, 10 to 12 learning-disabled children who are served by this program.

Learning disabilities programming at Pinehurst can be adequately and meaningfully discussed and conceptualized only as part of the larger class unit of more than 50 children. A general description of the entire open class program will therefore be given.

The following four primary objectives have been adopted by the Pinehurst team as goals for the open education program.

1. To develop motivation for learning
2. To develop tolerances for differences
3. To encourage academic achievement
4. To develop communication skills

Although these are important goals, the most important factor in this program is the "umbrella" that encompasses the entire concept, the constant striving to maintain the warm and accepting emotional climate necessary for growth and well-being of the children.

The basic philosophy of the program is possibly best represented by an attitude of genuine caring and concern for each child. Consistent with this philosophy, the teaching staff has adopted the following guidelines, stated in very personal terms.

If you say you *care* about children and are advocates for children, then:

1. You will gear your program to children, not children to the program.
2. You will *say* that each child should be accepted for himself, and you will *demonstrate* this acceptance.
3. Realizing that each child has his own set of abilities and liabilities, you will *say* that each individual has something to offer the group, and you will *look for and find* that something in each child.
4. You will *say*, "A child should not be compared to or in competition with others for grades," and you will *carry this out* by evaluating each in the context of his own ability and effort.
5. You will say, "Begin with the child where he is, and you will *help* him to find success at his level and then help him to reach out beyond and do even better. You will not label him and lock him in at "his" level.

When you can show the child that you not only tolerate, but go so far as to expect and even enjoy, the differences you find in him and his classmates, *then* perhaps he will believe you.

Teacher attitudes create a model for a change in attitude in the child. The child may then be able to say (and believe), "There are some things that I am that I cannot change: sex, race, age, physical characteristics, handicaps. There are other things that I *can* change, and I will try to change for the better." It is this change in attitude that the Pinehurst staff has tried to help children develop within themselves; this is what the Pinehurst program is all about.

The arrangement of the classroom is shown in Fig. 10. Within this facility a variety of activities take place at all times. Although this is an open setting, there is a fair degree of built-in structure. The following features are included in this program.

1. Multiple learning centers contain

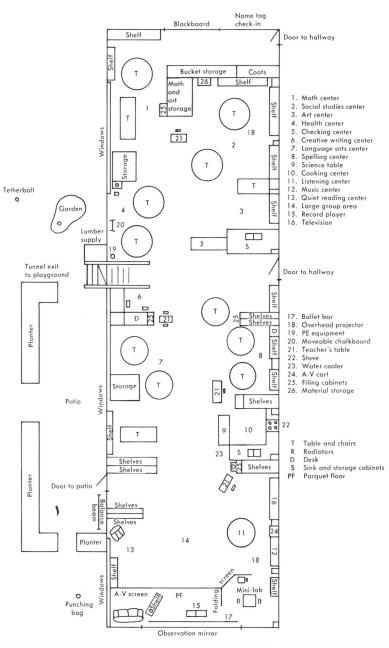

Fig. 10. Pinehurst Middle School fifth-grade classroom.

books and materials pertaining to the particular center. Centers include language arts, math, science, health, quiet reading, social studies, spelling, free choice centers, cooking, horticulture, physical education, free reading, music, art, viewing, listening, pets, and puzzles.

2. Children move from learning center to learning center.
   a. Each child has a weekly contract sheet on which he keeps a record of his activities within the school.
   b. Several different methods are used (in addition to the weekly contract sheet) to help children plan what they will do on a daily basis. The intent is to guide children in learning to plan for themselves.

3. Instructional approaches are varied. Small group instruction, large group instruction, and individual help are all provided. (Written units and teacher-pupil conferences guide students in their work). Special remedial classes are provided in math and reading.

4. Children are grouped in families with a family leader.
   a. The designated family center is a place for the family to meet to go to lunch and to clean up in the afternoon.
   b. The family serves to provide squad groupings for physical education instruction.
   c. On Monday, Wednesday, and Friday families work together on social studies skills for the entire afternoon. (This incorporates all areas of the curriculum.)

5. Children have three free choices per week to visit smaller interest centers— to work on songs for music, view a filmstrip, use musical instruments, visit the pet center (gerbils, mice, tropical fish, and others), or do free reading, creative writing, and art work. After the free period the child returns to his work.

6. Children within centers may group or regroup themselves to work as long as they do not disturb others.

7. Children are held responsible for their own and each other's behavior.

8. The teacher is viewed as a facilitator of education. He or she gathers materials suitable to each level of ability and to meet varying interests.

9. Each child is encouraged to do his best in competition with his own record. Each child may progress as far and as fast as he wishes.

10. Based on a variety of types of evaluation, children are placed at a level at which it is believed they can succeed yet be challenged. They are by no means "locked in" at this level; they may move up or down according to what they accomplish.

11. As the instruction depends on the child's ability as an individual, so does his evaluation. He is judged by his accomplishment according to his ability.

12. Written units guide children in their centers for most work; however, an individual approach is used in reading. Spelling and math are programmed. The child establishes his own goals and sets out to achieve them. He is tested either orally or by written tests at the completion of his work.

13. Modification of behavior, self-discipline, and development of a set of values are considered as important as academic achievement.

14. Parent and community volunteers are welcomed and sought after to share and work with children in activities that grow out of their special interests.

Learning disabilities programming is just one function of this total open program, an ideal way in which to avoid requiring children to leave their regular classroom to receive such services. Before school starts in the fall the teacher team reviews cumulative folders of children who will be in the class, searching for indications of possible learning problems. Previous test scores and teacher comments are helpful in indicating which children might be more closely observed once they arrive in class. Observations of team members and placement tests are used to determine instructional levels (for *all* children in the class) and provide additional guidance. Specific testing (educational or process tests) may be given as a part of the regular class procedure to determine any need for further investigation.

Children who appear to be having unusual difficulty are discussed carefully by the team and, if indicated, parents are contacted for a conference. They are told about potential difficulties and, if they give permission, additional tests may be given by school psychologists. When such tests indicate that the child is in the average range or above in intellectual ability, and if academic achievement tests indicate considerable educational retardation, the child will be scheduled into a "mini-lab" within the classroom (see Fig. 10). If IQ evaluations indicate a much lower intellectual level, children are not considered for the learning disabilities programming, but more information is available to the other teachers (all in the same room and working together regularly throughout the day) for more meaningful programming.

Prescription folders are made for each child served in the mini-lab, based on data similar to that used in the Robinson Primary School program. A daily record sheet with specific information on activities and accomplishments of each day is maintained.

In many respects the work in the mini-lab is similar to what may take place in any other effective learning disabilities program. Additional specialized programming will be planned by the learning disabilities resource teacher and implemented at other stations within the room. The unique feature of this program is the fact that all of this programming takes place in one room. A similarly advantageous feature is the fact that referrals during the year involve a team of teachers who are already working together; thus there is almost no communication gap.

The Pinehurst Middle School program is truly unique; it provides for a minimum of segregated activities and virtually no displacement of children during the year to initiate learning disabilities programming. The problems that may exist in some programs in getting the learning disabilities specialist and the regular class teacher together are nonexistent. They are together; in fact, they refer children for possible special help on a joint referral basis. This program can provide for individualization, for maintenance in the mainstream, and for meaningful specialized services all at the same time. But, like all educational plans that appear to be so unusually beneficial, there are additional factors to consider.

Perhaps the most negative factor in terms of general implementation of such a plan is the cost. Whereas the Pitt County program can provide an apparently meaningful level of service for an entire school at the salary cost of one teacher and one aide, this program would require an extra teacher at each grade level. Some cost advantage may be achieved through maximum use of aides, but this plan would appear to almost always cost more than the Pitt County plan.

A second problem is that of the required team teaching arrangement. Many teachers can function effectively as part of a team, but there are a number of indications that all teachers cannot do so. In addition, the open classroom concept is not accepted everywhere; even if it were, there would be significant cost factors involved in remodeling tens of thousands of school buildings.

In the final analysis the Pinehurst Middle School effort must be considered an interesting and important effort to try out a potentially valuable concept. There could be many types of variations of this plan such as combination grades to which high-risk children are assigned along with children making average and above-average progress or a learning disabilities resource teacher who spends one-half day in each of two such open classes in the same school. Perhaps none of these alternate arrangements would be as effective as the Pinehurst plan, but they might be used in more schools because they cost less. The Pinehurst program and others like it in North Carolina may help point the way to such potentially valuable organizational variations.

ANCHORAGE BOROUGH MODIFIED PRIMARY PROGRAM AND ALASKA LEARNING DISABILITIES RANKING SCALE

The Alaska Learning Disabilities Ranking Scale (ALDRS) and an accompanying educational component, the Anchorage Borough Modified Primary Program, were developed in cooperation with the Alaska Department of Education to provide an early identification and prevention program for children who are likely to have academic problems in the primary grades. An important goal for the project was to devise a screening procedure that could easily be completed by any kindergarten or first-grade teacher without an undue expenditure of time and purchase of expensive test materials and that could be easily replicated elsewhere in the state, including rural villages as well as larger districts.

The three-part screening process was developed as a result of solicited input from local kindergarten and first-grade teachers, research of the literature, and consultation with members of the learning Disabilities Leadership Training Institute of the University of Arizona. The first part of the scale (teacher ranking) allows teachers to identify, in rank order, the children in their class whom they consider high risks, listing the specific difficulties they are having. This procedure eliminates the vast majority of students from further consideration or evaluation.

Part 2, entitled individual checklist, is a compilation of behaviors, skills, and preacademic tasks that should be mastered to ensure average success in a typical first-grade class. A list of easily obtainable or teacher-made materials to be used in completing the checklist is included. This section allows an evaluator to deal with discrete or specific skills that a child may or may not have mastered.

The third and last part, the letter identi-fication test, simply and quickly provides for an assessment of a child's knowledge of the alphabet. The bottom half of the page is removed and used by the student; the teacher records the child's responses on the remaining portion.

The ALDRS is first administered by kindergarten teachers in late spring. The data are evaluated by at least one learning disabilities specialist (the project coordinator) and a school psychologist assigned to the program. No specific cutoff score has been established due to the wide range from school to school. Selection for modified primary placement is made on a need basis considering all of the referrals from the two or three schools that are grouped together to be served by each class. Each modified primary class has a maximum of 15 children. Those children selected for placement are preenrolled for class in the fall and the remainder are placed on a waiting list for consideration when openings occur.

In the fall of first grade (due to a high mobility rate) children are screened for a second time. This allows the reidentification of students who were earlier identified and then moved as well as students who are new to the district.

After parent permission is obtained and the child is placed in the class, the teacher begins assessing academic and behavioral skills. Instruction is individualized so that each child experiences success continuously. There is much emphasis on language development and social-emotional skills as well as the basic academic areas of reading, math, and writing.

If a child continues to experience difficulty in acquiring needed skills and concepts, referral is made for in-depth diagnosis by a psychologist. The results of this testing provide information for prescriptive instruction. A learning disabilities specialist who serves as a resource to each teacher of a modified primary class assists in developing a suitable learning program based on the psychological test data, classroom observation, and one-to-one instruction for these children.

Most children acquire the needed skills

Text continued on p. 190.

ALASKA LEARNING DISABILITIES RANKING SCALE
(Revised Spring 1975)

School _____ Date _____

Teacher _____ Grade _____

No. of children in class _____

I. Based on your professional judgment, please list those children in your class whose progress to date is such that you think they would *not* be likely to succeed in the regular first-grade program. Rank them in order of severity, beginning with the *most* severe case first. Please provide complete information for each child you identify.

II. State at least two specific reasons that you think a child will be likely not to succeed in grade one. State the *major interference* to the learning process *first*.

I. Name of child	Checklist score	Alpha. rec.	Sex (M or F)	Birthday	II. Specific reason(s) for identification
1.					
2.					
3.					
4.					
5.					

III. On completion of the above ranking scale, please complete a copy of the accompanying checklist for each child you identified. Complete every question for each child that you can answer from memory. After this take each checklist with unanswered questions and take the child aside and determine whether he/she has mastered those specific skills or behaviors. Please answer *all* questions.

ALASKA LEARNING DISABILITIES RANKING SCALE (INDIVIDUAL CHECKLIST)
(Revised Spring 1975)

Master score table

1 = 3%	6 = 20%	11 = 36%	16 = 53%	21 = 70%	26 = 86%
2 = 6	7 = 23	12 = 40	17 = 56	22 = 73	27 = 90
3 = 10	8 = 26	13 = 43	18 = 60	23 = 76	28 = 93
4 = 13	9 = 30	14 = 46	19 = 63	24 = 80	29 = 96
5 = 16	10 = 33	15 = 50	20 = 66	25 = 83	30 = 100

Student _____ Birth date _____

Teacher _____

Date _____

School _____

Raw score _____ Percentage _____

	Yes	No
1. Can this child count by rote to 10?		
2. Can this child say the alphabet by rote?		
3. When compared with his/her classmates, can this child listen attentively and follow oral directions without frequent repetitions or failure to complete them?		
4. When shown a picture of a single, common object (an animal, building, utensil, etc.) and asked to name it and use it in a complete sentence, can the child do so as well as the majority of his/her classmates?		
5. When shown a story picture (for example a picture from a basal reader), can the child make a story of at least three sentences to describe it?		
6. Can this child match any eight randomly selected pairs of lowercase letters of the alphabet? (For example, b, d, g, p, q, m, n, w and w, q, n, b, m, g, d, p.)		
7. Does this child demonstrate the ability to imitate letter sounds when requested to do so by the teacher?		
8. Does this child know two of the three following facts: first and last name, address, and telephone number?		
9. When shown the eight basic colors (red, yellow, blue, green, orange, purple, black, brown), can the child identify at least seven of them?		
10. Can this child present from memory the nursery rhymes, songs, and stories learned in class as well as the majority of his classmates?		
11. Does this child demonstrate a level of understanding comparable to the majority of his/her classmates for the concept of position and direction? (For example, can he/she describe the position of people and objects in the room and describe the location of his home or how to get there?)		
12. Can this child grasp a pencil properly in a three-finger position preparatory to writing or drawing?		
13. Can this child print his/her first name from memory?		

	Yes	No

14. Can this child reproduce a circle, square, and triangle from visual stimulus without serious distortion? (The triangle and square should possess three and four clearly defined sides and angles, respectively.)

15. Can this child write letters, numbers, and words without frequent reversals and/or rotations?

16. When presented with any 12 lowercase letters of the alphabet, can this child correctly identify at least 11 of them?

17. Can this child recognize at least two sight words (for example, red, yellow), excluding his name?

18. When utilizing concrete objects (blocks, tokens, rods, etc.), does this child demonstrate an understanding of the concepts of "one less" and "one more"?

19. Can this child manipulate concrete objects to add and subtract from 1 to 5?

20. Can this child match and recognize numerals and sets out of sequence from 1 to 10?

21. Does this child wash his/her hands and face properly without assistance (uses soap, uses and disposes of towel in wastepaper basket, etc.)?

22. Does this child usually put on and take off his/her coat, boots, etc. without assistance?

23. Is this child responsible for his/her own belongings (hangs up his/her coat, keeps his work area clean, etc.)?

24. Does this child display the ability to function independently outside the classroom (goes directly to get a drink and returns promptly, carries a message, etc.)?

25. Is this child's behavior average or better than the majority of his/her peers (minimal crying, pouting, withdrawal, and temper outbursts)?

26. Does this child demand or require *only* his fair share of attention (no more than the majority of his classmates)?

27. When compared with his/her classmates, would this child's behavior be termed typical in regard to hyperactivity (inability to sit still) and distractibility (inability to attend the task at hand)?

28. When compared with his/her classmates, does this child exhibit relatively consistent performance from day to day and/or subject area to subject area?

29. Does this child demonstrate the ability to cooperate with peers and follow rules?

30. Does this child display an understanding of the concepts of left and right equal to his/her classmates?

Total number of Yes responses _____

IV. After answering the 30 questions on the checklist, count the number of Yes responses. This is the raw score; write this on the first page of the checklist. To obtain the percentage score, use the table on the first page; enter this in the appropriate place. The lower the percentage, the more likely it is that this child will experience problems during the first grade and should be considered for special intervention.

LIST OF MATERIALS NEEDED TO COMPLETE CHECKLIST

The following numbers correlate with the items on the checklist. (In order to assess item No. 4 you need the item described after No. 4 below.)

4. Picture of one common object (example: animal, vehicle)
5. Picture depicting an activity that would encourage use of sentences for description
6. Two sets of letters for matching
9. Crayons for identification of eight basic colors
14. Circle, triangle, and square drawn on paper to provide the stimulus for the child to reproduce with a pencil or crayon
16. Use alphabet recognition test for this item
18. Blocks, tokens, rods
19. Blocks, tokens, rods
20. Set of cards with numerals 1 to 10 on one side and sets on the other

Stopwatch for letter identification test

ALASKA LEARNING DISABILITIES RANKING SCALE
LETTER IDENTIFICATION TEST
(Revised Spring 1975)

Cut along the dotted line and present to the student the student letter identification list. Determine the number of letters he/she can correctly identify in a timed *1-minute* interval. If the child cannot identify a letter in 5 seconds, instruct him/her to omit it and proceed to the next one. Should he/she identify all the letters on the page before the time limit is expended, instruct him/her to continue by proceeding again from the first line.

Use the following teacher's letter identification recording score sheet to score and record each student's performance. Please list all requested information for each student tested.

Student's name _____

Teacher's name _____

ALASKA LEARNING DISABILITIES RANKING SCALE

Teacher's letter identification recording and score sheet   Number correct (1 min.) _____

n	w	y	k	d	o	a	s	x	z	(10)
f	b	e	l	p	c	v	m	j	p	(20)
t	u	i	r	g	h	n	w	y	k	(30)
d	o	a	s	x	z	f	b	e	l	(40)
p	c	v	m	j	q	t	u	i	r	(50)

- -

ALASKA LEARNING DISABILITIES RANKING SCALE

Student letter identification list

n	w	y	k	d	o	a	s	x	z	(10)
f	b	e	l	p	c	v	m	j	p	(20)
t	u	i	r	g	h	n	w	y	k	(30)
d	o	a	s	x	z	f	b	e	l	(40)
p	c	v	m	j	q	t	u	i	r	(50)

to succeed in the regular primary grades after the modified primary experience. For those who continue to show evidence that their learning patterns are sufficiently different to make success in the regular elementary program unlikely, certification and placement in a more specialized program is also an option for Anchorage students.

This program continues to expand and now includes a majority of the elementary schools in the Anchorage Borough School District. Follow-up studies of former modified primary students have been undertaken and will be continued each spring to determine the rate of progress made by these children. Initial data suggest that these children are progressing at an average rate for the class in which they were placed, but further study must be undertaken to confirm this.

The ALDRS as used in Anchorage is reproduced on pp. 186-189. For many school districts it may be of value in the form shown here. With slight revisions it may be applicable in others.

EARLY CHILDHOOD RESOURCE UNIT
SCHOOL DISTRICT SIX

Greeley, Colorado

School District Six in Greeley, Colorado, has well-established, effective programs designed to assist children with learning disabilities. In addition another program focuses on prevention rather than remediation of learning problems. This program was developed because in Greeley, as in all communities, there are young children who display a wide variety of minimal learning problems. These children are normal in most respects, but they may puzzle their preschool or kindergarten teachers with difficulties in various learning tasks.

In 1971 the Early Childhood Resource Unit was established at the Laboratory School at the University of Northern Colorado, a joint venture of School District Six and the School of Special Education of the University of Northern Colorado. During the first year of operation 5- and 6-year-old chil-

dren were evaluated, and recommendations to teachers and parents were based on a diagnostic observation model (pp. 44-45). The description that follows will provide an overview of the Greeley version of an early intervention program in learning disabilities. Similar programs have been initiated in other communities; the Greeley program provides a model for many of them.

Philosophy

Early identification of children with potential learning problems is a multifaceted endeavor. Standard instruments related to suspected deficits can be used, but perhaps more relevant are the observations of teachers and other specialists using procedures that review the child's individual development and functional level on school-related tasks. Of even greater importance is the task of educational programming for such children.

To separate what we *know* from what we *believe* is difficult; however, the Greeley program is based on the following assumptions.

1. Prevention of school failure is preferable to remediation after the failure occurs.

2. The younger the child, the more difficult is the assessment of learning problems. (Many young children demonstrate some predictors of learning disabilities.)

3. The earlier the intervention, the more effective that intervention will be.

4. Keeping the child in his regular class will help guarantee the referring teacher's interest and feeling of responsibility. Removing the child from the class for even a short period of time may possibly create an undesirable label. Also, it may result in the teacher feeling that the child has become "someone else's problem."

5. Involvement in writing the educational prescription increases commitment; therefore it is preferable to have the regular class teacher accompany children to the diagnostic center. He or she can learn to assist in the informal testing and can experiment with new materials and strategies during this time. With the help of the educational diagnostician the teacher can write the educational prescription.

6. Although standardized screening instruments have value, teachers can be as capable and often more accurate in identifying children with potential learning problems if guidelines and assistance are provided.

Goals

Rather than emphasizing procedures of identification, classification, and special class placement, the Early Childhood Resource Unit focuses on prevention of learning disabilities in young children who display minimal problems. The major objectives are as follows:

1. To enhance the achievement resources of children experiencing learning difficulties in the regular class setting
2. To enhance the regular school program and to reduce the need for special class placement through early identification and planned educational programming in the regular class
3. To provide support for parents in attending to the special needs of their children
4. To provide assistance to the regular classroom teacher in selection, development, adoption, and implementation of remediation of the learning problems through educational prescriptions

Program details

Six children at a time attend the Early Childhood Resource Unit for 2 hours each afternoon for a period of approximately 2 weeks. The problems experienced by these children fall into several broad categories.

Maturational lags. Immaturity is one of the outstanding causes of school difficulty. "A lack of readiness not only aggravates learning problems where they exist but causes problems in cases where there is potential for good performance" (Ames, 1968). The problem of immaturity is not solved by passively allowing the child to grow older. The child who is not ready for kindergarten is the one who most needs to be there. An extended period of readiness may be planned for such a child. This might include enrichment activities at home and school, summer pro-

gramming, a prekindergarten curriculum, or later, a transitional setting between kindergarten and first grade.

Language deficits. The community in Greeley, Colorado, is rich with the culture of Mexican-Americans. Unfortunately the children from bilingual-bicultural homes may not be equipped for the kind of English language proficiency required in the classroom. Testing, communications to parents, and programming must be designed to prevent such children from falling further and further behind.

Other language problems include those related to receptive or expressive abilities. Analysis of such problems is followed by the development of strategies to enhance deficit areas.

Sensory or perceptual problems. Identification and diagnosis of sensory or perceptual problems is a relatively easy task. Remedial activities are incorporated into the educational plan and are usually implemented by a support person such as the learning disabilities teacher.

Behavioral problems. The child with disruptive, acting out behavior is commonly perceived to have a learning problem, and indeed, such behaviors do tend to interfere with the educational process. Solutions are sought through a task analysis approach, with consideration of the classroom environment, the home dynamics, the daily sequencing of activities, and the manner in which the teacher interacts with the child.

Regardless of the reason for referral, *any child* who continues to puzzle the regular classroom teacher and who is *not* a likely candidate for special class placement may be considered for the services of the early Childhood Resource Unit.

Referral

1. Currently children are referred by their regular classroom teachers, preschool teachers, or interested parents. (This is in support of the theory that teachers and parents may be as capable of selecting children as formal testing procedures.)
2. Children who can potentially remain in

the mainstream of education for their remedial program will be referred.

3. Children with more severe learning problems will be referred to psychological services for evaluation and appropriate placement.

4. Each school makes initial parent contact and obtains necessary permission for further testing and observation in the Early Childhood Resource Unit. (Parents are urged to accompany their children to the unit.)

5. Transportation and scheduling is arranged by the Early Childhood Resource Unit specialists. (The cost of transportation is minimal since the busing takes place during hours when the buses are not in demand.)

6. Whenever possible, the kindergarten teacher obtains permission from the building principal to accompany the children to the unit.

Evaluation

1. There is a period of observation prior to, during, and after the diagnostic testing. The observations are made in as many settings as possible such as on the bus, on the playground, in the cafeteria, and in the home as well as in the regular class settings.

2. Routinely the following tests are administered during the 2-week period of observation and evaluation.
   a. Kinetic Family Drawings
   b. Gesell Developmental Examination
   c. Complete speech and language evaluation
   d. Audiological evaluation
   e. Vision testing (using the Keystone Telebinocular, Dvorine Color Plates, Titmus Fly, etc.)
   f. Engelmann Basic Concepts Inventory
   g. Piagetian interview

3. Other tests (selected after initial observations) include the following.
   a. Illinois Test of Psycholinguistic Abilities
   b. KeyMath
   c. Peabody Individual Achievement Test

   d. Purdue Perceptual Motor Survey
   e. Frostig Developmental Test of Visual Perception
   f. Southern California Sensory Integration Tests
   g. Valett Developmental Survey
   h. Assessment of Children's Language Comprehension
   i. McCarthy's Scales of Children's Abilities

Information collected prior to prescription. As stated earlier, the identification of children with potential learning problems is a multifaceted endeavor. Standard instruments related to suspected deficits can be used, but probably more relevant are the *observations* of teachers and specialists using procedures that review the child's individual development and functional level. Prior to writing the educational prescription the following information should be collected.

Identifying information
1. Name and age of pupil
2. Person who referred pupil
3. General appearance (relative size, build, clothes, hair, grooming, etc.)
4. Initial impression

Behavior of individual
1. Coordination (large muscle activity and finer coordination)
2. Posture and gait
3. Activity of pupil (If active, under what conditions? Does pupil show purposeful activity, aimless fiddling, etc.?)
4. Handedness and skill in use of tools, etc.
5. Communication (Does pupil talk much? Formally or informally? In complete sentences or in words? How does pupil respond to others?)
6. Self-control and control of emotion (Are responses immediate or developed? Are they appropriate? Are they exaggerated?)
7. Attention span (Easily distracted? Interested? In what?)
8. Ways of solving problems (What does pupil do if he wants something?)
9. Response to others (Friendly? Shy? Withdrawn? Watching others? Disturbing others? Helping others?)
10. Dependence and independence (Busy? Wants too much attention?)
11. Fatigue level (Any evidence of variation?)

12. Nervous traits (Nail biting? Thumb sucking? Constant rocking?)

General health and physical development
1. Personal care (hair, hands, neatness of clothes, nails, independence in toileting, etc.)
2. Estimation of vision and hearing (in general)
3. Body structure, adequate sensory organs, respiration, condition of hands and feet, allergies, endurance, muscle tone, etc.

Social development
1. Control of expression of emotions, awareness of sex differences, variations in behavior to opposite sex, older people, younger people
2. Reactions of others to pupil (teacher's expectations, parents' attitudes)
3. Cooperation and competitiveness
4. Social conformity (acceptance of authority, rules, property regulations)
5. Adjustment to new environment, separation from mother, etc.

Cognitive development
1. Level of language development
   a. Use of words, speech defects, use of sentences, estimation of vocabulary
   b. Voice quality (soft, loud, pitch, etc.)
2. General information and environmental awareness
3. Response to interruptions and ability to return to original activity
4. Divergent thinking (Novel solutions? Variety of ideas?)
5. Ability in drawing, use of puzzles, copying designs, etc.
6. Approach to problem solving (Does pupil defend answers, etc?)

Work habits
1. Interest, use of time, ability to concentrate, etc.
2. Ability to get along with others
3. Willingness to try new things
4. Acceptance of criticism
5. Safety habits
6. Ability to follow directions
7. Service to others
8. Persistence

Educational data
1. Speed and rate of learning
2. Previous school experience
3. Factors that give an indication of how much the pupil knows, how to go about teaching him, how he learns, etc.
4. Learning style (Any indications of his strong channels of input and output?)

Program personnel. The *educational diag-nostician* is the key person in this program. In large programs there should be a full-time coordinator in addition to several educational diagnosticians, but in the Greeley program the diagnostician coordinates the program and performs the following functions.
1. Conducts both formal and informal evaluation procedures
2. Develops teaching plans or educational prescriptions (in conjunction with the teacher)
3. Consults with other professionals as necessary and appropriate in individual cases
4. Requests assistance or referral to other special services when needed
5. Conducts building-level staffing

The *educational aide* assists the teacher in many of the these functions. A good aide can be of great value. An inadequate aide or one assigned to this task by chance or to provide employment will be of little value. The educational diagnostician should be asked to play a major role in selecting the aide.

Parents are very much a part of the program. The classroom teacher is usually involved in teaching—introducing new skills and concepts through the child's areas of strength. In the Greeley Early Childhood Resource Unit the plan for remediation is developed so that the parents become involved with remedial efforts. Home activities are recommended by the educational diagnostician and demonstrated when necessary. These may include learning games, techniques to improve listening skills, visual memory, etc.

The *regular class teacher* selects children to be evaluated, assists in the observation and evaluation procedures, and plays the major role in the implementation plan. In the Greeley program the emphasis is on strengths, not weaknesses, and a serious attempt is made to provide a plan that will not take an undue amount of the regular class teacher's time. (This is in recognition of the fact that the teacher has from 25 to 30 children, and a plan that calls for a great deal of highly individual assistance probably will not be implemented.)

The *learning disabilities resource teacher* may play various roles as determined by the type and degree of disability being remedied. There is a learning disabilities resource teacher in each of the Greeley schools, and their assistance with this program may include the following.

1. Attendance at staffings and assist in interpretation of prescriptions
2. Demonstrating remedial techniques when needed
3. Assistance in providing ongoing evaluation
4. Liaison between the classroom teacher, educational diagnostician, school psychologists, speech clinician, etc.

The *learning resources center coordinator* assists in making the materials that are part of the center available to both the Early Childhood Resource Unit coordinator and the regular class teacher. All communities do not have such facilities, but the shortage of really good material for handicapped children and youth makes such a facility a near necessity for all programs for exceptional children.

Various other personnel are of significant help in this program. The type and degree of help they provide varies with the child and the setting. The *school psychologist* and the *school speech clinician* assist as the individual case indicates. The *school nurse* attends staffings and assists as needed. *Custodians* and *bus drivers* have indicated an interest in handicapped children in Greeley, and short orientation sessions have resulted in their being of genuine assistance.

The Greeley program was developed jointly with special education staff members from the University of Northern Colorado who continue to provide assistance. The program could certainly exist and perform successfully without this specialized assistance, but it has provided something "extra" that might not be easy to duplicate. Members of various medical disciplines are also involved in this effort. Pediatricians, neurologists, ophthalmologists, otolaryngologists, and others have been involved as required.

Some aspects of the Greeley Early Child-hood Resource Unit are undoubtedly enhanced by the presence of the university program, and other school districts who wish to emulate this program may have to employ additional professional personnel to compensate for lack of such assistance. This is a practical program that is actually not too difficult to implement. If reactions of Greeley school personnel can be used as a reliable guide, it serves its function well.

SUMMARY

A variety of methods and models has been used to serve the learning disabled. Resource rooms are the most common plan, but itinerant programs continue to be used in certain settings. Through practice and observation of what appear to be the most effective programs, certain guidelines for the establishment of effective resource room services have evolved. These were detailed in this chapter.

A hypothetical learning disabilities program, the Midville program, plus a description of the program in Winterville, North Carolina, were presented to provide a conceptualization of resource room programs in operation. The Midville description also provided other program alternatives.

An interesting open setting learning disabilities program in Pinehurst, North Carolina, was reviewed. This type of programming for the learning disabled has not been widely used, but it certainly provides some interesting concepts and components that may be implemented in a number of settings.

Preventive programs have grown in acceptance in recent years, and although there has been insufficient time to determine which preventive models are most effective, certain trends are emerging. Two of these programs, one in Anchorage, Alaska, and one in Greeley, Colorado, were discussed in this chapter. The emphasis of the discussion of the Anchorage program was screening and identification; the Greeley program was overviewed in total.

The area of learning disabilities is quite new, but due to rapid acceptance it has provided a number of program alternatives and models. The next several years may be a time of new program models but appears more likely to be a time when resource room programs and preventative programs will be expanded, refined, and polished. This process is already underway, and initial observation are indeed encouraging.

REFERENCES AND SUGGESTED READINGS

Alaska Learning Disabilities Ranking Scale (ALDRS). Anchorage, Alaska: Anchorage Borough School District, 1975.

Ames, L. Learning disabilities: a developmental point of view. In H. Myklebust (Ed.), *Progress in learning disabilities.* New York: Grune & Stratton, Inc., 1968.

Gearheart, B. R. *Learning disabilities: educational strategies.* St. Louis: The C. V. Mosby Co., 1973.

Pinehurst Middle School Open Program (Bulletin). Pinehurst, N.C.: Monroe County Schools, undated.

Pitt County Learning Disability Staff Development Center (Bulletin). Winterville, N.C.: W. H. Robinson Primary School, undated.

Reger, R. What is a resource room program? *Journal of Learning Disabilities,* 1973, *6*(10), 15-21.

11 Current issues and new directions

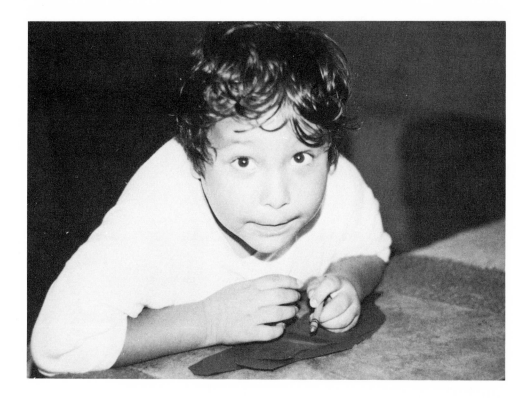

In many respects a major part of the 10 preceding chapters has been a discussion of current issues in learning disabilities. The field is new, and thus much of its history (since its recognition as an entity) is still current. As for new directions, some of these have been mentioned, but in this chapter they will be summarized and brought into sharper focus. In some areas of concern such as continuing research in brain functioning and the role of the medical profession we will consider a number of findings and inferences that were not included in preceding chapters.

ISSUES RELATED TO OTHER AREAS OF SPECIAL EDUCATION

Many of the issues and new directions in learning disabilities are closely related to or an integral part of issues and trends in the larger field of special education. They must be considered and dealt with in relation to learning disabilities, but their origin has been in concerns with educational provisions for other handicapping conditions or with education of all handicapped children. Among the more significant of these issues are concerns about labeling, self-contained class programs versus other service delivery systems, due process, the shortcomings of assessment tools, minority cultural and ethnic differences, and mainstreaming of the handicapped (Gearheart and Weishahn, 1976). These issues are highly interrelated, and it is difficult, if not impossible, to comprehensively discuss one without becoming involved with several of the others. Most readers of this text will have some appreciation of these concerns; therefore we will not review how and why they became issues but rather how they may have special implications for the development of learning disabilities programs and services.

Labeling has been thoroughly denounced for the stigma effect, which seems nearly inescapable (in particular for the mentally handicapped), and because of the so-called self-fulfilling prophesy potential. This has led to many other concerns, among them a feeling on the part of many that we must abandon all self-contained classes and service delivery structures that by their organizational nature automatically label a child. The idea of mainstreaming, of returning handicapped children to the general educational mainstream with a minimum of specialized help, grew out of this concern with labeling and the fact that the educational results of labeling and special class placement have not been particularly encouraging (Martin, 1974).*

Concern with labeling has had two very different effects on the development of learning disabilities programs. Because learning disabilities services are most often provided in a resource room or by an itinerant teacher, children are not placed in special classes and labeled with the same degree of definitiveness as in traditional programs for the educable mentally handicapped. Other children leave the regular class for special instrumental music instruction, for athletics, or to go to the

remedial reading teacher or speech clinician. Leaving to receive special help for a learning problem is not too different.

In addition, the term "learning disability" infers something temporary, and for many it means that the school or the system, not the child, is at fault. Mental handicap (or retardation) indicates that the *child* is defective, with no indication that the school program may be at fault. As a result of a more positive attitude toward learning disabilities, many children have been reevaluated and classified as learning disabled rather than mentally handicapped. Some of these children are more accurately classified as learning disabled, but there is little doubt that some have been inaccurately classified as such to avoid problems relating to labeling and the negative image of special classes for the mentally handicapped. Disenchantment with special classes and a mutiplicity of related factors have tended to crowd more and more children into programs for the learning disabled without sufficient concern for the accuracy of the assessment that led to placement.

An opposite effect has had an influence on another facet of learning disabilities programming, an influence that is not yet of any great magnitude but may well grow. Prevention programs at the kindergarten or first-grade level have become fairly common, and most would agree that prevention is more desirable than waiting to deal with a fully developed problem. (See Chapter 10 for a discussion of the Greeley, Colorado, and Anchorage, Alaska, program.) The problem with prevention programs in learning disabilities is one of identification. To know whom to serve in prevention programs, we must identify (label) children as having potential problems.

In learning disabilities it is difficult to identify young children with a high degree of accuracy except when they exhibit very severe learning problems. (In this case the efforts will not be preventive.) Thus we find ourselves in a real dilemma. If we provide early preventive programs, we must search out children who indicate some of the symp-

---

*In this and the following discussion of issues and influences that are part of the essential background of these issues, I will of necessity oversimplify many of these influences. The alternative—to discuss them in detail—would require an undue amount of emphasis and space.

toms that may indicate future learning disabilities. We thus label them as children with potential learning problems. If we wait until later, it is too late for prevention. In the meantime we will undoubtedly "label" some children inaccurately as potential problems, for such programs must be based on a composite of predictors that cannot be 100% accurate. In some communities this is no problem; in others it is. Where it is a problem, such plans may be abandoned rather than face serious public criticism.*

We should note that the concern about labeling children as potentially learning disabled or high risk relates to the problem of definition discussed in Chapter 1. A variety of questions, both philosophical and practical, about the issues of labeling, lowering of academic expectations, inadequate assessment tools, and minority cultural and ethnic differences will continue to affect planning and programming for learning disabilities. The magnitude of this effect will be related in part to our professional competence in launching new programs and improving existing ones, but in some instances it may be more significantly affected by feelings, emotional reactions, and biases. Sensitivity to these factors and the exercise of great care in what we call new programs and how we sell them to the public will continue to be highly essential.

Another issue that has developed as a result of litigation and general concern about misassessment, misplacement, labeling, and a tendency for educators to bypass parents in

*Through personal communication with a number of local directors of special education, I know of several school districts that dropped plans for initiation of high-risk first-grade programs because of strong opposition to the labeling (identification) necessitated by such plans. One vocal board member or other influential citizens can scuttle this effort if their perception is that this may lead to stigma, low expectations on the part of teachers, or other similar results. In one state, legislation that would have provided reimbursement for such preventive programs was effectively stopped by a small group of legislators. The nature of this information prevents the disclosure of specific sources, but the effect of concern about labeling is real.

planning educational programs is the problem of due process. When considered in relation to all of its many ramifications, the matter of due process is highly complicated, but a recent manual, *A Primer on Due Process: Education Decisions for Handicapped Children* (Abeson et al., 1975), has greatly simplified this complex topic. This guide, published by the Council for Exceptional Children, includes a discussion of the historical and legal background, the sequence of procedures required, how hearings must be held, and other related issues. It includes, in addition to basic essential information, a sample of most of the forms that might be required by a local school district involved in implementing appropriate due process procedures. It is technically accurate and easily understood and is the best available single source of information for those interested in a comprehensive overview of the entire issue.

Public Law 93-380, the Education Amendments of 1974, requires the states to provide for certain aspects of due process in their plans for the education of the handicapped. The following is from Public Law 93-380, Title VIB, Sec. 612(d) (13A):

(The states must) provide procedures for insuring that handicapped children and their parents or guardians are guaranteed procedural safeguards in decisions regarding identification, evaluation and educational placement of handicapped children including, but not limited to (A) (i) prior notice to parents or guardians of the child when the local or State educational agency proposes to change the educational placement of the child, (ii) an opportunity for the parents or guardians to obtain an impartial due process hearing, examine all relevant records with respect to the classification or educational placement of the child, and obtain an independent educational evaluation of the child, (iii) procedures to protect the rights of the child when the parents or guardians are not known, unavailable, or the child is a ward of the State including the assignment of an individual (not to be an employee of the State or local educational agency involved in the education or care of children) to act as a surrogate for the parents or guardians, and (iv) provision to insure that the decisions rendered in the impartial due process hearing required by this paragraph shall be binding on all parties subject only to appropriate administrative or judicial appeal.

The effects of this law and of the principle of due process will vary from state to state, but they must be considered in all we do in planning for handicapped children. The generalizable, major immediate effects are that parents must be fully informed and involved in all educational decisions, and educators must be more forthright and more fully accountable. Long-term effects remain to be seen.

In conclusion, many of the issues that confront learning disabilities practitioners and program planners are not a direct result of events that have taken place within the specific area of learning disabilities. Rather they are a part of a larger area of concern with the efficacy of special education programming; approaches, practices, and procedures in dealing with handicapped children; the use of inadequate or inappropriate assessment tools; and placement criteria and practices that have been careless and in some instances have violated the rights of both children and parents. The atmosphere created by such factors has led to the popularity of articles such as *Education's Latest Victim: The "LD" Kid* (Divoky, 1974) and *Chaining Children with Chemicals* (Vonder Haar, 1975). There is a measure of truth in the cases made by these and other authors with similar concerns, but the effect tends more to reaction than to considered correction of real problems.

Other writers take another side of the issue and claim miraculous recoveries for learning-disabled children while in the same article indicating that 20% to 30% of all children may be learning disabled. Some who make such claims are well-intentioned reporters; others are promoting some sort of questionable miracle cure. Those who work with children with learning disabilities, children who badly need their help, must be aware of this issue and attempt to bring order and common sense into such debates. Although spectacular claims of miracle cures or charges of scandalous misdiagnosis and improper treatment may sell magazines, they often do little more than spread misconception and misinformation.

DEFINITION OF LEARNING DISABILITIES

The variety of definitions accepted or suggested as acceptable remains an important issue in learning disabilities. However, it must be recognized that the resolution to this problem (if it were to occur) could affect the following.

1. Which children can be served in state reimbursed, special education programs funded as learning disabilities programs
2. Which professionals must certify the primary diagnostic findings (medical doctors, psychologists, other educational diagnosticians)
3. The appropriateness of use of various methods or techniques (for example, if it is a cause-oriented definition that implies that the cause must be corrected, then behavior modification techniques should not be used. If it is purely symptom oriented, then there will be much less reason to complete many of the diagnostic procedures presently used.)
4. The percentage of the student population included and thus how much money will be required to support specialized programming
5. The scope of research that may properly be included as learning disabilities research (This may be critically important as it relates to the amount and sources of resource funds.)
6. The relationship of learning disabilities to other specialized educational efforts— if in fact, learning disabilities is defined as an educational problem

The establishment of a hard-and-fast definition, particularly if it were very narrowly specific, could have a profound effect on the future of learning disabilities efforts; thus it is indeed a critical issue.

NEW HOPE FROM MEDICAL RESEARCH

It has been suggested throughout this text that specific evidence of brain injury is of little value in most educational settings. This is because such information provides little, if any, specific guidance as to how to assist the child educationally. In contrast a number of important research efforts related to brain function hold promise in the prevention or amelioration of learning problems. These research efforts in composite may provide one area of hope for the reduction of learning disabilities and perhaps of mental retardation.

In the following section we will consider several examples of recent medical research. These will be accounts of isolated research (isolated in the sense that these are not a part of some grand design or plan of action) that seem to be of potential value. They are of interest as an indication of what is happening in fields other than education, and their possible value should be evident.

Brain blood flow

Research summaries reported in two successive issues of the *Journal of Learning Disabilities* indicate that current research efforts may provide additional highly valuable information regarding hitherto little understood functioning of the human brain. In one instance research was conducted with humans; the other involves research with animals that may provide guidelines for prevention of brain damage in premature or small-for-age infants.

The first, actually a series of studies, is the outgrowth of brain blood flow pattern research at the Department of Clinical Neurophysiology of the University Hospital of Lund, Sweden. A regional blood flow technique was used to obtain a quantitative map of the dominant hemisphere regions that are activated by speech and reading. Changes in blood flow induced by speech and reading were compared with the resting pattern and with the pattern elicited by voluntary hand and arm movements.

The description of technical aspects of this research requires neurological nomenclature far beyond the assumed scope of readers of this text, but the essence of the research is that functions of the brain's language centers, the question of cerebral dominance and differences between "inner speech" and normal speech (as in reading aloud), are now open to quantitative investigation. A variety of language disorders may now be more meaningfully studied, and perhaps certain questions as to the nature of various manifestations of learning disabilities can now be determined.

This research indicates that certain previous assumptions about cerebral correlates to conscious mental activity were inaccurate. It was found that speech and reading activate different areas of the brain than problem solving, as in psychological testing. Implications of this research are of considerable importance, and the technique used opens new avenues of investigation that may permit us to much more fully understand the language functions of humans (McGlannan, 1975a).

A second report of brain blood flow research, conducted primarily with rhesus monkeys, indicates that the amount and duration of slow blood flow to the brain during the first few weeks of life is proportional to the amount of brain damage. This work, reported by Dr. Barker of the Institute of Rehabilitation Medicine at New York University School of Medicine, provides new hope for the prevention of brain damage in premature children. Therapy to increase brain blood flow can be successfully given to human infants and would thus probably reduce the incidence of brain damage in infants who were experiencing slow brain blood flow. A safe method of testing for adequate brain blood flow has been developed, and irreversible brain damage may be prevented when this technique is perfected.

Various animal infants (monkeys, rats, puppies) show a marked increase in brain blood flow as a function of age, and human infants may show a similar increase. Premature and developmentally young children may benefit greatly from this knowledge, and learning disabilities and mental retardation may be prevented in cases in which slow blood flow is a major cause (McGlannan, 1975b). These two and other studies of brain blood flow are characteristic of research that may pay excellent dividends in the not too distant future.

Human brain asymmetry

Efforts to better understand the separate and the interrelated functions of the two hemispheres of the brain (efforts that are not directed primarily at assisting the learning disabled) may soon prove to be of significant value. Although much of the nervous system is symmetrical, the functions of the two cerebral hemispheres are quite different. This difference has been known and widely accepted for some time, but only recently has the right hemisphere received much research attention. This is apparently because the left hemisphere plays the dominant role in speech, and we have been highly interested in functions and dysfunctions in the realm of speech.

As long ago as 1925 pioneers such as Samuel Orton postulated that lack of hemispheric dominance was one cause of what we would today call learning disabilities (Orton, 1937). His theories have been generally discounted, but recent investigations suggest that poor cross-hemispheric integration may be one cause of the more major learning disorders (Kershner and Kershner, 1973). Other research deliberately directed at right hemispheric functions indicates that we may have too long overlooked the functions of the right hemisphere and that it may make highly valuable contributions to the functioning of the left hemisphere. Samples (1975) suggests that "the emphasis on intellectuality and rationality has been an excursion into half the function of the brain." He indicates that when the right hemisphere of the brain is systematically stimulated and its functions enhanced, an increase in self-esteem and a related increase in performance of skills commonly associated with the left hemisphere results.

Samples' arguments are not totally accepted, but his success in special projects with urban youth certainly deserves more careful attention. The fact that we really do not know much about the right hemisphere, how it functions independently of the left and how it may function interrelatedly with the left, should spur us to further investigation. Samples postulates that the kind of

"street smart" or adaptive ability that some children and youth possess, which is not effectively measured by our best available tests of intelligence, may be related to right hemispheric abilities. As we learn more about the functioning of the whole brain, it is almost certain that we will increase our understanding of certain types of learning disabilities.

A variety of other research into the differing functions of the right and left hemispheres of the brain is taking place around the world. This research is related to a number of diverse interests and is being carried out by researchers from a variety of disciplines. One such study that received some mention in the popular press during 1975 was conducted by researchers associated with the Brain Research Institute of the UCLA Medical Center. Rogers et al. (1975) conducted a fascinating study in which Hopi Indian children were used to investigate the possibility that the two sides of the brain may participate differently in language processing of Hopi and English. This possibility was suggested by earlier language theorists' efforts to contrast Hopi and English after analyzing Hopi and concluding that it was uniquely different from English.

These postulated differences include the observation that Hopi emphasizes the concrete, is immediately and fundamentally involved with nature, links speech with its context, and by its very nature creates involvement with the perceptual field. In contrast, English leads its users to separation or abstraction from the perceptual field, is concerned with culture, and leads to a context-free and noncontradictory universe of discourse (Cicourel, 1974). An example of an obvious difference is that of the manner of conjugation of English verbs. We conjugate English verbs in relation to time (which is abstract). In Hopi it is not possible to separate time and space; therefore there cannot be similar verb conjugation. This type of difference occurs over and over again when the two languages are compared.

The Hopi-English study of hemispheric specialization and language was carried out in an elementary school in the Hopi Nation,

Arizona. A random sample of children in grades four, five, and six, all of whom were bilingual with English as a second language, was selected. All had learned English to some extent before entrance in school, and all (to be eligible as participants) were right-handed and spoke Hopi in their homes. Participation of the two sides of the brain in language processing was determined through electro-encephalographic (EEG) measurement.

A series of tasks were presented in random order, including two stories, "The Sparrow Hawk and the Lizard" and "Isaw Niq Pu Tutsvo" ("The Coyote and the Wren"). Complex analysis through use of a telemetry device, a series of electronic conversions, and analysis of variance of the independent, repeated measures yielded highly interesting results.

There were significant differences in right and left hemispheric EEG lateralization, indicating more right hemispheric participation during the Hopi story than the English story. Many details of this research would be required to communicate a full report of the results, but the fact that all language is not necessarily processed by the left hemisphere is most significant. Among the ideas that might be investigated in unusual cases are such possibilities as the use of some sort of substitute, more highly concrete language in cases of severe learning disabilities in which the left hemisphere is dysfunctional as regards language. (This was not a suggestion of Rogers et al. or other investigators, but it is one idea that occurred immediately on reading this research report.)

Whatever the outcome of this and related brain function studies, the results will be of value to those who are attempting to construct new approaches to assist children with learning disabilities. The possibilities that may develop as a result of such research, although not likely to reach fruition overnight, are almost limitless.

SERENDIPITOUS RESEARCH OF IMPORTANCE TO LEARNING DISABILITIES

Most educated individuals are aware of the manner in which research efforts directed at one problem or issue may eventually be of greater assistance in another direction or area of application. It is fairly safe to assume that the field of learning disabilities will benefit from this effect in the near future. In fact, this may be one of the positive results that will come from an otherwise mainly negative overprediction of the incidence of learning disabilities. If enough people think that learning disabilities are very widespread, there may be more attention paid to the problem and thus more likelihood of a variety of benefits. One such spin-off benefit, or potential benefit, will provide an example of how this may work.

Observations of dermatoglyphic (ridges of the skin) abnormalities on the hands of defective babies of mothers who had taken thalidomide or who had suffered from rubella infections led Dr. Ira Salafsky of the Evaluation Center for Learning and Genetic Service of the Evanston (Ill.) Hospital to conduct further investigations of this phenomenon (Salafsky, 1975). In his preliminary report published in April, 1975, Salafsky suggested a longitudinal study to attempt to verify his hypothesis. He believes that there may be sufficient dermatoglyphic indications of a high risk for learning disabilities that this may be used as one screening indicator in attempting to establish eligibility for preventive or early remedial programs. Salafsky noted that this was not an attempt to provide a scientific base for palmistry; the indications with which he is concerned have nothing to do with "life lines" or "love lines." According to Salafsky, these ridges are formed by the middle of the second trimester of pregnancy and are essentially unalterable after that time. Therefore the presumption would be that factors (such as rubella in the mother early in the pregnancy) that influence early fetal development also influence development of the ridges.

To some this may seem an unusual way to attempt to predict the potential need for learning disabilities assistance, but it should be remembered that many of the syndromes in which mental retardation is a prime risk are first identified by physical (appearance) characteristics. This preliminary finding, which must for now be listed among those of potential direct value in learning disabilities planning and programming, may prove to be unreliable or may be reliable only as used with other indicators. This is an excellent example of the potentially wide variety of research efforts that may prove of value in our evolving area of knowledge about learning disabilities. Salafsky's recommendation that "dermatoglyphic analysis be added to the multidisciplinary approach that is so necessary in the diagnosis and workup of children with learning disabilities" (Salafsky, 1975) is an appropriate comment with which to approach the next topic of consideration as we examine new directions and trends in learning disabilities.

DIAGNOSTIC-TREATMENT CENTERS FOR THE LEARNING DISABLED

Child development centers involved in diagnostic evaluation, prescription, and treatment of children with developmental problems have been in existence for many years; many of the early centers were part of a university medical school. These centers have worked with a variety of handicapping conditions, with considerable emphasis on mental retardation and psychiatric disorders in the past. In recent years there has been a rapid increase in both private and university-affiliated centers that address themselves primarily to learning disabilities. Usually these centers are headed by medical doctors and include a staff that provides the multidisciplinary emphasis advocated by Salafsky.

A problem that has emerged in some of these programs is an overdependence on one, or perhaps two, types of diagnosis or treatment. When the staff is assembled by a director who is quite drug treatment oriented the staff tends to be of the same bias; those who differ greatly generally sense the local emphasis and do not apply or do not remain interested in employment after they are interviewed. The same effect occurs no matter what the specific orientation, and the value of the multidisciplinary team approach is greatly reduced. In some cases the staff seems to have a low level of awareness of the variety of possible approach avenues; in others they are aware but are so certain of the value of their own bias that they ignore others.

In many ways this situation parallels the manner in which educational practitioners find one good approach and then try to make all children fit into that framework. The approach may work fine with some but is inappropriate or at least less than maximally effective with others. This has been a problem, but fortunately there appears to be a trend toward a multifaceted medical approach by teams of physicians who deliberately assess a variety of factors and influences and provide for a variety of types of treatment or remedial approaches. One institute that represents a worthwhile move in this direction is the New York Institute for Child Development, Inc. The following description of this institute should illustrate this broader approach to learning disabilities.

*The New York Institute for Child Development** is a medically directed diagnostic-treatment center for the hyperactive learning-disabled child and the underachiever. A generalizable assumption of those who direct this program is that most such children have a twofold problem. First, it is believed that the child's body chemistry may be out of balance and, second, he may suffer from general neurological disorganization.

Pharmacological (drug) approaches are not favored because they tend to have a superficial effect on these children. They become more subdued, but sensorimotor functioning and learning performance are not improved.

The New York Institute provides a two-pronged program of treatment following a laboratory workup and in-depth diagnostic

*My appreciation to William Mullineaux, Clinical Director of the New York Institute for Child Development, for information, including personal communication about the functions of the institute. Part of this descriptive narrative is also adapted from mimeographed materials distributed by the institute. I have attempted to be consistent with the information provided, but some interpretations were made for which I must take full responsibility.

tests. The first part is a carefully monitored nutritional program, and the other is a detailed sensorimotor program.

The program coordinates a weekly therapy session given at the institute with a daily home exercise schedule. Checks on progress are made monthly and reevaluation is made at 3-month intervals until the child is functioning reasonably normally and discharged.

During its 7-year history more than 2,000 children have been served by the New York Institute's program of therapy, and records there indicate beneficial results.

Nutrition and brain function

The New York Institute for Child Development has utilized a multifaceted medical-nutritional approach for many years and should be considered a leader in this field. They have pioneered in the elimination of sugar and chemicals from children's diets; the following statement expresses their beliefs in this area of concern.

> The role of nutrition in brain function has long been recognized. Nutrition to the brain is not just important for good brain function, it is critical. Too low or too high levels of nutrients will cause aberrant brain function. Too low a level of oxygen will cause the brain to behave in such a manner that symptoms of brain dysfunction or disease will appear. Too low sugar levels will also cause the brain to operate in a way that will be diagnosed as diseased, psychotic, brain damaged, etc.
>
> Nutrition is not only crucial for function, it is crucial for growth and development. We know that better nourished mothers produce smarter, better functioning infants. We know that better nourished children produce better athletes and students. Better nourished children produce better functioning adults. Conversely, we know that malnutrition produces brain damage.
>
> Today, we also know that nutrition plays a key role in many conditions we thought had no biochemical basis. Hyperkinesis is a condition in which nutrition can be the causative-curative factor.

The New York Institute for Child Development program also incorporates a sensorimotor training program based on specific evaluation in this area. Training, some of it on a group basis, is undertaken at the institute. Additional exercises and activities are outlined to be done at home as individual evaluation indicates necessary.

Many medically oriented treatment programs are in some ways similar to the New York Institute, and more are opening each year. Some are multidisciplinary in nature, start with complete diagnostic workups, and include regular reevaluations. Others are narrow in outlook and may be of little more value than some school programs for the learning disabled have been in the past. One of the more popular treatment approaches, the use of megavitamins, is one that may hold tremendous promise but also may become one of the most misused and misunderstood. Writing of the use of megavitamins to treat schizophrenia, Graber (1973) notes that "one of the side effects of orthomolecular medicine, because of the availability of vitamins and the growing body of popular literature on the subject, has been the tendency of patients to bypass the medical profession entirely and treat themselves."

This may become a serious problem with the use of megavitamins to treat learning disabilities. Graber also notes that "giving vitamins is a very simple way to treat a patient. In some cases, it's also an invitation for lazy practitioners with an M.D. degree to make some easy money" (Graber, 1973). These two possibilities must be considered when evaluating treatments such as megavitamin therapy and other similar approaches. The promise is great, but the path to exciting and revolutionary progress is strewn with pitfalls.

GROWING NUMBER OF PROFESSIONALS WHO WORK WITH LEARNING DISABLED

As has been indicated throughout this text, a growing number of professionals are making significant contributions in efforts to assist the learning disabled. This is as it should be, for with this multidisciplinary emphasis we will surely make more rapid progress in efforts to prevent learning disabilities in some children, reduce the effect of learning problems in others, and remedy problems in those children who have not received the benefit of or have not responded to early intervention. These efforts will be of maximum effect only as each of these disciplines makes every effort to do the following.

1. Work with other disciplines with full respect for the contributions of all and with conscious effort to place the needs of children above self-interest
2. Learn from parallel experiences of others
3. Recognize that learning disabilities are so varied that although a given type of professional assistance may be of significant value in some cases, it may be essentially useless in others
4. Share in research efforts, establishing multidisciplinary research thrusts whenever possible
5. Appreciate the complexity of a total effort that requires consideration of genetic factors, environmental influences, nutritional variables, and educational procedures to name just a few

We will not attempt to consider a comprehensive list of those professional groups who should attend to these considerations; the list may grow as we develop additional understanding of learning disabilities. We can, however, consider one professional group that has the potential for significant contribution, perhaps in direct proportion to how they learn from the experience of others.

Speech and hearing specialists have been among the major contributors to significant segments of the developing field of learning disabilities. Wepman, a long-time specialist in this area, provided a challenge to speech and hearing specialists when he said, "With relatively slight alteration in some curricula —and perhaps none in others—speech and hearing specialists can (and I strongly believe should) become the major educational resource for direct auditory perceptual training and become actively involved in parent and teacher guidance in the art of listening" (Wepman, 1975). Wepman's point regarding the potential contribution of the speech and hearing specialist is well taken; this group has excellent credentials and must pro-

vide a meaningful contribution in this arena, *but they must learn from the experience of others.*

As has been emphasized throughout this text, efforts to remedy perceptual processes without planned involvement and coordinated efforts to assist the child to use these newly developed abilities in the learning tasks (that is, reading and arithmetic) have not been overwhelmingly successful. Learning disabilities specialists have tried the "process only" route and have found it to be lacking. Although admittedly not established with total certainty, it appears that we must assist the child in the academic tasks concurrently with attempts to remedy perceptual, conceptual, or language disorders. *It also appears that one of the major roles of the professional working with the learning-disabled child is that of advising the regular classroom teacher as to how to proceed in teaching the child to read (or do arithmetic, or interpret material in social studies, etc.).*

In attempting to determine needed changes in curricula, university training program officials have learned from special educators in the field that if learning disabilities specialists do not have *teaching experience* or do not at least fully understand how, for example, reading is taught in the regular classroom, it is difficult for them to be of assistance to the classroom teacher (University of Northern Colorado Conference Proceedings, 1974). One of the problems is not fully understanding how the process works; the other is that teachers dislike taking instructions from specialists who "have never been there."

If the speech and hearing specialist is to be a part of a team approach, then their abilities can be used to the fullest. Little additional training will be required, and all will benefit. In practice, however, public school officials (superintendents, principals, etc.) do not understand the complexity of the problem. In cases I have observed, speech clinicians who knew their field well but had no experience and no formal training in how to teach reading were asked to tell well-qualified, experienced teachers how to improve a learning-disabled child's reading skills. They did little, if any, better than the previous "learning disabilities specialist" who had a master's degree in learning disabilities with too much emphasis on perceptual-motor problems and no teaching experience.

The preceding is an oversimplification of a complex problem, but it is an example of a problem that must be carefully considered. We must insist on a *team effort, in which the best abilities of a number of professionals may be tapped.* If, for example, any one specialist is likely to be assigned as the only specialist working with learning-disabled children and advising teachers in educational methodology, then training programs must be expanded and (in this case) teaching experience must be required.

A parallel problem exists with learning disabilities specialists who have much training in process dysfunctions and little teaching knowledge of methodology or experience. Some universities are now correcting this situation, but in some states the amount of training and experience required to be a learning disabilities specialist is so minimal as to be little short of ridiculous. If this is the only individual attempting to help the child and his teacher, it is no wonder that such programs are often unsuccessful. *More training and a multidisciplinary team effort is essential.*

One more example of this principle is that of medical intervention. If, for example, a 9-year-old child is helped through megavitamins or diet control to become an effective learner, he will not necessarily magically "catch up" in reading or in any of the academic areas. The medical sector may have "done its thing," but without carefully planned educational programming, the child will remain retarded educationally, and most of the positive effect will be lost. This principle is so simple; yet it has been so often overlooked that it must be regularly reiterated. All concerned with the child must plan together, must keep each other informed, must respect the ability and potential contribution of others; then perhaps we can

really help the child. Professional myopia must not be permitted to reduce the potentially valuable effects of the increasing number of professionals who are truly interested in the learning-disabled child. It is well to be dedicated to knowledge and the pursuit of truth in its highest form, but our point of focus must remain constant, on a *child* who needs our combined, coordinated best efforts.

SUMMARY

This final chapter can be summarized briefly. The field of learning disabilities is full of hope; there are new knowledge about the functions of the brain and the neurological system, new ways to overcome the basic learning problems of some learning-disabled children, and increased efforts to discover potential learning problems and establish prevention programs. More professional groups are becoming interested in the learning disabled and dedicated to providing meaningful assistance, and more public school learning disabilities programs are opened each year.

There is also the other side of the coin. A series of related problems that have beset the remainder of special education must be faced by those who work with the learning disabled. The problems of labeling, due process, varied interpretations of mainstreaming, and a concern about assessment tools and techniques, particularly as applied to minority groups, are among the major concerns. Professional groups do not always work together, and many potential gains may be lost due to lack of cooperative effort. A single definition of learning disabilities does not exist, and many proposed definitions could lead to little but more problems.

Perhaps the best, most descriptive final word that can be applied is *challenge!* Working with learning disabilities represents one of the most tremendous challenges available in education today.

REFERENCES AND SUGGESTED READINGS

Abeson, A., Bolick, N., and Hass, J. *A primer on due process: education decisions for handi-*

capped children. Reston, Va.: Council for Exceptional Children, 1975.

Cicourel, A. *Cognitive sociology: language and meaning in social interaction.* New York: The Free Press, 1974.

Divoky, D. Education's latest victim: the "L.D." kid. *Learning,* 1974, *3*(2), 20-25.

Gearheart, B., and Weishahn, M. *The handicapped child in the regular classroom.* St. Louis: The C. V. Mosby Co., 1976.

Geschwind, N. Language and the brain. *Scientific American,* 1972, *226*(4), 76-83.

Graber, D. Megavitamins, molecules, and minds. *Human Behavior,* 1973, *2*(5), 8-15.

Hoffman, M. A learning disability is a symptom, not a disease. *Academic Therapy,* 1975, *10*(3), 261-275.

Kershner, J., and Kershner, B. Dual brain asymmetry: another cause of learning disorders? *Academic Therapy,* 1973, *8*(4), 391-393.

Martin, E. Some thoughts on mainstreaming. *Exceptional Children,* 1974, *41*(3), 150-153.

McGlannan, F. Research of interest: brain blood flow. *Journal of Learning Disabilities,* 1975, *8*(2), 83-84. (a)

McGlannan, F. Research of interest: premature infant: brain blood flow. *Journal of Learning Disabilities,* 1975, *8*(3), 152-153. (b)

McNeil, M., and Hamre, C. A review of measures of lateralized cerebral hemispheric functions. *Journal of Learning Disabilities,* 1974, *7*(6), 375-383.

New York Institute for Child Development, Inc. Bulletin, New York: The Institute, 1975.

Orton, S. *Reading, writing, and speech problems in children.* New York: W. W. Norton & Co., Inc., 1937.

Richardson, K., and Spears, S. *Race and intelligence.* Baltimore, Pelican Books, 1972.

Rogers, L., et al. Hemispheric specialization and language: an EEG study of Hopi Indian children. Los Angeles: Brain Research Institute, UCLA Medical Center, 1975.

Salafsky, I. Babies hands may give clue to their development. *Journal of the American Medical Association,* 1975, *232,* 240-241.

Samples, R. Learning with the whole brain. *Human Behavior,* 1975, *4*(2), 17-23.

Shneour, E. *The mal-nourished mind.* New York: Doubleday & Co., Inc., 1975.

University of Northern Colorado Conference Proceedings (meeting of employers of special education practitioner/graduates). Greeley, Colorado, 1974.

Vonder Haar, T. Chaining children with chemicals. *The Progressive,* 1975, *39*(3), 13-17.

Walker, S., III. We're too cavalier about hyperactivity. *Psychology Today,* 1974, *8*(7), December, 43-48.

Wepman, J. New and wider horizons for speech and hearing specialists. *Journal of the American Speech and Hearing Association,* 1975, *17*(1), 9-10.

APPENDIX A

Pupil behavior rating scale

The Pupil Behavior Rating Scale reprinted here first appeared in *Learning Disabilities: Educational Strategies* (Gearheart, 1973). It is an adaptation of a scale developed under a U.S. Public Health Service research grant and used in the Aurora Public Schools, Aurora, Colorado. Since 1973 it has appeared in other publications and has demonstrated its value in continued use. It is similar to other rating scales in use in the elementary schools and is to be completed by the classroom teacher. Children are "rated" in five major areas of learning and behavior in comparison to their classmates. Thus the scale is most effective after a teacher has worked with a group of children for several weeks or, preferably, several months.

Completion of this scale leads to an objectification of the classroom teacher's observations of children in the class; the student screening profile indicates relative performance in 5 major areas and 24 subareas. Low ratings on this scale *do not* indicate the presence of a learning disability. They do indicate that the pupil's performance should be further investigated and evaluated. The various possibilities that might be indicated by low ratings may be illustrated by the case of a first-grade child rated who ranked quite low in section I, auditory comprehension and listening, and section II, spoken language.

This girl appeared more capable in other areas of first-grade work than in reading and, in contrast to the low ratings in sections I and II, had high ratings in parts of section III, orientation, and all of section V, motor. Her school performance was erratic; that is, she did very well in some tasks and scored relatively low in others. In many ways she seemed to be a learning-disabled child, perhaps one with auditory perception problems. However, after completing the rating scale and noting the low scoring areas, her teacher discovered that she had been absent during the week in which the audiologist had completed hearing screening with her class. On referral it was learned that she had a borderline mild to moderate hearing loss, but because she was quite intelligent (a fact discovered by individual intelligence testing) she was able to compensate for her loss to a considerable extent, and it had not been discovered. It was also discovered that her hearing loss was slowly becoming more severe, but medical intervention helped reduce the loss and stopped the deterioration.

In this case the Pupil Behavior Rating Scale was a "failure" in discovering a learning disability but a real success in assisting in educational assessment and (in this instance, medical) amelioration. The Pupil Behavior Rating Scale and others like it have been used most commonly in screening for children with learning disabilities, but in the process they have been highly valuable in providing a meaningful point of focus for further investigative efforts on behalf of children other than the learning disabled. Low scores on such scales indicate that we should look further (with certain children), and they tell us where to focus our investigation.

209

PUPIL BEHAVIOR RATING SCALE*
Instruction manual

One of the most important techniques for diagnosis in learning disabilities is the Pupil Behavior Rating Scale. This scale is used to assess areas of behavior that cannot be measured by standardized group screening tests. Therefore your careful rating of individual pupils is necessary.

You are asked to rate each child on these five areas of learning and behavior:

I.   **Auditory comprehension and listening**

In this section, you evaluate the pupil as to his ability to understand, follow, and comprehend spoken language in the classroom. Four aspects of comprehension of language activities are to be evaluated.

II.   **Spoken language**

The child's oral speaking abilities are evaluated through the five aspects comprising this section. Use of language in the classroom and ability to use vocabulary and language in story form are basic to this ability.

III. **Orientation**

The child's awareness of himself in relation to his environment is considered in the four aspects of learning that make up this section. You are to rate the child on the extent to which he has attained time concepts, knowledge of direction, and concepts of relationships.

IV.   **Behavior**

The eight aspects of behavior comprising this section relate to the child's manner of participation in the classroom. Self-discipline in relation to himself (that is, ability to attend) as well as in relation to others is critical to your rating in this section.

V.   **Motor**

The final section pertains to the child's balance, general coordination, and use of hands in classroom activities. Three types of motor ability are to be rated: general coordination, balance, and manual dexterity. Rate each type independently because a child may have no motor difficulties, only one type of difficulty, or any combination of those listed.

---

*Adapted from a project developed under Research Grant, USPHS Contract 108-65-42, Bureau of Neurological and Sensory Diseases.

Name_____No._____   School_____Grade_____

Sex_____Date_____   Teacher_____

PUPIL BEHAVIOR RATING SCALE*

1	2	3	4	5

I. Auditory comprehension and listening

Ability to follow directions

1	2	3	4	5
Always confused; cannot or is unable to follow directions	Usually follows simple oral directions but often needs individual help	Follows directions that are familiar and/or not complex	Remembers and follows extended directions	Unusually skillful in remembering and following directions

Comprehension of class discussion

1	2	3	4	5
Always inattentive and/or unable to follow and understand discussions	Listens but rarely comprehends well; mind often wanders from discussion	Listens and follows discussions according to age and grade	Understands well and benefits from discussions	Becomes involved and shows unusual understanding of material discussed

Ability to retain orally given information

1	2	3	4	5
Almost total lack of recall; poor memory	Retains simple ideas and procedures if repeated often	Average retention of materials; adequate memory for age and grade	Remembers procedures and information from various sources; good immediate and delayed recall	Superior memory for both details and content

Comprehension of word meanings

1	2	3	4	5
Extremely immature level of understanding	Fails to grasp simple word meanings; misunderstands words at grade level	Good grasp of grade level vocabulary for age and grade	Understands all grade level vocabulary as well as higher level word meanings	Superior understanding of vocabulary; understands many abstract words

II. Spoken language

Ability to speak in complete sentences using accurate sentence structure

1	2	3	4	5
Always uses incomplete sentences with grammatical errors	Frequently uses incomplete sentences and/or numerous grammatical errors	Uses correct grammar; few errors of omission or incorrect use of prepositions, verb tense, pronouns	Above-average oral language; rarely makes grammatical errors	Always speaks in grammatically correct sentences

*Adapted from a project developed under Research Grant, USPHS Contract 108-65-42, Bureau of Neurological and Sensory Diseases.

Continued.

PUPIL BEHAVIOR RATING SCALE—cont'd

1	2	3	4	5
II. Spoken language—cont'd				
Vocabulary ability				
Always uses immature or improper vocabulary	Limited vocabulary including primarily simple nouns; few precise, descriptive words	Adequate vocabulary for age and grade	Above-average vocabulary; uses numerous precise descriptive words	High level vocabulary; always uses precise words to convey message; uses abstraction
Ability to recall words				
Unable to call forth the exact word	Often gropes for words to express himself	Occasionally searches for correct word but adequate for age and grade	Above-average ability; rarely hesitates on a word	Always speaks well; never hesitates or substitutes words
Ability to formulate ideas from isolated facts				
Unable to relate isolated facts	Has difficulty relating isolated facts; ideas are incomplete and scattered	Usually relates facts into meaningful ideas; adequate for age and grade	Relates facts and ideas well	Outstanding ability in relating facts appropriately
Ability to tell stories and relate experiences				
Unable to tell a comprehensible story	Has difficulty relating ideas in logical sequence	Average ability to tell stories	Above average; uses logical sequence	Exceptional ability to relate ideas in a logical meaningful manner
III. Orientation				
Promptness				
Lacks grasp of meaning of time; always late or confused	Poor time concept; tends to dawdle; often late	Average understanding of time for age and grade	Prompt; late only with good reason	Very skillful at handling schedules; plans and organizes well
Spatial orientation				
Always confused; unable to navigate around classroom or school, playground or neighborhood	Frequently gets lost in relatively familiar surroundings	Can maneuver in familiar locations; average for age and grade	Above-average ability; rarely lost or confused	Never lost; adapts to new locations, situations; places
Judgment of relationships: big, little; far, close; light, heavy				
Judgments of relationships very inadequate	Makes elementary judgments successfully	Average ability in relation to age and grade	Accurate judgments but does not generalize to new situations	Unusually precise judgments; generalizes them to new situations and experiences

PUPIL BEHAVIOR RATING SCALE—cont'd

1	2	3	4	5
III. Orientation—cont'd				
Learning directions				
Highly confused; unable to distinguish directions as right, left, north, and south	Sometimes exhibits directional confusion	Average, uses R vs. L, N-S-E-W	Good sense of direction; seldom confused	Excellent sense of direction
IV. Behavior				
Cooperation				
Continually disrupts classroom; unable to inhibit responses	Frequently demands spotlight; often speaks out of turn	Waits his turn; average for age and grade	Cooperates well; above average	Cooperates without adult encouragement
Attention				
Is never attentive; very distractible	Rarely listens; attention frequently wanders	Attends adequately for age and grade	Above average; almost always attends	Always attends to important aspects; long attention span
Ability to organize				
Is highly disorganized; very slovenly	Often disorganized in manner of working; inexact, careless	Maintains average organization of work; careful	Above-average ability to organize and complete work; consistent	Always completes assignments in a highly organized and meticulous manner
Ability to cope with new situations: parties, trips, unanticipated changes in routine				
Becomes extremely excitable; totally lacking in self-control	Often overreacts; new situations disturbing	Adapts adequately for age and grade	Adapts easily and quickly with self-confidence	Excellent adaptation, utilizing initiative and independence
Social acceptance				
Avoided by others	Tolerated by others	Liked by others; average for age and grade	Well liked by others	Sought by others
Acceptance of responsibility				
Rejects responsibility; never initiates activities	Avoids responsibility; limited acceptance of role for age	Accepts responsibility; adequate for age and grade	Enjoys responsibility; above average; frequently takes initiative or volunteers	Seeks responsibility; almost always takes initiative with enthusiasm
Completion of assignments				
Never finishes, even with guidance	Seldom finishes, even with guidance	Average ability to follow through on assignments	Above-average ability to complete assignments	Always completes assignments without supervision

Continued.

PUPIL BEHAVIOR RATING SCALE—cont'd

1	2	3	4	5

IV. Behavior—cont'd

Tactfulness

Always rude	Usually disregards other's feelings	Average tactfulness; occasionally socially inappropriate	Above-average tactfulness; rarely socially inappropriate	Always tactful; never socially inappropriate

V. Motor

General coordination: running, climbing, hopping, walking

Very poorly coordinated; clumsy	Below-average coordination; awkward	Average coordination for age	Above-average coordination; does well in these activities	Exceptional ability; excels in this area

Balance

Very poor balance	Below-average falls frequently	Average balance for age; not outstanding but adequate equilibrium	Above-average; does well in activities requiring balance	Exceptional ability; excels in balancing

Ability to manipulate utensils and equipment; manual dexterity

Very poor in manual manipulation	Awkward in manual dexterity	Adequate dexterity for age; manipulates well	Above-average manual dexterity	Almost perfect performance; readily manipulates new equipment

STUDENT SCREENING PROFILE

Date of birth_____

Name_____ Sex_____ Date_____

School_____ Grade or level_____ Teacher_____

FOR OFFICE USE ONLY—DO NOT WRITE ON THIS SIDE

I. Auditory comprehension and listing

A. Ability to follow directions
  1   2   3   4   5

A._____

B. Comprehension of class discussion
  1   2   3   4   5

B._____

C. Ability to retain information
  1   2   3   4   5

C._____

D. Comprehension of word meanings
  1   2   3   4   5

D._____   Total I_____

STUDENT SCREENING PROFILE—cont'd

II. Spoken language

A. Ability to speak in sentences
   1   2   3   4   5
         A._____

B. Vocabulary ability
   1   2   3   4   5
         B._____

C. Ability to recall words
   1   2   3   4   5
         C._____

D. Ability to formulate ideas
   1   2   3   4   5
         D._____

E. Ability to tell stories
   1   2   3   4   5
         E._____ Total II_____

III. Orientation

A. Promptness
   1   2   3   4   5
         A._____

B. Spatial orientation
   1   2   3   4   5
         B._____

C. Judgment of relationships
   1   2   3   4   5
         C._____

D. Learning directions
   1   2   3   4   5
         D._____ Total III_____

IV. Behavior

A. Cooperation
   1   2   3   4   5
         A._____

B. Attention
   1   2   3   4   5
         B._____

C. Ability to organize
   1   2   3   4   5
         C._____

D. Ability to cope with new situations
   1   2   3   4   5
         D._____

E. Social acceptance
   1   2   3   4   5
         E._____

F. Acceptance of responsibility
   1   2   3   4   5
         F._____

G. Completion of assignments
   1   2   3   4   5
         G._____

H. Tactfulness
   1   2   3   4   5
         H._____ Total IV_____

Continued.

STUDENT SCREENING PROFILE—cont'd

V. **Motor**

    A. General coordination   A._____
        1   2   3   4   5

    B. Balance   B._____
        1   2   3   4   5

    C. Manipulative skills   C._____   Total V_____
        1   2   3   4   5

APPENDIX B

Sources of materials, equipment, and books for use in learning disabilities programs

The list of publishers and suppliers of materials, equipment, and books that follows is an expanded, updated version of a similar list published in *Learning Disabilities: Educational Strategies* in 1973. A response that indicated the value of this earlier listing led to its inclusion in this text in an updated form. Letters of inquiry to these various suppliers and publishers will bring catalogs or supply lists that will be more up to date than any list of actual materials that could be included here.

Some of these companies provide audiovisual materials, learning games, equipment, and a variety of other curriculum materials. Others produce or supply only one type of product, for example, professional books. The list that follows indicates six categories of products.

AV   Audiovisual materials
BK   Professional books
CM   Curriculum materials
EQ   Equipment
GA   Educational games
TE   Tests and testing equipment

Overlap between these six categories makes it difficult to "key" the list precisely, and various publishers and vendors add to or modify their product lines regularly. The list is provided as a starting point for further investigation and does not imply qualitative endorsement.

Academic Therapy Publications — AV, BK, CM, EQ, TE
1539 Fourth St.
San Rafael, Calif. 94901

Acropolis Books — BK, CM
2400 17th St. N.W.
Washington, D.C. 20009

Allied Educational Council — BK, CM, GA
Distribution Center
P.O. Box 78
Galien, Mich. 49113

Allyn & Bacon, Inc. — BK
470 Atlantic Ave.
Boston, Mass. 02210

American Educational Publications — BK
245 Long Hill Rd.
Middletown, Conn. 06457

American Guidance Service — AV, BK, CM, EQ, GA, TE
Publishers Building
Circle Pines, Minn. 55014

Ann Arbor Publishers — CM
611 Church St.
Ann Arbor, Mich. 48104

Appleton-Century-Crofts — BK
440 Park Ave. S.
New York, N.Y. 10016

Association for Childhood Education — BK, CM
3615 Wisconsin Ave. N.W.
Washington, D.C. 20016

Audio-Visual Research — CM
1317 Eighth St. S.E.
Waseca, Minn. 56093

Baggiani & Tewell   BK, CM
4 Spring Hill Court
Chevy Chase, Md. 20015

Barnhart, Clarence L., Inc.   CM
Box 250
Bronxville, N.Y. 10708

Basic Books, Inc.   BK
404 Park Ave., S.
New York, N.Y. 10016

Behavioral Research Laboratories   CM, GA
Box 577
Palo Alto, Calif. 94302

Bell & Howell   AV
7100 McCormick Rd.
Chicago, Ill. 60645

Bobbs-Merrill Co., Inc.   BK, CM, TE
4300 West 62nd St.
Indianapolis, Ind. 46206

Borg-Warner Educational Systems   CM, EQ
7450 N. Natchez Ave.
Niles, Ill. 60648

Bowmar   AV, CM, EQ
622 Rodier Dr.
Glendale, Calif. 91201

Brown, Wm. C.   BK
135 S. Locust St.
Dubuque, Iowa 52001

Burgess Publishing Co.   BK, CM
4265 6th St.
Minneapolis, Minn. 55415

California Association for Neurologically
    Handicapped Children   AV, BK
P.O. Box 1526
Vista, Calif. 92083

California Test Bureau   TE
Del Monte Research Park
Monterey, Calif. 93940

Chandler Publishing Co.   BK, CM
124 Spear St.
San Francisco, Calif. 94105

Chicago (University of) Press   BK
5750 Ellis Ave.
Chicago, Ill. 60637

Childcraft Education Corp.   CM, GA
964 Third Ave.
New York, N.Y. 10022

Children's Music Center, Inc.   AV, BK, CM
5373 West Pico Blvd.
Los Angeles, Calif. 90019

Concept Records   AV
Box 250
Center Conway, N.H. 03813

Constructive Playthings   AV, CM
1040 East 85th St.
Kansas City, Mo. 64131

Consulting Psychologists Press   BK, CM, TE
577 College Ave.
Palo Alto, Calif. 94306

Continental Press   AV, CM
Elizabethtown, Pa. 17022

Control Development, Inc.   GA
3166 Des Plaines Ave.
Des Plaines, Ill. 60018

Council for Exceptional Children   BK, CM
1411 S. Jefferson Davis Highway
Arlington, Va. 22202

Craig Corp. & Industrial Division   CM
921 W. Artesia Blvd.
Compton, Calif. 90220

Creative Playthings   CM, EQ, GA
Edinburg Road
Cranbury, N.J. 08512

Day, John, Co.   BK, CM, TE
257 Park Ave. S.
New York, N.Y. 10010

Developmental Learning Materials BK, CM, EQ, GA
7440 Natchez Ave.
Niles, Ill. 60648

Dick Blick, Inc.   CM, GA
P.O. Box 1267-F
Galesburg, Ill. 61401

Dimensions Publishing Co.   BK, CM
Box 4221
San Rafael, Calif. 94903

Dryden Press, Inc.   BK
901 N. Elm
Hinsdale, Ill. 60521

Educational Activities, Inc.   AV, BK, CM
Box 392
Freeport, N.Y. 11520

Educational Development Laboratories CM, GA
284 Pulaski St.
Huntington, N.Y. 11744

Educational Progress Corp.   AV, CM
Box 45663
Tulsa, Okla. 74145

Educational Projections Corp.   AV, CM
1911 Pickwick Ave.
Glenview, Ill. 60610

Educational Service, Inc.   CM, GA
P.O. Box 219
Stevensville, Mich. 49127

Educational Teaching Aids   CM, GA
159 W. Kinzie St.
Chicago, Ill. 60610

Educational Testing Service   TE
Princeton, N.J. 08540

Educators Publishing Service   AV, BK, CM,
75 Moulton St.   EQ, GA, TE
Cambridge, Mass. 02138

EduKaid of Ridgewood   CM, GA
1250 E. Ridgewood Ave.
Ridgewood, N.J. 07450

Essay Press   CM
P.O. Box 5, Planetarium Station
New York, N.Y. 10024

Expression Co., Publishers   CM, GA
P.O. Box 11
Magnolia, Mass. 01930

Eye Gate House   AV, CM
146-01 Archer Ave.
Jamaica, N.Y. 11435

Fearon Publishers   BK, CM, TE
6 Davis Dr.
Belmont, Calif. 94002

Field Educational Publications, Inc.   AV, CM
2400 Hanover St.
Palo Alto, Calif. 94304

Filmstrip House, Inc.   AV
432 Park Ave. S.
New York, N.Y. 10016

Follet Educational Corp.   BK, CM, TE
Box 5705
Chicago, Ill. 60680

Gamco Industries, Inc.   CM, EQ, GA
P.O. Box 1911
Big Springs, Tex. 79720

Garrard Publishing Co.   BK, CM
1607 N. Market St.
Champaign, Ill. 61820

Ginn & Co.   BK, CM
125 Second Ave.
Waltham, Mass. 02154

Grune & Stratton, Inc.   BK, TE
111 Fifth Ave.
New York, N.Y. 10003

Gryphon Press   BK, CM
220 Montgomery St.
Highland Park, N.J. 08904

Guidance Associates   TE
1526 Gilpin Ave.
Wilmington, Del. 19800

Hale, E. M., & Co., Publishers   BK
1201 S. Hastings Way
Eau Claire, Wis. 54701

Harcourt Brace Jovanovich, Inc.   BK, TE
757 Third Ave.
New York, N.Y. 10017

Harper & Row, Publishers   BK
49 E. 33rd St.
New York, N.Y. 10016

Heath, D. C., & Co.   BK
125 Spring St.
Lexington, Mass. 02173

Hoffman Information Systems   AV, CM
5623 Peck Rd.
Arcadia, Calif. 91006

Holt, Reinhart & Winston, Inc.   BK
383 Madison Ave.
New York, N.Y. 10017

Houghton Mifflin Co.   BK, TE
2 Park St.
Boston, Mass. 02107

Ideal School Supply Co.   AV, CM, GA
11000 S. Lavergne St.
Oak Lawn, Ill. 60453

Illinois (University of) Press   BK, CM, TE
Urbana, Ill. 61801

Imperial International Learning Corp.   AV, CM
P.O. Box 548
Kankakee, Ill. 60901

Incentive Products Educational   CM, TE
1902 Coral Way
Miami, Fla. 33145

Instructo Corp.   CM, EQ, GA
200 Cedar Hollow Rd.
Paoli, Pa. 19301

International Reading Association   BK, CM
6 Tyre St.
Newark, Del. 19711

Interstate Printers, Inc.   BK, CM
Jackson at Van Buren
Danville, Ill. 61832

Intext Publishing Co.   BK
Scranton, Pa. 18515

Johns Hopkins Press   BK
Baltimore, Md. 21218

Journal of Learning Disabilities   BK
5 N. Wabash Ave.
Chicago, Ill. 60602

Kansas (University of) Press   BK
366 Watson
Lawrence, Kan. 66044

Kenworthy Educational Service, Inc.   CM, GA
P.O. Box 3031
Buffalo, N.Y. 14205

Keystone View Co.   GA, TE
Box D
Meadville, Pa. 16335

Kingsbury Center   CM, GA
2138 Bancroft Pl.
Washington, D.C. 20008

Kismet Publishing Co.   CM, GA, TE
P.O. Box 90
South Miami, Fla. 33143

Knowledge Aid   CM
6633 W. Howard St.
Niles, Ill. 60648

Kutz Corp.   CM, GA
P.O. Box 140
McLean, Va. 22101

Laidlaw Brothers   BK
Thatcher and Madison Sts.
River Forest, Ill. 60305

Language Research Associates   BK, TE
Box 95
Chicago, Ill. 60637

Lawson Book Co.   CM
9488 Sara St.
Elk Grove, Calif. 95624

Lea & Febiger   BK
600 S. Washington Square
Philadelphia, Pa. 19106

Learning Pathways   CM
Rt. R, Box 723
Evergreen, Col. 80439

Learning Research Associates, Inc.   AV, CM, TE
1501 Broadway St.
New York, N.Y. 10036

Learning Systems Press   CM, GA
P.O. Box 909-E
Rantoul, Ill. 61866

Learning Trends   AV, CM, GA
115 Fifth Ave.
New York, N.Y. 10003

Lippincott, J. B., Co.   BK
E. Washington Square
Philadelphia, Pa. 19105

Little, Brown & Co.   BK
34 Beacon St.
Boston, Mass. 02106

Litton Instructional Materials, Inc.   CM, EQ, GA
1695 W. Crescent Ave.
Anaheim, Calif. 92801

Love Publishing Co.   BK, CM
6635 E. Villanova Pl.
Denver, Col. 80222

Lyons & Carnahan, Publishers   BK, CM
407 E. 25th St.
Chicago, Ill. 60616

Macmillan Co.   BK
866 Third Ave.
New York, N.Y. 10022

Mafex   BK, CM, GA, TE
111 Barron Ave.
Johnstown, Pa. 15906

Math Media, Inc.   CM, GA
P.O. Box 345
Danbury, Conn. 06810

McGraw-Hill, EDL   CM, EQ, GA
284 Pulaski Rd.
Huntington, N.Y. 11743

McKay, David, Co., Inc.   BK
750 Third Ave.
New York, N.Y. 10017

Mead Educational Services   CM, GA
245 N. Highland Ave.
Atlanta, Ga. 30307

Media   CM
P.O. Box 1355
Vista, Calif. 92083

Medical Motivation Systems   EQ
Research Park, State Rd.
Princeton, N.J. 08540

Merrill, Charles E., Publishing Co.   BK, CM
1300 Alum Creek Dr.
Columbus, Ohio 43216

Milton Bradley Co.   CM, EQ, GA
74 Park St.
Springfield, Mass. 01106

Mosby, The C. V., Co.   BK
11830 Westline Industrial Dr.
St. Louis, Mo. 63141

MultiMedia Education, Inc.   AV, CM, GA
11 West 42nd St.
New York, N.Y. 10036

**New York Association for
   Brain-Injured Children**   BK
305 Broadway
New York, N.Y. 10007

Noble & Noble, Publishers, Inc. CM
750 Third Ave.
New York, N.Y. 10017

Open Court Publishing Co. CM
P.O. Box 599
LaSalle, Ill. 61301

Orton Society BK
8415 Bellona Lane
Towson, Md. 21204

Owen, F. A., Publisher BK
7 Bank St.
Dansville, N.Y. 14437

Oxford University Press BK
200 Madison Ave.
New York, N.Y. 10016

Peek Publications BK
P.O. Box 11065
Palo Alto, Calif. 94303

Phonovisual Products, Inc. CM
12216 Parklawn Dr.
Rockville, Md. 20852

Prentice-Hall, Inc. BK, CM
Englewood Cliffs, N.J. 07632

Preston, J. A., Co. CM, EQ, GA, TE
71 Fifth Ave.
New York, N.Y. 10003

Priority Innovations BK, CM
P.O. Box 792
Skokie, Ill. 60076

Project Life—General Electric AV
P.O. Box 43
Schenectady, N.Y. 12301

Pruett Publishing Co. BK, CM
P.O. Box 1560
Boulder, Col. 80302

Psychological Corp. (The) TE
316 E. 45th St.
New York, N.Y. 10017

Psychological Test Specialists TE
Box 1441
Missoula, Mont. 59804

Psychotechnics, Inc. CM, EQ, GA
1900 Pickwick Ave.
Glenview, Ill. 60025

Research Press Co. BK
CFS Box 3327
Champaign, Ill. 61820

Response Systems Corp. AV, EQ
Edgemont, Pa. 19028

Rheem Mfg., Califone Division EQ
5922 Bowcroft St.
Los Angeles, Calif. 90016

Scholastic Magazines, Inc. CM, EQ
50 West 44th St.
New York, N.Y. 10036

Science Research Associates BK, CM, GA, TE
259 E. Erie St.
Chicago, Ill. 60611

Scott, Foresman & Co. AV, CM
11310 Gemini Lane
Dallas, Tex. 75229

Slosson Educational Publications TE
140 Pine St.
East Aurora, N.Y. 14052

Society for Visual Education, Inc. AV, CM, GA
1345 W. Diversey Pwy.
Chicago, Ill. 60614

Special Child Publications BK
4535 Union Bay Pl., N.E.
Seattle, Wash. 98105

Speech & Language Materials, Inc. CM, GA
P.O. Box 721
Tulsa, Okla. 74101

Stanwix House, Inc. CM, GA
3020 Chartiers Ave.
Pittsburgh, Pa. 15204

Steck-Vaughan Co. BK, CM
P.O. Box 2028
Austin, Tex. 78767

Stone, R. H., Products CM
18279 Livernois
Detroit, Mich. 48221

Syracuse University Press BK
Box 8, University Sta.
Syracuse, N.Y. 13210

Teachers College Press BK
1234 Amsterdam Ave.
New York, N.Y. 10027

Teachers Publishing Corp. BK, CM
Darien, Conn. 06820

Teaching Resources Corp. AV, BK, CM, EQ, GA, TE
100 Boylston St.
Boston, Mass. 02116

Teaching Technology Corp. CM, GA
7471 Greenbush Ave.
North Hollywood, Calif. 91609

Thomas, Charles C, Publisher BK
301 E. Lawrence Ave.
Springfield, Ill. 62703

Topaz Books   BK
Five N. Wabash Ave.
Chicago, Ill. 60602

Tweedy Transparencies   AV
208 Hollywood Ave.
East Orange, N.J. 07018

United Transparencies, Inc.   AV
P.O. Box 688
Binghamton, N.Y. 13902

Webster Division/McGraw-Hill
  Book Co.   AV, BK, CM
13955 Manchester Rd.
Manchester, Mo. 63011

Wenkart Publishing Co.   BK, CM
4 Shady Hill Sq.
Cambridge, Mass. 02138

Western Psychological Services   BK, CM, EQ, GA, TE
12031 Wilshire Blvd., Dept. E
Los Angeles, Calif. 90025

Wiley, John, & Sons, Inc.   BK
605 Third Ave.
New York, N.Y. 10016

Word Making Productions   CM, GA, TE
P.O. Box 1858
Salt Lake City, Utah 84100

APPENDIX C

Pitt County resource room program: forms and additional information

The learning disabilities referral form and parent permission forms for individual testing and placement are included to indicate the type of information that may be asked or required for these purposes. The diagram of the diagnostic-prescriptive center and the brief descriptions of the purposes of each of the stations within this center may be of value in better conceptualizing this resource room.

Many school districts may wish to use a different approach or different wording than used in these forms. These are given here as a guide to the type of form that has worked successfully in one school district. The diagram and description of the purposes of each of the stations in this actual classroom may provide new ideas for existing programs or a starting point for programs just being organized. This information, along with the narrative description on pp. 177-180, should provide sufficient information to permit readers to determine if this model has merit for their local situation.

For additional information about the diagnostic-prescriptive center, write to Blanie A. Moye, Principal, or Betty Quinn, Learning Lab Teacher; W. H. Robinson Primary School, P.O. Box 505, Winterville, North Carolina 28590. For information about the Pitt County Learning Disability Staff Development Center (the teacher training function), write to Jean Averette, L.D. Staff Development Coordinator, W. H. Robinson Primary School, P.O. Box 505, Winterville, North Carolina 28590, or to Betty Levey, Dr. John Richards, or Alan Sheinker, Department of Special Education, East Carolina University, Greenville, North Carolina 27834.

PITT COUNTY SCHOOLS

LEARNING DISABILITIES REFERRAL FORM

To: _____, Learning disabilities teacher

From: _____ Date of Referral _____

Name of child: _____ School _____

Parents: _____ Grade _____ Birthdate _____

Address: _____ Phone _____

Intelligence level (est.) _____ (Superior, Bright, Average, Dull)

Academic: (Estimates based on last achievement test results and present observations)

  1. Present reading level   _____

  2. Area of difficulty in reading   _____

  3. Level of spelling   _____

  4. Level of arithmetic   _____

  5. Areas in which he or she is most   _____
     interested

Place a check by the characteristics that apply to this child. ($\sqrt{}$ = Noticeable, $\sqrt{}+$ = Very noticeable)

_____ 1. Hypoactive (passive)

_____ 2. Distractible (short attention span)

_____ 3. Impulsive, unpredictable

_____ 4. Usually slow in completing work

PITT COUNTY SCHOOLS

LEARNING DISABILITIES REFERRAL FORM—cont'd

_____ 5. Poor handwriting

_____ 6. Does not follow directions

_____ 7. Clumsy or awkward

_____ 8. Disorganized work habits

_____ 9. Writes with either hand

_____10. Confuses right and left

_____11. Trouble finding or keeping place

_____12. Frequent reversals or inversions in reading and writing

_____13. Can word call but not comprehend

_____14. Has difficulties using and understanding language

_____15. Poor self-concept

_____16. Spatial orientation (cannot find his way around school)

Teacher notes and observations: (Include both strengths and weaknesses—amplify academic level estimates above as appropriate)

Please include samples of his work.

PITT COUNTY SCHOOLS
GREENVILLE, NORTH CAROLINA
PERMISSION FOR TESTING

Date: _____

School: _____

Principal: _____

Teacher: _____

Grade: _____

To: _____

    In order to provide adequate school experiences for your child, we would like to have your permission for individual educational testing. This will enable us to meet _____ needs as we plan a program of individualized instruction.

PLEASE DETACH AND RETURN

    I give my permission for _____ to have individual educational testing.

_____
(Parent or guardian)

PITT COUNTY SCHOOLS

PERMISSION FOR PLACEMENT

Date: _____

School: _____

Principal: _____

Teacher: _____

Grade: _____

To: _____

Your child is being considered for placement in a resource class for children with learning disabilities. This class is designed to provide individualized instruction in areas in which your child has shown deficiencies.

PLEASE DETACH AND RETURN

- -

I give my permission for _____ to be placed in a resource class for children with learning disabilities.

_____
(Parent or guardian)

_____ I waive the right to receive a registered letter concerning my child's placement.

PITT COUNTY SCHOOLS
DIAGNOSTIC-PRESCRIPTIVE LEARNING CENTERS

READING AND LANGUAGE CENTER

Purpose: To provide learning experiences that will improve word attack skills, sight word recognition, reading comprehension, interest in reading, and oral and written language

WRITING CENTER

Purposes: To provide opportunities for the development of fine motor skills leading to improvement in manuscript and cursive writing and to provide creative writing experiences offering improvement in written language skills

MATH CENTER

Purpose: To provide experiences in number readiness skills, computational skills, and time and money concepts that will enable the child to gain speed and accuracy

AUDITORY PERCEPTION CENTER

Purpose: To provide opportunities for the development of good listening skills in the areas of auditory discrimination, auditory memory, auditory figure-ground perception, auditory closure, and sound blending

VISUAL PERCEPTION CENTER

Purpose: To provide opportunities for the development of good visual skills in the areas of visual memory, visual discrimination, and visual motor activities

KINESTHETIC-TACTILE CENTER

Purpose: To provide experiences in the improvement of tactile perception (related to the sense of touch via the fingers and skin surfaces) and kinesthetic perception (obtained through body movements and muscle feeling)

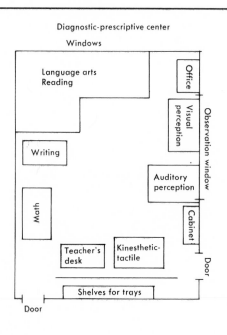

Diagnostic-prescriptive center

APPENDIX D

Reading evaluation tools, reading materials and programs, and high-interest, low-vocabulary level books

READING EVALUATION TOOLS
Reading survey tests

Botel Reading Inventory, Follett Corp. (group and individual, grades 1 to 12, 40 minutes to 1 hour)

The inventory is used to determine instructional, frustration, and free reading levels, measures word recognition, listening comprehension, and phonics.

Gates MacGinitie Reading Tests, Teachers College Press (group, grade 12, 40 to 45 minutes)

Tests are available on different levels. They are designed to give diagnostic information about a child's silent reading skills such as vocabulary, comprehension, and speed.

Iowa Silent Reading Tests, Houghton Mifflin Co. (group, grades 4 to 13, 45 to 50 minutes, designed on two levels: grades 4 to 8 and grades 9 to 13)

Assessment includes comprehension skills, word meaning, and location of information.

Metropolitan Reading Test, Harcourt Brace Jovanovich, Inc. (group, grades 2 to 9, 40 to 60 minutes)

The primary tests assess word knowledge and word discrimination; the elementary test adds reading comprehension; and the intermediate and advanced tests measure word knowledge and reading comprehension among other skills.

SRA Achievement Series: Reading, Science Research Associates (group, grades 1 to 9, 65 to 120 minutes)

The series measures comprehension, vocabulary, verbal-pictorial association, and language perception.

Stanford Reading Tests, Harcourt Brace Jovanovich, Inc. (group, grades 3 to 9, 35 to 40 minutes)

Tests measure reading comprehension and vocabulary.

Diagnostic tests

Durrell Analysis of Reading Difficulty, Harcourt Brace Jovanovich, Inc. (individual, grades 1 to 6, 30 to 45 minutes)

This test is recommended for less severe cases of reading difficulties. It includes assessment of word recognition and assessment of oral and silent reading levels and auditory comprehension.

Gates-McKillop Reading Diagnostic Tests, Teachers College Press (individual, grades 1 to 8, no time limit)

The tests diagnose specific deficiencies in reading performance. Assessment includes oral reading, oral vocabulary, and auditory discrimination.

Monroe Diagnostic Reading Examination, C. H. Stoelting Co. (individual, grades 1 to 6, 45 minutes)

This examination diagnoses specific difficulties in word recognition.

Monroe-Sherman Group Diagnostic Reading and Achievement Tests, C. V. Nevins Printing Co. (group or individual, grades 3 and up)

Achievement tests assess paragraph meaning, speed, word discrimination, arithmetic, and spelling. Aptitude tests include visual memory, auditory memory and discrimination, motor speed, and vocabulary.

Roswell-Chall Diagnostic Reading Test of Word Analysis Skills, Essay Press (individual, grades 2 to 6, 5 minutes)

The test is designed to supplement information obtained from standardized silent and oral reading tests. Word recognition and analysis are assessed.

Screening Tests for Identifying Children with Specific Language Disability, Educators Publishing Service (grades 1 to 2, 2 to 3, and 3 to 4)

Tests include visual copying, memory, discrimination. There are three auditory group tests, one individual.

Spache Diagnostic Reading Scales, California Test Bureau (individual, grades 1 to 8, 1 hour)

Vocabulary, comprehension, word analysis, and auding are assessed as well as levels in oral and silent reading.

Oral reading tests

Gilmore Oral Reading Test. Harcourt Brace Jovanovich, Inc. (individual, grades 1 to 8, 15 to 20 minutes)

Measures comprehension, speed, and accuracy.

Gray Oral Reading Paragraphs, The Bobbs-Merrill Co., Inc. (individual, grades 1 to 12, 7 to 15 minutes)

The test assesses rate and accuracy of oral reading to obtain a grade level score. Comprehension questions are provided but not included in scoring.

Leavell Analytical Oral Reading Test, American Guidance Service, Inc. (individual, grades 1 to 8, 20 minutes)

The test measures accuracy and comprehension of oral reading.

READING MATERIALS AND PROGRAMS
Filmstrips, discs, and slides

EDL Controlled Reader Program, Coast Visual Education Co., Inc., 5610 Hollywood Blvd., Hollywood, Calif. 90028

This program uses a projector in which reading materials are presented in a left-to-right manner at a predetermined rate to develop a wide range of visual functioning and interpretive skills. Material can be presented at 60 to 1000 words per minute. A moving slot is designed to encourage left-to-right perception and improve visual mobility and coordination. A variety of materials are available from games to silent reading stories.

Project Life/General Electric Program, General Electric Co., P.O. Box 43, Schenectady, N. Y. 12301

This program consists of programmed instruction filmstrips that are used in connection with a device called a Student Response Program Master. This device is about the size of a small radio and has a number of keys that the student presses to select his choice of answers to questions. If the student selects the correct key, a light is turned on, and he is able to advance to the next frame of the filmstrip.

Cenco Filmstrip Program, Cenco Educational Aids, 2600 S. Kostner Ave., Chicago, Ill. 60623

This program is used in connection with a mechanical device called the Projection Reader/Tachistoscope. It eliminates the need to remove film from the projector to present a story on a line-by-line basis and introduces new vocabulary tachistoscopically without removing the filmstrip from the projector. Materials are available from readiness level through grade 6.

EDL-Flash-X, Coast Visual Education Co., Inc., 5610 Hollywood Blvd., Hollywood, Calif. 90028

The EDL Flash-X is a small, inexpensive hand tachistoscope employing four ¾-inch discs. Each disc contains 40 exposures. Materials range from readiness levels through college.

Craig Reader Programs, A. F. Milliron Co., Inc., 1198 S. La Brea, Los Angeles, Calif. 90019

The Craig Reader Programs utilize a fully automated individual reading training instrument resembling a miniature television set. It has variable speed control features that permit the student to set his own pace in laboratory-applied serial tachistoscopic, expanded line, and perceptual training techniques. Speeds range from 100 to over 1600 words per minute. Programs are available from elementary grades through college.

Multimodal systems

Borg-Warner System 80, Coast Visual Education Co., Inc., 5610 Hollywood Blvd., Hollywood, Calif. 90028

System 80 consists of a boxlike device that provides simultaneous visual and auditory stimulation. It utilizes a 12-inch vinyl record and a filmstrip. A child responds to a recorded voice by pressing one of the five selection buttons. The instrument moves forward when a correct answer is given and repeats if an incorrect answer is given. Every fourth lesson serves as a review. This program can be used for developmental or remedial reading.

Hoffman Audiovisual Instructional System, Hoffman Information Systems, 5623 Pick Rd., Arcadia, Calif. 91006

The system uses an instrument that presents a simultaneous visual and audio signal. Study units consist of 40-minute lessons in 10-minute modules. Questions that are presented audiovisually are printed in the student's answer book. Lessons are self-correcting. This program can be used for developmental or remedial reading as well as enrichment.

Language Master, Bell & Howell Co., 7100 McCormick Rd., Chicago, Ill. 60645

The Language Master provides simultaneous auditory and visual stimulation. The unit functions as a dual-channel audio recorder and playback device. The student may listen to the master track when he views the material in printed form. He may then record his own version on the student track. The student can check his own responses with the master track recording. The unit can be used for developmental or remedial reading.

Aud-X Mark 3, Coast Visual Education Co., Inc., 5610 Hollywood Blvd., Hollywood, Calif. 90028

Aud-X Mark 3 consists of a cassette player and a projector. The Listen-Look-Learn System provides instruction in readiness, word attack skills and comprehension skills. The program is geared for elementary students. Each recorded lesson has a playing time of 13 minutes. With each cassette-filmstrip set there is a workbook that provides reinforcement learning. The Learning 100 System serves older students who are nonreaders or who are reading at grade levels 1 to 3. The program consists of paired story and word study lessons. Workbook activities provide reinforcement to student learning.

Tape recordings

EDL Listen and Think Programs, Coast Visual Education Co., Inc., 5610 Hollywood Blvd., Hollywood, Calif. 90028

EDL Listen and Think Programs develop listening comprehension and thinking skills. Each program provides a sequence of 15 lessons. The student alternates between listening to the taped material and responding in a lesson book to the taped instruction. Compressed speech is used during later lessons. Materials are presented for levels kindergarten through grade 9.

St. Louis Program, Coast Visual Education Co., Inc., 5610 Hollywood Blvd., Hollywood, Calif. 90028

The St. Louis Program consists of 28 tapes and accompanying pupil response booklets. It was written to help disadvantaged primary children, but portions of the program are recommended for use by children of all ability levels as an introduction to the sounds of consonants and vowels.

SRA Listening Skills Program, Science Research Associates, Inc., 259 E. Erie St., Chicago, Ill. 60611

SRA Listening Skills Program consists of a series of recordings designed to develop and strengthen children's listening abilities in grades 1 through 6. The student responds to taped activities with paper and pencil.

Ginn Word Enrichment Program, Ginn & Co., 125 Second Ave., Waltham, Mass. 02154

Ginn Word Enrichment Program is designed to teach successful application of word analysis skills, build vocabulary, and extend word meaning. This program is designed for use with primary grades employing a basal reading series and is suitable for remedial work in intermediate grades.

Califone Audio Reader Program, Rheem Califone, 5922 Bowcroft St., Los Angeles, Calif. 90016

Califone Audio Reader Program is multilevel and is designed to stimulate vocabulary growth, oral reading skills, and comprehension. Each level contains 20 prerecorded tape lessons recorded in both directions to eliminate the necessity to rewind. This program can be used for grades 1 to 6.

Multilevel books and workbooks

Specific Skill Series, Barnell Loft, Ltd., 111 S. Centre Ave., Rockville, N.Y. 11571

The Specific Skill Series consists of 42 workbooks with worksheets. The latter permit optional self-correction.

Reading Skill Builders, Reader's Digest Services, Inc., Pleasantville, N.Y. 10570

Reading Skill Builders are adapted for different reading levels, in grades 1 through 8. Two series are available, the original and the new. There are audio lessons for portions of the new series.

New Rochester Occupational Reading Series, Science Research Associates, Inc., 259 E. Erie St., Chicago, Ill. 60611

SRA's New Rochester Occupational Reading Series provides reading instruction and information about the world of work. Material is mature in content but scaled as low as second-grade reading level. Material would be suitable for grades 9 through 12 and adult.

HIGH-INTEREST, LOW–VOCABULARY LEVEL BOOKS

This is a partial listing of books with high interest and low vocabulary levels recommended for pupils who read below their assigned grade level. The interest level immediately follows the title.

The Bobbs-Merrill Co., Inc., 730 N. Meridian St., Indianapolis, Ind. 46307

The Childhood of Famous American Series, intermediate through junior high school

Benefic Press, 1900 N. Narragansett, Chicago, Ill. 60639

Butternut Bill Series, primary
Button Family Adventure Series, primary
Cowboy Sam Series, primary
Dan Frontier Series, primary and early intermediate
Easy-To-Read Books, primary
Jerry Series, primary through intermediate
Sailor Jack Series, primary through intermediate
Space Age Books, late primary and early intermediate
Space Science Fiction Series, intermediate through junior high school
Tom O'Toole Books, primary through intermediate

Bowmar, 622 Rodier Drive, Glendale, Calif. 91201

Reading Incentive Program, junior and senior high school

D. C. Heath & Co., 125 Spring St., Lexington, Mass. 02173

Our Animal Story Books, intermediate
Teen-Age Tales, junior and senior high school

Doubleday & Co., Inc., Garden City, N.Y. 11530

The Signal Books, junior and senior high school

Educational Guidelines Co., Division of The Economy Co., 1901 N. Walnut, Oklahoma City, Okla. 74103

Better Reading Series, junior and senior high school

Field Educational Publications, Inc., 510 Merchandise Mart Plaza, Chicago, Ill. 60654

The Checkered Flag Series, late intermediate through senior high school
The Deep Sea Adventure Series, late primary through intermediate

The Jim Forest Readers, primary through intermediate
Morgan Bay Mystery Series, intermediate and junior high school
The Time Machine Series, primary and early intermediate
Wildlife Adventure Series, late primary and intermediate

Garrard Publishing Co., 1607 N. Market St., Champaign, Ill. 61820

The Basic Vocabulary Series, primary

Houghton Mifflin Co., 2 Park St., Boston, Mass. 02107

The Piper Books, intermediate
Read-by-Yourself Books, intermediate

McGraw-Hill Book Co., Inc., Webster Division, 1221 Avenue of the Americas, New York, N.Y. 10020

The Everyreader Series, intermediate through senior high school
The Junior Everyreader Series, intermediate through junior high school

Random House, Inc., 457 Madison Ave., New York, N.Y. 10022

Beginners Books, primary and intermediate
The Landmark Books, intermediate through junior high school

Science Research Associates, Inc., 259 E. Erie St., Chicago, Ill. 60611

Science Research Associates Pilot Libraries, intermediate and junior high school

Scott, Foresman & Co., 433 E. Erie St., Chicago, Ill. 60611

Scott Foresman Easy Reading Books, intermediate and junior high school
Simplified Classics, junior and senior high school

Thomas Y. Crowell Co., 432 Fourth Ave, New York, N.Y. 10016

The Clyde Bulla Books, intermediate

References and suggested readings

Abeson, A., Bolick, N., and Hass, J. *A primer on due process: education decisions for handicapped children.* Reston, Va.: Council for Exceptional Children, 1975.

Allen, R., and Allen, C. *Language experiences in reading.* Chicago: Encyclopedia Britannica Press, 1966.

Ammons, R., and Ammons, H. *Full-Range Picture Vocabulary Test.* Missoula, Mont.: Psychological Test Specialists, 1958.

Applegate, E. *Perceptual aids in the classroom.* San Rafael, Calif.: Academic Therapy Publications, 1969.

Aukerman, R. *Approaches to beginning reading.* New York: John Wiley & Sons, Inc., 1971.

Ausubel, D. *The psychology of meaningful verbal learning.* New York: Grune & Stratton, Inc., 1963.

Ayres, J. *Sensory integration and learning disorders.* Los Angeles: Western Psychological Services, 1972.

Ayres, J. *Southern California Sensory Integration Tests.* Los Angeles: Western Psychological Services, 1972.

Baker, H., and Leland, B. *Detroit Tests of Learning Aptitude.* Indianapolis: The Bobbs-Merrill Co., Inc., 1959.

Balow, B. Perceptual-motor activities in the treatment of severe reading disability. *Reading Teacher,* 1971, *24,* 513-525.

Bangs, T. *Language and learning disorders of the pre-academic child.* New York: Appleton-Century-Crofts, 1968.

Bannatyne, A. *Language, reading, and learning disabilities.* Springfield, Ill.: Charles C Thomas, Publisher, 1971.

Barakat, M. A factorial study of mathematical abilities. *British Journal of Psychology,* 1951, *4,* 137-156.

Barsch, R. *A movigenic curriculum* (Bulletin No. 25). Madison, Wis.: State Department of Public Instruction, 1965.

Barsch, R. *Achieving perceptual-motor efficiency.* Seattle: Special Child Publications, 1967.

Beery, K. *Developmental Test of Visual Motor Integration: administration and scoring manual.* Chicago: Follett Corp., 1967.

Beery, K. *Remedial diagnosis.* San Rafael, Calif.: Dimensions Publishing, 1968.

Behrmann, P. *Activities for developing visual perception.* San Rafael, Calif.: Academic Therapy Publications, 1970.

Bellak, L. *The Thematic Apperception Test and the Children's Apperception Test in clinical use* (2nd ed.). New York: Grune & Stratton, Inc., 1971.

Bereiter, C., and Englemann, S. *Teaching disadvantaged children in the preschool.* Englewood Cliffs, N.J.: Prentice-Hall, Inc., 1966.

Bereiter, C., and Hughes, A. *Teacher's guide to the Open Court Kindergarten Program.* LaSalle, Ill.: Open Court Publishing Co., 1970.

Bernstein, B. *Everyday problems and the child with learning difficulties.* New York: The John Day Co., Inc., 1969.

Berry, M. *Language disorders of children: the bases and diagnoses.* New York: Appleton-Century-Crofts, 1969.

Birch, H., and Belmont, I. Auditory-visual integration in brain-damaged and normal children. *Developmental Medicine and Child Neurology,* 1965, *7,* 135-144.

Birch, H., and Gussow, J. *Disadvantaged children: health, nutrition, and school failure.* New York: Grune & Stratton, Inc., 1970.

Blau, H., and Blau, H. A theory of learning to read. *The Reading Teacher,* 1968, *22,* 126-129.

Bloomer, R. The cloze procedure as a remedial reading exercise. *Journal of Developmental Reading,* 1962, *5,* 173-181.

Bloomfield, L., and Barnhart, C. *Let's read.* Detroit: Wayne State University Press, 1961.

Boehm Test of Basic Concepts. New York: The Psychological Corp., 1970.

Bond, G., and Tinker, M. *Reading difficulties; their diagnosis and correction* (2nd ed.). New York: Appleton-Century-Crofts, 1968.

Brainerd, C. The origins of number concepts. *Scientific American, 228*(3), 1973, 101-109.

Bruner, J., and Goodnow, J., and Austin, G. *A study of thinking.* New York: John Wiley & Sons, Inc., 1956.

Buckley, N., and Walker, H. *Modifying classroom behavior* (Rev. ed.). Champaign, Ill.: Research Press, 1970.

Burns, R. *New approaches to behavioral objectives.* Dubuque, Iowa: William C. Brown Co., Publishers, 1972.

Bush, W., and Giles, M. *Aids to psycholinguistic teaching.* Columbus, Ohio: Charles E. Merrill Publishing Co., 1969.

Carter, H., and McGinnis, D. *Diagnosis and treatment of the disabled reader.* New York: Macmillan Publishing Co., Inc., 1970.

Cazden, C. *Child language and education.* New York: Holt, Rinehart & Winston, Inc., 1972.

Chalfant, J., and Scheffelin, M. *Central processing dysfunctions in children: a review of research.* (NINDS Monograph No. 9). Washington, D.C.: U.S. Government Printing Office, 1969.

Chall, J. *Learning to read: the great debate.* New York: McGraw-Hill Book Co., 1967.

Chaney, C., and Kephart, N. *Motoric aids to perceptual training.* Columbus, Ohio: Charles E. Merrill Publishing Co., 1968.

Cheves, R. *Visual-motor perception teaching materials.* Boston: Teaching Resources Corp., 1967.

Chomsky, C. *The acquisition of syntax in children five to ten.* Cambridge, Mass.: M.I.T. Press, 1969.

Cicourel, A. *Cognitive sociology: language and meaning in social interaction.* New York: The Free Press, 1974.

Cobb, J. *Survival skills and first grade achievement* (Report No. 1, Center for Research and Demonstration in the Early Education of Handicapped Children). Eugene, Ore.: University of Oregon, 1970.

Colarusso, R., and Hammill, D. *The Motor-Free Test of Visual Perception.* San Rafael, Calif.: Academic Therapy Publications, 1972.

Copeland, R. *Diagnostic and learning activities in mathematics for children.* New York: Macmillan Publishing Co., Inc., 1974.

Copeland, R. *How children learn mathematics— teaching implications of Piaget's research* (2nd ed.). New York: Macmillan Publishing Co., Inc., 1974.

Cott, A. Megavitamins: the orthomolecular approach to behavioral disorders and learning disabilities. *Academic Therapy,* 1972, 7 (Spring), 245-259.

Cratty, B. *Developmental sequences of perceptual-motor tasks.* Freeport, N.Y.: Educational Activities, 1967.

Cratty, B. *Movement behavior and motor learning.* Philadelphia: Lea & Febiger, 1967.

Cratty, B. *Psychology and physical activity.* Englewood Cliffs, N.J.: Prentice-Hall, Inc., 1968.

Cratty, B. *Social dimensions of physical activity.* Englewood Cliffs, N.J.: Prentice-Hall, Inc., 1968.

Cratty, B. *Perceptual-motor behavior and educational processes.* Springfield, Ill.: Charles C Thomas, Publisher, 1969.

Cratty, B. *Active learning: games to enhance academic abilities.* Englewood Cliffs, N.J.: Prentice-Hall, Inc., 1971.

Cratty, B., Ikeda, N., Martin, M., Jennett, C., and Morris, M. *Movement activities, motor ability and the education of children.* Springfield, Ill.: Charles C Thomas, Publisher, 1970.

Cruickshank, W. *The brain-injured child in home, school, and community.* Syracuse: Syracuse University Press, 1967.

Cruickshank, W. (Ed.). *The teacher of brain-injured children.* Syracuse: Syracuse University Press, 1966.

Cruickshank, W., Bentzen, F., Ratzeburg, F., and Tannhause, M. *A teaching method for brain-injured and hyperactive children.* Syracuse: Syracuse University Press, 1961.

Dallmann, M., Rouch, R., Chang, L., and DeBoer, J. *The teaching of reading* (4th ed.). New York: Holt, Rinehart & Winston, Inc., 1974.

de Hirsch, K., Jansky, J., and Langford, W. *Predicting reading failure: a preliminary study of reading, writing, and spelling disabilities in preschool children.* New York: Harper & Row, Publishers, 1966.

Dechant, E. *Diagnosis and remediation of reading disability.* Englewood Cliffs, N.J.: Parker Publishing Co., 1968.

Dechant, E. *Linguistics, phonics, and the teaching of reading.* Springfield, Ill.: Charles C Thomas, Publisher, 1969.

Dechant, E. *Improving the teaching of reading*

(2nd ed.). Englewood Cliffs, N.J.: Prentice-Hall, Inc., 1970.

Deese, J. *Psycholinguistics.* Boston: Allyn & Bacon, Inc., 1970.

Delacato, C., and Moyer, S. Can we teach word meaning? *Elementary English,* 1953, *30* (February), 102-106.

Delacato, C. *Treatment and prevention of reading problems.* Springfield, Ill.: Charles C Thomas, Publisher, 1959.

Delacato, C. *The diagnosis and treatment of speech and reading problems.* Springfield, Ill.: Charles C Thomas, Publisher, 1963.

Delacato, C. *Neurological organization and reading.* Springfield, Ill.: Charles C Thomas, Publisher, 1966.

Dember, W. *Visual perception: the nineteenth century.* New York: John Wiley & Sons, Inc., 1964.

Deutsch, C. Sociocultural influences and learning channels. In H. Smith (Ed.), *Perception and reading.* Newark, Del.: International Reading Association, 1968.

Divoky, D. Education's latest victim: the "L.D." kid. *Learning,* 1974, *3*(2), 20-25.

Doll, E. *The Vineland Social Maturity Scale.* Circle Pines, Minn.: American Guidance Service, 1965.

Doll, E. *Preschool Attainment Record.* Circle Pines, Minn.: American Guidance Service, 1966.

Downing, J. *The Initial Teaching Alphabet reading experiment.* Chicago: Scott, Foresman, 1965.

Downing, J. The Initial Teaching Alphabet. In J. Downing, Ed., *The First International Reading Symposium.* New York: John Day, 1966.

Dunn, L. *Peabody Picture Vocabulary Test.* Circle Pines, Minn.: American Guidance Service, 1965.

Durkin, D. *Teaching them to read* (2nd ed.). Boston: Allyn & Bacon, Inc., 1974.

Ebersole, M., Kephart, N., and Ebersole, J. *Steps to achievement for the slow learner.* Columbus, Ohio: Charles E. Merrill Publishing Co., 1968.

Egg, M. *Educating the child who is different.* New York: The John Day Co., Inc., 1968.

Ellis, R. The stimulus trace and behavioral inadequacy. In N. Ellis (Ed.), *Handbook of mental deficiency.* New York: McGraw-Hill Book Co., 1963.

Ellson, W. Programmed tutoring: a teaching aid and a research tool. *Reading Research Quarterly,* 1965, *1,* 77-127.

Engelmann, S., and Osborn, J. *DISTAR: an instructional system.* Chicago: Science Research Associates, Inc., 1970.

Fernald, G. *Remedial techniques in basic school subjects.* New York: McGraw-Hill Book Co., 1943.

Flesch, R. *Why Johnny can't read and what you can do about it.* New York: Harper & Row, Publishers, 1955.

Forness, S., and MacMillan, D. The origins of behavior modification with exceptional children. *Exceptional Children,* 1970, *37*(October), 93-99.

Freeman, R. Drug effects on learning in children: a selective review of the past thirty years. *Journal of Special Education,* 1966, *1*(1), 17-44.

Friedus, E. *New approaches in special education of the brain-injured child.* New York: New York Association for Brain-Injured Children, 1957.

Friedus, E. The needs of teachers for specialized information on number concepts. In W. Cruickshank (Ed.), *The teacher of brain-injured children.* Syracuse: Syracuse University Press, 1966.

Frierson, E., and Barbe, W. (Eds.). *Educating children with learning disabilities.* New York: Appleton-Century-Crofts, 1967.

Fries, C. *Merrill Linguistic Readers: a basic program.* Columbus, Ohio. Charles E. Merrill Publishing Co., 1962.

Fries, C. *Linguistics and reading.* New York: Holt, Rinehart & Winston, Inc., 1963.

Frostig, M. *Frostig Developmental Test of Visual Perception.* Palo Alo, Calif.: Consulting Psychologists Press, 1963.

Frostig, M. *Movement education: theory and practice.* Chicago: Follett Corp., 1970.

Frostig, M. *Selection and adaptation of reading methods.* San Rafael, Calif.: Academic Therapy Publications, 1973.

Frostig, M., and Horne, D. *The Frostig Program for the Development of Visual Perception: teacher's guide.* Chicago: Follett Corp., 1964.

Frostig, M., and Horne, D. Marianne Frostig Center of Education Therapy. In M. Jones (Ed.), *Special education programs: within the United States.* Springfield, Ill.: Charles C Thomas, Publisher, 1968.

Frostig, M., Lefever, D., and Whattlesey, J. *The Marianne Frostig Developmental Test of Visual Perception.* Palo Alto, Calif.: Consulting Psychologists Press, 1964.

Furth, H. *Thinking without language.* New York: The Free Press, 1966.

Gagné, R. The acquisition of knowledge. *Psychological review,* 1962, *69,* 355-365.

Gagné, R. *The conditions of learning* (2nd ed.). New York: Holt, Rinehart & Winston, Inc., 1970.

Gattegno, C. *Words in Color.* Chicago: Encyclopedia Britannica Press, 1962.

Gearheart, B. *Education of the exceptional child: history, present practices and trends.* Scranton, Pa.: Intext Press, Inc., 1972.

Gearheart, B. *Learning disabilities: educational strategies.* St. Louis: The C. V. Mosby Co., 1973.

Gearheart, B., and Weishahn, M. *The handicapped child in the regular classroom.* St. Louis: The C. V. Mosby Co., 1976.

Gearheart, B., and Willenberg, E. *Application of pupil assessment information: for the special education teacher.* Denver: Love Publishing Co., 1974.

Gerstmann, J. Some notes on the Gerstmann syndrome. *Neurology,* 1957, *7,* 866-869.

Geschwind, N. Language and the brain. *Scientific American,* 1972, *226*(4), 76-83.

Getman, G. The visuomotor complex in the acquisition of learning skills. In J. Hellmuth (Ed.), *Learning disorders* (Vol. 1). Seattle: Special Child Publications, 1965.

Getman, G. *Pathway School Program.* Boston: Teaching Resources, 1969.

Getman, G., and Hendrickson, H. The needs of teachers for specialized information on the development of visuomotor skills in relation to academic performance. In W. Cruickshank (Ed.), *The teacher of brain-injured children.* Syracuse: Syracuse University Press, 1966.

Getman, G., and Kane, E. *The physiology of readiness.* Minneapolis: Programs to accelerate School Success, 1964.

Getman, G., Kane, E., Halgren, M., and McKee, G. *Developing learning readiness: teacher's manual.* New York: McGraw-Hill Book Co., 1968.

Gibson, E. *Principles of perceptual learning and development.* New York: Appleton-Century-Crofts, 1969.

Gibson, J. *The senses considered as perceptual systems.* Boston: Houghton Mifflin Co., 1966.

Gillingham, A. *Collected papers* (Orton Society Monograph III). Pomfret, Conn.: The Society, 1967.

Gillingham, A., and Stillman, B. *Remedial work for reading, spelling, and penmanship* (6th ed.). New York: Hackett & Wilhelms, 1946.

Gillingham, A., and Stillman, B. *Remedial training for children with specific disability in reading, spelling, and penmanship* (7th ed.). Cambridge, Mass.: Educators Publishing Service, 1965.

Goins, J. *Visual-perceptual abilities and early school progress.* Chicago: University of Chicago Press, 1958.

Goldman, R., Fristoe, M., and Woodcock, R. *Goldman-Fristoe-Woodcock Test of Auditory Discrimination.* Circle Pines, Minn.: American Guidance Service, 1970.

Goodman, D. (Ed.). *The psycholinguistic nature of the reading process.* Detroit: Wayne State University Press, 1968.

Graber, D. Megavitamins, molecules, and minds. *Human Behavior,* 1973, *2*(5), 8-15.

Guilford, J. *The nature of human intelligence.* New York: McGraw-Hill Book Co., 1967.

Guszak, F. *Diagnostic reading instruction in the elementary school.* New York: Harper & Row, Publishers, 1972.

Hainsworth, P., and Siqueland, M. *The Meeting Street School Screening Test.* Providence, R.I.: Crippled Children and Adults of Rhode Island, 1969.

Hallahan, D., and Cruickshank, W. *Psychoeducational foundations of learning disabilities.* Englewood Cliffs, N.J.: Prentice-Hall, Inc., 1973.

Hammill, D., and Bartel, N. (Eds.). *Educational perspectives in learning disabilities.* New York: John Wiley & Sons, Inc., 1971.

Haring, N. *Attending and responding.* San Rafael, Calif.: Dimensions Publishing Co., 1968.

Haring, N., and Schiefelbusch, R. (Eds.). *Methods in special education.* New York: McGraw-Hill Book Co., 1967.

Haring, N., and Whelan, R. (Eds.). *The learning environment: relationship to behavior modification and implications for special education.* Lawrence, Kan.: University of Kansas Press, 1966.

Harris, A. *Harris Test of Lateral Dominance* (3rd rev. ed.). New York: The Psychological Corp., 1958.

Harris, A. *How to increase reading ability* (5th ed.). New York: David McKay, Co., Inc., 1970.

Harris, O. *Goodenough-Harris drawing tests.* New York: Harcourt Brace Jovanovich, Inc., 1963.

Hartman, N., and Hartman, R. Perceptual handicap or reading disability? *The Reading Teacher,* 1973, *26,* April, 684-695.

Hartstein, J. (Ed.). *Current concepts in dyslexia.* St. Louis: The C. V. Mosby Co., 1971.

Hebb, D. *The organization of behavior.* New York: John Wiley & Sons, Inc., 1949.

Hellmuth, J. (Ed.). *Learning disorders* (Vols. 1 to 4). Seattle: Special Child Publications, 1965 to 1971.

Hewett, F. *The emotionally disturbed child in the classroom.* Boston: Allyn & Bacon, Inc., 1968.

Hinshelwood, J. *Congenital word blindness.* London: H. K. Lewis, 1917.

Hoffman, M. A learning disability is a symptom, not a disease. *Academic Therapy,* 1975, *10*(3), 261-275.

Homme, L. *How to use contingency contracting in the classroom.* Champaign, Ill:. Research Press, 1971.

Jansky, J. The phenomenon of plasticity in relation to manipulating numbers and early learning of arithmetic. In J. Hellmuth (Ed.), *Learning disorders* (Vol. 1). Seatle, Wash.: Special Child Publications, 1965.

Jastak, J., and Jastak, S. *Wide Range Achievement Test.* Wilmington, Del.: Guidance Associates, 1965.

Johnson, D., and Myklebust, H. *Learning disabilities: educational principles and practices.* New York: Grune & Stratton, Inc., 1967.

Jongsman, E. *The cloze procedure as a teaching technique.* Newark, Del.: International Reading Association, 1971.

Kaliski, L. Arithmetic and the brain-injured child. *The Arithmetic Teacher,* 1962, *9,* 245-251.

Kaluger, G., and Kolson, C. *Reading and learning disabilities.* Columbus, Ohio: Charles E. Merrill Publishing Co., 1969.

Karlin, R. *Teaching elementary reading.* New York: Harcourt Brace Jovanovich, Inc., 1971.

Karnes, M. *Helping young children develop language skills.* Washington, D.C.: Council for exceptional Children, 1968.

Kass, C. Psycholinguistic disabilities of children with reading problems. *Exceptional Children,* 1966, *32,* 533-541.

Kelly, T. *Crossroads in the mind of man.* Stanford, Calif.: Stanford University Press, 1928.

Kephart, N. *The brain-injured child.* Chicago: National Society for Crippled Children and Adults, 1963.

Kephart, N. *The slow learner in the classroom* (Rev. ed.). Columbus, Ohio: Charles E. Merrill Publishing Co., 1971.

Kershner, J., and Kershner, B. Dual brain asymmetry: another cause of learning disorders? *Academic Therapy,* 1973, *8*(4), 391-393.

Kimmell, G., and Wahl, J. *The Screening Test for Auditory Perception.* San Rafael, Calif.: Academic Therapy Publications, 1969.

Kirk, S., and Kirk, W. *Psycholinguistic learning disabilities: diagnosis and remediation.* Urbana, Ill.: University of Illlinois Press, 1971.

Kirk, S., McCarthy, J., and Kirk, W. *Illinois Test of Psycholinguistic Abilities: examiner's manual* (Rev. ed.). Urbana, Ill.: University of Illinois Press, 1968.

Kleinmuntz, B. (Ed.). *Concepts and the structure of memory.* New York: John Wiley & Sons, Inc., 1967.

Kolstoe, O. *Mental retardation: an educational viewpoint.* New York: Holt, Rinehart & Winston, Inc., 1972.

Koppitz, E. *The Bender Gestalt Test for Young Children.* New York: Grune & Stratton, Inc., 1963.

Kosc, L. Developmental dyscalculia. *Journal of Learning Disabilities,* 1974, *7*(3), 46-59.

Lane, A. Severe reading disability and the Initial Teaching Alphabet. *Journal of Learning Disabilities,* 1974, *7*(8), 23-27.

Lerner, J. *Children with learning disabilities: theories, diagnosis, and teaching strategies.* Boston: Houghton Mifflin Co., 1971.

Luria, A. *Higher cortical functions in man.* New York: Basic Books, Inc., Publishers, 1966.

Mackintosh, H. *Current approaches to teaching reading.* Washington, D.C.: National Education Association, 1965.

Mann, P., and Suiter, P.: *Handbook in diagnostic teaching: a learning approach.* Boston: Allyn & Bacon, Inc., 1974.

Martin, E. Some thoughts on mainstreaming. *Exceptional Children,* 1974, *41*(3), 150-153.

Matthes, C. *How children are taught to read.* Lincoln, Neb.: Professional Educators Publications, 1972.

McGlannan, F. Research of interest: brain blood flow. *Journal of Learning Disabilities,* 1975, *8*(2), 83-84.

McGlannan, F. Research of interest: premature infant: brain blood flow. *Journal of Learning Disabilities,* 1975, *8*(3), 152-153.

McNeil, M., and Hamre, C. A review of measures of lateralized cerebral hemispheric functions. *Journal of Learning Disabilities,* 1974, *7,* 375-383.

Mechan, M., Jex, J., and Jones, J. *Utah Test of Language Development.* Salt Lake City: Communication Research Associates, 1967.

Menyuk, P. *The acquisition and development of language.* Englewood Cliffs, N.J.: Prentice-Hall, Inc., 1971.

Money, J. (Ed.). *The disabled reader: education of the dyslexic child.* Baltimore: The Johns Hopkins University Press, 1966.

Money, J., Alexander, D., and Walker, H., Jr. *A Standardized Road-Map Test of Direction Sense.* Baltimore: The Johns Hopkins University Press, 1965.

Monroe, M. *Children who cannot read.* Chicago: University of Chicago Press, 1932.

Montessori, M. *The Montessori method.* Cambridge, Mass.: Robert Bentley, Inc., 1965.

Moore, O., and Anderson, A. The Responsive Environments Project. In R. Hess and R. Bear (Eds.), *The Challenge of Early Education.* Chicago: Aldine Publishing Co., 1967.

Moskovitz, S. Some assumptions underlying the Bereiter approach. *Young Children,* 1968, *24* (1), 24-31.

Murray, H. *Thematic Apperception Test.* Cambridge, Mass.: Harvard University Press, 1943.

Myers, P., and Hammill, D. *Methods for learning disorders.* New York: John Wiley & Sons, Inc., 1969.

Myklebust, H. *Auditory disorders in children.* New York: Grune & Stratton, Inc., 1954.

Myklebust, H. Language disorders in children. *Exceptional Children,* 1956, *22,* 163-166.

Myklebust, H. Learning disorders: psychoneurological disturbances in childhood. *Rehabilitation Literature,* 1964, *25,* 354-359.

Myklebust, H. *Development and disorders of written language.* New York: Grune & Stratton, Inc., 1965.

Myklebust, H. (Ed.). *Progress in learning disabilities.* New York: Grune & Stratton, Inc., 1968.

Myklebust, H., and Boshes, B. *Minimal brain damage in children.* Evanston, Ill.: Northwestern University Press, 1969.

New York Institute for Child Development, Inc. Bulletin. New York: The Institute, 1975.

Orton, J. *A guide to teaching phonics.* Cambridge, Mass.: Educators Publishing Service, 1965.

Orton, S. *Reading, writing, and speech problems in children.* New York: W. W. Norton & Co., Inc., 1937.

Orton, S. Specific reading disability. *Bulletin of the Orton Society,* May, 1963, *13,* 7-17.

Orton, S. Collected papers (Orton Society Monograph II). Pomfret, Conn.: The Society, 1966.

Orton Society. *Specific language disabilities* (Vol. 3). Pomfret, Conn.: The Society, 1963.

Orton Society. *Dyslexia in special education* (Vol. 1). Pomfret, Conn.: The Society, 1964.

Osgood, C. A behavioristic analysis. In J. Bruner (Ed.), *Contemporary approaches to cognition.* Cambridge, Mass.: Harvard University Press, 1957.

Osgood, C., and Sebeok, T. (Eds.). *Psycholinguistics.* Bloomington, Ind.: Indiana University Press, 1965.

Otto, W., and McMenemy, R. *Corrective and remedial teaching, principles, and practices.* Boston: Houghton Mifflin Co., 1966.

Paraskevopoulos, J., and Kirk, S.: *Development and psychometric characteristics of the Revised Illinois Test of Psycholinguistic Abilities.* Urbana. Ill.: University of Illinois Press, 1969.

Piaget, J. *Play, dreams and imitation in childhood.* New York: W. W. Norton & Co., Inc., 1951.

Piaget, J. *The growth of logical thinking in the child.* New York: Basic Books, Inc., Publishers, 1958.

Piaget, J. *The origins of intelligence in children.* New York: W. W. Norton & Co., Inc., 1963.

Piaget, J. *The Child's Conception of Number.* New York: W. W. Norton & Co., Inc., 1965.

Piaget, J. *The language and thought of the child.* New York: World Publishing Co., 1967.

Piaget, J. *Science of education and the psychology of the child.* New York: Grossman Publishers, 1974.

Pitman, J. *Evidence submitted to the Bullock committee of inquiry into reading and the use of English* (Foundation Publication No. 18). New York: Initial Teaching Alphabet Publications, Inc., 1973.

Rambusch, N. *Learning how to learn—an American approach to Montessori.* Baltimore: Helicon Press, 1962.

Reger, R., Schroeder, W., and Uschold, K. *Special education: children with learning problems.* New York: Oxford University Press, Inc., 1968.

Reisman, F. *A guide to the diagnostic teaching of arithmetic.* Columbus, Ohio: Charles E. Merrill Publishing Co., 1972.

Reynolds, G. *A primer of operant conditioning.* Glenview, Ill.: Scott, Foresman & Co., 1968.

Richardson, E., and Bradley, C. ISM: a teacher-oriented method of reading instruction for the child-oriented teacher. *Journal of Learning Disabilities,* 1974, *7*(6), 19-27.

Richardson, K., and Spears, S. *Race and intelligence.* Baltimore: Pelican Books, 1972.

Roach, E., and Kephart, N. *The Purdue Perceptual-Motor Survey.* Columbus, Ohio: Charles E. Merrill Publishing Co., 1966.

Robins, D. *Special education guide to the Open Court Program.* LaSalle, Ill.: Open Court Publishing Co., 1970.

Robinson, R. *An introduction to the cloze procedure, an annotated bibliography.* Newark, Del.: International Reading Association, 1971.

Rogers, L., et al. Hemispheric specialization and language: an EEG study of Hopi Indian children. Los Angeles: Brain Research Institute, UCLA Medical Center, 1975.

Salafsky, I. Babies hands may give clue to their development. *Journal of the American Medical Association,* 1975, *232,* 240-241.

Samples, R. Learning with the whole brain. *Human Behavior,* 1975, *4*(2), 17-23.

Slosson, R. *Slosson Intelligence Test for Children and Adults.* East Aurora, N.Y.: Slosson Educational Publications, 1963.

Smith, R. *Teacher diagnosis of educational difficulties.* Columbus, Ohio: Charles E. Merrill Publishing Co., 1969.

Spache, G. *Spache Binocular Vision Test.* Meadville, Pa.: Keystone View Co., 1961.

Spache, G. *The teaching of reading: methods and results.* Bloomington, Ind.: The Phi Delta Kappa Educational Foundation, 1972.

Spache, G., and Spache, E. *Reading in the elementary school* (3rd ed.). Boston: Allyn & Bacon, Inc., 1973.

Sptizer, H. *Teaching elementary school mathematics.* National Education Association, 1970.

Stafford, R. Negative relationship between ability to visualize space and grades in specific courses. *Journal of Learning Disabilities,* 1972, *5*(1), 38-40.

Stephens, T. *Directive teaching of children with learning and behavioral handicaps.* Columbus, Ohio: Charles E. Merrill Publishing Co., 1970.

Stern, C. *Children discover arithmetic.* New York: Harper & Row, Publishers, 1949.

Strang, R. *Diagnostic teaching of reading* (2nd ed.). New York: McGraw-Hill Book Co., 1969.

Strauss, A., and Lehtinen, L. *Psychopathology and education of the brain-injured child.* New York: Grune & Stratton, Inc., 1947.

Terman, E., and Merrill, M. *Stanford-Binet Intelligence Scale, manual for third revision.* Boston: Houghton Mifflin, Co., 1961.

Thompson, L. *Reading disability.* Springfield, Ill.: Charles C Thomas, Publisher, 1969.

Ullman, L., and Krasner, L. *Case studies in behavior modification.* New York: Holt, Rinehart and Winston, Inc., 1965.

Valett, R. *The remediation of learning disabilities.* Palo Alto, Calif.: Fearon Publishers, 1967.

Valett, R. *A psychoeducational inventory of basic learning abilities.* Palo Alto, Calif.: Fearon Publishers, 1968.

Valett, R. *Modifying children's behavior.* Palo Alto, Calif.: Fearon Publishers, 1969.

Valett, R. *Programming learning disabilities.* Palo Alto, Calif.: Fearon Publishers, 1969.

Van Riper, C. *Speech correction: principles and methods.* Englewood Cliffs, N.J.: Prentice-Hall Inc., 1972.

Vonder Haar, T. Chaining children with chemicals. *The Progressive,* 1975, *39*(3), 13-17.

Walker, S. III, We're too cavalier about hyperactivity. *Psychology Today,* 1974, *8*(7), 43-48.

Waugh, K., and Bush, W. *Diagnosing learning disorders.* Columbus, Ohio: Charles E. Merrill Publishing Co., 1971.

Wechsler, D. *The Revised Wechsler Intelligence Scale for Children (WISC-R).* New York: The Psychological Corp., 1974.

Wepman, J. *Wepman Auditory Discrimination Test.* Chicago: Language Research Associates, 1958.

Wepman, J. New and wider horizons for speech and hearing specialists. *Journal of the American Speech and Hearing Association,* 1975, *17*(1), 9-10.

Wickelgren, W. Memory. In J. Swets and L. Elliot (Eds.), *Psychology and the handicapped child.* Washington, D.C.: U.S. Government Printing Office, 1974.

Wolinsky, G. The application of some of J. Piaget's observations to the instruction of children. *Teaching Exceptional Children,* 1970, *2*(4), 189-196.

Woodcock, R. *Peabody Rebus Reading Program.* Circle Pines, Minn.: American Guidance Service, 1967.

Worell, J., and Nelson, M. *Managing instructional problems: a case study workbook.* New York: McGraw-Hill Book Co., 1974.

Zeaman, D., and House, B. The role of attention in retardate discrimination learning. In N. Ellis (Ed.), *Handbook of mental deficiency.* New York: McGraw-Hill Book Co., 1963.

Zigmond, M., and Cicci, R. *Auditory learning.* San Rafael, Calif.: Dimensions Publishing, 1968.

Zintz, M. *Corrective reading* (2nd ed.). Dubuque, Iowa: William C. Brown Co., Publishers, 1972.

INDEX